NAILING THE NEW SAT

NAILING

THE NEW SAT

EDWARD B. FISKE & BRUCE G. HAMMOND

SOURCEBOOKS, INC.
NAPERVILLE, ILLINOIS

Published by Sourcebooks, Inc.
P.O. Box 4410, Naperville, Illinois 60567-4410
(630) 961-3900
Fax: (630) 961-2168
www.sourcebooks.com

The Library of Congress has cataloged the first edition as follows:
Fiske, Edward B.
Fiske New SAT Insider's Guide / Edward B. Fiske, Bruce G. Hammond
      p. cm.
ISBN 1-4022-0163-X (alk. Paper)
1. Scholastic Assessment Test—Study guides. I. Hammond, Bruce G. II. Title.
LB2353.57.F59 2004
378.1'662—dc22

2004003978

Printed and bound in the United States of America
DR 10 9 8 7 6 5 4 3 2 1

To Brent Colley, the world's
greatest Hokie fan

CONTENTS

INTRODUCTION

Cutting through SAT Hysteria

There are many stressful moments in the life of a teenager—like hearing your name on the school intercom followed by the words, "Please report to the main office." Or the awkward silence on a phone line just before you summon the courage to ask, "Are you busy Saturday night?" For pure humiliation, nothing beats the sight of your mom striding close on the heels of the tour guide at First Choice U, notebook in hand, asking yet again about campus safety and whether it is really true that boys and girls share the same bathrooms.

But these moments are kid stuff compared to the phrase that strikes like a thunderbolt through the heart of every high school student:

"Open your test booklet, read the directions, and begin."

Welcome to your worst nightmare: the SAT.

The SAT wasn't always this scary. Though it has existed in its modern form for nearly sixty years, only in the last two decades has the hype become hysteria. Before 1957, students weren't even informed of how well they did on the test. (The College Board communicated directly with the colleges and the student was left out of the loop.) But those were the days when getting in had more to do with where you went to school and who your parents were than your SAT scores. Since the mid-1970s, there has been a steady ratcheting up of the pressure on test-takers as competition to get into the nation's elite colleges has intensified. In the past fifteen years alone, applications to the Ivy League have spiked about 50 percent. At the most desirable colleges in hot locations—like Columbia and NYU in New York City or George Washington in D.C.—applications have more than doubled.

> "Approach the SAT as a series of problems to solve, not as a test that will determine the rest of your life."
>
> —700 V, 760 M

Competition has also heated up among the colleges, which are almost as obsessed with looking good in the rankings as the students are with getting in. Average SAT scores are an important yardstick for the colleges; though they never admit it publicly, the colleges are somewhere between eager and desperate to enroll students with high scores. At colleges that offer merit scholarships, such awards are often available only to students who meet minimum score cutoffs. Despite a growing backlash against standardized testing, and the decision of a few dozen selective colleges to make the test optional, the importance of the SAT for college admission is greater than ever before.

Does all this make you a little nervous? Join the club. Colleges say that a high SAT score is only a small part of the formula for getting in—and certainly less important than your high school transcript. It is true that you can't get in at a selective college without top grades. But thousands of students nationwide rank at or near the top of their high school classes, and you can bet that these students also write good essays and get great recommendations. When the colleges evaluate their hordes of eager applicants, only one part of the application ranks each student neatly on a universal scale: the SAT.

It is no coincidence that the nation's most prestigious colleges have the highest average SAT scores. In 2004, the average scores of students admitted to the likes of Harvard or Stanford hovered around 750 on both the Verbal and Math sections—scores achieved by less than 1 percent of the test-takers. At Brown, a slightly less selective institution, the averages were closer to 700 Verbal and 700 Math. (All SAT sections are graded on a scale of 200–800, with the national average on each hovering just over 500.) Indeed, the average SAT scores at virtually all selective colleges can be predicted almost exactly by their place in the admission pecking order. To put it another way, students with high test scores are much more likely to be admitted at selective schools than those with lower scores.

The link between SAT scores and admission chances is strong—and would be good reason by itself to make students nervous about taking it. But the scariest part of the SAT is not the fact that it is important, but rather that the results are so unpredictable. From the time they are fresh-faced babes in elementary school, students get grades from a teacher to tell them how they are doing. There is no mystery about grades in school—if you master the material, you get an A. Study hard and you will be rewarded. Though a few slacker-geniuses can get A's without doing much, and though some teachers give grades that seem arbitrary, in most classes grades make sense and students know what to do in order to improve them.

The SAT replaces the predictability of school grades with a new standard. SAT scores are reported on a precise numerical scale, yet exactly why particular students get particular scores is often a mystery. The scores usually reflect school grades, more or less, but they also invariably rewrite the pecking order of who is "smarter" than whom. Consider two students who take the same classes in the same school and get the same grades. Call them 2200 Tom and 1900 Nancy. Both have 3.93 grade point averages in the toughest courses, and both took the same prep course for the SAT and studied the same amount. Yet Tom scored 300 points higher. Was it luck? Test-taking skills? Is Tom really a better student than Nancy, even though they have been

COLLEGE BOARD AND ETS: WHO ARE THEY?

Even many educators don't understand the difference between the College Board, which owns the SAT, and Education Testing Service (ETS), a test-development organization that has a contract to design and administer it for the Board. Often, we'll refer to these two collectively as "the test-makers." The Board will be our primary subject when we're talking about policies and public statements related to the SAT, including the types of test questions. ETS will be our focus when we take a closer look at how particular questions are designed.

running neck and neck since middle school? Is Tom better prepared for college? In the big picture, both students scored far above the national average, but that is small consolation to Nancy, who will be less likely to qualify for admission and scholarships because of her lower score. Nobody will ever be able to say for sure why Tom scored 300 points higher, or what, if anything, Nancy could have done to close the gap.

There are several reasons for the confusion surrounding the SAT. Most importantly, nobody can agree on what the SAT measures. Even the test-makers don't have a ready answer. Academic skills are obviously important, but so too are test-taking techniques. The imprecision of standardized testing is another source of uncertainty. Like public opinion polls quoted in the media, the SAT is not a perfect measure of what you know because it doesn't test all your knowledge, but only a sample of it. On the SAT, everybody has a "real" score—the average of what they would get if they took the test an infinite number of times. The odds are about one in three that your score on any particular section will vary from your real score by at least 30 points, and there is about a 10 percent chance that your score will be off by at least 60 points. And that doesn't factor in what could happen if you simply have a bad day.

With such an air of mystery surrounding the SAT, it is no wonder that the test causes such fear and loathing among high school students and their parents. Admission officers try to downplay its importance, but their assurances ring hollow. The test-makers say that the SAT is a test of reasoning, but who really believes that?

The combination of the pressure surrounding the SAT, and all the double-talk about the test from the higher education establishment, paved the way for another player on the college-prep scene: the multimillion-dollar SAT coaching industry. Skillfully playing on the anxieties that so many students logically feel, many prep outfits promise top-secret techniques that will help students outwit the test. Others administer hour upon hour of drills and homework. Many do both. The tab for all this extra cramming frequently tops $1,000.

There has always been a large fly doing the backstroke in the ointment of test-prep. No one has been able to prove whether it really works. Ask the College Board and you'll learn that the SAT "measures skills developed over a long period of time." Translation? Forget studying because there's nothing you can do.

According to the Board, taking a coaching course to prepare for the SAT is unlikely to increase your combined score by a total of more than 30 points. Various studies, most done at the request of College Board and ETS, show this to be true. No surprise here—if test prep were found to be effective, the validity of the test would be undermined. For their part, the test-prep companies have claimed eye-popping average score gains of as much as 140 points and more on a student's combined Verbal + Math score. They have commissioned studies of their own that (surprise!) back up their side of the story, chapter and verse.

> "Students who aren't self-motivated and won't study alone benefit most from a classroom prep course. One-on-one tutoring should be for people who are behind or don't understand what to study. Self-motivated students should prepare on their own."
>
> —710 V, 720 M

Suspicious of the test-makers, and not quite trusting the coaching outfits, families can be forgiven if their thinking about the SAT is all over the place. The boy next door says his combined SAT score went up 150 points with Princeton Review? Take a prep course. Cousin Amanda says her score went down 20 points after a Kaplan course? Don't take a prep course. But isn't there a guarantee that my score will go up? Take a prep course. My college counselor says I can probably prepare just as well on my own? Don't take a prep course.

Under the stress of the college search, the allure of the test-prep companies is often irresistible. Facing tens of thousands of dollars in tuition payments, many families are willing to cough up an extra grand on the chance that it might help.

The Truth about the SAT

The purpose of this book is to clear up the confusion once and for all. Hype and hysteria have been swirling around the SAT for years, and all the more so since the redesign of the test in March 2005. We begin the book with straightforward answers to questions such as:

- What does the SAT really measure?
- How important is the SAT?
- Is it possible to psych out the SAT?

After a balanced look at each these issues, we found that the truth differs in important ways from the party line offered by the colleges, the College Board, and the giants of test prep. In Chapter 2, we move on to another old chestnut that has bedeviled families for years:

- Are coaching courses really worth the money?

In over twenty years of writing and counseling about college admission, we have heard variations of this question over and over again. Prior to doing the research for this book, even we did not have a ready answer. Unbiased information about prepping for the SAT is hard to get. Even among education professionals, attitudes toward SAT preparation and coaching courses have always been shaped by biases and hunches rather than hard information. Many educators resent the College Board and its stranglehold on the college admissions process. Believing that the SAT is arbitrary and discriminatory, they are inclined to believe the claims of the test-prep companies that the SAT is a rigged game that can be outsmarted if you know the rules. On the other side are educators—including most admissions officers—who believe the SAT has a useful role in college admissions even if it does have flaws. These people are generally suspicious of the slick marketing and dubious claims of the test-prep companies.

> "I think that what I got out of my prep course was stronger vocab and experiences from taking practice tests. If I had bought a good vocab book and made my own schedule, I think that I could have been just as effective."
>
> —610 V, 800 M

For many years, we quoted an admissions officer who said "you pay your money and you take your chances." A pithy turn of phrase but not particularly enlightening. To get beyond the propaganda of the test-makers, the admission officers, and the test-prep giants, we needed an independent voice. It occurred to us that with all the purportedly "inside" information circulating about the SAT, there was one source conspicuously lacking: the students who have actually taken the test.

Since 1981, the *Fiske Guide to Colleges* has offered the inside story on the nation's best and most interesting colleges by reporting straight talk from students coast to coast. This book brings the same kind of insight to the SAT.

In what turned out to be one of the largest independent studies ever conducted about preparing for the SAT, we distributed nearly 1,400 surveys to students and received responses from 815 students at 67 high schools. We sought a broad sample of students that included both those who paid for test prep and those who prepared on their own. Our main priority was simple: Find out what works. How did students who did well prepare for the SAT? Which prep techniques did they find useful? We also wanted to take a hard look at coaching courses. Would those who got tutoring or coaching score higher than those who did not? Would those who paid big money see results?

After reading and tabulating 815 surveys, the answer came back loud and clear. The 425 students who did not take a prep course or get a tutor scored a combined 1291, while the 390 students who did take a prep course averaged 1257. The average score for the 119 students who took a course or got tutoring from Princeton Review or Kaplan was 1278.

Surprised? We were. But the more we analyzed our results, the more they made sense. Here are a few of the many insights that you will learn in this book:

- Why the highest-scoring SAT-takers seldom benefit from prep courses
- How high-scoring students use their wits to beat the SAT
- Why taking full-length practice tests—and analyzing the results—is the single most effective way to prepare

Most importantly, you'll get the collective wisdom (and occasional wit) of 815 students who averaged a combined score of over 1270. If your goal is to score high, there is no better source than students who have recently done so. You'll learn how they prepared for the test—what worked for them, what didn't work, and what they wish they had done differently.

Doing It on Your Own

This book differs from most SAT prep guides because it does not offer a sure-fire formula for acing the test. Our bottom line, reinforced by the hundreds of surveys we received from students with firsthand experience, is that most students will be best served by devising their own strategy rather than using a prepackaged approach designed by others. Our job is to report the findings of our surveys—including countless techniques used by real students—and let you choose the methods that make the most sense. We'll offer plenty of guidance on how to shape your approach to the SAT, but you're the one in control.

The most important impact of this book, we hope, will be to unleash the initiative of America's brightest students. We wrote this book with you in mind because we found compelling evidence that *strong students are the least likely to benefit from prep courses and the most likely to increase their scores by designing their own prep programs.*

As our survey makes clear, the savviest students have known all along that they could beat the test on their own. But hype and peer pressure can be powerful forces, and untold thousands of parents and students have been buffaloed into wasting their money on tutors and prep courses. We'll tell more than a few sad stories of such experiences.

There is a strong basis in learning theory for the effectiveness of preparing on your own. Modern research on the brain has proven that initiative and learning go hand in hand, and that active learners retain far more than those who passively listen to others. Memory, it turns out, is constructed rather than absorbed. Students are far more likely to retain knowledge that they themselves have shaped into a meaningful whole. Test prep is not brain surgery or theoretical physics. Every student who takes the SAT has already studied the subject matter on the test. Some students may not want to put out the effort to design their own approach, but all can do it if they put their minds to it.

There is an old saying that the best way to learn a subject is to teach it to someone else. Ever wonder why that is so? In the process of explaining something to another person, we are forced to design our own way of ordering the information. We may have already "learned" the material, but we will know it much better after creating a mental blueprint for how to teach it. This blueprint stays in our head and is the context for remembering. When the chips are down, we are far better able to recall information from a blueprint we have made ourselves than one that was handed to us on a silver platter. In studying for the SAT, the most successful students are the ones who teach themselves.

Another insight from our survey that is backed up by learning theory is this: The best way to master the SAT is through focused practice. Instead of cramming their heads full of tricks, top-scoring students experiment with problem-solving methods under conditions that simulate the real test. They learn to handle SAT questions through repetition, and they try various techniques until they find what works for them. They learn how to deal with time pressure by repeatedly facing that pressure in practice and then developing strategies for dealing with it. And what about all those secret ways to psych out the test advertised by the test-prep companies? Suffice it to say that such gimmicks are more effective at selling prep courses than helping real students score high on the SAT.

> **"It seemed that the instructors became talking books. Everything they told us I had already read."**
>
> —610 V, 690 M

We could probably sell more books with a foolproof, patented, guaranteed-or-your-money-back system to beat the SAT, but that would be dishonest. Students learn differently. A great technique for one student may befuddle and unnerve another. Take reading comprehension. Some students swear by reading the questions first, then reading the passage. Others get distracted by reading the questions first. Still others skim the passage and then focus on the questions. The strategy you choose is less important than making a choice—your choice.

This book offers a menu of all the best techniques from hundreds of high-scoring students, including:

- How to get your brain in shape and the importance of pacing yourself
- How to get inside the minds of the test-makers and understand what they are looking for
- How to zero in on the correct answer even if you are not sure what it is
- How to overcome your anxiety and approach the test with confidence

Along the way, you'll learn strategies that cover every type of question you'll encounter on the SAT. We'll lay them all out, then guide you toward your own unique strategy for conquering the test.

According to our survey, the number-one reason why students take an SAT prep course is to pay an adult to force them to focus on the SAT. With that kind of attitude, no wonder students do better when they have the initiative to prepare on their own. With the publication of this book, there are no more excuses. Think of us as a $17 alternative to a $1,000 prep course.

THE POWER OF LEARNING BY DOING

Imagine two people learning how to play a new game. Like basketball. Suppose one of them listens to weeks of lectures on the finer points of the game—how to dribble, how to shoot, how to run a back-door play, how to execute a baseline spin move from the low post. Suppose another person spends all that time actually playing the game. Who do you think will be the better player? Like basketball, taking the SAT is a game that is best learned by actually doing it, not by listening to experts talk about it.

Let's Get Started

We hope that you will find the layout of this book logical and easy to follow.

Chapter 1, "Inside the New SAT," gives you the essential facts about the SAT: the nuts and bolts of the new (and old) versions, what the changes mean for students like you, the role of the SAT in the college admission process, a rundown of exactly what the SAT measures, and an inside look at whether you can psych out the test. We'll also cover the Preliminary SAT (PSAT) and give you tips on the other major standardized test, the ACT.

Chapter 2, "SAT Prep Courses: Straight Talk from Students," lays out the findings of our survey. It is chock-full of quotes from students who did well on the test about their strategies for beating the SAT, and whether they thought their SAT prep courses improved their scores. If you still want to take a prep course after reading this chapter, be our guest.

Chapter 3, "Taking Charge of Your SAT Prep," offers advice on how to prepare for the SAT, including when to take the SAT, how many times to take it, and how to design your own prep course. Based on our surveys, we'll reveal how focused practice can help you devise all-important strategies for skipping problems, making educated guesses, and honing your speed and stamina.

Chapters 4–6 provide a closer look at the Writing, Critical Reading, and Math sections that comprise the New SAT. Instead of offering long-winded explanations of topics you already understand, we'll give you an inside view of the nastiest tricks the test-makers will throw your way—and how you can beat them at their own game.

Following Chapter 6, we offer perhaps the book's most unique feature—the Fiske SAT Practice Tests. As you read this book, you will quickly discover that we harp on the importance of taking practice tests. Most of the time, we'll refer you to *The Official SAT Study Guide* published by the College Board, but for an extra challenge, you should also take the Fiske Practice Tests—the only tests available that give you a workout on the hardest questions. Take these tests to diagnose your strengths and weaknesses, increase your test-taking speed, and hone your personal strategy. If you can handle our practice SATs, the real thing will be a snap.

To help you navigate the book, the first three chapters begin with an "Answers to Your Questions" box that outlines the topics, in order, covered in that chapter. The chapters on the three sections of the SAT begin with a box that summarizes the types of questions that will be discussed in each.

So what are you waiting for? Don't let procrastination slow you down. You can do it, and the time is now.

The SAT and the Meaning of Life

Stress can kill you, both in life and on the SAT. As this book shows, staying calm is crucial for doing your best. Many students and parents get stressed out over today's college admission climate—understandable when the nation's most selective colleges are accepting less than 10 percent of their applicants. There's no denying that good SAT scores can give you a leg up on the competition.

But let's not get carried away. We have yet to meet a college student who walks the campus with SAT scores tattooed on his or her forehead. And while many families have a window decal on their car that announces a college choice, is anybody really looking? We suspect that the getting-in stakes are not as high as you may think. Lesser-known schools generally try harder than the big names, and many of them offer bigger scholarships, smaller classes, more attention from faculty, and better mentoring for opportunities after graduation. There are a lot of unhappy people at the Harvards of the world, and thousands more at places you've never heard of who are doing just fine.

Work hard, score high, and play the game. Aim for Dream U and maybe you'll get there. But don't count on the college search to give your life meaning. If you're getting straight A's but also getting stressed out, that's a sign that your priorities may need tweaking. You'll enjoy your life more—and you just might get a higher score on the SAT.

In that spirit, we offer the following slightly tongue-in-cheek "pledges" for the college admission process that we hope students and parents will take to heart.

FISKE'S

College Admission Pledge
for Students

I have accepted the fact that my parents are clueless. I am serene. I will betray not a tremor when they offer opinions or advice, no matter how laughable. My soul will be light as a feather when my mother elbows her way to the front of my college tour and talks the guide's ear off. I am serene.

Going to college is a stressful time for my parents, even though they are not the ones going. I recognize that neurosis is beyond anyone's control. Each week, I will calmly reassure them that I am working on my essays, have registered for my tests, am finishing my applications, have scheduled my interviews, am aware of all deadlines, and will have everything done in plenty of time. I will smile good-naturedly as my parent asks four follow-up questions at College Night.

I will try not to say "no" simply because my parents say "yes," and remain open to the possibility, however improbable, that they may have a point. I may not be fully conscious of my anxieties about the college search—the fear of being judged and the fear of leaving home are both strong. I don't really want to get out of here as much as I say I do, and it is easier to put off thinking about the college search than to get it done. My parents are right about the importance of being proactive, even if they do get carried away.

Though the college search belongs to me, I will listen to my parents. They know me better than anyone else, and they are the ones who will pay most of the bills. Their ideas about what will be best for me are based on years of experience in the real world. I will seriously consider what they say as I form my own opinions.

I must take charge of the college search. If I do, the nagging will stop, and everyone's anxiety will go down. My parents have given me a remarkable gift—the ability to think and do for myself. I know I can do it with a little help from Mom and Dad.

FISKE'S

College Admission Pledge

for Parents

I am resigned to the fact that my child's college search will end in disaster. I am serene. Deadlines will be missed and scholarships will be lost as my child lounges under pulsating headphones or stares transfixed at a Game Cube. I am a parent and I know nothing. I am serene.

Confronted with endless procrastination, my impulse is to take control—to register for tests, plan visits, schedule interviews, and get applications. It was I who asked those four follow-up questions at College Night—I couldn't help myself. And yet I know that everything will be fine if I can summon the fortitude to relax. My child is smart, capable, and perhaps a little too accustomed to me jumping in and fixing things. I will hold back. I will drop hints and encourage, then back off. I will facilitate rather than dominate. The college search won't happen on my schedule, but it will happen.

I will not get too high or low about any facet of the college search. By doing so, I give it more importance than it really has. My child's self-worth may already be too wrapped up in getting an acceptance letter. I will attempt to lessen the fear rather than heighten it.

I will try not to say "no" simply because my son or daughter says "yes," and remain open to the possibility, however improbable, that my child has the most important things under control. I understand that my anxiety comes partly from a sense of impending loss. I can feel my child slipping away. Sometimes I hold on too tightly or let social acceptability cloud the issue of what is best.

I realize that my child is almost ready to go and that a little rebellion at this time of life can be a good thing. I will respect and encourage independence, even if some of it is expressed as resentment toward me. I will make suggestions with care and try to avoid unnecessary confrontation.

Paying for college is my responsibility. I will take a major role in the search for financial aid and scholarships and speak honestly to my child about the financial realities we face.

I must help my son or daughter take charge of the college search. I will try to support without smothering, encourage without annoying, and consult without controlling. The college search is too big to be handled alone—I will be there every step of the way.

INSIDE THE NEW SAT

Most readers already know what the letters "SAT" stand for—or think they know. Scholastic Aptitude Test? Think again. That name bit the dust in 1990. Scholastic Assessment Test? The College Board ran that one up the flag pole in the early '90s, but no, "SAT" does not stand for that either. The truth is that "SAT" no longer stands for anything. It is a brand name—like Kmart or Exxon.

The story of the SAT's incredible changing name is convoluted but crucial to understanding the test. The roll-out of the revised SAT in March 2005 represented a major change in the way the test is put together.

Understanding how and why the test was changed is crucial for any student who wants to master it.

The Scholastic Aptitude Test was first administered back in 1926, when everybody thought they knew what aptitude meant. The SAT was an intelligence test, designed to distinguish students who had the potential for higher education from those who did not. In the days when people believed in the validity of IQ—intelligence quotient—it was a perfectly logical exercise. By the 1960s, the selective colleges and universities widely used the SAT. Previously, the most important questions in college admissions had been: "Where'd you go to school?" and "Who's your daddy?" The SAT played a crucial role in opening doors to gifted students who were not born with a silver spoon.

The College Board's fondest hope was that the SAT would become a universal measure of scholastic aptitude—not to be confused with scholastic achievement. The latter was the domain of the ACT (discussed below), the Achievement Tests (now called "SAT Subject Tests"), and the Advanced Placement tests. Unlike all of these, the SAT was not intended to measure what students learned in school. It aimed higher.

> **"The most important thing about the SAT is not to be surprised."**
> —730 V, 720 M

But the old SAT was like a spiffy new shirt with a teensy-weensy thread hanging from the sleeve. Give that thread a yank and the whole thing might come unraveled. The root of the problem with the SAT lies in the complexity of the human brain and in the fact that modern research has figured out that intelligence is a complicated, multifaceted thing. Some people have excellent spatial understanding but are lousy in interpersonal awareness. Some people can speak brilliantly but are unable to translate their insight into writing. Some people are speedy in processing information; others process more slowly but produce thoughtful, nuanced answers to complex questions. Three hours of oval blackening will reward students who excel in the particular set of skills and abilities measured by the test, but this exercise may also punish students who have other skills that are just as important—or even more important—for success in college and in life.

The realization that intelligence cannot be measured by two numbers was a major problem for the College Board and its SAT. The SAT was not supposed to be an achievement test, and it clearly was not an adequate measure of intelligence. So what did it measure?

Answering this question is complicated by a few inequities. Students from families with higher incomes consistently score better on the SAT than they should in relation to lower income students with similar grades. At the same time, members of some minority groups score lower than their school performance suggests they should. In addition, girls, who on average get better grades than boys, score lower on both sections than do boys. The College Board says that the test merely reflects the inequities already present in society.

By 1990, the word "aptitude" had become an anachronism. It suggested that the ingredients of success were inborn rather than learned. But "scholastic assessment" was no better. By design, the SAT did not measure classroom-acquired knowledge. The College Board already had a complete line of scholastic assessment tests in the form of what is now known as the SAT Subject Tests.

Faced with the problem of defending a test that measured neither intelligence nor achievement, the College Board gamely soldiered on. Its brain trust hit upon a new unifying concept for the test—"developed reasoning ability." In effect, the Board was claiming that the SAT measured ability that was linked to schoolwork yet was broader than school learning and, at the same time, was neither a measure of innate ability nor a proxy for socioeconomic status. Is that confusing enough for you? Interviewed in 1999 by the PBS television program *Frontline*, Wayne Camara, head of the College Board's office of research, summed up the argument this way:

> [The SAT] is not an IQ test. It's far from it. Developed reasoning skills measured on a test like the SAT will link directly to the breadth and the depth of the curriculum students have been exposed to in school, but also out-of-school learning. Students who have read an incredible amount, whether it's in-school assignments or out-of-school assignments, are more likely to do better on tests like the SAT but also in college.
>
> So it's not an achievement measure, which would be redundant with what grades are. But it's certainly not an IQ test, which would be an innate measure of ability. It's much more developed reasoning— the type of skills students develop over an extended period of time.

The idea that the SAT measured reasoning ability—but not necessarily reasoning ability developed in school—would prove to be untenable. If life outside of school was part of the equation, there was too much probability that SAT scores would be shaped by factors such as family income, ethnicity, and other socioeconomic factors. The notion of "developed ability" was like blood in the water for the critics.

The mortal blow for the old SAT was a thunderbolt unleashed in February 2001, by then-president of the University of California, Richard Atkinson. Out of the blue, he announced that he would recommend that UC drop the SAT as an admissions requirement. Atkinson, a psychologist, lashed out at the SAT as "aligned neither to standards nor school curriculums" and went on to say:

> Simple fairness tells me this is wrong. We are, after all, a society built on twin notions: first, that actual achievement should be what matters most; and second, that people should be judged on the basis of what they have made of the opportunities available to them. Therefore, it seems only right that college-bound students should be judged on what they have accomplished during four years of high school, not on the basis of a single standardized exam designed to test undefined notions of "aptitude." For those reasons, I am recommending to the faculty that the SAT no longer be required for students applying to UC.

Atkinson stressed that he is not against standardized testing per se—just tests that are not connected to high school curriculum. He reaffirmed UC's use of the SAT Subject Tests, describing them as a better predictor of college performance than the SAT, and called for the design of new standardized tests geared toward what students learn in school.

It would have been interesting to be a fly on the wall at College Board headquarters when Atkinson's announcement came over the wire. "To drop the SAT would be like deciding you're going to drop grades," responded Gaston Caperton, president of the Board. With 175,000 students on eight campuses, UC was the SAT's largest institutional user and a client that College Board could not afford to lose. Almost before the ink had dried on

Atkinson's statement, the Board was busily working on a new version of the SAT that would appease Atkinson and the critics. Barely four months later, the Board announced plans for the changes scheduled to be implemented in March 2005.

Goodbye 1600, Hello 2400

The most obvious change in the SAT is the new way of computing combined scores. The old SAT consisted of the familiar Verbal and Math sections graded on the 200–800 scale. The revised version has three sections: Writing, Critical Reading, and Math. Total testing time has increased from 3 hours to 3 hours and 45 minutes. With three sections instead of two, the holy grail of standardized test-taking is now 2400—a combined perfect score on all three.

It should surprise no one that the New SAT has a split personality. Its roots as an aptitude test are still apparent, yet it has been dressed up with new material to make it a more credible indicator of what students learn in school. The Verbal section, renamed Critical Reading, has one major change: the much-dreaded analogies have been deleted. (See the comparison on the next page.) In their place, students get a bigger dose of reading comprehension. There are still reading passages of up to 850 words, but additional short passages, called Paragraph-Length Critical Reading, have been added.

> "Cramming does not help at all for the SAT, but reading widely and looking up unfamiliar words is useful."
>
> —780 V, 800 M

The Math section has two significant changes: there is more higher-level math, and quantitative comparison questions have been dropped. Most of the new math topics are normally learned in Algebra II. They range from radical equations and negative exponents to quadratic equations. Geometric notation will now be used, and basic trigonometry may be used as an alternative method to solve some problems. New statistics concepts will include scatterplots and geometric probability. The role of a calculator, scientific or graphing, will expand.

Few students will shed any tears over the axing of the analogies. A fixture on the SAT since 1936, analogies have long been synonymous with the test. But in recent years, they have also been a poster-child for the disconnect between SAT and the typical high school curriculum. An example:

ANALOGIES : COLLEGE BOARD ::
(A) achievement : ACT
(B) aptitude : test
(C) essay : writing
(D) calculator : math
(E) albatross : Ancient Mariner

British literature buffs will immediately recognize that the correct answer is (E) albatross : Ancient Mariner. Just as the albatross symbolized the

OLD SAT   NEW SAT

Total Time: 3 hours	**Total Time: 3 hours and 45 minutes**
Sections	**Sections**
3 Verbal (2 of 30 minutes, 1 of 15 minutes)	3 Critical Reading (2 of 25 minutes, 1 of 20 minutes)
3 Math (2 of 30 minutes, 1 of 15 minutes)	3 Math (2 of 25 minutes, 1 of 20 minutes)
	3 Writing (2 of 25 minutes, 1 of 10 minutes)
1 unscored section	1 unscored section
Types of Questions	**Types of Questions**
Verbal	**Critical Reading**
Sentence completions	Sentence completions
Analogies	Passage-based reading (500–850 words)
Critical reading	Paragraph-length reading (100 words)
Math	**Math**
Conventional multiple-choice	Conventional multiple-choice
Quantitative comparisons	Grid-ins (student-produced responses)
Grid-ins (student-produced responses)	
	Writing
	Student-produced essay
	Identifying sentence errors
	Improving sentences
	Improving paragraphs

Mariner's guilt in Samuel Taylor Coleridge's epic poem, so the analogies were a symbol of the SAT's failure to keep up with the times. UC's Atkinson said he was moved to consider dropping the SAT when he visited an elite private school where the curriculum in the middle grades included cram sessions on SAT-style analogy questions. The College Board itself now admits that the analogy questions encouraged rote memorization of vocabulary. If only the Board had fessed up to that fact a few years ago.

Also dropped were the Quantitative Comparison questions, which asked students to evaluate two mathematical expressions with four possible answers. Here is an example:

SUMMARY DIRECTIONS FOR COMPARISON QUESTIONS
<u>Answer</u>:
A if the quantity in Column A is greater;
B if the quantity in Column B is greater;
C if the two quantities are equal
D if the relationship cannot be determined from the information given

$$6x - 12 = 42$$

Column A	Column B
x	8

Answer: A. (Since x must equal 9, Column A is greater than Column B.)

Like the analogies, this type of problem never sees the light of day in a classroom and therefore will be axed. As with the old SAT, a few math questions will require students to produce their own answer. The bulk of the questions will remain in the conventional five-question multiple-choice format.

The biggest change in the test has come in the form of a new section, Writing, created with material lifted from the former SAT II: Writing Test. Multiple-choice questions, also in the format of those on the SAT II: Writing Test, come in three types: identifying sentence errors, improving sentences, and improving paragraphs. All three kinds are in multiple-choice format and require students to choose the most appropriate word or phrase to be inserted to correct an error or make an improvement.

Unless you have been living under a rock for the last five years, you know that the Writing section includes a 25-minute essay. A writing test had been high on the University of California's list of priorities. As with the multiple-choice questions, the format of essay is similar to that of the old SAT II: Writing Test and features open-ended prompts that allow students to express a personal opinion. An example:

"Necessity is the mother of invention." Plan and write an essay in which you develop your point of view on this issue. Support your position with reasoning and examples taken from your reading, studies, experiences, or observations.

As with the old SAT, the new version includes one unscored "experimental" section that will be used to test new questions and may be Critical Reading, Writing, or Math. This section does not count toward a student's score.

> "Don't freak out! That's the best advice. The SAT is serious but if you are too tense it won't help and it will cause physical and emotional distress."
>
> —710 V, 800 M

The addition of the Writing section will be accompanied by a slight decrease in the time devoted to Critical Reading and Math. Taken as a whole, the changes added 45 minutes of testing time and increased the registration fee to about $41.50. As a footnote, UC's Atkinson hailed the changes as soon as they were announced. He stated, "I give enormous credit to the College Board and to its president, Gaston Caperton, for the vision they have demonstrated in bringing forward these changes and for their genuine commitment to improved educational attainment in our nation."

And the part about UC dropping the SAT? Didn't happen. Having successfully prodded the College Board into action, Atkinson and UC reversed their decision soon after Caperton announced his plan to change the test.

OLD PSAT

Total Time: 2 hours and 10 minutes

Sections
2 Verbal (25 minutes each)
1 Writing (30 minutes)
2 Math (25 minutes each)

Types of Questions
Verbal
Sentence completions
Reading comprehension (500–800 words)
Analogies

Writing
Identifying sentence errors
Improving sentences
Improving paragraphs

Math
Conventional multiple-choice
Grid-ins (student-produced responses)
Quantitative comparisons

NEW PSAT

Total Time: 2 hours and 10 minutes

Sections
2 Critical Reading (25 minutes each)
1 Writing (30 minutes)
2 Math (25 minutes each)

Types of Questions
Critical Reading
Sentence completions
Passage-based reading (500–850 words)
Paragraph-length reading (100 words)

Writing
Identifying sentence errors
Improving sentences
Improving paragraphs

Math
Conventional multiple-choice
Grid-ins (student-produced responses)

The New PSAT and the National Merit Program

Although most of the hype has been about the revised SAT, there is also a new version of the Preliminary SAT. The Preliminary SAT is a modified version of the real thing, administered once a year in October to eleventh graders and many tenth graders depending on high school policy. The PSAT is also the qualifying test for the National Merit Scholarship Program, the largest and best-known scholarship/recognition program in the country.

The changes to the PSAT were less significant than those to the SAT. The PSAT has consisted of Verbal, Writing, and Math sections since 1997, when a Writing section like the one on the revised SAT was added. A major difference: The PSAT consists only of multiple choice questions (no essay). The Verbal portion, renamed Critical Reading, includes the same kinds of questions as those on the revised SAT with the analogy questions likewise eliminated. As with the SAT, the PSAT math section has axed the Quantitative Comparisons and features more higher-level math, but the PSAT does not include anything from Algebra II. Though there is *not* an essay on the new PSAT, schools will be given the option of administering one for practice. Total testing time is two hours and ten minutes—an hour and thirty-five minutes shorter than the SAT. If you are reviewing for the PSAT, all the advice in this book applies.

Unlike the SAT, students register for and take the PSAT through their high schools, which have the option of administering the test on a Wednesday or a Saturday. Students who are homeschooled should contact a local high school and arrange to take the test there. Students occasionally run into problems if their school arranges a Saturday administration that conflicts with an athletic contest or other event. In such cases, they are allowed to take the test at a school other than their own, and those with conflicts should investigate local schools that may be giving it on Wednesday. If all else fails, missing the PSAT is not a disaster. The scores are not generally reported to the colleges and carry little significance once a student completes an SAT. The main value of the PSAT is practice. Most schools keep each student's test booklet on file, and when the score reports come back in December, students can see exactly which questions they missed. The PSAT is scored in a similar way to the SAT, but instead of 200–800, the scale is 20–80.

The long form of the Preliminary SAT's acronym is PSAT/NMSQT, the latter part standing for National Merit Scholarship Qualifying Test. Eleventh graders who take the PSAT are automatically entered in the competition. Each student's scores in the Critical Reading, Writing, and Math sections are added together to create a Selection Index. The top 1.25 percent of eleventh grade scorers, more or less, earn the status of National Merit Semifinalists. The next-highest 3 percent are designated as Commended Students and receive a certificate for their efforts. One footnote: The 1997 decision to add a Writing section to the PSAT was made under the threat of legal action. At that time, many more boys than girls were earning Merit Scholarships, and since girls tend to do relatively better than boys in writing, the new section was intended to boost the number of female winners. It did, though the goal of a fifty/fifty gender split remains elusive.

Since National Merit mandates a fixed proportion of winners from each state tied to its population, your odds of qualifying can vary depending on where you live. That spells trouble for students from highly educated states like Massachusetts, where the Selection Index necessary for Semifinalist status has traditionally been about 221. In less high-falutin' places like Wyoming or Mississippi, the qualifying score has been closer to 200. (The exact score in each state may vary from year to year depending on the number of high scorers.)

Once the Semifinalists are announced—in September of twelfth grade—they have about a month to write an essay and complete a short application that is coupled with a counselor recommendation. Advancing to Finalist is a snap as long as the student's grades are in the A range. About 90 percent of Semifinalists become Finalists when the new crop is announced in early February. From here, about 2,400

> "Thinking like the test-maker was good and bad because sometimes I forgot to just think about what I thought."
>
> —590 V, 720 M

of the highest scorers are awarded one-time scholarships from National Merit of up to $2,500. Major corporations also make awards, usually to Finalists who are dependents of their employees or residents of areas where the corporations do business. About two hundred four-year colleges offer scholarships to Finalists, including some that make a cottage industry of enrolling Finalists with full-ride scholarships. But don't count on anything but a yawn from Ivy-caliber schools, which are overrun with applications from National Merit honorees.

In all, just over half of the Finalists receive a scholarship. Whether or not Finalists get money may have less to do with merit than where they choose to go to college, where they live, and where their parents work.

National Merit also sponsors the separate National Achievement Scholarship Program for outstanding black American high school students. The mechanics of the program are similar to those of the main program, and just over 775 students are ultimately named as Finalists and are thereby eligible for scholarships. African American students can enter both the National Achievement and National Merit programs.

How Important Is the SAT?

To hear students talk, you'd think that college admission was all about SAT scores—with maybe a quick glance at a student's transcript and letters of recommendation. Keenly aware of the hype, colleges are quick to downplay the importance of scores. High school counselors fall somewhere in the middle; they seek to ease student overemphasis on the SAT while believing in their heart of hearts that the SAT is more important than the colleges are willing to admit.

> **"Studying beforehand seems to me less useful than pacing yourself and thinking clearly during the test itself."**
>
> —800 V, 710 M

We spoke to several college admission officers to get their views. "The SAT is one factor in our evaluation of academic achievement and potential," says Jerome Lucido, vice provost for enrollment at the highly selective University of North Carolina at Chapel Hill. "This evaluation includes coursework, grades, rank in class (or its many proxies), awards, achievements, and teacher recommendations. We also consider many personal factors. It is clear, then, that SAT plays a much smaller role in the overall decision than students would believe from the rumors they hear, from the rhetoric of the coaching companies, or from the popular press."

If you polled the admissions directors of fifty highly selective colleges, every one of them would probably agree with this statement. While downplaying the importance of the SAT, admission officers defend its usefulness as one part of the application. In doing so, they walk a fine line. Even the College Board admits that grades in school are the best indicator of college readiness. But the colleges (and the College Board) maintain that the combination of high school grades and SATs is a better predictor than either measure by itself. "The tests are a national measure for all applicants, so it helps to equalize consideration of candidates across a wide national and international spectrum," says Karl Furstenberg, dean of admissions and financial aid at Dartmouth College.

David Erdmann, dean of admissions and enrollment at somewhat selective Rollins College, expands on this reasoning: "Our experience is that grading systems, rigor, curriculum, standards, and expectations vary from school to school. Recommendations have the same flaw. The best recommendation for the top student at one high school may have the same praise that might have been heaped on the middle student at another high school. We believe that recommendations typically favor independent school students where the teaching load is lighter, where putting the best foot forward is an expectation, and where the recommendation is generally in greater depth. Essays suffer the same inherent flaw, or can, where the opportunity for assistance is greater. SAT or ACT scores help to level the playing field."

We suspect that many admissions officers would also agree with this statement. Yet if it is true that the SAT is the only universal yardstick—or at least true that admission officers perceive it to be—that fact strengthens the hand of those who say that the SAT may be more important than the colleges say it is. Public perception of the SAT as a universal yardstick also plays a role. To a greater or lesser degree, all admissions offices feel pressure to maintain high average SAT scores among their entering classes—high scores look good, and scores are a factor in the rankings produced by *U.S. News & World Report*.

The correlation between high scores and admission to top colleges is exceptionally strong. Dartmouth and UNC at Chapel Hill provide the following figures based on combined scores from the old SAT:

SAT SCORE	PERCENT ACCEPTED	
	Dartmouth	UNC
1600	80	95
1400–1590	36	68
1200–1390	14	39
1000–1190	11	22
800–990	0	11
600–790	0	2

Of course, the colleges would be quick to point out that students who have high scores tend to bring other qualities that make them stand out. Then again, many of the low scorers who get in are athletes or others with special talents.

The gulf in perception that separates those on the high school side and those in college admission offices may lie in how each one sizes up the competition. Top students see themselves as competing against other top students. The student with a 2.5 GPA in a particular high school is not likely to be applying to the same colleges as classmates with a 3.7 or 3.8. Given that students with similar academic records apply to the same schools, what makes the difference? These students all get good recommendations and can generally write a good essay. Today's trend toward grade inflation accentuates the issue. Capable, hard-working students inhabit an increasingly narrow band of grades in the A/A–/B+ range. The SAT is often the only factor that puts meaningful distance between them. A strong student who does not test well may score in the 500s or 600s on each section for a combined score in the 1200s; a student with the same A average who is an SAT whiz may get 700s for a combined score in the 1400s or 1500s.

All this begs an important question: Does the SAT measure real abilities? Or merely test-taking skills? We'll weigh in on this raging debate a bit later. For now, suffice it to say that if you're an able student with a strong transcript, your SAT score will determine your fate at selective institutions as much as or more than any other part of your application.

Before we leave the topic of the SAT's importance in admission, it is worth noting that most public universities that are less selective than UNC at Chapel Hill use a different model. With lots of applicants and relatively few admission officers, these institutions tend to rely on test score cut-offs for admission, though there is often an alternate route to getting in for students who do not achieve the requisite score. The University of Arizona is a typical example. For in-staters, U of A requires that students meet one of the following four criteria for automatic admission: 1.) rank in the top 25 percent of the high school class, or 2.) have a 3.0 GPA, or 3.) a 1040 SAT, or 4.) a 22 ACT. Students who do not meet any of these requirements may be admitted if they fulfill other criteria.

Still other schools create a formula for admission that encompasses minimum GPA and test score requirements. Depending on the formula, it is sometimes possible to compensate for a low test score with a high GPA. Most colleges that use a specific score formula are up-front about it on their websites. Standardized test scores are not necessarily more important at these institutions than at the highly selective places, but at least you know where you stand.

What about the ACT?

Ask someone from Connecticut about the ACT and you may get a blank stare. The same goes if you ask about the SAT in Iowa. The world of college admissions is divided into two fiefdoms of roughly equal size. The SAT was created by a group of Ivy Leaguers as a sorting mechanism for elite East Coast institutions. It is also the dominant test on the West Coast, thanks in part to the influence of the University of California. The original purpose of the SAT was to make subtle distinctions between the abilities of above-average students. The ACT was conceived by professors at the University of Iowa in the late 1950s and has historically served the Midwest and Mountain West. It was initially designed to assess the academic preparation of students of a wider cross-section of students. The SAT is more than thirty years older, and with 1.4 million test-takers a year, it is still the most widely used college entrance exam. But the ACT, with 1.2 million test-takers per year, has been gaining ground in recent years as more students on the coasts seek an alternative to the SAT.

> "I would say buy a prep book; don't pay $900 for a prep course.... My friends who took courses were bored and did worse than me. I learned the same techniques for $17.99 from a nice paperweight."
> —800 V, 770 M

The ACT includes sections in English, math, reading, and science reasoning that are scored on a 36-point scale. The average composite ACT score is between 20 and 21. The vast majority of colleges will accept either the SAT or ACT to satisfy their core testing requirements. A few highly selective institutions, especially those that are technically oriented, prefer the SAT because it makes finer distinctions on the high end of the score scale. (The extremely short list of institutions that will accept only the SAT includes Harvey Mudd College, St. Mary's College of Maryland, and Wake Forest University.)

For students who are disappointed with their SAT scores, the ACT offers another chance to do well on a standardized test. Though the two tests are used interchangeably, their personalities are far different. While the SAT has always been a sorting mechanism for selective institutions, the ACT was originally created less to help with admission decisions than to determine course placement. While the SAT purports to measure "reasoning," the ACT is an achievement-based test. In practical terms, that means the ACT has more straightforward questions about material you have learned in school while the SAT offers riddles that test big-picture thinking ability. The SAT has always emphasized vocabulary to a much greater degree than has the ACT, which focuses mainly on grammar and usage in its English section.

In math, the ACT has stressed knowing the right formulas to solve problems while the SAT gives students the formulas and asks them to solve problems that require more creativity. Time pressure is often a factor on both tests.

The introduction of the revised SAT has blurred these distinctions somewhat. The College Board is trying to make the SAT more achievement-oriented—and more like the ACT. For its part, the ACT now offers an optional 30-minute essay similar to the one on the revised SAT. Many selective colleges require students to take the ACT with essay if they submit ACT scores. Other colleges will accept the ACT with or without essay. If your colleges do not require the essay and you don't want to deal with writing one, you may prefer to take the ACT rather than the SAT.

SAT vs. ACT: How the Scores Stack Up

Here is how scores on the old SAT correlated with those on the ACT. If a student got a 23 on the ACT, for example, that was roughly the same as getting a 1070 on the SAT. Look for a revision of these numbers when data on the New SAT become available. Students who score significantly better on one test or the other should consider submitting only these scores to the colleges. If a student takes both tests and the scores are about even, submitting both sets of scores is probably the best strategy.

ACT–SAT CONVERSION CHART

ACT	SAT	ACT	SAT
36	1600	25	1140
35	1580	24	1110
34	1520	23	1070
33	1470	22	1030
32	1420	21	990
31	1380	20	950
30	1340	19	910
29	1300	18	870
28	1260	17	830
27	1220	16	780
26	1180	15	740

Is It Possible to Psych Out the SAT?

The biggest brouhaha over the SAT concerns the extent to which it measures real abilities as opposed to mere test-taking savvy. Critics say that knowledge of test-taking techniques plays an outsized role in doing well. The most extreme version of this argument holds that an SAT score is simply a measure of how well a student takes the SAT. By getting inside the mind of the test-maker, the theory goes, students can find the answers to many questions without regard to the subject matter that the question addresses. The most prominent advocate of this view is Princeton Review, which grosses millions each year selling this approach. Independent testing watchdog groups, which generally oppose high-stakes exams such as the SAT, have also bought into this theory because it helps bolster their arguments against the test.

The kernel of truth to this view relates to how ETS designs the SAT. As with many tests that attempt to measure broad abilities, on the SAT most of the questions are chosen based not on whether the answer is an important piece of knowledge, but on how many students get the question right or wrong. For each SAT, there must be a constant proportion of easy and hard questions so that the scores come out right. A 600 on one administration of the SAT must mean the same thing as a 600 on the next administration. Since the easy questions come at the beginning and the hard questions at the end in all sections except Reading Comprehension, students must be wary of obvious answers near the end of each section because they are often tricks designed to fool average test-takers. Princeton Review illustrates this principle with a fictitious character, Joe Bloggs, who represents the average student. Joe Bloggs gets the easy questions right and the hard questions wrong. Here is an example:

If $4^r = s$, which of the following equals $16s$?

(A) 64^r
(B) 4^{16r}
(C) 16^r
(D) 4^{2+r}
(E) 4^r

This problem is a relatively hard one that Joe Bloggs is likely to miss. In order to get it right, students must understand how to manipulate exponents. For those who don't know the math, response (A) may seem like a logical answer. If we multiply s by 16, shouldn't we also multiply 4^r by 16, thereby giving us 64^r? Of course not. 64^r is a wildly different expression than 4^r, depending on the value of r. The answer is (D) because by changing the exponent from r to $2 + r$, we are multiplying 42, which is 16, by the original expression 4^r.

The technical term that test designers use for a Joe Bloggs answer is a "distracter"—an answer made to appear right that is actually wrong. The SAT is full of distracters because ETS and the College Board want only a few students to score high. At this point, a tip of the cap is due Princeton Review for highlighting an insight that can be summarized as follows: Watch out for easy-looking questions at the end of sections. Much of the hoopla related to getting inside the mind of the test-makers has its origin in this technique.

> "I always skip hard questions so that I won't be rushed and mess up the easy questions."
>
> —710 V, 740 M

As far as we can tell, there is not much more than this to "psyching out the test-maker." Everybody knows the test is tricky—but which tricks do you usually fall for? The way to find out is by taking the test over and over and learning from your mistakes. We recommend that students be wary of venturing too far into the realm of reading the test-makers' minds, a tangent that can take you away from focusing on your own strengths and weaknesses. The material on the test, based as it is on subjects that all students have studied, is almost always a more reliable guide to finding the answer than shadowy theories about the test-makers' tendencies. If you have the brain power to outsmart the test-maker, the chances are excellent that you can solve most problems based on the content of the questions.

In our survey of 815 students nationwide, we found few students who referenced test-taking techniques of this nature as the most important part of their test prep—or even as a useful part. The allure of learning inside secrets is powerful, but most students find the reality of it less than they imagined. "Making the test into a mental game is distracting and can be demoralizing," says one student who scored 640 V, 760 M. Says another student, who got 590 V, 720 M, "Thinking like the test-maker was good and bad because sometimes I forgot to just think about what I thought." A Princeton Review prepper who scored 620 V, 620 M was simply confused: "I didn't know when to apply their methods. With dozens of kinds of math tricks, it's difficult to know when to use what." Adds another student who took a Princeton Review course and scored 620 V, 620 M, "Joe Bloggs answers and educated guesses don't always work and I found it more difficult to figure out when to use them than to just do the problem." A third student with 600 V, 600 M maintains that "trying to think like the test-maker wastes too much time."

POLITICAL CORRECTNESS AND THE SAT

Pity the poor white male. Once the top dog in American society, he is fast becoming a pariah—at least if you judge by portrayals in the SAT. We analyzed the Sentence Completion questions in ten SATs administered from 1995–2002 that form the contents of the third edition of *10 Real SATs*, a book published by the College Board. In these questions, the test-makers invent sentences and leave blanks for students to fill in. The subject matter of the sentences does not directly relate to the questions, but it does reveal the extent to which the test-makers are trying to combat the perception that the test is biased against females and minorities. There were a total of 181 Sentence Completion questions in 20 sections, and most of them dealt with fictitious characters. But 32 real people were mentioned. The list included 22 women, 8 African Americans, 5 Hispanics, and 3 Asian Americans. The 10 males included 7 minorities and 2 from overseas. The lone American white male was Thomas Jefferson, referenced in a question about his decision not to condemn lotteries.

The questions mentioned a total of 13 fiction writers by name. Nine were from minority groups and the other 4 were white women. Included were distinguished authors such as Maya Angelou, Toni Morrison, and Virginia Woolf, and somewhat lesser-known figures such as Toni Cade Bambara, Maxine Hong Kingston, Clara Rodriguez, and Li-Young Lee. The diversity was admirable in all respects but one: no white males.

Males took it on the chin in the questions that referenced fictitious individuals. The females included Veronica, the gifted physicist; Gwen, who decided to become a medical ethicist; and Carmen Sanchez, the company president who set a good example for her employees. The males included some shadier characters; every negative reference was to a male. One lad committed an act so "heinous" that it was "appalling" even to him. A certain Mr. Edwards "shocked his associates by reacting violently" without provocation. Another poor bloke "is no scholar" even though he "can regurgitate isolated facts."

A young man named Steven, presumably watching his weight, "found it particularly difficult to forgo chocolate." The behavior of other males was "bizarre," "inexplicable," and "dilatory," while another stirred "violent enmity." A boy named Andrew apparently avoided these pitfalls, though he turned out to be "excessively cerebral."

The closest thing we found to a negative reference to a woman was to a female doctor who "vacillated so frequently on disease prevention" and a female prime minister who "was notoriously intransigent regarding issues of national security."

Our purpose is not to question the value of diversity. We're simply saying that on a test where speed is crucial, it is an advantage to be able to size up female- and minority-centered questions at a glance. For instance, you may find yourself puzzling through pairs of words in which you know the definition of one word in the pair but not the other. If so and the question deals with women or minorities, pick the pair with the most positive word.

The test-makers emphasize female- and minority-friendly content because white males do better on the test. Students of all backgrounds can use this tendency to boost their scores.

The biggest problem with the psych-out-the-test approach is that it adds to the mental burden that students carry into the test. Students responding to our surveys told us that the most important key to doing well on the SAT is a relaxed mind-set. Yet prep courses often make the SAT more complicated and stressful than it needs to be. "I feel the program's pressure truly made me nervous and resulted in my lower scores," says one student who took a prep course and was "greatly disappointed" with his 610 V, 590 M. Another student took a prep course and scored 550 V, 590 M on his first SAT. For the second and third, he "slept more and told myself it isn't that big of a deal." His final scores: 620 V and 650 M.

Students told us that course instructors are often less concerned about the needs of their students than in bragging about how they can outsmart the test-makers. "The prep course concentrated too much on stressing that ETS is trying to trick you instead of spending time doing practice tests," says a student who scored 570 V and 610 M. We are inclined to agree with the 680 V, 670 M scorer who says, "I feel that the people who pay hundreds of dollars for tutors, study and practice for the test for hours, and take the test like eight times, do less well than those who just relax."

The people who emphasize getting inside the mind of the test-makers are cashing in to the tune of millions of dollars. But they've got it all wrong: the real key isn't to psych out the test but to psych up yourself. Instead of trying to cram your head full of someone else's tricks, focus on your own preparation:

- Your way to beat test anxiety
- Your way to increase your test-taking speed
- Your way to approach the Reading Comprehension
- Your way to figure out the tough math problems

Just as an athletic team should focus mainly on its own play rather than worry about what the other team will do, so must SAT-takers be primarily concerned with conditioning their minds to score high.

What It Takes to Beat the SAT

Everyone wants to know what the SAT really measures. Intelligence? Reasoning ability? Factual knowledge? Mere test-taking wizardry? Good guesses all—but all wrong.

Nominally, the revised SAT includes sections on reading, writing, and math skills. Strong ability in each of these is essential to scoring well. Some students may need to brush up on math, others may need to work on their vocabulary or their mastery of written English. Subject matter matters.

But just as important are qualities that you'll never read about in a College Board brochure. Here is our assessment of what really matters on the SAT:

A Clear Head under Pressure

Nothing is more important to success than the ability not to stress out. A tense brain processes information more slowly and makes more mistakes than a relaxed one. In the primeval forest of 10,000 years ago, anxiety meant fight or flight. Anybody who takes a 3-hour-and-45-minute test while fighting that impulse is bound to score lower than someone who is less anxious. The students who do best on the SAT are generally calm and confident. The heightened alert of a testing situation may actually help them think more clearly.

Speedy Thinking

Students who think faster do better on the SAT. Students who think more slowly do not have time to finish the test, or they miss questions because they are worried about not having enough time. Speed takes the pressure off and gives students time to go back and check their work. Speed is especially crucial on the critical reading, where many students get bogged down and stressed out. And what about trying to write a decent essay in 25 minutes? Quick thinkers are not always the deepest thinkers or the most nuanced. But as long as the College Board and ETS use time pressure as a sorter, fast workers will come out on top. The College Board has never provided an adequate educational reason why the test should be timed. (The Board does argue that the SAT reflects the fact that many tests in college are timed.)

> "Because the multiple-choice answers are supposed to mess you up, if you dwell on any one too long you'll probably get tricked and miss it."
>
> —790 V, 800 M

Ability to Stay Focused

Chess players make good SAT-takers. Why? Because they know how to put their minds inside a game that has many angles. A good test-taker never loses focus on what the game is—to get the questions right. Some students make the mistake, for instance, of getting really interested in the reading comprehension passages. Bad idea. They waste valuable time learning about a fascinating subject when they should focus on the questions and then move on. Some bright students get confused because they let outside knowledge intrude into the logic of a question and its answer. Many SAT questions have more than one answer when removed from their context. A good test-taker edits out this noise without thinking about it. She is focused, surgical, and sequential. Gets the right answer—moves on to the next.

A Feel for Proper English

Don't count on your literature class to give you the skills necessary to do well on Critical Reading and Writing. Exposure to good grammar from the time you were knee-high is much more important. Many students, for instance, cannot define the subjunctive mood but know that "if I was going to the store" is incorrect. (It should be "if I were going to the store.") Many students can get sentence completion problems without even looking at the answers by being familiar with words commonly paired together. For example, you might encounter a problem such as, "Because there were ------- circumstances, he

NEW SKILLS FOR A NEW SAT

The main keys to success on the New SAT are the same as those on the old one. But the relative emphasis has changed. Here are the most important new developments:

✔ **Verbal skills will be twice as important as math.** With the addition of the Writing section, verbal skills outweigh math by 2:1. Cynics see this as partly an effort to boost the scores of girls, much as the College Board did in adding a Writing section to the PSAT.

✔ **Vocabulary will be less important.** The analogies hinged largely on word definitions. Though some sentence completion and reading comprehension questions will still emphasize vocabulary, word meanings in these questions can be figured out in the context of a sentence or paragraph.

✔ **Advanced math knowledge will matter more.** The old SAT included math rooted in simple formulas that everyone had learned by first-year algebra and geometry. The trick has always been knowing how to set up the problem. This emphasis will remain strong, but the new math will require more formula know-how.

✔ **Students must write an essay.** Bet you're glad to get this breaking news. The emphasis is on composing thoughts quickly and getting them down in an organized way with concrete examples to back up your point of view. Preparation will potentially make a bigger difference here than anywhere else on the test.

was not punished for his misdeed." The answer to this portion of the question is "extenuating"—easy for someone who knows that "extenuating" and "circumstances" often go together.

Reading and Word Power

Though the decision to drop the analogies will mean that the New SAT has less emphasis on knowing definitions, vocabulary will still be very important. The Sentence Completion questions in Critical Reading are really vocabulary questions, and the Reading Comprehension section also tests vocabulary. The number-one, all-time best way to prepare for the SAT—even better than having dinner every night with your college-educated parents—is to read, read, read (with a dictionary). Reading helps you recognize words and know their meaning, but that is only the beginning. Most students don't realize that the SAT math is also in large measure a reading test. The math questions spin scenarios that must be kept straight in the student's mind—a skill that is developed by reading. Readers develop the focus necessary to stay tuned to the test and the ability to move through it quickly.

Problem-Solving Ability and Short-Term Memory

Notice we didn't say "mathematical" ability? The SAT Math section uses math to test students, but it isn't about math. The Math section takes problems that everyone knows how to solve and disguises them. Or it adds a tricky twist, like asking for the greatest integer that is less than the solution to a particular computation. We offer an overview of such shenanigans in our chapter on the Math section. For now, suffice it to say that knowing how to solve math problems is less important than understanding how to stay on top of complicated scenarios. A lot of it boils down to simple short-term memory. Many questions are difficult not because they require challenging computations, but because they stack up elementary ones in confusing ways. Keeping it straight is the name of the game.

Stamina

Though less important than speed, stamina will get more important with the 3-hour-and-45-minute format of the SAT. In your daily school life, when do you ever focus for 3 hours and 45 minutes nonstop? Maybe at exam time but probably not even then. Taking the SAT is like running a marathon—it takes training to discipline your mind and body to focus for that period of time. Students who do poorly on the SAT generally lose focus halfway through the test.

Developing Your Own Approach

As usual, the truth about the SAT is somewhere between the College Board's public pronouncements and the overheated rantings of the critics. The SAT does measure real abilities that are important to academic success. If your academic skills are limited, no amount of hocus-pocus will get you a high score. On the other hand, there is no good reason why these particular characteristics should be valued more than many other skills and characteristics that lead to success in college and in life, skills that the SAT does not measure. Is the SAT tilted in favor of certain types of people and against others? Definitely.

The good news is that preparation can make a difference. If you're a white-knuckle test-taker, practicing the test can help you increase your comfort level. If speed is your problem, techniques can be learned to buy you some extra time. By fine-tuning the pace at which you move through the test, you can further ease your anxiety. If you are uncertain in your writing skills—or even if you're not—some concentrated planning for the new essay is likely to improve your score. If math gives you trouble, focused preparation will increase your comfort level and make you a little more intuitive when the chips are down. By trying out various problem-solving strategies, you can find the ones that will help you most.

> "Making the test into a mental game is distracting and can be demoralizing."
> —640 V, 760 M

A miracle is probably not in the cards, but there is plenty you can do to raise your score. We'll tell you how—based on the insight of hundreds of high-scoring students.

SAT PREP COURSES
STRAIGHT TALK FROM STUDENTS

2

ANSWERS TO YOUR QUESTIONS

✔ **Do coaching courses really work?**

✔ **If not, why are they so popular?**

✔ **What do students say about prep courses?**

✔ **What advice do students have about preparing?**

Anyone who managed to remain semiconscious in AP English may have a vague recollection of Odysseus and his encounter with Scylla and Charybdis. Don't remember that one? It was when Odysseus had to steer his ship between Scylla, a six-headed monster, and Charybdis, who swallowed boats in a whirlpool and then spit them back out. Still doesn't ring a bell?

When it comes to taking the SAT, the seas are ruled by two giants that are just as powerful, if slightly less menacing.

One of them is a two-headed monster, the College Board and ETS, which uses the SAT to create a mixture of fear, confusion, and exhaustion in its prey. After the reasoning test has neutralized the reasoning powers of each hapless student, College Board and ETS proceed to one of their most important tasks: extracting fees. Under the cover of an acorn logo and nonprofit status, they devise ever-more creative ways to bring in the loot: fees to take the tests, late fees, fees to report scores to the colleges, fees to rush scores even faster to the colleges, and fees to learn scores by phone. For the College Board and ETS, the SAT is a cash cow. They roar with rage when anyone suggests that the test can be beaten with coaching.

> **"Don't buy into the frenzy out there. Some of these prep companies try and sell you packages you don't need."**
>
> —680 V, 640 M

The other giant of standardized testing seduces its victims with a soothing melody about acing the SAT. It whispers things like, "The SAT is a scam" and "We guarantee your SAT score will improve by at least 200 points." Ah, the siren song of Princeton Review—the biggest name among the legions of tutors and test-prep gurus nationwide that offer a magic bullet to slay the standardized test monster. While College Board and ETS create fear and loathing, the test-prep giants play on it. Though not a whirlpool exactly, the test-prep industry can suck you under and spit you out—minus $1,000 and a few dozen hours of your time.

Are the College Board and ETS correct in their claims that coaching for the SAT won't help (much)? Can the right coaching guarantee that your score will rise? It occurred to us that one way of answering this question might be to ask people with firsthand experience. We went to the ultimate source for straight talk about the SAT—the students who had just finished taking it. By reporting the collective wisdom of hundreds of students from dozens of schools, we hope to give families the information they need to make smart choices.

The Story behind the Survey

In February–April of 2003, we conducted one of the largest independent surveys of SAT preparation practices ever done. We began by enlisting the help of high school guidance counselors who had been generous as expert consultants to the *Fiske Guide to Colleges* and the *Fiske Guide to Getting into the Right College*. Of this group, seventy agreed to distribute and collect the survey from up to twenty students. A high proportion of these counselors work at private and suburban public schools, and a few are independent counselors. We chose this population because we knew that it would include a high proportion of top scorers—useful for their insight into scoring high on the test—and a high proportion of students who paid for test-prep services.

Most previous studies—whether sponsored by the test-prep companies, the test-makers, or someone else—consisted of a before-and-after analysis of a particular group. Their method: Give the SAT to a group of students who know nothing about it, give them a prep course, and test them at the end. But studies such as these, typically done at the behest of the test-prep giants, are open to the possibility of manipulation. The first SAT taken by the students— the one used as a benchmark to measure improvement—is often not a real SAT but an imitation designed by the company doing the study. Assuming that these imitations approximate a real SAT, they carry none of the pressure of a real one. Furthermore, there is no guarantee that the students chosen to be part of the studies are typical of all test-takers— indeed, some studies are conducted on a sample of students whose scores are known beforehand.

> "I just felt stupid after I left the sessions because I hadn't remembered half that stuff we went over. I think preparing on your own is better because people can easily stress you out."
>
> —580 V, 520 M

Most importantly, these before-and-after studies were asking the wrong question. The issue is not whether preparing for the test can make a significant improvement in your score. Just about everyone would agree that it can. The real issue is: Can a coaching course or tutoring improve your score more than preparing on your own with books and software?

Our first order of business was to divide the surveys into two piles: those who had received face-to-face instruction and those who had not. Among the first group were students who had paid for one-on-one tutoring and those who had participated in a coaching course offered by a private firm or at their school, including a few students who had received a prep course for the PSAT. Many in this group had paid hundreds of dollars for their course, though those who took a school-based course typically paid less, and a few got the course for free. This group also included a handful of those who had taken an online prep course.

Since it was conducted in 2003, the survey necessarily included students who took the old SAT. Throughout the book, our references to students in the survey cite their scores on the Verbal and Math sections, the former of which corresponds to the current Critical Reading section. In addition, we supplemented our main survey with follow-up questions for students who had taken the Writing Subject Test, the forerunner of the Writing section on the current SAT.

Eye-Opening Results

From the total of 815 students, 390, or 48 percent, had received coaching while 425, or 52 percent, had prepared on their own. Our most important question was whether those who had face-to-face instruction earned higher scores than those who had not. Based on the highest verbal and highest math score of each student, we found that students who did not take a prep course scored higher than those who did.

> Average score for **coached** students:
> 636 Verbal, 621 Math
> Average score for **uncoached** students:
> 645 Verbal, 646 Math

The distribution of combined scores for coached and uncoached students, based on highest verbal and highest math, is below. Included are the total number of students, coached and uncoached, who earned a combined score in each range. Percentage figures represent the proportion of the total within that range:

Score	Coached	Uncoached
Below 1000	31 (53%)	28 (47%)
1000–1090	32 (50%)	32 (50%)
1100–1190	64 (56%)	50 (44%)
1200–1290	87 (48%)	93 (52%)
1300–1390	87 (49%)	90 (51%)
1400–1490	74 (48%)	79 (52%)
1500–1600	15 (22%)	53 (78%)

Two surprising findings emerge from these data. First, students who got face-to-face coaching for the SAT actually scored lower, on average, than those who did not. Those who took a prep course received an average combined score of 1257, while those who did not averaged 1291. In each score interval below 1500, there are approximately equal numbers of those who received coaching and those who did not.

Second, among students who scored above 1500, a much smaller fraction received coaching than among students who scored lower. High scorers typically prepared for the test on their own. And as we will see below, students in this group who did take a coaching course or tutoring generally found it to be a waste of time. The difference of 34 points between the combined scores of the two groups is due primarily to the fact that those who scored above 1500 were less likely to have taken a prep course.

Princeton Review and Kaplan

An important emphasis of our study was to examine the results achieved by students who took coaching courses from the two major national test prep companies, Princeton Review and Kaplan. Of the 815 students in our survey, 72 reported that they took a Princeton Review classroom course, 46 took a classroom course from Kaplan, 5 went to Princeton Review for one-on-one tutoring, and 1 took an online course from Princeton Review. These totals include students who took a standard classroom course from the two firms—typically lasting about 40 hours—and students who took a school-based course of variable length offered by one of the two firms. Five ambitious souls took a class or tutoring from both Kaplan and Princeton Review.

The combined group of Kaplan and Princeton Review preppers included 119 students from 44 schools in 21 states. The results? The Kaplan preppers had an average score of 637 Verbal and 665 Math for a combined score 12 points higher than those who did not take a prep course. Princeton Review's averages were 624 Verbal and 640 Math, 26 points below the non-prep average.

These differences are probably meaningless. It may be that students with high verbal scores are less likely to take a prep course, or that prep courses have slightly better success in raising math scores. But the bottom line is that prepping with Kaplan or Princeton Review did not correlate with higher scores among our survey participants.

Below is the combined distribution of scores, based on each individual's highest verbal and math score, of the 119 students who prepped with Kaplan or Princeton Review. The first percentage figure refers to the percentage of Kaplan/Princeton Review preppers who were in that interval. The second is the percentage of all students in the survey who scored in that interval.

Score	# Kaplan/ Princeton Review Prep	% Kaplan/ Princeton Review Prep	% of entire survey
Below 1000	6	5	7
1000–1090	7	6	8
1100–1190	24	20	14
1200–1290	27	23	22
1300–1390	22	18	22
1400–1490	27	23	19
1500–1600	6	5	8

These numbers show that the distribution of scores of those who took a Princeton Review or Kaplan course differs little from the distribution of those who did not. Some students who took Princeton Review or Kaplan scored high, others scored low, still others scored in the middle.

It should be noted that while many of these students took the standard Princeton Review or Kaplan course, others took school-based courses offered by personnel from these companies. Such school-based courses can be shorter in duration than a full-blown Princeton Review or Kaplan course.

Nevertheless, our survey offers strong evidence that a prep course with Princeton Review or Kaplan is not likely to be more effective than preparing for the SAT on your own. Because many of the students who do prepare on their own use Princeton Review or Kaplan materials, one obvious piece of advice is to save your $1,000 and buy the book for about $15. But we also have our doubts about the techniques of the test-prep giants, which we will address below.

Score Increase Claims: A Closer Look

It should come as no surprise that our results are at odds with what the big test-prep companies say. In recent years, Princeton Review has advertised an average score increase of 140 points for students who take its classroom prep course. The company cites a study conducted at its behest in 2002 by a corporate communications firm. The sample included 693 students, out of which 138 provided usable responses. The average combined score increase for the latter group was 136 points. We have three observations about the study:

- Princeton Review selected the students who would be included in the survey pool
- An unknown number of the score increases were computed based on a Princeton Review diagnostic test rather than a real SAT
- Only 20 percent of the students in the initial sample were included in the results

WHEN MOM AND DAD PUSH THE PREP COURSE

A majority of the students in our survey who paid for SAT coaching said that the idea came from mom and dad. That's understandable—parents are the ones who pay the bill. But our questionnaires found numerous instances when over-stressed parents crammed a cram course down the throat of an unwilling student. One my-mom-made-me-do-it prepper describes his course as "a waste of time and money," adding that "what helped was sitting down by myself and becoming comfortable with the format." He scored 700 V and 730 M. Another student says his math tutoring was "worthless" and that he reacted negatively "because it was not my choice." His scores were 760 V, 690 M and he advises students to take practice tests and prepare on their own. Yet another student was prodded by his parents to get tutoring in math after he scored "only" 640 the first time. "It was boring and I wasn't told anything I didn't already know. I'm just glad my parents paid for it, not me," he tells us. And his math score the second time? 640 again. Asked about the benefits of her prep course, another student who scored 520 V and 630 M replied: "It pleased my parents." Were the benefits worth the cost? "No!"

> "My mother and I considered a prep course but decided that, because of my limited time and good study and test-taking abilities, it was not the best option for me. The books allowed me to work at my own pace when I had pieces of time and to concentrate on what I knew I needed to work on rather than spending time on things I was already comfortable with."
>
> —800 V, 720 M

Kaplan does not claim an average score increase for its students. According to a statement from Justin Serrano, the Executive Director of Kaplan Test Prep, "Score improvement statistics can be manipulated to create the appearance of a particular test score improvement, when, in fact, those results were based on small samples of students with nonrepresentative score distributions."

There are no guarantees in college admission—unless you sign up for an SAT coaching course from the leading test-prep companies. "We guarantee you'll raise your score at least 200 points, or we'll work with you again until you do, for free," says Princeton Review. In other words, there is good news and bad news: You don't get your money back, but you can enjoy another free year of the same preparation that didn't work the first time. Kaplan does offer a money-back guarantee. The hitch: Kaplan guarantees only a score increase. If you go up 10 points, no dice. Given that the College Board says that the typical student goes up nearly 30 points between tests anyway (from eleventh to twelfth grade), this guarantee is less than scintillating. In order for the guarantees to apply, students must attend all the sessions and do all the homework.

Why the Myth Won't Go Away

If the case for an SAT prep course is so weak, why do families continue to spend millions on them every year? The reasons are complex. With the cost of a year at Prestige U now more than $40,000, some families don't seem to mind ponying up another $1,000 with an "it-can't-hurt" philosophy. Common sense says that preparing for the SAT—whether on your own or through a course—can indeed improve your score. The fallacy, skillfully perpetuated by the test-prep giants, is the notion that families face a choice between spending big dollars for a prep course or doing nothing. But that's not the way it is.

Part of the reason for the test-prep mania lies with the College Board's lack of credibility on this issue. For decades, the Board insisted that preparation could have no meaningful impact on a student's score. While still pooh-poohing the impact of test prep, the Board now sells its own line of test-prep books and software. Hmm. Also crucial was the Board's inability to develop a convincing explanation of what the SAT really measures. Is the test really about "reasoning?" Or does it merely use simple subject matter to create tricky questions?

The disconnect between how College Board talked about the test and how students experienced it created an opening for anybody who could sell straight talk. Prior to 1980, test prep was a relatively sleepy industry dominated by Stanley H. Kaplan, the forerunner of today's Kaplan that was founded in the 1940s by its avuncular proprietor. But the industry took off in the 1980s with the rise of Princeton Review and its hipper-than-thou image and aggressive guarantees of score improvement. Countless other regional, local, and online companies have gotten into the game.

In the world of SAT coaching, perception is reality. Many students will never know for sure whether or how much their scores have increased because they take a prep course before their first SAT (or PSAT). But if you've been told again and again that your scores will increase, the common tendency is to believe it. Naturally, there are some instances when test scores do increase dramatically: from coaching, a good night's sleep, lack of a headache, the

THE VOICE OF EXPERIENCE

We found a true expert on test-prep in the person of a 540 V, 670 M scorer who took three coaching courses—one from Princeton Review, one from Kaplan, and a third with another commercial firm. What did he learn?

"Hey, it's a business. You're just fooling yourself when you think that money will buy you knowledge."

He says his family spent "a lot" on prep courses that "became tedious and a burden." The bottom line? "I advise preparing on your own with books or software. Keep in mind that the prep courses work with the same books. Buying them and not attending classes can save a lot of money."

imponderables of fate, or the statistical margin of error in the SAT. When this happens after a prep course, students are sure to attribute the rise to their course and spread the word far and wide, leading to the "so-and-so increased by 200 points" buzz. Students whose scores do not go up after a prep course are disappointed and embarrassed. They're also a lot less likely to brag about it in school. It's a bit like people who talk about their experience in the stock market. They're not likely to bend your ear about the clinkers.

Students Talk about Their Prep Courses

Many people assume that an adult standing in the front of the room, with students listening attentively, will automatically raise scores. But studies among college students have shown that those who listen to a lecture learn no more than those who get a transcript of what was said. That bodes ill for national test-prep companies because many instructors are recent college graduates who rely heavily on company books. "What was taught in the classroom was the exact same thing printed in the Kaplan book I bought from the bookstore," complains a 740 V, 690 M scorer. Another student who prepped at a local firm and scored 610 V, 690 M writes, "It seemed that the instructors became talking books. Everything they told us I had already read.... The instructors often didn't know the answers to questions outside our homework."

> "Actually doing test questions was far more effective than rote memorization of vocabulary words or math formulas."
>
> —800 V, 800 M

Despite the subjectivity involved, we wanted to know about students' perceptions of whether coaching increased their scores. The survey gave students a choice of five responses to how much they thought their composite score increased: None; 50 points or less; 60–100 points; 110–150 points; or 160+ points. The most common response was 60–100 points, followed by 50 points or less. Together, these two responses formed a solid majority across all score intervals and all test-prep companies. Lesser and approximately equal numbers of students believed that their score went up not at all, or 110–150 points, and a smaller fraction believed that its scores had gone up 160 points or more. There was only one systematic difference in the responses. Those who scored lower than 1100 were less likely to believe that their score had jumped more than 100 points.

Of the students who thought that their prep course was worthwhile, few cited test-taking strategies or the insight of the instructor as the reason why it was useful. The most commonly cited benefit was access to practice tests; a close second was having someone on the scene to make sure they got done. "The course itself did not provide many helpful hints but did force me to take practice tests," says a 600 V, 600 M scorer. "My tutor made me do the work on the tests," admits another student who scored 690 V, 710 M. "If he hadn't forced me to do it, I probably wouldn't have done it."

Many students tended to be forgiving when coaching courses failed to deliver the promised score increases. "I learned a lot of great strategies but did not improve my score by the 100 points that were guaranteed," said a 650 V, 550 M Princeton Review student of her prep course. "I would still recommend it to other students because I know that it can be very helpful for many students."

"I only increased 10 points," wrote a 540 V, 560 M Princeton Review prepper who elsewhere noted, "I would recommend this course. It was very helpful learning the tips on how to take the SATs." Another Princeton Review student with a combined score of 550 V, 630 M had an interesting hypothesis about score increases: "Each time I took a practice test my score improved. I think the tests they gave got easier, because my real SAT score was a lot lower than my final practice score." One 640 V, 590 M scorer was perturbed by what she perceived as Princeton Review's lack of follow-through. "Princeton Review did not keep its word about private tutoring if I didn't go up 100 points from my first practice test. I had to find a tutor on my own." (Princeton Review's guarantee for private tutoring is the same as for its classroom courses.)

> "Cramming does not help at all for the SAT, but reading widely and looking up unfamiliar words is useful."
> —800 V, 780 M

The Test-Prep Syndrome

A final reason why families don't balk at ineffective prep courses might be styled "The Test-Prep Syndrome." This is the tendency to identify with one's tutor after long hours in captivity cramming for the SAT. It is human nature, especially among adolescents, to bond with adults who give them time and attention. "I had an amazing and inspiring tutor who motivated me to do well on the SATs," wrote one student who scored a combined 1090. "My tutor opened my mind to so many wonderful things. Her and I established a close relationship and I enjoyed working with her so much." Unfortunately, this student's scores went down 10 points after working with the tutor to the tune of $110 per hour. Were the benefits of this tutoring worth the cost? Perhaps. The tutor is probably a fine person who will get a solid endorsement when another family is seeking an SAT coach.

From a mixture of hype, anxiety, and the very real student/tutor relationship, SAT coaching has become a fixture on the landscape of the college admission process. Faced with the anxiety of a high-stakes test, families find comfort in the belief that buying a service will help cope with the problem. Just be forewarned that extra hand-holding might not mean a higher score.

A Closer Look at the Questionnaires

Below, we summarize the responses to our survey with reference to the highest combined score achieved by the students: those who scored 1500 or better in the first cohort, those who scored 1300–1490 in the second cohort, etc. Each group seemed to have its own personality, which hinted at why the students got the scores they did.

> "The SATs test my emotional state more than anything else."
>
> —760 V, 680 M

The surveys offer a revealing glimpse of attitudes and experiences of today's students related to the SAT and preparing for it. They also provide strong evidence of the overwhelming importance of the SAT in the lives of ambitious, high-achieving young people. By grouping the responses according to test score, we are consciously accentuating that emphasis for the purpose of this study. The reader can draw his or her own conclusions as to whether emphasis on the SAT has gone too far.

Readers should also be reminded that students in the survey are part of a selective group. In many cases, they attend schools where the average SAT score is 1200 or higher. Their perceptions of a "good" or "bad" SAT score are shaped accordingly.

Students Who Scored 1500–1600

You know who they are. You've seen them in your honors classes. They're the geniuses, the uber-testers, the disgustingly smart people who are always

ANATOMY OF A 1600

Julie Zhou is anything but a test-prep geek. From rock climbing to the math club, she did it all. But when the time came to take the SAT, she was focused. On her first try, she notched a spiffy 1550 with 750 Verbal and 800 Math. Good enough for most people, but not for Julie. "I realized from the results of my first SAT that my vocabulary skills needed the most improvement," she recalls. "I really focused on that aspect of the test and scraped together a long list of words provided by my school, prep books, and books I read for enjoyment and studied until I knew them all." Her regimen also included plenty of practice tests. "They were effective in letting me get the feel for the test. I usually didn't work an entire test all the way through, instead concentrating on my most difficult sections." Julie describes her preparation for the math section as "finding new ways to check my answers." By knowing the angles backwards and forwards, she could leave herself more ways of solving a problem and more methods to ferret out mistakes. Another piece of advice from Julie: "Towards the end of each section, the most tempting answers are always wrong." Her hard work paid off when she took the SAT a second time and nailed a 1600. "Be cautious but confident," she advises, "You are all capable of owning this test with adequate preparation."

Julie Zhou graduated from The Westminster Schools in Atlanta, Georgia. She now attends Harvard University.

busting the curve in AP Calculus BC. On the SAT, they scored in the top one-half percent of test-takers and most of them will attend places like Harvard and Brown. They make you want to blow chunks.

But who are these people and how did they get such high scores? By studying day and night? Prep courses up the wazoo? Not exactly. It turns out that students who scored above 1500 were mostly nonchalant about their achievement. A total of 68 students in our survey scored 1500 or better—including four that registered a perfect 1600—but only fifteen had coaching of any kind. "Test prep is stupid. The less I prepped the better I did," chirped a 790 V, 720 M scorer. This lad says he prepared less than five hours for his first SAT and got a combined 1380, then did nothing before the second test and went up 130 points. In response to a question about how he prepared for his second SAT, a 770 V, 800 M scorer replied, "I ate breakfast." As a group, the 1500s were more confident and less likely to take the test multiple times. Forty-three percent didn't bother to take it twice, including two who scored 1590 on the first try and apparently felt no desire to go for a 1600.

It may be that the 1500+ scorers had good reason to be confident, and perhaps they only took the test once because they got the score they needed, but we think their relaxed air may have something to do with why they aced the test. "Don't freak out," declares a 710 V, 800 M scorer bound for University of Illinois at Urbana–Champaign, "The SAT is serious but if you are too tense it won't help and it will cause physical and emotional distress."

Despite the laid-back tenor of the high scorers, plenty of them worked hard to improve their scores. One student prepared on her own for more than 30 hours per week for her first SAT and got a combined 1290. For two subsequent tests, she accelerated her efforts, working more than 40 hours per week with a study book she created herself. The result was a 1510. Another student finally pulled a 1600 on her fourth try with more focus on prep books.

As a group, the 1500 scorers undermined the idea that coaching courses are the route to a stratospheric score. Of the fifteen students who got tutoring or coaching, most said it was not worth the cost. "I didn't learn anything!" writes a frustrated 760 V, 790 M scorer, "Kids should prepare on their own."

"Too simplistic, did not cover material for the highest scores," says a student who scored 750 V, 760 M in evaluating his prep course. Of her school's prep course, a Harvard-bound student says, "It did me no good. I already knew or had heard all that they told me." Of the six students who took a

Princeton Review or Kaplan course, five said that the benefits were not worth the cost.

While coaching courses were generally panned, the 1500s cited practice tests again and again as their single most important mode of preparation. "I took 10 practice SATs starting two weeks before the test, and it helped me take a look at all the things I was consistently missing," writes a 740 V, 780 M scorer who says his coaching course was not worth the cost. "Practice, practice, practice—the best way to become comfortable with the material," writes a Yale ED admit who scored 1510.

The following quote from a 1580 scorer will gladden the hearts of English teachers nationwide: "Cramming does not help at all for the SAT, but reading widely and looking up unfamiliar words is useful." No one should be surprised that many of the 1500+ scorers say that they are dedicated readers.

Mere mortals will be relieved to learn that the 1500 scorers do, like everybody else, have their challenges with the SAT. "Reading comprehension questions occasionally seem to have more than one or even no good answer depending on your opinion," says a Princeton-bound student, citing a common complaint among students of all ability levels. She says that practice "helps you learn what sort of answer the test is looking for." Another issue: high scorers frequently have trouble with basic math, especially geometry, that they may not have studied since eighth grade. Prone to overconfidence in their ability to resurrect that material, some high-scoring students learn the hard way that they need to brush up.

> "They shouldn't guarantee points. Going up depends on how much time one spends on the work outside class on the test in a specific day."
>
> —800 V, 700 M

The clear message of the 1500+ scorers can be summarized in one word: self-reliance. In the words of a 800 V, 720 M scorer, "My mother and I considered a prep course but decided that, because of my limited time and good study and test-taking abilities, it was not the best option for me. The books allowed me to work at my own pace when I had pieces of time and to concentrate on what I knew I needed to work on rather than spending time on things I was already comfortable with."

Students Who Scored 1300–1490

At least these people show signs of being mortal. "I wanted to show colleges I was right for them, but was scared my scores wouldn't be good enough," says one student whose chances were probably not scuttled by her 1340. Another student writes that she disliked her SAT prep course for a surprising reason. "Everyone was comparing their scores, and even though mine were perfectly decent, I felt bad about how I had done.… I wish I had done a couple of practice tests on my own," she writes. What were these "perfectly decent" scores? 760 Verbal, 630 Math.

There is one difference between this group and the 1500s—attitude. The 1300 and 1400 scorers are more likely to take a test-prep course, more likely to spend hours on the preparation, and more likely to be feeling stress. Not that the stress is universal. "I didn't study much," crowed a student who scored 1450, "Studying is just making up for all the wasted time playing video games instead of doing homework and reading books." Touché.

As with the 1500 scorers, timed practice tests were considered crucial. "I took about six of the sample tests from the *10 Real SATs* book in preparation for my second test and it helped me a great deal," says a Bucknell ED admit. His scores went from 600 to 650 on the Verbal and 710 to 780 on the Math.

WHEN A SCORE INCREASE ISN'T EVERYTHING

A student at a prestigious East Coast boarding school who scored 490 V, 600 M on her first SAT was determined to improve her verbal score. "I have never done well on standardized testing.… The reading comprehensions scared me!" So she hired a tutor for once-a-week sessions. "I spent countless hours studying for vocabulary and devoting time to prepping for the test. After only going up 10 points, I was furious because I had put so much effort into it," she writes. Despite the fact that her score barely went up, this student rates her tutoring as more effective than her classroom course from Princeton Review. "I don't regret it because the tutoring has helped me in the long run, especially in school," she says.

As high scorers know, a test-taking state of mind is key. "Mental readiness is more important than academic," advises a 690 V, 780 M scorer, "It is the difference between good test-takers and bad ones." Or, in the words of a Bates-bound student, "Don't get psyched out about the damn test!" (He chose not to do a prep course.)

One student had an unusual 190 point jump in her scores on the third time she took the test—to 710 V and 680 M—after being mired at a combined 1200 on the first two. Reason? She took more practice tests before the third time, but she believes that her state of mind was the key. "The first two times I was anxious because so much pressure is put on this one test. The third time I went in very confident.... I just told myself it didn't matter and I could crush the test—and I did." (She also got in ED at Washington U in St. Louis.)

There was plenty of diversity on the subject of coaching. "Human interaction, for me, is usually more fun and effective because books and software can't really change their way of explaining to suit my needs," writes a convincing advocate for test prep who scored 650 V, 710 M. Her other advice includes "get enough sleep, eat breakfast, do practice tests." A student who scored 1390 credits one-on-one tutoring with Princeton Review with raising her score 350 points. "We worked at a pace that was suited to my needs and therefore very beneficial," she writes.

> "Time pressure was my biggest problem. Other than that, the questions were not that hard."
>
> —540 V, 500 M

"I think the SAT is a ridiculous, unfair system," writes a 1360 scorer who took Princeton Review and endorses its assessment of the test. "Although I felt that I was acquiring an unfair advantage because my family could afford to pay for the course, the course was effective." This girl identified practice tests as her most useful tool in preparing and estimated that her prep course—which cost about $1,000—raised her scores by 60–100 points.

One Princeton Review prepper found that a brand name is less important than the instructor. "Princeton was horrible. The prep class did nothing to make sure I was improving and when I had a tutor first from them she was flaky and late," writes the student, who nevertheless managed a 1330. An instructor with the right pedigree is not necessarily the solution. A 690 V, 700 M scorer reports that her course "was utterly boring, and our teacher, an

MIT graduate with a major in nuclear engineering and a score of 1590 on the SAT, seemed as clueless half the time as we were."

One student who scored 680 V, 660 M voiced a common complaint about prep courses: "You had to go at the pace of people who did not understand things you did.... I felt that if I used the prep book independently, I could do the same exercises at a pace that suited me," he writes. Says another student who scored 640 V, 740 M after one-on-one tutoring, "We used Kaplan books and I could have learned just as much without the tutor and just the book."

A 690 V, 710 M scorer says if he had it to do over again, he would skip his prep course and "have my parents force me to do practice tests."

Students Who Scored 1100–1290

If the 1300–1490 scorers were somewhat stressed, this group was positively manic. As a whole, the 1100–1290 cohort was the most stressed out in the survey. Students in this group scored in roughly the 62nd to 89th percentile nationally, yet in their high-powered schools, their scores were no better than average. "Because this is a standardized test, I get nervous thinking about the weight this has on my future," writes a 670 V, 520 M scorer. "I was nervous because I heard all the horror stories and forgot my calculator and I fell asleep," says a student who scored 580 V, 570 M despite these difficulties.

> "I would recommend not reading too much into the questions and making sure you understand what the question is asking."
>
> —800 V, 800 M

Does stress cause these students to score lower? Probably. Is the stress caused by anxiety about keeping up with higher scoring peers? Perhaps. These students were more likely to express negative attitudes toward standardized tests, but the comments had a different tenor than the nonplussed disdain of many 1500 scorers. "Keep in mind that the SAT is meaningless and a poor judge of one's person," writes a 1270 scorer who describes himself as "very anxious" before taking the test.

Lack of time was a major factor for many in this group. "It was the hardest trying to finish, and doing the problems under time pressure made me lose my train of thought a lot," says a 570 V, 530 M scorer. Students who prefer to deliberate over problems find themselves rushed, as do slow readers. "I find the reading comprehension questions the most challenging. I was very nervous and it is very tough to concentrate on long passages when your mind is wandering and thinking about other things," notes a student who scored 1160.

WHERE THE STUDENTS CAME FROM

Our survey included students at 67 schools in 29 states, as well as a handful of students who were clients of participating independent counselors. Our goal was not a representative sample of the nation as a whole, but rather a representative sample of students likely to consider SAT coaching. As a result, most of the students came from suburban public or private schools. The list consists of:

Albuquerque Academy (NM)

The Athenian School (CA)

Birmingham High School (CA)

Bishop Brady High School (NH)

Brookfield Academy (WI)

Carol Gill Associates (NY)

Carolina Friends School (NC)

Cherry Creek High School (CO)

Cody High School (WY)

The Colorado Springs School (CO)

Columbus School for Girls (OH)

Crystal Springs Uplands School (CA)

Cypress Falls High School (TX)

Deerfield Academy (MA)

Durham Academy (NC)

Dwight-Englewood School (NJ)

Eaglecrest High School (CO)

Episcopal School of Dallas (TX)

The Gunnery (CT)

Hathaway Brown School (OH)

Highland High School (ID)

Iolani School (HI)

John Burroughs School (MO)

Holy Innocents' Episcopal School (GA)

La Pietra Hawaii School for Girls (HI)

Lake Ridge Academy (OH)

Lakewood High School (CO)

Los Angeles Center for Enriched Studies (CA)

Los Angeles Unified School District (CA)

Mandarin High School (FL)

McClure, Mallory & Baron (CA)

Mercersburg Academy (PA)

Milton Academy (MA)

Montclair High School (NJ)

Moravian Academy (PA)

Newton North High School (MA)

North Central High School (IN)

Northfield Mount Hermon School (MA)

Pace Academy (GA)

Peddie School (NJ)

Polytechnic School (CA)

Providence Day School (NC)

The Putney School (VT)

Ravenscroft School (NC)

Ridgewood High School (NJ)

Rockhurst High School (MO)

Rocky River High School (OH)

Rowland Hall–St. Mark's School (UT)

St. Andrew's–Sewanee School (TN)

St. Andrew's Episcopal School (MS)

St. Catherine's School (VA)

St. Cecilia Academy (TN)

St. John's Country Day School (FL)

St. Mary's Hall School (TX)

Salesianum School (DE)

San Ramon Valley High School (CA)

Seven Hills School (OH)

Shaker Heights High School (OH)

Shawnee Mission South HS (KS)

Steinbrecher & Partners (CT)

Trinity Christian Academy (TX)

University of Illinois Laboratory
   High School (IL)

University Preparatory Academy (WA)

The Urban School of San Francisco (CA)

Vail Mountain School (CO)

Vermont Academy (VT)

Webb School of Knoxville (TN)

The Westminister Schools (GA)

Weston High School (CT)

Wyoming Seminary (PA)

Real academic weaknesses accentuated the test-taking difficulties for some in this group. Whereas higher scorers had trouble with their rusty geometry, this cohort was more likely to struggle with the algebra—a problem that has been accentuated because the New SAT added more Algebra II problems. On the verbal side, a number of students reported difficulty with vocabulary and word definitions.

Some in this group also benefited from elementary test-taking techniques. A student who scored 990 on her first SAT bought a prep book and increased her focus. "My mistake on the first test was omitting too many questions instead of taking an educated guess," she writes. After studying five hours, her scores went up 160 points to 580 V, 570 M.

Assessments of test prep did not differ greatly from the 1300–1490 scorers. One student who took both a classroom course and tutoring from Princeton Review said she went up "only" 100 points. "I liked one-on-one because I needed someone to explain to me the answers I got wrong. If someone can understand the explanations in a book, go for it!" says this 650 V, 590 M scorer. A Kaplan student noted what many experts believe—that prepping for the math yields more results than for the verbal because vocabulary and reading are harder to improve in a short period of time. Another Kaplan prodigy who scored 510 V, 630 M said his course was "maybe" worth the cost and cautions that coaching is not a panacea. "When you take a course, you actually need to work on your own in order to get better. I only did what I was told to do inside the classroom and I didn't see results," says this student, who rates prep books as his most useful study tool. More so than the higher scorers, students in this range cite a lack of motivation as the reason why they took a prep course. "There needs to be structure and needs to be hand-holding," says a 580 V, 560 M scorer. "If my tutor hadn't checked my homework every time, I probably wouldn't have done it."

> "[The class] was too long and spent too much time attending to the individuals with the poorest score, leaving me very bored."
>
> —710 V, 710 M

A Princeton Review student who said that her score had improved 100 points in verbal and math nevertheless said that her course was not worth the cost. "The company was helpful, but again, I didn't know when to apply their methods. With dozens of kinds of math tricks, it is difficult to know when to use what." This girl, who scored 1240, rates practice tests as her most important prep tool.

One student who did not take a prep course devised a novel prep method. "I found that reading was a greater preparatory pastime than studying. The prep books and CD-ROM focus on 'beating the system' through strategy, but I found I used knowledge as a better weapon," she writes. Well enough to get a 1230.

Students Who Scored 1090 and Below

Though their scores place them near the national average for SAT test-takers, students in this cohort were largely a dispirited and/or disengaged group. "I'm a horrible test-taker," says a 450 V, 400 M scorer, "I space out when taking a test such as the SATs." Another student who scored 470 V, 540 M says, "I did not want to take the test. I hate standardized tests," adding that students "should prepare for a long and pointless Saturday." A 540 V, 540 M scorer reports that the primary usefulness of his prep course was "to help me get the damned thing over."

Again and again, students in this cohort spoke of the clock as their primary nemesis. "Time pressure was my biggest problem. Other than that, the questions were not that hard," says a student who scored 540 V and 500 M. Adds a 520 V, 420 M scorer, "The time was the worst because no matter how confident you were, it was always on your mind."

This cohort seemed to divide into two groups. The first, which generally did not take a coaching course, seemed to know little about the test and care less. "I wasn't concerned about getting a high grade because the colleges I applied to don't require a high SAT score," writes a student who scored 550 V, 440 M. A student who scored 1030 attributed his struggles to the fact that he was not taking a math course and had a demanding work schedule outside of school. A 970 scorer said that she "knew enough to get a high enough score, I just didn't prepare at all."

On the other side of the ledger were students who had a real commitment to improving their scores. Many of these took prep courses, though the results were often disappointing. One student who scored 450 V, 480 M says that his family spent $1,000 on a prep course. "When I was taking this prep course I felt my scores would improve, but they didn't." He identified practice tests as his most important prep tool. Self-esteem issues cropped up for one student in her coaching course. "I took the prep course with very intelligent and competitive students. For this reason, I was embarrassed to ask questions and did not receive the attention that I needed," she says. This student scored 520 V, 530 M.

Of the twelve students in this cohort who said they had worked with Princeton Review, six estimated that their scores had gone up 50 points or less. "If I had their books, I could have done it on my own," says a 500 V, 520 M scorer. "The program forced me to study rather than sleep or waste time. I was able to survive the actual SAT without passing out at the end," reports a 500 V, 500 M scorer. She estimates that the course increased her score 60–100 points but was not worth the cost because "I was grouped with people who didn't share my same problems and concerns." The most prominent Princeton Review backer in the cohort estimates that his scores went up 110–150 points, to a total of 500 V and 510 M, and says that a prep course is worthwhile "because you can talk to someone and get tips that no book can give you."

There was at least one ray of hope amid the general gloom of the many students who scored low in the context of their schools. "Don't worry! I got

PREP COURSE CONCLUSIONS

Readers may draw their own conclusions from the responses we've cited. Here are the most important:

- Practice tests are the single most crucial element of any prep program. Students, particularly high scorers, say so again and again.

- High scorers tend to be much more confident than low scorers. They are more likely to prepare for the SAT on their own.

- Paying for test prep is an uncertain proposition at best. Many students are adamant that their coaching course was not productive; most are uncertain as to the benefits.

- The most commonly cited benefit of a coaching course is that it helps students who lack the initiative, discipline, or confidence to prepare on their own.

- Initiative, discipline, and confidence are among the most important ingredients of scoring high on the SAT.

Next, we make the case as to why preparing on your own is the best way for most students to tackle the SAT.

into every college I applied to even though my test scores were poor. There is so much more to a person than their testing abilities," she writes. This student scored 520 V, 460 M and was accepted by Alfred University, Hartwick College, Earlham College, Lesley College, and Warren Wilson College. Congratulations to her!

TAKING CHARGE OF YOUR SAT PREP

3

ANSWERS TO YOUR QUESTIONS

✔ What are the benefits of preparing on my own?

✔ When should I take the SAT?

✔ How many times should I take it?

✔ How do I register?

✔ How should I design my preparation program?

✔ What are the most important strategies for success?

How much would you pay for a spiffy SAT score? $500? $1,000? We recently saw a prep course advertised on the Internet for $1,775. That's a serious price tag for SAT tutoring, but with four years of tuition bills around the corner, a prep course suddenly may not seem so expensive.

Our problem with SAT coaching isn't the expense. We don't recommend coaching courses for most students because we have come to believe, after doing our homework, that preparing on your own is likely to be more effective. We say this not simply because so many of the students in our survey—particularly the high scorers—said coaching was a waste of time. Nor were we swayed merely by the fact that the students in our survey without coaching scored higher than the students who got it—maybe the uncoached students just didn't need the coaching.

The real issue is attitude. The students who prepare on their own do so because they have faith in themselves. They're self-directed and willing to get organized. They're independent. Students who seek coaching, whether they realize it or not, are making a tacit admission that they feel helpless. They want someone else to show them the way, or to give them the magic bullet. Over and over again, students will say things like "I needed the course to force me to study" and "I could never have done it on my own."

But if the SAT is really so important, why can't you do it your own? And why, if you aren't motivated to do it on your own, do you think attending a course will help? If the subject were Calculus or AP Physics, you might need somebody to guide you. But the SAT isn't like a class in school where the goal is to master new or hard material. The "stuff" is easy. You've already learned it. The hard part is getting yourself accustomed to a new test-taking process.

> "I am a firm believer that it is more beneficial to prepare to take the test than it is to study the material."
>
> —690 V, 690 M

Forget the idea that there is a mysterious secret to acing the SAT that someone else must teach you. There is only an obvious secret: practice. Think about the way you learn any new skill, like singing, dancing, drawing, writing, skateboarding, throwing a Frisbee, or playing a new game on your Xbox. The first step is to get familiar with the basics. If you're on a skateboard, you fall down a lot. If you're drawing or writing, a lot of paper gets tossed in the trash. If you're throwing a Frisbee, your first toss will start off straight and then hook at a crazy angle and crash-land in the neighbor's tulips. Only after hours, days, months, or years of practice do you get the feel of what you're doing. Only then can you begin to master advanced techniques. You learn foreshortening to make your drawings appear 3-D. You master the art of beginning your essays with an anecdote. You start doing tail-whips or curb-stalls on your skateboard. And how do you learn all this? Practice. Along the way, it helps to get some advice on the finer points—that is why we've written this book. But advanced information is useful only when you know how to use it.

By preparing on your own, you can construct your own strategy for taking the test rather than trying to ape someone else's. You can weigh various techniques and choose the ones that work best for your learning style. You'll develop far greater mastery than if you merely tried to copy the latest guaranteed plan. By trusting yourself, you'll begin to build the confidence that will be a crucial element of your success. Is doing it on your own a challenge? Of course! That's why it has the potential to raise your score.

We know all this may sound scary, and we sympathize. Fear and procrastination are powerful enemies. We know you'll probably think of a million reasons to put off focusing on the test. Does that mean you should go running to a tutor? We think not. A tutor may provide a temporary security blanket, but until the day when the College Board and ETS allow them in the test center, the effects of tutoring will usually wear off about the time you blacken your first oval. The SAT is all about you—alone with the test—and your preparation should be the same.

> "[A prep course is worthwhile] if you are willing to pay, because it is more motivating because you have to go to class."
>
> —660 V, 800 M

When Should I Take the SAT?

Left to their own devices, some parents would start their kids on SAT prep in about seventh grade. Easy there, mom. Better take a chill pill if you feel those thoughts coming on.

The main risk from starting too early goes something like this: Mom and dad are nervous about the SAT. Mom and dad transmit their nervousness to son or daughter. Instead of helping, test prep simply makes son or daughter more nervous.

A second pitfall is nearly as destructive as the first. It follows a basic law of parenting: When mom or dad exert a force in one direction, son or daughter exert an equal and opposite force in the other direction. Let's say mom wants son to start preparing for the SAT. That means son probably wants to do anything but start preparing for the SAT. Not to be outdone, mom forces son to start preparing. To get back at mom, son goes through the motions of preparing but never really tries.

Given the crucial importance of a positive attitude, we think the student should make the call about when to start preparing—though we don't rule out periodic parental nudges. That said, there are several advantages to starting early for top students. A number of higher scorers in our survey recalled taking the SAT in middle school as a positive experience. (Most did so in preparation for "Talent Search" summer programs based at Duke, Johns Hopkins, Northwestern, or University of Denver.) These students said that a good score in seventh or eighth grade gave them confidence that they would do well in eleventh grade.

We suspect, however, that this dynamic might work the opposite way for a student who is not so advanced. A poor score in middle school doesn't help anyone. Also, the SAT now includes math from Algebra II, which few students get until ninth grade. It remains to be seen how much the Talent Search programs will continue to rely on scores from the SAT, but even if they do, we would recommend that only students who typically score in the top 1st–3rd percentile on standardized tests consider this option. SAT prep for middle schoolers is over-the-top and likely to fuel anxiety and frustration.

> "Practice, practice, practice—the best way to become comfortable with the material."
>
> —800 V, 710 M

A second early-bird option is becoming more popular among top scorers: taking the test in tenth grade. Several of the high-scoring students in our survey suggested this option. There are two rationales:

The Math Is Fresher

"The most challenging thing for me was just that I hadn't done any of this type of math since about seventh grade," said a Pomona ED admit who scored 770 V, 680 M. Another student with 760 V, 680 M described the math section as "hard to do when you're in a calculus frame of mind." These comments were echoed by many, many students who told us that the hardest part of the math was overcoming rustiness.

The Pace of School Is Slower

"Since school course work is more difficult junior year, there is more free time to study for the SAT sophomore year," says a 700 V, 800 M scorer who recommends taking it in March of grade ten. He adds that students can begin studying vocabulary as soon as ninth grade. Though most students will probably take a pass on that, it is true that eleventh grade is when everything hits the fan in the life of a high school student, including AP courses, varsity sports, and leadership positions.

Most students wait until at least the summer after tenth grade to prepare, usually before the PSAT or their first SAT. Though some students seem to need the experience of bombing their first SAT before they get serious for the second, the best strategy is to get it right the first time. Below are some pros and cons of preparing for and taking the SAT on the various possible test dates:

October SAT. Too early for eleventh graders. Get the PSAT under your belt. Twelfth graders can consider this date as the last one definitely in time for early decision or early action.

October PSAT. Prepping before this test makes particular sense for students who are gunning for recognition in the National Merit Scholarship competition. Students with busy school schedules may choose to do a chunk of their work in the summer, then maintain a moderate pace in September before ramping up in early October. The main pitfall to the PSAT strategy is the fact that summer is a long time from mid-October, and work done then may be a distant memory. In addition, some students are simply not ready to cope with major test prep so early in eleventh grade.

November SAT. Eleventh graders who prepped before the PSAT can take their first SAT on this date as part of a kill-two-birds-with-one-stone strategy. Since the date is only two to three weeks after the PSAT, the material should still be fresh. Early November is not a bad time in the school calendar—midsemester exams are over but the end-of-term crunch has not yet hit. The timing is also good for athletes: fall sports are generally over and winter sports have not yet begun. On the down side, you won't yet have your results from the PSAT, which might help you identify strengths and weaknesses. For most eleventh graders, November will be too early.

December SAT. An unlikely choice except for last-minute twelfth graders who want one last shot. Not near any major breaks and too close to first-term exams.

January SAT. Students with school exams in December should seriously consider this one. Winter break is not a time that most students would prefer to prepare for the SAT, but busy superachievers must take time where they can get it. The results from the October PSAT will arrive before the break, and students can generally get their test booklets from the guidance office and go over every question they missed. Two weeks of leisurely study in late December can be followed by another two or three weeks in early January, when school work is light because the new term has just begun. This date may not be appropriate for those who play winter sports and those who have exams in January.

March or April SAT. In some years, this administration of the test is given in mid to late March. In others, it is early April. This is a reasonably good date for many students, though it often arrives before spring break. Mid-March fits well with the sports season; winter sports are generally over but spring ones are not yet in full swing. Some high school counselors recommend this date as part of a March-and-May strategy. The theory behind this approach is that taking it twice in quick succession will allow students to do better the second time because the memory of the first one will be fresh.

May SAT. Though May is a popular date, it is not particularly convenient for many students because AP exams also hit in the first half of the month. On the plus side, students who have spring break in April can use that time to ramp-up their preparation. Year-end academic demands will not have reached a crescendo, especially at schools that continue through early June.

June SAT. Applicants to highly selective institutions will want to reserve this date for the Subject Tests. For students not taking Subject Tests, this date may work well, especially for those students who get out of school in late May.

After taking the SAT I once or twice in grade eleven, most students will want to take it again in grade twelve, generally in October or November. A second pass at the Subject Tests may also be on the agenda, usually in November or December.

How Many Times Should I Take It?

The standard advice has always been to take the SAT twice in eleventh and/or twelfth grade—and a third time if you have a particular reason to want one more crack at it. But that was the old SAT. The current SAT has three sections, and since colleges generally add the highest scores in each category, our hunch is that students are going to want every opportunity to increase all three scores.

THE COLLEGE BOARD'S FEE MACHINE

When it comes to finding clever ways of extracting cash from the pockets of high school students and their families, nobody does it better than the College Board. In spring of 2005, a few of its fees were as follows:

Taking the SAT	$41.50
Taking three SAT Subject Tests	$41.00
Late registration	$20.00
Standby registration	$35.00
Score reports after the test date	$9.00 per college
Rushed score reports	$26.00 plus $9.00 per college

It doesn't take a genius to figure out why the College Board can charge such inflated prices. The people who decide that you must take College Board tests—the colleges—are not the ones who pay for it (you do). Though students can theoretically take the ACT as an alternative to SAT I and II, in reality students in many parts of the country feel little choice but to take the SAT.

One of the most egregious examples of College Board money-grubbing occurred several years ago when it hatched the idea of making students pay for the privilege of viewing their scores "early" via its website. Though scores would be made available to everyone on the Web about three weeks after the test date, the College Board charged $13.00 to those who wanted to see their scores seven to ten days ahead of time. Though the College Board billed the scheme as a way to ease student anxiety, critics charged that the Board was attempting to profit from that anxiety. The College Board has since quietly dropped the fee to view scores online, though students can still pay $10.00 to get their scores early by phone.

Look for more price hikes in the future. As long as the colleges and the College Board have a stranglehold on standardized testing, there is little to restrain future fee increases. The paying customers (you) have no leverage.

Like all standardized tests, the SAT has a built-in margin of error. This is because the SAT does not test all the knowledge out there, but only a small sample of it. One test might have "scrupulous"—a word you happened to learn in English class last year—while another might have "apocryphal," a word you've never seen in your life. ("Scrupulous" means "honest" while "apocryphal" means "of questionable origin or authenticity.") Because of differences like this from exam to exam, the score you get on a particular test may vary from your "real" score—the average score you would get if you took the test a large number of times.

> **"I would not take the [prep] course again, nor would I recommend it. The teacher was awful."**
>
> **—780 V, 660 M**

Score jumps caused by random variations are amplified by events in the life of the student who takes the test. Maybe you didn't drink enough water on the morning of the test, got dehydrated, and got a headache. Maybe you drank too much water, got nervous, and got the runs. For a hundred different reasons, your score can fluctuate depending on whether you had a good day or a bad day.

Of the 815 students we surveyed, 137 (or 17 percent) increased their combined scores by at least 100 points from their first SAT to their second, third, (and in a few cases) fourth SAT. Like the colleges, we looked at only the highest verbal and math scores. For instance, if a student scored 600 Verbal and 650 Math on the first SAT, then 670 Verbal and 630 Math, we counted that as a 70 point increase despite the 20 point decline in Math. If on the third time the student scored 650 Verbal and 680 Math, the combined score increase from the first test to the third would be 100 points.

There is a distinct possibility of increasing your score significantly on the second or third try, and that possibility will be magnified now that the SAT has three sections instead of two.

Registering for the Tests

This part should be simple. Right?

Guess again. Registering for the SAT is a maze with enough twists and turns to confuse even the savviest applicant. The key is to get on top of it early. Each year's dates are listed on the College Board's website and in the annual registration bulletin mailed to high school guidance offices. The registration deadline is about thirty-five days ahead of each test date. There is no sense in procrastinating—go ahead and register. In addition to all the usual personal information, you will need the following:

Your High School's Code. This six-digit number will ensure that your school gets a copy of your scores. Many schools report SAT scores on the back of your transcript.

Your Social Security Number. Another milestone on the road to adulthood. You probably have no clue what your social security number is; now is a perfect time to memorize it.

Your Choice of Test Center. Your best move is to consult current twelfth graders (or your counselor) about the best place in your area to take the test. You want a test center with big desks instead of those narrow ones that are an extension of the armrest—especially if you're left-handed. You also want a center where the heat works without making the room ninety degrees. The most popular test centers sometimes fill up. Register early for the best shot at your first choice.

A List of Colleges to Receive Your Scores. Students are always leery of this one when they take the test for the first time. Most would rather see their scores before they send them to the colleges. We understand. It doesn't really matter if you designate colleges to receive scores until the last time you take the SAT or the Subject Tests, when you must send scores to all colleges that

WON'T SOME STUDENTS DO BETTER WITH A TUTOR?

Possibly. If a student has trouble with the subject matter on the SAT—particularly the math—a tutor may be the best choice. If a student has a learning disability, or is motivated but simply can't get organized, a tutor may provide a helpful touchstone. Too often tutors are hired simply because a student is anxious or has low self-confidence. This is exactly the kind of student who would benefit most from working through the test on his or her own rather than developing dependence on an adult. Some students say that they learn better through human interaction, and we don't doubt it. But taking the SAT is not about learning subject matter. It is an individual process that is best mastered through experience. The best a tutor can offer is a structured and encouraging space for the student to do the same things they could do on their own.

require them. Designating these colleges when you register will save you money since College Board lets you send scores to up to four colleges for free if you do so at registration. If you wait, you'll need to send in an Additional Score Report Form with a per-college fee.

Along with the nuts and bolts information, the registration form features the SAT questionnaire. It includes everything from your family income and religious preference to your own assessment of your scholastic ability. Is your mathematical ability "Highest," "Above Average," "Average," or "Below Average?" The questionnaire asks about your experience with computers, what you intend to major in, and whether you have a disability.

Why all the questions? The College Board explains, "The SAT Questionnaire allows you to provide information about your academic background, activities, and interests to help you in planning for college and to help colleges find out more about you." Translation: The College Board wants to sell your address to colleges who are interested in recruiting students with your characteristics. It will also use your responses in evaluating the test. To

FINDING THE RIGHT STUDY SPACE

This may sound like a mundane detail, but it is really make or break. To get the maximum effect from your work, you should find a spot that simulates the testing conditions as exactly as possible. For practice tests or extended study sessions, we recommend a place outside of where you live your normal life that tells you "This is where I am preparing for the SAT." One option would be to stay after school if you can find study space there, or to go to mom or dad's office during non-business hours. A nearby library is another possibility. For routine study sessions, choose a space at home away from clutter and confusion. Silence is essential. If all your studying is done with music in the background, you will recall less on the real SAT when there will be no music in the background. (Research shows this—we're not making it up.) One other hint: Make sure you have a good stopwatch. If you're like most students, you get nervous at the idea of timing yourself. All the more reason to use that stopwatch.

keep adding to your pile of college mail, choose "yes" on the question that asks if you would like to participate in the Student Search Service.

If this is your second or third time taking the test, there is no reason to bother with the questionnaire. If you do fill it out, you can always leave any questions blank that you choose.

As you complete the registration form, you'll also have an opportunity to sign up for SAT Answer-Reporting Services. If you take the test in October, January, or May, you can get the Question and Answer Service, which gives you all the questions and whether you got them right or wrong. On other test dates, you can get the Student Answer Service, which offers a breakdown of the types of questions you

> "If you are one to cheat yourself, to take short cuts and to lose motivation, take an SAT course with outlined rules and requirements."
>
> —560 V, 650 M

answered right and wrong and their level of difficulty. In a recent year, these services cost $24.00 and $9.00, respectively. Dates and costs may change, but these services are worthwhile if you plan to take the test again.

Late Registration and Score Reporting

If you space out and miss the registration deadline, don't have a conniption. The College Board can still accommodate you—for a fee. For a week or two after each deadline, students can register late. If you miss the boat entirely, you can still show up on test day with a shot at getting in as a standby. There are no guarantees with standby registration. You must show up at a test center with a completed registration form in hand and a check for the registration fee plus an additional $35.00 or so. If you are thinking of doing standby, we recommend that you call your test center of choice on Monday or Tuesday before the test. Ask to speak to the SAT coordinator. He or she may be able to tell you whether there is likely to be space. In most cases, there will be.

A variety of issues can crop up related to reporting scores to the colleges. First, be aware that the report sent to you and your school is not considered "official." Even though your college application may ask you to fill in your scores—and even though your high school transcript may include your scores—most colleges ask that you have the College Board send scores directly to them.

WHY YOU DON'T NEED A PHONEBOOK-SIZED PREP BOOK

You know we recommend *The Official SAT Study Guide* as a valuable resource. What about other books? By all means try them if you have the time and energy, but don't get too bogged down. This book is relatively short because we don't want to take too much time from your main job: taking practice tests. Instead of throwing everything but the kitchen sink at you, we've boiled it down to our most essential insights about the SAT.

Unlike the ACT, which allows students to send scores from a particular date, the SAT operates on a send-one-send-them-all system. Suppose you take the SAT in April, two Subject Tests in June, and another SAT in October. If you want to send the October score to Middlebury, the report will automatically include the June and April scores.

It hasn't always been this way. When Big Sis took the Subject Tests, she may have had the option of withholding the scores under a program called Score Choice. Alas, College Board abolished Score Choice in 2002. That said, most students are more worried about the colleges seeing bad scores than they need to be. Remember, your highest scores will be what they look at. The same goes for the Subject Tests—if you bomb one, you can always take it again and the first score is unlikely to count against you.

If you have a nervous breakdown while taking the SAT, there is one recourse. Until the Wednesday following the test, you can cancel your scores—meaning that your scores will disappear forever and no one (including you) will see them.

The most common issue with score reports is getting them to the admission office fast enough. Reports are generally sent to the colleges about three weeks after the test date. So if you're applying with a January 1 deadline and take the test in December, your score will arrive in plenty of time at the colleges you designated to receive your scores. The hitch? Sometimes students decide to apply to a college after they have taken their last SAT. In this case, students must use an Additional Score Report Form (or go to www.collegeboard.com) and pay a fee to get the scores sent. Under normal circumstances, additional reports take a poky three to five weeks to arrive at Most Desirable U. That's a problem if your deadline is next week. Not to worry. For the incredible low price of $26.00—plus $9.00 per college—the College Board will rush your scores within two business days to all the schools on your list. (Prices subject to increase every year.) We should hasten to add that rush reporting will not speed initial scoring but only helps after you have received your scores.

> "Mental readiness is more important than academic—it is the difference between good test-takers and bad ones."
>
> —690 V, 780 M

Students should always make every effort to have their scores arrive by the application deadline. But generally speaking, scores that arrive within a few weeks of the deadline are in time for consideration. For early decision, scores from the October date are always in time and scores from November often are. For regular decision, if you bomb your Math II subject test in December and want one more crack at it, January will probably work.

Students who are concerned about their scores being reported in time should contact the college. An admission officer may be able to advise you as to whether you really need to rush a score, or whether a particular score will arrive in time for consideration. If your school already has a copy of the score report, your counselor may be able to report the score pending arrival of an official report.

Students with Disabilities

As this book makes clear, the ability to cope with time pressure can be a major factor in determining your score. Why fight it if you don't need to? Students with diagnosed physical and learning disabilities have the right to take college admission tests with special accommodations, most notably extended time, large print, or an audio version of the test. In 2003, the College Board discontinued its long-time practice of "flagging" the scores of students who tested with disabilities. Since such scores are no longer identified in any way, there is no downside to testing with accommodations if you qualify.

Schools file the paperwork with College Board, and there are two basic requirements:

- A diagnostic evaluation and recommendation for extended time by a qualified professional. In cases where the original diagnosis was made more than three years ago, follow-up testing must confirm the original diagnosis.
- Evidence that the school has acknowledged the disability and is granting the same accommodations in day-to-day work that are being requested for the SAT.

For students in public schools, this generally means having an Individualized Education Plan (IEP) that is the product of at least one meeting between parents, teachers, and the student. A comparable plan is necessary for private school students. If you have been diagnosed with a disability or are thinking of having an evaluation, do it as soon as possible.

> "It's better to get all the easy questions done that you can, so you aren't rushing through them later and making stupid mistakes."
>
> —790 V, 720 M

Speak to your high school counselor to get the ball rolling. The best time to ask the College Board for accommodations is at the end of ninth grade—before your first PSAT—at which time your school accommodations must already be in place.

A last-minute rush to get accommodations may increase your likelihood of getting denied. College Board has begun to clamp down on perceived abuses by students who seek extended time based on a questionable diagnosis, and a student who suddenly petitions for accommodations in eleventh grade may raise red flags. A high proportion of the students who seek special testing come from wealthy areas, and the College Board recently implemented a School Compliance Review that is aimed at schools with a suspiciously high percentage of students seeking extended time.

Students who are approved for testing with up to 50 percent additional time generally take the SAT at national test centers on the same day as other students. Students needing more than 50 percent additional time take the test at their home schools during a short window of time beginning on the national test date.

WHAT ABOUT ELECTRONIC PREP MATERIALS?

Despite all the hi-tech gadgetry crowding the lives of today's students, the vast majority still prepare for the SAT using books rather than CD-ROMs or the Internet. As long as the SAT is administered on paper, books will offer the nearest facsimile of the real thing. Books also allow students to scan several dozen questions on the same page while computers typically have a narrower field of view and must be scrolled up and down.

But technology has its advantages. A CD-ROM, or programs available on the Internet, can immediately tell students how many questions they got right on a practice test and identify areas where they are weak. Some programs will also adjust their degree of difficulty automatically based on questions answered right and wrong. Others offer video instruction segments that spice up the routine. "The CD-ROM kept me engaged and I was less likely to get bored or distracted," says a student who scored 660 V, 690 M. Our electronic program of choice is the College Board's Official SAT Online Course for the simple reason that all of its questions are from real SATs.

Along with software available for use or purchase on the Internet, students can also opt for online courses that include live chat with an instructor. Only a handful of students in our survey paid for such a course, and most who did were disappointed with the results. One little gem on the Internet that might be worth a look is Number2.com, a site that offers a free test-prep tutorial. For building word power, try www.thefreedictionary.com, a comprehensive source where the definitions of synonyms, antonyms, and related words are one click away.

Making Your Own Prep Course

There are many things in life that are less than pleasant—but which must be done anyway. Like eating broccoli, going to the dentist, or sitting beside mom and dad at a college night presentation.

Add SAT prep to the list. But like most challenges, preparing for the SAT is also an opportunity. With you in control of the process, you'll learn more while boosting your confidence.

KNOWING WHAT YOU NEED TO DO

Scoring for the SAT is straightforward. Your raw score equals the number you get right minus a fraction of those you get wrong. The raw score is then converted to a score on the venerable 200–800 scale. As we explain below, it is generally to your advantage to answer every question. Assuming that you do, the chart below tells you roughly how many questions you need to get right and wrong for various scores. The data is based on a version of the test given in May 2000.

Target Score	Number Right	Number Wrong	Percent Right
Verbal			
800	74	4	95
700	69	9	88
600	60	18	77
500	51	27	65
Math			
800	58	2	97
700	63	7	88
600	44	16	73
500	39	21	65

The exact number of questions a student must get right to achieve a particular scaled score will fluctuate slightly from test to test. In school, 88 percent is a B+—a disappointing grade for many ambitious students. But on the SAT, 88 percent means a score of roughly 700, outstanding by almost anyone's standards. The bottom line: You can probably miss 5–10 questions and still get the score you are looking for. Don't come undone if there are a few that you have no clue how to solve. Focus on getting the ones that you do know how to solve. (Computations based on data from *10 Real SATs*, Third Edition.)

It is no easy task to shoehorn SAT prep into the hectic schedule of an eleventh grader, and planning ahead is essential. First, students should figure out how much time they want to spend. In as little as ten hours, students can take two full-length practice tests and have another four hours of study—a minimal review but better than nothing. A fuller commitment of about forty hours will allow students to do half a dozen or more full-length tests along with plenty of work focused on particular areas of strength and weakness. Anything more than fifty hours is probably overkill, though if a student is motivated and has the time to spend, there is no reason not to keep going. Students who need significant brush-up on SAT math or grammar may want to do a more extended review, as will students who want to take a long-term approach to building their vocabulary.

Generally speaking, we recommend starting about 45 days, more or less, before your exam date. If your life is hectic, two months ahead might be better. If you have a break from school or plenty of free time, one month may do. Though you don't need to plan every minute of your prep regimen ahead of time, it is helpful to have a clear sense of your path from the beginning. We recommend that you do a tentative schedule at the outset to give yourself a clear idea of where you are going. You can always revise your plan as you go.

Often, the biggest hurdle is getting started. Here are some tips:

Begin with a Bang
Starting in dribs and drabs may make it more difficult for you to build momentum. The best way to get your head around SAT prep is to find a weekend or school break where you can begin with at least five hours of focus in the span of a day or two.

Don't Make Your Sessions too Long
Once you get started, it is better to do four 45 minute study periods per week than one that lasts 3 hours. This is a flaw with most SAT prep courses, which are built for the convenience of the instructor, not you. The longer you focus on your task, the lower your efficiency will be. The more frequently you study, the more you will learn.

Schedule Down-time After
Research suggests that there is a period after focused thought when the knowledge sinks in—literally. Try to wind down after you study. Vegetate in

front of the TV. Read *Cosmo* or *Sports Illustrated* for twenty minutes and then go to bed. Take a break before studying something else.

Make Sure That at Least 75 Percent of Your Work Is Practice

You may need to look up words or go back to your tenth grade math book to learn about a specific type of problem. But don't stray too far from doing actual SAT problems.

Schedule Practice Tests for Saturday Mornings

As test day approaches, nothing gets you ready better than taking practice tests at 8:00 a.m. on the Saturdays before your SAT. We recommend that you find a quiet place like a library or office. Simulate the real thing as closely as possible.

Aside from buying this book, your first move should be to get the latest edition of the College Board's *Official SAT Study Guide*, the only book in which every question is a real question. Since the Board does not allow others (like us) to publish complete SATs, the practice tests in any book not published by the Board are put together by authors trying to mimic the real thing. The practice tests in this book are an exception because we designed them to be harder than a real SAT. We intend our practice tests to complement rather than replace those in the *Official SAT Study Guide*.

Getting started with SAT prep is like sizing up an ice-cold swimming pool. Some people stick a toe in the water and then procrastinate. Others wade in cautiously—and begin yelping when the water reaches their knees. But a few hardy souls avoid all the nonsense and simply take the plunge.

This is the strategy we recommend with SAT prep. A full-length, timed

CONSIDER EAR PLUGS

Do you ever get distracted when the person behind you has the sniffles? Consider ear plugs. They're cheap and easy to use. Try them out on a practice test and see if they help you focus. One potential hitch: make sure you can hear the proctor when time is called.

practice test is a good way to start. If you are using the *Official SAT Study Guide*, turn to the answer key and tally your score. This is your first benchmark of where you are and offers a realistic idea of the score you can shoot for as you prep. Compare your score on the practice test with your PSAT score(s). If they are close, you have an excellent indication of where you stand. Go back and look at how many you got right and wrong in each section. What are the patterns?

Another possibility would be to start with one of the practice tests at the end of this book. If this is your strategy, don't pay too much attention to your score and don't be rattled by the fact that the questions are tough. Our tests are designed to give you a better idea of how to handle the hardest problems.

Even before blackening their first oval, many students will have a clear idea of what they need to work on. After a practice test or two, we advise students to focus on the types of problems that give them the most difficulty. You may feel uncertain about the

> "My problems were never a problem of knowledge, but of making dumb mistakes and losing focus, something that is easy on such a long and boring test."
>
> —700 V, 760 M

subject matter on the test—especially the math—but resist the temptation to go running for your ninth grade geometry book. You've had the material before; use practice problems rather than non-test-related material to resharpen your skills. "Actually doing test questions was far more effective than rote memorization of vocabulary words or math formulas" says a Princeton-bound 800 V, 800 M scorer.

After reaching a minimum comfort level with each kind of question, your attention should turn to one of the most important issues of SAT prep: how to pace yourself to avoid anxiety and make sure you spend the right amount of time on each kind of question.

Beating Anxiety and Time Pressure

Why do you fear the SAT? If you're like most students, it isn't because the grammar is too hard or because you can't handle a few multiple-choice tricks. You're probably taking trigonometry, pre-calculus, or calculus in math—are you really going to get worked up over an exam that ends with Algebra II?

We know what scares you: time pressure. We read about it over and over again in our surveys:

- "Whether or not you are a fast or slow test-taker, time is always attacking you," writes a 730 V, 720 M scorer.
- "Time pressure really affects the way my brain processes things," writes a student who scored 550 V and 590 M.
- "The time pressure is exhausting. I know I could do better if I had fifteen more minutes to do each section," says a student with 670 V and 700 M.

The vicious cycle goes like this: Time pressure causes anxiety, and anxiety increases susceptibility to time pressure. Students get anxious because of the fear that they won't have time to finish. Anxiety slows their processing speed and they fall behind the pace necessary to finish—which makes them even more anxious. Most students gamely fight through their stress, and many earn a good score. Nevertheless, these students will score far below what they could have gotten had they been stress-free.

One of the most striking findings of our survey was the extent to which the highest scorers—those who scored a combined 1500 or above—were able to remain stress-free. In most cases, they were relaxed because they did not feel time pressure. It is no doubt true that many of these students possess outstanding academic skills that allow them to excel. But the characteristic that defines them more than any other is their relaxed, clear-headed approach. The students who scored 1200–1400 were much more stressed out, and we suspect that many of them had the skills but not the temperament to score even higher. Had the 1370 scorer quoted above not been so exhausted by fighting the time pressure, he might not have needed those additional 15 minutes at the end of each section, and he might have scored 1470 or 1570.

Another thing we learned is that a clear head is more important than preparation. "The SATs test my emotional state more than anything else," says a student who scored 760 V, 680 M. She reports that she improved her verbal score by 90 points on her second SAT simply because she was more relaxed. Another student who admitted to being very nervous before his first SAT scored 540 V, 550 M. He prepared less for his second test, was less nervous, and improved to 650 V, 670 M.

BUILDING YOUR PREP COURSE:
A SAMPLE TIMELINE

Eight Weeks
Total Time: Approximately 45 hours

The following is merely a guideline. If you have a break from school near your test date, you can follow a more concentrated schedule. If this pace seems too intense, you can spread out your prep over 9–12 weeks.

1. Full-length practice tests:
Time frame: 1–2 weekends

Do two of these on your first weekend, one more on the following weekend if necessary. Get the feel of the test. Diagnose strengths and weaknesses.

2. Practice each problem type:
Time frame: 3–4 weeks, 4–6 sessions per week

Begin 45-minute sessions after your first weekend of practice tests. Develop a strategy for each kind of problem. Experiment with various approaches. Do subject-matter review if necessary. Target areas in need of improvement.

3. Sections under timed conditions:
Time frame: 3–4 weeks, 4–6 sessions per week

Fine-tune your pace on each type of section. Do two sections per session (45–50 minutes total). Accelerate your speed and examine the impact on your accuracy. Experiment with skipping and guessing. Get a feel for the clock.

4. Whole test under timed conditions:
Time frame: 2–3 weekends

Do two to four full-length, timed tests in the last two weekends before the test. Work on staying focused in the last two sections of each test. If overly fatigued or stressed, experiment with resting during the last several minutes of each section rather than checking work. Learn to pace yourself.

Your Game Plan

Perhaps the best way to lower the pressure is to be familiar with the test, and specifically, to know what lies ahead. This chapter lays out a complete game plan for beating SAT stress that can be executed with a month or two of preparation.

Step One: Getting Comfortable

Telling students to relax before taking the SAT is like telling them to ignore the pink elephant floating in the corner of the room. It won't work. Relaxation comes only with mastery and a feeling of control. Students must conquer their fear of time pressure by proving to themselves, again and again if necessary, that they can finish the test.

If you're preparing to take the SAT, consider yourself in training. Throughout this book, we have spoken of timed practice tests as the single most important way to condition your mind for the rigors of the SAT. After your first practice test or two—which should act as an overall diagnostic of your strengths and weaknesses—turn your attention to the sections that make up the test. Which ones are the toughest for you? Focus on the most difficult, but don't ignore others that you may already be good at. Use your stopwatch. Subconsciously, you probably won't want to time yourself because timing causes stress. That's the main reason why you need to time yourself. Get used to it.

As you work through your practice sections, record your observations for later review, either in a notebook or a Word file on the computer. A student who scored 750 V, 790 M used this approach for learning grammar. She did numerous practice sections, and for every question she missed, she typed the error and the corrected sentence—along with an explanation of the error in her own words. By the time test day neared, she had accumulated 25 pages of problems that she reviewed every 48 hours.

Learning from Your Mistakes. Look for patterns in the questions you get right and wrong. In College Board's *Official SAT Study Guide*, the answer key for each test rates the questions on a scale of 1–5, with 1 being the easiest and 5 being the hardest. One of the most important secrets to doing your best on the SAT is to get the easy questions right. You should be acing the 1s and 2s, which generally account for between 25 and 30 percent of the test. You might miss a handful of 3s—which generally make up about 40 to 45 percent of the questions—and even more of the 4s and 5s, which together comprise an additional 25 to 30 percent of the test.

After you take a practice test or section, go back to look at the ones you missed. Did you really not know the answer? Or did you make a bonehead mistake? Nothing is more important than getting the ones you should get—either because ETS defines them as easy, or because you know you should have gotten them after seeing the answer. The fix might be as simple as reading more carefully, or checking alternative answers even after you think you've found the right one. Maybe you're forgetting to do the final step in too many math problems and falling for distracters. Keep doing practice problems and review the strategies in this book.

Part of the problem may be that you are putting too much pressure on yourself to finish the entire test. Since speed is at a premium, our first advice is to push yourself to see how fast you can go. But if the thought of trying to finish makes you break out in a cold sweat, maybe you shouldn't try. For students who have particular difficulty with time pressure, the best strategy may be to aim for completing the first two-thirds or three-fourths of the questions of each type—and doing the rest only if there is time. An alternative strategy, skipping problems, is discussed below.

> "Since school coursework is more difficult junior year, there is more free time sophomore year to study for the SAT."
>
> —700 V, 800 M

Step Two: How the SAT Is Different

Forget everything you've learned about taking tests in school. The SAT is different. In school, you learn a unit of material and then take a test on it. If you get all or almost all of the questions right—say, 90 percent of them—you do well. Get 65 percent and you're staring at a D. Let's say you get 65 percent of the questions right on your SAT Math section. That means you score about 500—roughly the national average. But most students probably aim higher—say 650 or so. To reach that goal, you'll need to get about 49 out the 60 questions—82 percent. Even if you're shooting for an 800, you can still generally miss two or three on the math section and three or four on the verbal.

The point is simple: Hardly anyone gets them all right. Too many students take the SAT as if it were a normal school test—and stress themselves out trying to get 100 percent. The right approach is to come into the test with a mindset of cool efficiency, knowing that you probably won't get them all. The SAT has more questions on it than a typical school test, and in every section, each one is worth the same amount. Get the easy ones right, don't sweat the hardest ones, and have a strategy to deal with the ones in-between.

Each time you approach an SAT problem, there are four possible outcomes:

1. Solve the problem and move on
2. Can't solve the problem—skip and come back
3. Can't solve the problem—guess and move on
4. Linger and try to solve the problem

Obviously, you hope that most problems fall into the first category. The key issue is what to do with problems that you do not know immediately how to solve. On school tests, the natural tendency is to grit your teeth and hang in there. Giving up quickly isn't in the nature of most good students. You'll think a little harder, try a different approach, re-do your calculations one more time, and...Grrrrr. Before you realize it, five minutes have passed. If you don't get the problem after spending all that time, you're going to be demoralized and stressed-out. Even if you do get it, you'll be playing catch-up for the rest of the section. A hard-won victory over a difficult problem is not worth the cost if you miss an easier one later because you are hurrying to finish, or if you can't get to two problems at the end because time runs out. We cannot emphasize enough: Committing more than two minutes to one problem is almost never a good strategy unless you have finished everything else in the section.

> "I regret waiting too long to take practice tests, and I would tell tenth and eleventh graders to start practicing months before the test, even if it's once a week."
>
> —690 V, 770 M

Step Three: Are You a Skipper or a Guesser?

Since you're too smart to fret and pull your hair out over a tough problem, there are two options. You can either skip it and come back, or you can guess.

Our survey included many advocates of skipping. "I took practice tests and found out a target score and the number I could skip to get the score," says a matter-of-fact student who got 700 V, 690 M. According to a 770 V, 800 M scorer, "It's better to get all the easy questions done that you can, so you aren't rushing through them later and making stupid mistakes." Another student was not satisfied with her 690 V, 710 M on her first SAT. "I knew I could do better because I hadn't managed my time very well, so I taught myself to skip hard questions. (It really does help, even though it feels wrong after taking too many tests in school where you had to answer every question.)" With the new strategy, her score jumped to 760 V and 740 M.

Despite widespread praise for skipping, there were some dissenting voices. One student who scored 610 V, 630 M writes that skipping "misleads an average student into thinking that he or she cannot do a question." Another potential drawback: Skipping means that you must read the question twice, and you may need to remind yourself of its context. This can be especially damaging in the Passage-Based Reading, where students who skip are forced to reacquaint themselves with an entire passage. Says a Princeton-bound 730 V, 770 M scorer, "Too much jumping around can be discouraging and/or time-consuming rather than time-saving." There is also the nightmare scenario of skipping a problem in the test booklet but forgetting to skip on the answer sheet.

If you do skip, watch your oval-blackening with extra care. Write some quick notes in the test booklet next to the problem if you have a thought worth remembering when you come back. If you can eliminate possible answers before moving on, leave a mark to remind yourself which ones you have eliminated.

Students should experiment with the amount of questions they skip. Between three and five is a reasonable number. If you find yourself skipping more than ten, you may need to start trying harder to get an answer before you skip, or making a few more guesses before moving on.

Students who are generally unable to finish the test—but who also get distracted by skipping—can try a modified version of this strategy. Because test questions of each type go from easy to hard (with the exception of Passage-Based Reading), some students may prefer to answer every question through the first two-thirds or three-quarters of each section, and then skip around among the hard questions at the end. This strategy allows unbroken concentration at the beginning while limiting time-pressure anxiety. After completing most of the test, students can use the remaining time to decide which of the relatively hard questions at the end of the section they will answer. This method is preferable to working straight through until time runs out because it is always possible that an easy question or two—or perhaps a "hard" question to which you happen to know the answer—will be lurking near the end.

In lieu of skipping, your second alternative for a stumper question is to guess. Which option is best? It depends on the question. If your gut feeling is that more thought will give you a chance to solve the problem, skip it. If you size it up and conclude that more thinking is not going to help, make a guess and move on. As you take your practice tests, ask yourself: Do you often skip a problem and then come back to it, only to make a guess because you still can't figure it out? If so, you would have been better off to guess the first time and put the question out of your mind.

Our practice tests are a useful tool for the skip/guess dilemma. Because our tests have a higher proportion of hard problems, you will likely encounter a concentrated batch of them that stump you the first time.

One thing you should never do is leave a question blank. On the multiple-choice questions that form the majority of the test, ETS awards one point for each question you get right and subtracts one-quarter of a point for every one you get wrong. That means that if you randomly guess at five, the odds are that you will get one right and miss four—with no affect on your score. The idea is to ensure that on average, random guessing will neither hurt nor help you. But guesses on the SAT are rarely random. In most cases, you can eliminate at least one bonehead response. On questions where you have any clue, no matter how faint, a guess is better than no answer.

To gauge the effectiveness of your guessing, we recommend that you monitor how many of your guesses are right and wrong when you take your practice tests. You can do so by making a mark beside each response that is a guess, then checking to see if you got them right. "Taking timed practice tests and making educated guesses sort of go hand-in-hand," says a student who scored 730 V, 800 M, "By taking mock SATs, I was able to get used to the answers that the test-makers were looking for, and was thus able to reason out answers on the actual test." Another student who scored 800 V, 730 M says that practice tests "help you find out how good of an 'educated guesser' you are so you'll know how much to trust that skill."

Step Four: Speed, Speed, Speed

By the time you get to Step Four, you should be reasonably comfortable with the SAT. One student who scored 710 V, 800 M described the importance of getting "into the groove of test-taking, to go with the flow." If you have done enough practice tests to develop a "feel" for the test, it is time to push yourself even harder.

As part of their training for track meets, distance runners increase their speed by running intervals. A person who runs the 1,600 meters, for instance, might do ten consecutive sprints of 200 or 400 meters. The person will probably never sprint like that in competition, but speed drills help to build capacity by forcing runners to go faster in practice than they do in a meet.

The SAT is the testing equivalent of a distance run, and speed work can pay big dividends. Can you finish a section in five minutes less than the time allowed? Ten minutes less? See how fast you can go before your efficiency drops. If you get your mind accustomed to finishing every section five minutes before time is called, you'll have plenty of time on the real test.

You may not think it is possible to save that much time. Try it and see. Perhaps you already take all the right shortcuts. But if you're a good student, you may be the kind who listens to the teacher when she says to show all your work, and not to skip steps. Maybe you always set up problems according to the formula, and carefully double-check each answer. Great strategies for school, lousy strategies for the SAT.

> "I tried to play it safe by spending more time making sure my answers were correct. I didn't have enough time to answer the hard ones and got a 740 [on the math]. On my second SAT, I strategically raced through the test to get to the hard questions."
>
> —720 V, 800 M

The SAT rewards people who live on the edge, get the test done, and don't stress out. So if you usually read the whole passage, experiment with skimming. Don't bother reading all the other answers if you are sure that (A) is the right one—move on. If you can solve a math problem with a quick estimate, don't bother doing the computations to confirm that you are right. Trust yourself and get to the next problem.

Even the highest scorers can benefit from accelerating their pace. Says one such student, "I tried to play it safe by spending more time making sure my answers were correct. I didn't have enough time to answer the hard ones and got a 740 [on the math]. On my second SAT, I strategically raced through the test to get to the hard questions." The result? A sparkling 800.

Another obvious benefit of moving faster is more time to go back to the problems you have skipped and/or to check your work. Students who have finished can breathe a sigh of relief and come back with a clear head. See how many skipped problems you can get on the second time around. If a skipped problem is a lost cause, five more minutes of puzzling over it will be a waste. Make a guess and move on. Your time might be better spent checking the ones you think you got right—especially if you can catch a blunder or two. We recommend that you experiment with how best to use your time at the end of a section.

> "I took practice tests and found out a target score and the number I could skip to get that score."
>
> —700 V, 690 M

As you ramp up your speed, keep an eye on your score. If you start to miss problems you'll need to slow down. But we wager that most students can go faster than they think. Speed will help you triumph over fear of the clock and give you a clearer head throughout the test.

Step Five: Stamina and Focus

With the advent of the New SAT, testing time has ballooned to a whopping three hours and forty-five minutes—more than an hour longer than the world's best runners take to run a twenty-six-mile marathon. Talk about exhausting. Even the best students can hit a wall about two-thirds of the way through. They lose focus. They slow down. They start looking out the window. "My problems were never a problem of knowledge, but of making dumb mistakes and losing focus, something that is easy on such a long and boring test," says a Dartmouth ED admit who scored 700 V, 760 M.

In the final weeks before the exam, students should return to taking full-length, timed practice tests. We recommend at least three. Just as preparing for a marathon requires running long distances, so too taking the SAT requires practice of sustained mental focus. Take a look at how well you do on your last section—the one you do when you're the most tired. Are you missing a few that you should get? If so, pay special attention to staying sharp on that section when you take your next practice SAT.

If you are one of those students who has persistent trouble with exhaustion at the end, we have two possible strategies. First, if you finish some sections early, consider resting instead of checking your work. Close your eyes, clear your head, and relax as much as possible. Over the course of four hours, a few breaks like this may make a difference.

Another possibility is that you are running out of gas due to a lack of food. Fortunately, the College Board has recently lifted its ban on taking food into the test center. At the midway point of your practice test, see if eating half a sandwich or a piece of candy perks you up. Don't eat enough to get full—and possibly sluggish—or enough to give yourself a sugar high that may become a sugar crash within an hour. As with most other aspects of the SAT, the best approach is to experiment until you find the snack that seems to give you the most energy.

One of your last items of business before test day is to get a clear sense of your preferred pace so that you can stick to it. On a Math section with 20 questions and 25 minutes, where do you want to be when 15 minutes are gone? Question 12? 15? Since the section lengths vary, it may be impractical to try to memorize the exact place you want to be when there are, say, fifteen minutes remaining. But students should have a well-honed sense of roughly where they ought to be as time winds down.

Of the numerous testimonials to taking timed practice tests, we found particularly noteworthy a young man who scored 600 V, 710 M on his first SAT but was not satisfied.

After he completed six full-length practice tests, his scores went up to 650 V, 780 M. "The one most important bit of advice I can give to potential test-takers is to keep taking timed practice tests," he says. A second student had taken a number of practice tests but had never timed himself and had generally gone over. "The second time around, I limited my work to the allotted time and found I was much more successful on the actual exam," he writes. How much more successful? He improved 160 points, from 670 to 750 on Verbal and from 640 to 720 on Math.

No matter how much you prepare, the SAT is bound to bring a few anxious moments. But with focused practice, you can teach yourself what to expect and thereby increase your comfort level. The best SAT-takers are proactive about staying calm. They attack the test with cool efficiency and preempt anxiety by getting to the end quickly. "The key is to stay smooth and avoid letting any difficulty lead to indecision or nervousness," says a 710 V, 800 M scorer.

The Zen of Test Day

Test day is all about being relaxed and focused. On the night before, do what will make you feel comfortable at 8:00 a.m. the next morning. Go to a movie. Hang out with friends. Watch mindless TV. If you're the type who feels more comfortable thinking about the test, go over a few last-minute details in your head. But don't do a full-blown cram session. Relax.

Go to bed at your regular time for a school night. This is the wrong night to experiment with going to bed early. If you try to hit the sack at 8:00 p.m.—and you're not tired—you may find yourself tossing and turning in bed until 2:00 a.m. If you do fall asleep, you'll be in bed ten hours instead of your usual eight and risk being groggy all day.

It should come as no surprise that staying up late is also a bad idea. Even if you're 100 percent convinced that your brain can function just as well on six hours sleep as it does on eight, we guarantee that you're wrong. Trust us—and get your normal amount of sleep.

On test morning, don't cut anything close. Get up in time for a leisurely breakfast. Leave the house in time to get there a little before 8:00 a.m. If you don't know exactly where you're going, make sure you have a map. Leave extra time once you arrive to find the room where the test will be given. At all costs, bring:

- Your admission ticket. Even if you registered via the mail, you can print a copy of it from www.collegeboard.com.
- A photo ID. Usually a driver's license or passport. If you don't have an ID, your school can make you one. See your counselor.
- Your calculator. The one you use in school, with fresh batteries.
- At least three No. 2 pencils. Make sure they are slightly dulled to better blacken those ovals.
- A watch or stopwatch. You never know if you'll be sitting near a clock. Make sure the alarm is turned off.
- A snack to eat in the middle of the test.

TEST DAY ADVICE FROM THE EXPERTS

Our survey participants were full of test-day advice. Here is some of the best:

"Put together all your materials the night before so you don't forget anything like a calculator or ID card." —660 V, 690 M

"Sleep is the most important thing to get a good score. Also, knowing that it is not the end of your life if you don't get a good score helps you relax."
—660 V, 730 M

"Keep the date well-marked on a calendar so that it doesn't sneak up on you. Eat a good breakfast so that your stomach doesn't growl, but not too many liquids. Know how to get to the testing center and where to park. Bring a jacket and dress in layers."—730 V, 670 M

"Arrive early at the test center—it takes away anxiety to be one of the first to show up." —700 V, 640 M

"Make sure you go to the bathroom before the test." —710 V, 720 M

WRITING 4

TOTAL TESTING TIME: 60 MINUTES

SECTIONS:

✔ 2 of 25 minutes
✔ 1 of 10 minutes

QUESTION TYPES:

✔ Student-Produced Essay
✔ Identifying Sentence Errors
✔ Improving Sentences
✔ Improving Paragraphs

We begin with Writing because the essay comes at the beginning of each SAT. Every version of the test also includes 49 multiple choice questions in three varieties: 1.) *Identifying Sentence Errors* problems, which test grammar, word choice, and knowledge of idiomatic English; 2.) *Improving Sentences* problems, which focus on grammar and modification of sentences to improve their flow and make them more concise; and 3.) *Improving Paragraphs* questions, which highlight how sentences fit together to form a coherent whole.

The Essay

As if regular college essays weren't stressful enough, along comes the SAT. At least the agony of this one will be over quickly. Regular college essays inflict their stress for weeks and even months. With the SAT, the torture is compressed into 25 gut-wrenching minutes. Lucky you.

You may be wondering how anybody can expect you to write a decent essay in a mere 25 minutes. A lot of people are asking the same question. The College Board's response is that the essay is not supposed to be perfect. "At the College Board, we recognize that an essay written in a short amount of time will not be polished but represents the initial phase of the writing process: the first draft," says a brochure describing the new test. The brochure reminds students that essays can get a top score with some errors in spelling, punctuation, and grammar.

But let's get real. Even if readers are instructed to overlook a limited number of syntactical errors, essays that do not have such errors are likely to make a better impression than those that do. On the more important issues of organization and marshaling evidence to back up your opinion, you will have less margin for error.

> **"Get a word-of-the-day email or calendar and try to incorporate new words into your vocabulary."**
>
> **—660 V, 690 M**

There is no sugar-coating the fact that the SAT essay is a race against the clock. The challenge is to learn how to write an essay in 25 minutes that looks similar to one you could produce in two hours. Sound impossible? The trick is to come to the test with a blueprint in mind. The subject matter of your essay will be dictated by the question, but the structure of the essay should already be in your head. You'll need to master—or remaster—the art of writing a five-paragraph essay in which you state an opinion and back it up with evidence. After fine-tuning your approach with plenty of practice under timed conditions, you should be able to go on autopilot when you sit down to write. You'll be in trouble if you don't. With only 25 minutes, there will be no time to experiment or ponder your approach. For this reason, preparation is more crucial for the essay than any other section of the SAT. Come in cold and you may draw a blank. Practice, and you can ace it.

There is one silver lining for anyone who is stressed out about the essay: It accounts for only about 30 percent of your Writing score. Notwithstanding all the hype surrounding the essay, the writing multiple-choice questions are actually worth twice as much. Go figure.

The most common type of question asks you to respond to an excerpt or quotation. Typically, the excerpt expresses an opinion on an issue that does not have one correct answer. It doesn't matter whether you agree or disagree with the statement. You may think the excerpt is completely true, partly true, or totally false. The test-makers want to know how skillfully you can back up your opinion with relevant evidence.

Here is an example:

Directions: Think carefully about the issue presented in the following excerpt and the assignment below.

People are always blaming their circumstances for what they are. I don't believe in circumstances. The people who get on in this world are the people who get up and look for the circumstances they want, and, if they can't find them, make them.
From George Bernard Shaw, Mrs. Warren's Profession (1893)

Assignment: What is your view of the idea that people make their own opportunities in life and are not controlled by their circumstances? Plan and write an essay in which you develop your point of view on this issue. Support your position with reasoning and examples taken from your reading, studies, experiences, or observations.

DO NOT WRITE YOUR ESSAY IN YOUR TEST BOOK. You will receive credit only for what you write on your answer sheet.

The first order of business is to demonstrate that you understand the meaning of the passage and can restate it in your own words. From there, you need to take a position on whether and to what extent the statement is true. Finally, you must back up your opinion with specific evidence from the subject areas listed in the question. The finished product should be about 400–550 words.

Sounds easy enough, right? OK, maybe it's not so easy. Let's take a closer look at the writing process.

Getting Your Brain in Gear

Before you sit down to practice, get familiar with the kind of thinking you will be required to do. Your task is to link the excerpt to something in "your reading studies, experiences, or observations." The quotation above suggests that people can control their circumstances rather than their circumstances controlling them. Let's say you agree with this proposition—your first step is to think of evidence and anecdotes to back up your view. In literature, Anne Frank comes to mind, the girl who wrote a world-famous diary about hiding from the Nazis during World War II. She faced horrible circumstances and rose above them. In the performing arts, Ludwig van Beethoven composed many of his greatest works while battling deafness.

Science? Thomas Edison was so persecuted by his teacher at an early age that his mother pulled him out of school. Then he later endured repeated failures before inventing the electric light.

> "People should take tutoring if they have money to burn.... Prepare on your own."
>
> —760 V, 690 M

These are all good possibilities that could be expanded upon. But you could just as easily think up evidence to support the other side. Suppose you have just finished reading *Manchild in the Promised Land* in English class, a novel about life in Harlem in the 1940s and '50s. Though the narrator, Sonny, manages to escape from his world of violence and mayhem, virtually all the other characters in the book fail to escape from their situations. Circumstances obviously play a huge role in the lives of those characters. The same applies to characters in *The Autobiography of Malcolm X*, *The Grapes of Wrath*, and hundreds of other books, fiction and nonfiction, that you study in school.

Evidence can also come from the world of current events. Consider the rising cost of a college education. With tuition climbing and government grants falling, fewer low-income students can afford to go to college—a circumstance beyond the control of those born into poor families. In politics, the family dynasties of Kennedy and Bush suggest that not everyone has an equal chance at a career on the national stage, or of being president, and that circumstances (family connections in this case) play a significant role in who gets elected.

How are you supposed to know all of this? Relax—you're not supposed to know any particular facts to write your essay. You simply need some practice in connecting facts that are in your head—whether from the classroom or your own reading—to quotations such as the one above. Trust us—you've got plenty of useful information in your brain. The trick is to pull it out at the right time.

The next ingredient is an anecdote from your life. As above, most essay questions leave open the possibility of citing evidence from your own experience to back up your opinion. Occasionally, you may see a question that asks you to write primarily about your personal experiences. We recommend that you take the opportunity to write about your life or your perspective as often as you feel comfortable. A personal angle, especially when combined with references to academic topics, will give your essay extra breadth. When you cite William Shakespeare or Maya Angelou, you demonstrate that you can think like a professor. When you offer an anecdote from your own experiences, you show the ability to connect abstract issues to your personal life. Doing both demonstrates that you can combine analytical insight with personal reflection.

WHO ELSE MIGHT READ YOUR ESSAY?

Sending your essay to the College Board is scary enough. But there might be someone else who reads it: an admissions officer at Most Desirable U. The College Board's plan is to make an electronic copy of every essay and send them via the Internet to graders in remote locations. But the Board will also allow admissions officers at particular colleges to access the essays of students who have designated those colleges to receive their scores. Not only will colleges be able to evaluate your essay for themselves; they'll also have a chance to compare your SAT essay with the ones on your application. Make sure the same person— you—writes all of them.

Some students are afraid to use the first person in the essay because teachers have said that the use of "I" is a no-no. It is true that the first person is not appropriate for some kinds of writing. But you definitely should use "I" in the SAT essay. Look again at the question. It begins with "What is your view?" and goes on to give advice on how to support "your position." The best way to respond to a "you" question is with an "I" answer. In fact, students who do not use "I" generally come off sounding stilted and are often forced into using the passive voice.

The First Paragraph

Picture one of the hapless English teachers recruited by the College Board to read SAT essays. There she sits with bloodshot eyes, slogging through her 247th essay on how people make their own opportunities in life and are not controlled by their circumstances.

That essay could be yours, and if it is, you'd better have a strong first paragraph. The impression from the first sentence or two can last throughout the essay. If your essay tails off at the end, the reader's attention may also tail off. Whatever the case, you'll get a good score if the opening shows that you can write.

Your first paragraph should be about three to five sentences, and there is a reliable formula. You need to do three things:

1. Rephrase the main idea of the quotation, preferably with new information or in a new context.
2. Take a position on the main idea that can be backed up in the rest of the essay.
3. Provide a roadmap for the rest of the essay.

Before we go further, a word of warning. This chapter includes some sample paragraphs and sample essays that we have designed to set a high standard for you. A few of them are pretty good, but most are downright sick. Don't let it bother you. We don't expect you to write essays this good, but we do want to you to aim high and get as close as you can.

And finally, a procedural note: SAT essays are graded on a 1–6 scale by two separate readers for a combined scale of 2–12. When readers disagree by more than two points, the essay is referred to a third reader and reassessed. A student's essay score is combined with his or her score on the multiple choice questions in the Writing section before being converted to the 200–800 scale. For the details of the grading standards, see the chart at the end of this chapter.

Let's get started. Below is a reminder of the assignment, then a reasonably good opening that restates the excerpt's main idea:

Assignment: What is your view of the idea that people make their own opportunities in life and are not controlled by their circumstances?

Abundant evidence shows that people make their own opportunities in life regardless of their circumstances. History is full of people who were born humble but seized opportunities and developed into leading figures. Examples such as Andrew Carnegie and John D. Rockefeller come to mind of people who began with nothing and rose to the top. Though not everybody can become as rich as these two men, everyone can succeed if they work hard.

This looks like the beginning of a "3" essay, possibly a "4." In the first sentence, the author demonstrates understanding of the excerpt with a competent paraphrase of it. There is no clumsy sentence like "I believe this statement is true." Instead, the author shows what she believes in the process of restating the main idea of the excerpt. Yet the first sentence lacks sparkle and does not expand on the quote. The second sentence is OK but vague; only in the third sentence does the author use specifics. As we will see below, strong writers are capable of integrating specific examples into their general statements that can help guide the entire essay. This author's references to Carnegie and Rockefeller are not particularly convincing because the lives of these two men were not typical of late-nineteenth-century America. She helps her cause by acknowledging as much in her final sentence, but better examples would not need to be qualified in this way. Grammar hawks will note the minor agreement error in the last sentence ("everyone" should be followed by a singular pronoun). Overall, this opening is competent but flawed.

A better opening paragraph is as follows:

> *The idea that people have the power to make their own destiny is a thoroughly modern notion. Had Shaw been writing 400 years earlier, in the time of William Shakespeare, he would almost certainly have had a different view. In the Shakespearean world, human life was controlled by the vagaries of Fate. I believe that the truth lies in the middle. Human beings can change some of their circumstances, but much of life is still controlled by the happenstance of birth, location, and social class.*

This opening paragraph is superior to the first on a variety of fronts. It rates at least a "5" and perhaps a "6." Note how the first sentence goes beyond merely restating the main idea of the excerpt. By telling the reader that the idea of free will is a "modern notion," the writer signals that he or she understands the question and gives the impression of having thought about it before. The ability to contrast the excerpt to a major theme in Shakespeare's works is impressive and on target. For his thesis, the author takes a middle ground between the two, and his task will be to cite evidence on both sides of the issue. A weakness is that he fails to differentiate between the part of life controlled by circumstance and that which human beings can change. He will have the rest of the essay to do so, but his focus would be clearer if he had taken care of business in the beginning.

We don't want to give the impression that there is a right answer to this question, so here is a fine opening paragraph that takes the other side:

> *In Mrs. Warren's Profession, George Bernard Shaw restates a classic tenet of modern enlightenment rationalism. It is not Fate or birth that dictates life's path, says his character, but the free will of every human being. Though the modern world cherishes this view, the realities of race, class, and gender limit our prospects far more than most of us realize. And modern science, far from liberating us, has highlighted the extent to which our genes may foreshadow our life outcomes. In a world where both nature and nurture conspire to rein us in, we humans have less real freedom than we think.*

This essay looks like a "6" in the making. In the first two sentences, the author gives a clear restatement of the excerpt's main idea while placing it in the context of the development of Western civilization. But rather than supporting the excerpt, the author challenges it, suggesting that though we like to think we have free will, in reality our parents and our genes have much to do with who we are. The range of vocabulary is superb—words like "foreshadow" and "conspire" show strong mastery of language without being unnecessarily stilted. The paragraph also provides a quick outline of the body of the essay, which could include a paragraph elaborating on each of the last three sentences. The author demonstrates creativity by suggesting that nature and nurture "conspire," a creative twist on the more commonly referenced tension between nature and nurture. Most of all, this student shows independence of mind in challenging a statement that most students will probably go along with.

We have already given you the two primary keys for a good opening paragraph. Here are two corollaries:

Be Specific. Many students mistakenly believe that any mention of specifics should wait until the body of the paper. Nothing could be further from the truth. The opening paragraph should be an examination of broad themes, but it should also be as specific as possible. Getting specific early allows you to probe more deeply in the body of the paper. Vagueness at the beginning shows that you lack clarity. Essays that begin vaguely have a meandering

FINDING YOUR VOICE

Funny things happen when students begin to write essays for a grade—or for the SAT. Remember the Professor on Gilligan's Island? Some students begin to sound like him, using stilted and distant language. SAT essay readers look for a range of vocabulary, including big words where appropriate, but also simple and direct ones where appropriate. On the other hand, some students seem to think that all manner of slang and street talk will pass muster. Think again. Direct language is good; sentences that include words such as "dude," "phat," and "da bomb" should be avoided. Your best bet is to write the way you would talk to your English teacher—naturally but not too informally.

quality as the author uses the process of writing the essay to figure out his main point. Only at the conclusion do such essays arrive at insights that ideally should be made in the introduction.

Use Complex Sentences. A simple sentence has only one clause. "I went to the store" is a simple sentence. So is "I was hungry." But "I went to the store because I was hungry" is a complex sentence. See the difference? The two simple sentences express disconnected thoughts that don't say anything about the cause of the action. The complex sentence joins the two and establishes a relationship between motive and action. Without complex sentences to connect thoughts, there is no way to deal efficiently with ideas that must be modified, qualified, and fine-tuned to achieve just the right meaning. To put it another way: Weak writers use simple sentences and strong ones use complex sentences.

This is not to say that you can never use a simple sentence. Everyone should sprinkle them in for variety if nothing else. If you use mainly complex sentences, the occasional simple one will be eloquent in its simplicity.

In suggesting that you use sentences with more than one clause, we are not advocating that you pad your prose with unnecessary verbiage. Each

THE RHYTHM OF THE OPENING PARAGRAPH

Since practice makes perfect, we offer three more excerpts below that are typical SAT Writing fodder. Your assignment: write the first paragraph of an essay that takes a position on the excerpts with reference to "reasoning and examples taken from your reading, studies, experiences, or observations." Once you have written your three opening paragraphs, turn to the box on pages 100-101 for our suggested opening paragraphs on these three topics:

- No one should underestimate the power of heartbreak to sharpen and motivate the human mind. Happiness may soothe us, but grief grants us wisdom.

- It is safe to say that no other superstition is so detrimental to growth, so enervating and paralyzing to the minds and hearts of the people, as the superstition of Morality.

- I have thought about it a great deal, and the more I think, the more certain I am that obedience is the gateway through which knowledge enters the mind of the child.

clause should be as lean as possible. Try to express the relationship between ideas as simply as possible while still doing justice to their complexity. Be precise, but also be concise.

Simple sentences can also be put to good use at the beginning of an essay to reach out and grab the reader. For most students, we recommend beginning with a conventional complex sentence that restates the main idea of the quotation while putting it into perspective. Pithy zingers may not come to mind under time pressure, and there is no reason to get hung up on stylistic wizardry when straightforward competence will do just fine. But maybe you're one of those gifted writers who always do it with style. Here's how your opening might look:

> *George Bernard Shaw obviously never read Shakespeare. At least his character in Mrs. Warren's Profession never did. Shakespeare's enduring relevance is due to his skill in chronicling how human lives are ruled by forces we can neither comprehend nor control. Has human nature changed in 500 years? I am skeptical of neat and tidy theories about human nature that gloss over issues of identity, power, and hierarchy. Not everybody has an equal chance to control their circumstances.*

The first sentence of this essay has real flair. The detour into Shakespeare takes most of the first paragraph but is worth the trip. This writer also highlights the not-so-subtle political implications of the excerpt, which, by suggesting that everyone has the power to control his circumstances, implicitly downplays the concerns of minorities and others who may get a raw deal from society. By taking exception to the quotation on these grounds, the author has set himself up to defend the perspectives of those who are bypassed or left out. With the second-to-last sentence, the author has left open the possibility of devoting the three paragraphs of the body to identity, power, and hierarchy. Just to make yourself feel better, note a few flaws. In the second sentence, the author mixes the third and first person with "human lives" and "we." The repetition of "human nature" is slightly awkward, and technically the last sentence should read "to control his or her circumstances." But all in all, this is a great opening paragraph.

CLEANING UP THAT NASTY HANDWRITING

SAT essay readers are under strict orders not to allow handwriting quality to color their assessment of an essay. Will they succeed? Probably not. Readers are under pressure to read a huge number of essays, and they have little time to puzzle through chicken-scratch. Even in cases where hand-writing is legible, a subtle advantage may go to the essay with immaculately formed letters as opposed to the one that looks like it was written during an earthquake. If you are among those who have offending handwriting—and you know who you are—we recommend that you pay special attention to penmanship as you practice. Print instead of writing in cursive, and write big. You may get a better score—and you'll definitely make your second-grade teacher proud.

To recap: Your first sentence should generally be a complex sentence that restates the main idea of the excerpt but also sheds new light on it. Move directly to your best insights in as much detail as you can muster in two or three sentences. As you summarize your position, introduce topics that will be developed in the main body.

The Body and the Conclusion

If you do the first paragraph right, everything else should be a piece of cake. We recommend that you make your essay five paragraphs: one of introduction, three of main body, and one of conclusion. Don't forget the paragraph breaks. Each of the three paragraphs in the body should be focused on developing an example from "your reading, studies, experiences, or observations" to back up what you said in the first paragraph. Our preferred strategy is to choose topics from two of the many possible academic topics and then to offer a personal experience or observation in the third and final paragraph of the main body. It is always possible to devote more than one paragraph to the same piece of evidence, but without a supply of facts at hand, students will find it difficult to do so except in the case of personal experiences that can be written about from memory.

On the following pages, we offer two complete essays with comments.

Directions: Consider carefully the following excerpt and the assignment below it. Then plan and write an essay that explains your ideas as persuasively as possible. Keep in mind that the support you provide—both reasons and examples—will help make your view convincing to the reader.

The human mind cannot stand prosperity. The solution to one problem often contains the seeds of the next, and today's dream can easily turn into tomorrow's nightmare. As an ancient sage once said, "Be careful what you wish for—you may get it."

Assignment: What is your view of the idea that successes and achievements often create more problems than they solve? In an essay, support your position by discussing an example (or examples) from literature, the arts, science and technology, history, current events, or your own personal experience or observation.

DO NOT WRITE YOUR ESSAY IN YOUR TEST BOOK. You will receive credit only for what you write on your answer sheet.

Our answer:

The ability to plan for the future is among the traits that distinguish human beings from the rest of the animal kingdom. At least since the time of Moses, people have looked beyond the troubles of the present toward a new beginning—a promised land. Yet as the Israelites were to learn, sometimes achieving a goal can create new and unexpected problems.

The early settlers of New England learned just such a lesson. In the early 1600s, the Puritans landed in Massachusetts, seeking the freedom to practice their particular brand of Protestantism. They were tired of being pushed around in England and wanted a new start. They got what they wished for—a safe place, far removed from the long arm of the Church of England. Yet they failed in their mission of creating a model religious community, the fabled "city upon a hill." Freed from persecution, they had less need to stick together. With vast stretches of fertile land extending to the horizon, the Puritans drifted apart and lost their sense of shared purpose. The leadership under John Winthrop and others desperately tried to hold things together, and the result was a new coercion not much different from what the Puritan fathers had experienced in the old world. While the standard of living among the Puritan emigrants was among the highest in the world, a crisis of spiritual identity was at least indirectly responsible for events such as the persecution of Anne Hutchinson, the backward-looking "Half-way covenant," and a few decades later, the Salem witch trials.

In more recent times, the growth of technology offers a second example of this phenomenon. Modern people seem to have an insatiable desire for new gadgets that will make life easier. First, we invented computers. Then cell phones and the Internet. Have these wonderful inventions eased our stress? Quite the contrary, people today work harder than ever partly because these new inventions have extended the time we can work. It is laughable to think that in the 1970s, many people believed that new technology would result in everybody working four-day weeks. Today's TV commercials would have us believe that there is nothing so liberating as sending a fax from a wireless computer on the beach during a vacation, or checking email from atop a mountain paradise. Images like these glamorize the rat race that we collectively share in as we continue to strive harder and worry more about what we don't have. It was Alexis de Tocqueville who commented on the neurotic obsession with material gain that seems to have always defined the United States. Each generation has wished for new inventions and each has gotten them—along with more anxiety, stress, and over-work.

When I was in elementary school, I always dreamed of what it would be like to be a big kid. Now I am in high school and feeling stressed about homework, college admission, and the question of what to do with the rest of my life. I look forward with great anticipation to the time when I will be an adult and will finally be able to do what I please. Hmmm. On second thought, maybe being a teenager is not so bad after all. Perhaps it is better to enjoy the here and now, and to be careful what you wish for.

This essay is definitely a "6." Don't let it stress you out. We use it to illustrate what to shoot for (and you may note that it contains a few minor errors).

Let's focus on the body—a paragraph about history, a paragraph about technology, and a personal insight. Each is an illustration of why we should be careful what we wish for. The paragraph on New England begins with a seamless transition from the opening. The first sentence is not a conventional thesis for the paragraph but a segue (transition) reaching back to the introduction. After two sentences of factual background, the author echoes the excerpt with a note that the New Englanders "got what they wished for" but failed in their mission.

The middle paragraph examines the paradox of technology that is supposed to make our lives easier. The subject matter in this paragraph is slightly less complex, allowing for simple sentences to provide a punchy break from the multiclause analytical ones. The author asks a rhetorical question in the fifth sentence, an effective device in a persuasive essay (and one that you will see throughout this book).

The first use of "I" comes in the fourth paragraph, where the author relates an anecdote that shows that she understands the proposition on a personal level. Though students may cite personal experiences at various points in the essay, first-person insight is often best placed at the end. Beginning with too many personal experiences can undermine your credibility in talking about other topics. You may use "I" in your opening paragraph, but we generally recommend that you build your case with academic or current-events facts and then use a personal anecdote as your clincher.

The essay ends with a flourish of humor that will help make it memorable.

To make you feel better, the following is a not-quite-so perfect essay in response to the same question:

I agree that successes and achievements often create more problems than they solve. There are many instances in history in which a scientific "advance" actually caused unintended consequences. The problem is that while people often focus on short-term goals, they fail to see the long-term consequences of their actions.

The prevalence of genetically modified foods is a good example. The U.S. and other countries have produced large quantities of genetically modified foods to feed hungry people and put money in farmers' pockets. But there has been too little consideration for the long-term impact on the environment and on people. People may get resistance to antibiotics, for instance. The people who defend genetically modified foods are the ones making a profit from it.

Another good example is all the famous people who become drug addicts and even die. So many people want to go into show business. Yet once they achieve it, many stars seem desperately unhappy. The number who have committed suicide is large. It includes people like Kurt Cobain and Ernest Hemingway. All of these people chose to try to become famous artists, but once they achieved their goal they still weren't happy.

When I was in middle school, my life's goal was to be a cheerleader. In eighth grade, my best friend and I both tried out. I was chosen for the squad but my friend was not, and to make a long story short, I gained a spot as a cheerleader but lost my best friend. By the time the season ended, I had had enough of cheerleading but I was never going to get my best friend back.

"Be careful what you wish for" is a good motto. Many of the world's problems come after people get what they want.

We give this essay a "3" or "4." On the plus side, it is well organized with an opening, a closing, and three paragraphs of body. The examples are generally well-conceived, and the essay is competently written for the most part.

But there are still plenty of issues. The first sentence is weak. Words such as "I agree with" or "I think that" are unnecessary in an essay like this. Your writing should be strong enough to show what you agree with and what you think. The rest of the first sentence is a mere restatement that does not convey any new insight—we would recommend cutting it if the writer were to do a second draft. The first paragraph includes good ideas but lacks the specifics necessary to give the essay a strong focus. The writer talks about scientific advances, discussed in the first paragraph of the main body, but does not do a good job of setting up the last three paragraphs.

The first paragraph of the main body contains good insight but is flawed in execution. The first sentence of the paragraph is OK but could elaborate more on what, exactly, genetically modified foods exemplify. The third and fourth sentences could be combined, as in an Improving Paragraphs question, and the last sentence is an assertion that lacks evidence to back it up. Note also the clumsy repetition of the word "people."

In the second body paragraph, the author's discipline breaks down with awkward word choice and simple sentences. She needs to be clearer about whether she is writing about a universal irony of human nature or a problem specific to rock stars.

In the third body paragraph, talking about herself, the author regains her rhythm and tells a nice story, followed by a straightforward one-sentence conclusion.

The total length of the essay is about 300 words, a middling amount. A better essay would get to 400 or 500 words. Overall, this essay is good but not stellar.

The Nitty-Gritty of How to Prepare

There are three keys to doing your best on the SAT essay: 1.) good writing 2.) good examples, and 3.) speed.

You've got the first of these—at least we hope so. The basics of good writing are no secret: organization, vocabulary, word choice, and variation of sentence structure are the biggies. If you need a refresher, the criteria are spelled out in the grading standards on pages 141-142.

While you can't teach yourself to write in a month or two, you can definitely make headway on your ability to think of and use examples. Many students develop a working list of examples that they can call upon in a pinch. You won't know the exact subject of your SAT essay question until you crack open your test booklet, but there are variations of certain themes that pop up over and over again. A few of them include:

- Overcoming obstacles or failure
- Encountering people from other cultures or backgrounds
- Dealing with peer pressure and social expectations
- Maintaining individual values and a sense of self
- Being underappreciated or ignored
- Balancing relationships with others and commitment to oneself

Can you identify a theme that relates to "reasoning and examples taken from your reading, studies, experiences, or observations"? Let's take peer pressure and social expectations. Can you think of an historical figure who defied them? Henry David Thoreau comes to mind. Or Margaret Sanger, who crusaded for birth control in the early 1900s. In the arts, consider Oscar Wilde, the gay playwright, or Spike Lee, the African American filmmaker.

THE RHYTHM OF THE OPENING PARAGRAPH II

Back on page 92, we asked you to write opening paragraphs for essays in response to three prompts with reference to "reasoning and examples taken from your reading, studies, experiences, or observation." Here again are the questions along with a sample opening paragraph from us. How does yours compare? There are many possibilities for an excellent opening paragraph and we offer only one. Our hope is that you can use these models to sharpen your own ideas.

"No one should underestimate the power of heartbreak to sharpen and motivate the human mind. Happiness may soothe us, but grief grants us wisdom."

It is no coincidence that grief has touched the lives of so many luminous figures in history. From statesmen such as Abraham Lincoln and Theodore Roosevelt to creative geniuses like Charles Dickens and Virginia Woolf, great lives seem to go hand in hand with great tragedy. I believe that we learn lessons about ourselves in failure that we cannot learn from success. Those who have always been successful may try hard, but those who have known failure generally try harder.

The first sentence restates the main idea while placing it in historical perspective. The second cites four examples that might be addressed in the main body. The author shifts to first person for the last two sentences and develops the link between wisdom and motivation. The rest of the essay will fall neatly into place. The first paragraph of the main body can be devoted to Lincoln, Roosevelt, and other public figures. The second paragraph will probably deal with literary figures and perhaps delve into some complexities. For instance, while Charles Dickens' early grief seemed to feed his creative energy, Virginia Woolf was ultimately overwhelmed by her creative demons and committed suicide. Personal perspectives in the fourth and/or fifth paragraph will round out the essay.

"It is safe to say that no other superstition is so detrimental to growth, so enervating and paralyzing to the minds and hearts of the people, as the superstition of Morality."

Excessive moralizing is a convenient target for liberal intellectuals. Yet we should not be so fast to dismiss the importance of a moral code. From scandals on Wall Street to lies in the White House, we see everywhere the breakdown of morality. It is true that excessive moralizing can lead to oppression, as recent hate crimes against gays and lesbians amply demonstrate. But true morality affirms humanity rather than limits it, and our democratic society cannot function without a moral code.

This quotation comes from a turn-of-the-century radical, and the first sentence of the opening paragraph shows excellent awareness of who might make such a seemingly outlandish statement about morality. The author does a fine job of weighing the pros and cons of morality, with specific evidence on both sides, but also takes a strong position as the paragraph ends. The main body of the essay can mirror this structure with the first body paragraph devoted to the problems caused by a lack of morality and the second to the dangers of excessive moralizing. The author does not include a first-person element in this paragraph but the door is open for a personal anecdote in the fourth and/or fifth paragraph to tie the two strands together.

"I have thought about it a great deal, and the more I think, the more certain I am that obedience is the gateway through which knowledge enters the mind of the child."

Since the beginning of time, adults have been imposing their will on children while rationalizing it as being "for their own good." But real learning is never the product of slavish obedience. To truly learn, children must have the freedom to make their own mistakes—impossible if they spend all their time obeying their elders. Thomas Jefferson once said that "a little rebellion is a good thing." Anyone who works with children should heed these words.

This opening is not as strong as the two above, mainly because it includes fewer pieces of concrete evidence that can be expanded on in the body of the essay. Although the quotation from Thomas Jefferson does have the potential for elaboration, ideas from the author's head dominate the paragraph. As a result, there are fewer topics that can be developed in the body of the essay. That said, this is still a fine opening paragraph that argues cogently.

The technology figure could easily be the contrarian Albert Einstein, though you might also choose Galileo, who was condemned by the Roman Catholic Church in the 1600s for saying that the Earth revolved around the sun. Lastly, can you think of a time in your life when you confronted harmful social expectations? What happened?

Some coaching firms advise students to spend hour upon hour perfecting several essays covering themes such as this before taking the SAT. When the students sit for the actual exam, the thinking goes, they can adapt their essays from memory to the particular question they encounter. This approach worked at least part of the time for the SAT II: Writing Test, and if you want to try it, here's how: Write several generic essays on the themes above, then crack open your copy of *The Official SAT Study Guide* and see if your essays give you an edge on a random selection of the ones therein. If it works, you'll have a tool to carry with you to the SAT.

> "I think it is more worthwhile to just buy a practice test book and do it on your own."
>
> —610 V, 610 M

However, we are leery of advising you to spend too much time crafting generic essays. The College Board and ETS are aware of this little game, which has been widely reported in the press, and they have tinkered with the format of the essay section. We expect to see more SAT essay questions with a narrow focus that will be more resistant to generic essays. For instance, a practice question circulated in 2003 asked students to respond to the idea that appreciation of the arts "may actually worsen us, diminishing our ability to respond to actual situations..." An unexpected question—and not the sort likely to be addressed by boilerplate material. We fear that students who spend a lot of time perfecting a few generic essays may get blindsided by a question that does not fit what they prepared. The result will be frustration, panic, and probably, a lower score.

We recommend a more flexible approach. Instead of focusing huge energy on perfecting a few generic essays, think broadly about figures in literature, the arts, science and technology, history, politics, and current events who may relate to these themes. You can think of events or social trends, too, but since most SAT essay themes apply to the human condition, the life experiences of people tend to be the most useful. You may want to

THE GRADERS: WHO ARE THEY?

In the years before the launch of the New SAT, College Board materials describing the test included a sales pitch: "If you are a teacher who would like to become more involved in the New SAT, think about becoming a reader for the New SAT essay. Teachers of English, writing, or language arts courses are particularly welcome."

brainstorm four or five people in each area, or choose areas such as history or literature with which you are familiar, and then concentrate mainly on them. Pick people that you already know about and if necessary, remind yourself of their life stories by reading a few encyclopedia entries. Generally, you will only need to write about two to four figures per essay, preferably from different walks of life, to get the job done.

Once you have collected a body of examples that could apply to a variety of topics, consider crafting some phrases or sentences that express key ideas. For instance, "Anne Frank epitomizes the ability of the human spirit to adjust to the most horrendous circumstances," or, "W.E.B. Dubois demonstrated that in order to foster lasting social change, activists must target the ideological roots of discrimination rather than merely attempt to control its effects." The more sophisticated you can get in your allusions, the better. Anne Frank is fine, but Albert Camus (to cite another figure from the World War II era) is better. W.E.B Dubois is better than Martin Luther King, Jr., but Sojourner Truth or Henry Highland Garnet might be best of all. Be sure to avoid anything that appears on the reading list of a typical ninth grader, like *Lord of the Flies* or *Harry Potter*. One purpose of the brainstorming process is merely to help you get accustomed to the sort of writing that plays well. But you may be surprised at how versatile some of your examples may be.

Armed with a list of possible historical figures, literary works, and significant events, think about brainstorming a few dozen words, like "epitomize" or "foster," that will add an elevated tone to your essay. You don't need to make every word a fifty-cent special, but a few well-chosen vocabulary words will get you credit for "varied, accurate, and apt vocabulary." If you use only two or three words from your list, it will have done its job.

So far, we have talked mainly about the academic side of your essay, but personal reflections from your own life can be just as valuable. Theoretically, you get the same credit for telling a story from when you were in third grade as you do from citing an existential philosopher. We suggest doing the equivalent of both. The intriguing thing about the personal side of your essay is that you can make it up as you go. Facts are facts if you're talking about history or science, but only you know about the experiences in your life. If you need a personal anecdote to illustrate a point, you can always embroider one out of your experiences, or even pull one from out of thin air. Some students may not feel comfortable with this approach; others will want to experiment with various degrees of storytelling related to events from their own experience.

> "Too much jumping around can be discouraging and/or time-consuming rather than time-saving."
>
> —730 V, 770 M

Once you've assembled a supply of academic evidence and have thought about how you will handle the personal side of your essay, tackle one of the essay questions in this book, or one of those in the *Official SAT Study Guide*. Writing these essays will give you experience in drawing on your pool of words and examples and help you master factual details about your chosen themes that may come in handy when you take the actual SAT. Work on integrating anecdotes from diverse people and subject matter with perspectives drawn from your own life. Write your first several essays untimed so that you can get the feel of writing a good one.

Know Your Audience

Your high school English teacher has probably taught you the importance of knowing your audience. It is fitting that your audience on the SAT essay will be...high school English teachers. What do we know about them? They're intellectual, they're liberal, and they're female. The minority of males sprinkled in will generally be cut from the same cloth. Like any other group,

English teachers have their preferences and pet peeves. Here are some themes that will resonate with them.

The World Is Complicated. The SAT is not the best place to dust off your essay about how self-discipline is the key to success, or how persistence always pays off. Save that for the American Legion essay contest. English teachers want to hear about conflict, complexity, and alienation. Instead of writing about black-and-white issues, probe some gray areas. Don't forget the complex sentences.

The Road Less Traveled. English teachers love the unexpected. On many questions, there is an obvious direction that most students will take their essays. For instance, most students would probably agree with the proposition that "the best things in life are free." A student who disagrees with this statement—and proposes that the best things in life must be earned—is likely to stand out. Don't be afraid to go a different direction or add a new twist. We are not advising that you go against your own instincts, but if you see multiple ways to approach a question, consider choosing the unconventional route.

Respect for Diversity. An essay about your ability to see things from the perspective of others is always solid gold, especially if the others are different from you in important ways. If you are from a minority group, don't be shy about tapping into that experience. Minority or not, show that you can learn from interactions with others, and don't be afraid to question or redefine your own sense of self in light of these interactions.

Lest there be any doubt, we are not suggesting that you concoct a phony essay based on what you think an anonymous reader wants to hear. English teachers can spot nonsense a mile away. These are general themes that may—or may not—be appropriate for any particular essay.

Hitting the Fast-Forward Button

Got your track shoes on? You'd better. Twenty-five minutes is precious little time. After mastering the art of writing your essay, you'll need to learn how to get it done before time is called. The only way to do it is with practice. By repeating the process, over and over if necessary, you can develop a sense of how much time you should spend on each phase.

When you hear the magic words—"open your test booklet and begin"—your first impulse may be to begin writing frantically. Easy there, partner. Too many students get caught up in the pressure of the moment and cut loose with the first thing that pops into their heads. Consider making a brief outline. This might include two or three major examples and at least one personal anecdote that could be covered in the body of the essay, and then some secondary points related to each. Not everybody functions best with an outline, but even if you're not accustomed to making one, try it and see for yourself.

From there, experiment with how much you can put on the page before time is called. If you're consistently getting caught before you finish, cut down your introduction or consider going to a three or four paragraph format rather than five paragraphs. Find out how much detail you can give on one example while still having time to get to one or two others. Always try to have a conclusion, or at least a coherent way to finish. The beginning is more important than the end, but the end matters.

You may also want to experiment with leaving two or three minutes at the end to proofread. Are you the kind of person who leaves out key words when you are writing in a hurry? If so, writing until time is called may not be your best approach. Again, the key is to experiment and find out what works best for you. If you find glaring errors in your unproofed essays, leave time at the end for a quick check.

A final strategy: Do at least several practice essays in only 20 minutes. If you find that your writing remains just as coherent despite the fact that you are moving faster, that's a sign that you could probably speed up, cover more ground, and have an even better essay. When you get accustomed to writing an essay in 20 minutes, having 25 minutes will be a luxury.

Keys to Success

1. Find a comfort level. We've loaded you up with advice, but your first priority should be to write a coherent essay with sentences that flow with a reasonable range of vocabulary. Use practice to figure out what you can—and cannot—accomplish in 25 minutes. Find a rhythm with your practice tests that you can repeat on the exam.

2. Get more specific. Your English teacher has told you over and over again—concrete detail is what makes an essay sing. SAT graders are taught to reward specific examples, and more is better. See how specific you can make your first paragraph, and use complex sentences to express shades of meaning. An opening paragraph with specifics will give your essay focus and allow you to develop your analysis in the main body, where you should cite as many concrete facts as gracefully possible.

3. Longer is better. English teachers are constantly telling their students that longer is not necessarily better, and students never believe them. In this case, the students' gut feeling is right. A lot of bad writing won't get a good score, but the more fully you can develop your essay with specific examples, the more likely that you will get a high score. Practice the art of finishing as close as possible to when time is called without getting caught by the clock.

4. Forget the "right" answer—go for the interesting answer. Repeat after us: There is no right answer to the SAT essay. Pick what you think is the "right" answer and you'll end up belaboring the obvious along with thousands of other students. Oddball questions deserve free-wheeling responses. Any answer is right as long as it is backed up by logic and examples.

5. Lose your perfectionism. Are you the kind of writer who sweats over every word? You can afford to do it on a term paper—but not on a 25-minute essay. We're not suggesting that you write a sloppy essay or one that is full of mistakes. But perfectionism is one of the major inhibitions to writing an excellent essay. Let your writing flow. Pause over key phrases, but don't sweat them all. You can't write a perfect essay in 25 minutes, and trying to do so may prevent you from writing an excellent one.

Identifying Sentence Errors

Studying grammar is nobody's idea of a good time. Even many English teachers hate the stuff—a big reason why so many students can analyze a Victorian novel but have never heard of the subjunctive mood and think that a gerund is a small furry animal found in pet stores. Even if you didn't know that a gerund is an "-ing" form of a verb that functions as a noun—

as in "I did the cleaning for Mom"—you know perfectly well how to use one. And if your ability to define the objective case is a little fuzzy, your ear will tell you that "Paul and me are going to the store" is incorrect. (The sentence needs the nominative "I" in that spot.)

If you don't learn this stuff in school, where do you get it? This is part of what the College Board calls "developed ability." It comes from reading, from conversations at the dinner table, and from listening to correct English. If your parents are college professors, you're in good shape. If you come from a home where grammar is not a priority, you may need to devote a little more practice to this material.

A few students may want to do a formal grammar review, though we suspect that this would be a waste of time in most cases. While we have no doubt that learning about modifiers, antecedents, and idioms would be highly entertaining, a better approach is to take practice tests that will identify trouble spots within these categories. You don't need to know fancy grammar terms; you merely need to know a mistake when you see one.

Identifying Sentence Errors is all about your ear for correct grammar. Most of the rules should be second nature. But there are a few tricky spots where the words that feel right may not be technically correct—and you can count on the SAT to dredge them up. In each version of the test, you'll get eighteen Identifying Sentence Error problems (not including those that may be included in the ungraded section). In the section that follows, we give you sixteen questions that are intended as examples of the problem areas that students most often encounter. The answers are in the paragraph immediately following the questions—don't peek until you've given them a good shot.

Directions: The following sentences test your ability to recognize grammar and usage errors. Each sentence contains either a single error or no error at all. No sentence contains more than one error. The error, if there is one, is underlined and lettered. If the sentence contains an error, select the one underlined part that must be changed to make the sentence correct. If the sentence is correct, select choice E. In choosing answers, follow the requirements of standard written English.

1. Everyone <u>who is</u> interested <u>in going</u> to the
          A   B

   game should <u>proceed to</u> the front door with
                C

   <u>their</u> hat and coat. <u>No error</u>
    D   E

2. If Grandma <u>was</u> still able <u>to feed</u> herself,
             A   B

   she <u>would not</u> need to consider
      C

   <u>moving into</u> a nursing home. <u>No error</u>
    D   E

3. Neither the teacher <u>nor</u> the principal
                 A

   <u>were</u> <u>willing to forgive</u> Ben's absence
    B   C

   because it <u>was</u> his third since the
         D

   beginning of October. <u>No error</u>
               E

4. Steve <u>observed</u> that the novels of Jane
       A

   Austen, <u>unlike Dickens</u>, <u>did not rise</u> to
         B   C

   the level of literary masterpieces in the

   eyes of <u>contemporary</u> critics. <u>No error</u>
         D   E

5. Although he <u>earned</u> a lower grade than
           A

   Sally and Joy, John firmly <u>believed that</u>
                    B

   he <u>was</u> the <u>better</u> of the three at
     C   D

   writing essays. <u>No error</u>
             E

GO ON TO THE NEXT PAGE

6. Amy proposed a plan <u>where</u> we
                         A
<u>would split up</u>, go dancing <u>with</u> our
     B   C
respective partners, and then <u>meet back</u>
                                    D
at the ranch. <u>No error</u>
                   E

7. The team, <u>which</u> consisted of ten-year-
               A
olds and nine-year-olds who

<u>had never played</u> the game,
        B
<u>were assembled</u> for the <u>purpose of</u>
        C   D
learning the rules. <u>No error</u>
                         E

8. The orange signs <u>entreat</u> motorists
                        A
<u>to drive</u> <u>slow</u> as they <u>come near</u> the
   B   C   D
construction zone. <u>No error</u>
                        E

9. If I <u>had known</u> that she <u>was going</u> to
         A   B
the show, I <u>would</u> have suggested that
              C
we <u>share</u> a cab. <u>No error</u>
      D   E

10. As she <u>turned from</u> the chalk board,
              A
Ms. Jones <u>shot</u> a disapproving glance at
             B
<u>Tony and I</u> and asked that we stop
    C
<u>talking</u>. <u>No error</u>
   D   E

11. <u>Uncomfortable with</u> our plan
       A
<u>to drive via</u> Atlanta, my father
    B
<u>suggested</u> that <u>Tony and I</u> consider
    C   D
changing our route. <u>No error</u>
                         E

12. Tomatoes and carrots <u>are</u> <u>an example</u> of
                           A   B
<u>the kind of</u> food that Americans should <u>eat</u>
   C   D
in larger quantities. <u>No error</u>
                           E

GO ON TO THE NEXT PAGE

13. Media coverage and alumni <u>support of</u>
                                   A

the university <u>has increased</u> rapidly since
                    B

the <u>hiring of</u> a new president <u>about</u> four
       C   D

years ago. <u>No error</u>
             E

14. The novel, <u>written by</u> Jules Verne, <u>follows</u>
                   A   B

the <u>exploits of</u> Phineas Fogg as he
       C

<u>circumcises</u> the globe in 80 days. <u>No error</u>
    D   E

15. <u>Located in</u> eastern Utah, Delicate Arch <u>is</u>
        A   B

one of the <u>most unique</u> landforms in the
               C

continental United States, and also one of

the <u>most photographed</u>. <u>No error</u>
       D   E

16. <u>Be they</u> adjectives or adverbs, modifiers
        A

<u>should</u> always <u>be placed</u> as near as possible
    B   C

to the words <u>they modify</u>. <u>No error</u>
                 D   E

The Answers

1. (D) 2. (A) 3. (B) 4. (B) 5. (D) 6. (A) 7. (C) 8. (C) 9. (E) 10. (C) 11. (E) 12. (B) 13. (B) 14. (D) 15. (C) 16. (E). Got 'em all? If so, feel free to skip to the next section. These are typical of the toughest sentence error questions, so don't feel bad if you missed some or even most of them.

The Explanations

1. Can't We All Agree?

This question illustrates the exalted principle of subject-pronoun agreement. With ordinary nouns and pronouns, this is a snap. Depending on whether the subject is singular or plural, you can make an easy pronoun adjustment. I get my coat and they get their coats. But there are a few renegade pronouns—such as "everybody," "everyone," "somebody," "someone," "nobody," "no one," "anybody," and "anyone"—that are singular but an awkward mate to third person singular pronouns. "Somebody needs to get their act together!"

yells mom from the upstairs bathroom after finding a wet towel in the middle of the floor. Tell her that technically speaking—and especially on the SAT—it should be "somebody needs to get his or her act together." **Answer: (D).**

2. The Moody (Subjunctive) Blues

"If I were the Grammar Guru," said Tess testily, "I would abolish the subjunctive mood." SAT-takers everywhere would heartily agree. The subjunctive connotes a conditional situation that would, could, or should happen if some other condition were to prevail. All well and good. The problem comes in the first and third person singular, where "were" is the correct usage in the "if" part of the sentence instead of the more normal-sounding "was." If Tess were the Grammar Guru, you would not need to waste your time learning this stuff. **Answer: (A).**

3. Agreement, Take II

"Neither...nor" and "either...or" are examples of singular constructions masquerading as plural ones. Since the teacher and principal are both mentioned in the beginning of the sentence, it would be easy to conclude that they are part of a compound subject with a plural verb, as in "Neither the teacher nor the principal were willing to forgive." But "neither" and "either" refer to only one of them. A hint: Substitute the word "one" for "the teacher nor the principal." The sentence would now read, "Neither one were willing to forgive"—an obvious error. The singular "was" is the correct verb form. **Answer: (B).**

4. The Importance of Parallelism

Parallelism is the idea that things being compared should correspond logically to one another. Were everything spelled out, the passage would read, "The novels of Jane Austen, unlike the novels of Charles Dickens..." There is nothing wrong with avoiding repetition of the word "novels," but a place-holder pronoun must remain because comparing the novels of Austen to Dickens himself does not make sense. The correct form: "The novels of Jane Austen, unlike those of Dickens..." **Answer: (B).**

5. Comparatives and Superlatives

This one is a no-brainer, but students can miss it because the incorrect usage does not stand out. A not-so-subtle hint: think good-better-best, bad-worse-worst, easy-easier-easiest. Got the idea? In comparing quantities, the -er form refers to the amount or degree when comparing two. The -est form refers to three or more. There are a few variations, like "worse" instead of "worser" and the fact that "lesser" drops its -er in many situations. In the question, "the better of the three" does not sound awful, but "the best of the three" is correct. **Answer: (D).**

6. Idiot's Guide to Idioms

Talk about sneaky. This sentence looks perfectly fine except for the fact that "where" is not the right preposition to go with "proposed a plan." The right usage is "in which." Questions of this type test your knowledge of idioms. Idioms are preferred combinations of words that sound right together. Often, but not always, they are verb and preposition combinations. You know most of them instinctively: "talk with," "go to," "flee from," "recommend that," and so on. Idioms only get dicey occasionally, as with "different from" rather than the incorrect "different than." **Answer: (A).**

7. Subject-Verb Agreement

This one is such a dirty trick that it makes us blush. The sentence starts with a collective subject that is singular even though it has more than one part. The sentence proceeds with a diversionary clause designed to make the reader forget that the subject is singular. On subject-verb agreement questions such as this, the key is to edit out the modifying clause. "The team was assembled" is correct. **Answer: (C).**

8. Adjectives and Adverbs

Call this "the -ly rule." A word that modifies a noun is an adjective, and a word that modifies a verb is an adverb. A person may have a soft voice, but that person speaks softly. Likewise, a driver may be slow, but only if he or she drives slowly. Adverbs are often beside the verbs they modify. If your first glance at a sentence does not reveal an error, take a look beside the verb to see if there is an adjective that needs an -ly. **Answer: (C).**

9. The Subjunctive Shakedown

There's nothing like puzzling over a past perfect subjunctive to brighten your day. Did you figure out immediately that this sentence had no errors? Or did you keep looking and looking until a phantom error surfaced? This is exactly the kind of conundrum ETS loves to create. At least they're not tearing the wings off butterflies. **Answer: (E).**

10. Getting on Your Cases

This question takes us back to the nominative and objective cases. When it comes to "I" and "me," students tend to remember the nominative. As everyone knows, "Me and Pauline are going to the store" doesn't cut it. Me and Pauline are the subject, so the correct usage is "Pauline and I." But question 10 includes Tony and I as the object of Ms. Jones's action. Correct wording: Tony and me. **Answer: (C).**

11. Nominative and Objective Again

If you've been paying close attention, you know the difference between this and question 10. This time, "Tony and I" has its own clause that is linked to the sentence by a conjunction, "that," rather than a preposition, which would mean the objective case. The father is suggesting that they take an action, and "Tony and I" is the subject of the last clause. Hence, the nominative case is correct. **Answer: (E).**

12. More Issues with Agreement

This problem involves agreement between three entities: the subject, a "to be" verb, and the object of the sentence. A prepositional phrase with a singular collective noun, "the kind of food," is inserted to distract students from the necessity of matching the plural subject and verb. Tomatoes and carrots are plural "examples" of foods within the category of the kind of food that should be eaten in larger quantities. **Answer: (B).**

13. Another Dirty Trick

Like problem 12, this sentence has a compound subject. If the sentence included only "media coverage of" or "alumni support of" as the subject, "has increased" would be a correct usage. But together, "media coverage and alumni support" is a compound subject, which requires a plural verb, "have increased." **Answer: (B).**

14. How's Your Diction?

OK, this one is comic relief. But it does illustrate what the College Board calls a "diction error." These generally occur when the writer is searching for one word and incorrectly uses another. In this case, "circumnavigate" is the word the writer was looking for. Another example: "Regretfully, he was absent on the day I gave my presentation." Correct word: "regrettably." **Answer: (D).**

15. Can't We Both Be the Best?

This is a diction error of a different sort than that of 14. According to *American Heritage*, "unique" means "the only one of its kind." Therefore, one thing cannot be more unique than another or most unique among a group of three or more. Substituting "unusual" for "unique" or eliminating "most" would make this sentence correct. **Answer: (C).**

16. Sick of the Subjunctive?

Sorry, you don't have a choice. In addition to its use with "if...would" statements, the subjunctive applies to present tense statements of what *should* be. For example, "I recommend that all students be exempted from taking final exams" uses "be" without "should." Another example: "The teacher insisted that Sheila do her homework." Since the present subjunctive form is identical to the base form of the verb, the subjunctive is noticeable only in the third person singular. In problem 16, the sentence is correct with the subjunctive form "be" in the first clause. **Answer: (E).**

Verb Tenses

There are two ways to learn a language. You can either memorize the rules, or you can start using the language and develop a feel for it. Good language instruction emphasizes the latter. As in most other areas of learning—including test prep—true mastery comes not from memorizing abstract rules, but from developing a working knowledge through practice.

That said, there is one area of grammar where a bit of review may be in order. Verb tense is the most important subject area in Identifying Sentence Errors. Though most of the questions related to it are easy, some students may need to brush up. There are six tenses and each has a variation to indicate progressive action. Each form conveys a specific meaning that is relevant to particular situations. At the risk of insulting your intelligence, here is an example of each:

Present:	She climbs the mountain.
Progressive:	She is climbing the mountain.
Past:	She climbed the mountain.
Progressive:	She was climbing the mountain.
Future:	She will climb the mountain.
Progressive:	She will be climbing the mountain.
Present Perfect:	She has climbed the mountain.
Progressive:	She has been climbing the mountain.
Past Perfect:	She had climbed the mountain.
Progressive:	She had been climbing the mountain.
Future Perfect:	She will have climbed the mountain.
Progressive:	She will have been climbing the mountain.

Between these twelve forms, a speaker of English can place climbing the mountain in any imaginable time frame. For Identifying Sentence Errors, make sure that the verb agrees with the nouns and pronouns in the sentence. As you may be aware, there are six pronoun variations that must match the verb form:

1st Person Singular:	**1st Person Plural:**
I	we
2nd Person Singular:	**2nd Person Plural:**
you	you
3rd Person Singular:	**3rd Person Plural:**
he, she, it, one	they

If none of this makes sense, or if you simply want to relive your seventh grade language arts class, you may want to do a grammar review. Most students will be able to iron out the kinks with more practice problems. Here are three that focus on some of the toughest cases:

1. Since June had not <u>been climbing</u> Pike's Peak since
              A

   1996, she <u>was</u> nervous about <u>getting</u> back on the
            B   C

   mountain, particularly because three hikers <u>had been</u>
                                              D

   lost there in the past year. <u>No error</u>
                                    E

Answer: A. The phrase "been climbing" is an incorrect usage of the past perfect progressive form because the action is not continuing at the time of the main clause. Instead of "been climbing," the correct usage is "climbed." A correct usage of the past perfect progressive would be, "June had been climbing Pike's Peak for four hours when she encountered a snake."

2. When June and Joe <u>have reached</u> the summit, they
                          A

   <u>will have been</u> climbing for six hours and <u>will</u>
     B   C

   probably <u>be fighting</u> dehydration. <u>No error</u>
                 D   E

Answer: A. The main clause of the sentence includes phrases in the future and future perfect. The past perfect is inappropriate for the first clause because the past and future do not make sense in combination. Instead of "have reached," the correct form is the present "reach."

3. Everyone in the group <u>will be</u> an expert hiker,
                             A

   even <u>those</u> who <u>have struggled</u> thus far, when
          B   C

   <u>they have climbed</u> the mandatory total of
          D

   eight 14,000-foot peaks. <u>No error</u>
                               E

Answer: D. We couldn't resist throwing in another shifty pronoun agreement question. The action in the sentence takes place in the future and present perfect tense. The middle clause is a curve ball, designed to distract attention from the singular subject "everyone." Therefore, "they have climbed" should be replaced by "he or she has climbed."

GRAMMAR GOOFS YOU SEE EVERY DAY

Everybody makes mistakes, especially when it comes to grammar. If you split an infinitive now and then, or mangle a modifier, don't let it get you down. The following are five grammar errors committed by folks who ought to know better: the *New York Times*, the Associated Press, and the good old College Board. Can you find the incorrect word in each of the excerpts below? Go to page 121 for the answers.

1. Roger Thompson trails the Crimson Tide across the South. He knows there are few college spectacles as grand as football and, as the head of admissions for the University of Alabama, he is out to draw a crowd. The road show might not be necessary, of course, if Alabama's pool of high school graduates was expected to grow enough to feed the university's ambitions. But that is not the case, not in Alabama nor in many other states across the nation.
   —*New York Times*, February 5, 2005

2. There is no shortage of theories, nor is there a lack of debate, about why American middle-distance running has declined…. American women, on the other hand, have largely been more successive at the middle distances. The consensus is, that compared with women in other countries, especially those in the developing areas of the world, American women have enjoyed significantly superior facilities, opportunities and economic support.
   —*New York Times*, July 15, 2004

3. Officials in Thailand have formally identified the body of a British fashion photographer who was killed by the Asian tsunami while holidaying with his

girlfriend.... A spokesman for the Foreign Office confirmed that the body had been found and was identified on March 3. She said his family were aware and British officials were working on having the body repatriated.

—Associated Press, March 8, 2005

4. A new study says 42 of the 65 teams playing in the men's NCAA tournament graduated less than 50 percent of their players.... If the NCAA's new academic reform plan was in place, the teams less than 50 percent graduation rates would face penalties that include loss of scholarships and a ban on postseason play.

—Associated Press, March 16, 2005

5. Colleges and universities throughout the world offer credit and/or placement for qualifying Advanced Placement Program Exam scores....You will see two things for each school that has provided their AP credit policy info:

* A link to the college's own Web page that details its AP credit and placement policies.
* A statement by the college or university about their AP policy.

—The College Board, AP Credit Policy Information flier, 2004

Keys to Success

1. Listen for the answer. As with the sentence completions, we recommend that you read the questions while listening to the voice inside your head, and if necessary, moving your lips. In most cases, you will "hear" the incorrect word or phrase.

2. Use practice to identify weaknesses. This kind of question does not take long to answer, so you can do lots of them in a short period of time. Make a list of the kinds of questions you miss and categorize them in a way that makes sense to you. In most cases, simple repetition will help you make the necessary adjustment.

3. Make sure your mind doesn't play a trick. You know ETS is trying to sucker you, but sometimes your own head helps ETS do it. It happens when you read a sentence that has an error in it, yet somehow your eye slides over the mistake as if it were correct. Most of the sentences you read in your life are correct, so your brain somehow substitutes a correct usage for the incorrect one—and you never notice your mistake. Weird how that works. If you have this problem, it is possibly a sign that you are reading too quickly. In problems in which the first reading shows no error, do a second one, reading more slowly to make sure you do not bypass the error.

4. Work through the "no error" dilemma. If you're stuck after two readings, ETS is probably trying to camouflage the error beneath a phrase that might pass muster in informal speech but is technically wrong. Unfortunately, students commonly miss these questions and choose "no error" when there really is an error. On the flip side, students who fear that they have answered "no error" too many times may convince themselves that there is an error where one does not exist. The solution: Keep track of the questions in which you do not see an obvious error after the first reading. Do you tend to get these questions right when you choose "no error"? Or are you more likely to get them right if you choose a response that you think may be an error but you're not sure? Each person has different tendencies. Some students need to have more trust in themselves and believe that when they don't see an obvious error, there isn't one. Other students tend to miss errors and need to look more carefully if their initial reading reveals no error. Use practice tests to find out which tendencies you have.

Improving Sentences

There is one universal rule for Improving Sentences: shorter is better. Some people wish to do their writing with lots of clauses, putting many participles in their prose, and having lots of repetitiveness, and generally mucking things up. Others get right to the point. Some people try to show their perspicacity by elucidating their ideas with erudite words that would look good

GRAMMAR GOOFS: DID YOU FIND THEM?

The excerpts on page 118 contain the grammar errors. The corrections are as follows:

1. …if Alabama's pool of high school graduates <u>were</u> (not "was") expected to grow…

2. American women, on the other hand, have largely been more <u>successful</u> (not "successive") at the middle distances.

3. She said his family <u>was</u> (not "were") aware…

4. If the NCAA's new academic reform plan <u>were</u> (not "was") in place…

5. You will see two things for each school that has provided <u>its</u> (not "their") AP credit policy info….A statement by the college or university about <u>its</u> (not "their") AP policy.

in an analogy question but don't fit their sentences. Others write hard-hitting prose. Some writers subscribe to the more-is-better theory, thinking that because there are many words on the page as well as many pages, that people won't notice a certain convoluted quality that may begin creeping into their writing because they can't seem, no matter how hard they try, you know, to get to the freakin' point.

Your job in Improving Sentences is to clean up this mess. Here's an example:

Directions: Choose the option below that changes the underlined phrase to make the sentence better. If no change is best, choose (A).

Jane wrote <u>stories and they capture</u> the feeling of alienation that she felt in her youth.

(A) stories and they capture
(B) stories, capturing in them
(C) stories, which were designed to capture
(D) stories, being the explanations of
(E) stories that capture

The correct answer is (E) because that response says in three words what the others say in four, five, or six words. This pattern repeats itself over and over. Of course, ETS knows you know that the short answer is generally best, so there will be plenty of cases when a longer answer is the right one. But incorrect short answers are often obvious. They tend to leave out important facts or change meanings, whereas too-long answers are plausible in their meaning but include unnecessary clutter. When in doubt, always choose the shortest answer.

As powerful as the shortest-is-best technique may be, it is not a substitute for knowing the relevant grammar. Improving Sentences questions include the grammar topics in Identifying Sentence Errors, plus some additional ones related to writing style. We covered verb tenses, a major topic, in detail on pages 116-117. Here is a quick review of other key grammar topics, some of which are also discussed in the section on Identifying Sentence Errors. The examples below illustrate some common mistakes.

Noun-Pronoun Agreement

A first person singular noun, called the antecedent, must be referred to later in the sentence by a first person singular pronoun. The same goes for second person plural, and so on. Third person singular accounts for most mistakes.
Common mistakes:
- No one should take *their* pencils. (*his* or *her* pencils)
- The team used a secret ballot to choose *their* captain. (*its* captain)
- Neither of them remembered *their* pencils. (*his* or *her* pencils)
- Each promised *they* would bring a friend. (*he* or *she* would)

Subject-Verb Agreement

Nouns and verbs must match in every sentence according to whether they are singular or plural, and whether they are first, second, or third person. Many subject-verb problems are easy. The tough ones generally have to do with singular subjects that look plural and plural subjects that look singular.
Common mistakes:
- A fleet of one hundred ships *sail* tomorrow. (*sails* tomorrow)
- Neither John nor Susan *visit* their old home anymore. (*visits* their old home)
- Tanya, Jeff, and George, the most dynamic jazz trio in town, *plays* at the club on Saturday. (*play* at the club)

Subjunctive Mood

The subjunctive expresses a condition that does not reflect reality but would or could if some other condition prevailed. The subjunctive is also used to describe actions done "as if" or "as though" a condition prevailed. First and third person "was" changes to "were."

Common mistakes:

- If I *was* gone, you would be sad. (If I *were* gone)
- He acted as though he *was* a king. (as though he *were* a king)
- If I *would have* noticed the frog, I would have tried to avoid stepping on it. (If I *had* noticed the frog)

Comparisons

Adjectives and adverbs generally have two forms by which to make comparisons: comparative (i.e., bigger, stronger) and superlative (i.e., biggest, strongest). The comparative form should be used when there are two items; the superlative applies to three or more.

Common mistakes:

- She is the *better* of the three. (*best* of the three)
- He is the *best* of the two. (*better* of the two)

Parallelism

The toughest of these questions tend to be comparisons. In everyday speech, many people use shortcuts when making comparisons, as in "I thought Lincoln's speech was better than Douglas," rather than "better than that of Douglas" or "better than Douglas's." To preserve parallelism, you must refer to the thing being talked about with at least a pronoun in the second half of the comparison.

Common mistakes:

- The defense attorney's closing argument was more effective *than* the prosecutor. (more effective *than that of* the prosecutor)
- The skiing in Colorado was *better than* Vermont. (was *better than that* in Vermont)

Idioms

These make people new to the English Language pull their hair out. There are no rules; just a pattern that everybody follows. Why should people "lace up" shoes but "shut down" a computer? Why should a boat be "dead in the water" instead of "dead on the water"? The toughest problems with idioms on the SAT are generally related to verbs and their propositions. Unfortunately, there is not much advice to give other than to suggest you look for phrases that sound slightly wrong.

Common mistakes:
- Vince is qualified for joining the tennis team. (qualified to join)
- She lives at Chicago. (lives in Chicago)
- I remember the chapter where Harry meets Ron. (in which Harry meets Ron)

Style and Sentence Structure

Improving Sentences questions cover more terrain than Identifying Sentence Errors questions. The latter require students to identify a word or two that violate the rules of grammar in the context of a sentence.

Improving Sentences questions require students to examine the effectiveness of a sentence as a whole. While some questions hinge on a single offending word, many offer more than one grammatically correct answer choice. The key is to evaluate the overall fluency of the sentence. Is it concise? Is the meaning clear? Is there a more effective way of conveying the meaning of the sentence? Errors that must be corrected include:

- Fragments and run-on sentences
- Misplaced adjectives and adverbs
- Wordiness and awkwardness
- Passive voice

In each SAT, you will encounter twenty-five Improving Sentences questions. A batch of eleven will begin the 25-minute writing section (generally near the middle of the test), and another selection of fourteen will stand alone in the 10-minute Writing section, which generally comes at the end of the test.

Below are some sample questions that include commonly missed concepts. Answers and explanations follow.

> **Directions:** The following sentences test correctness and effectiveness of expression. Parts of each sentence or the entire sentence is underlined; beneath each sentence are five ways of phrasing the underlined material. Choice A repeats the original phrasing; the other four choices are different. If you think the original phrasing produces a better sentence than any of the alternatives, select choice A; if not, select one of the other choices.
>
> In making your selection, following requirements of standard written English; that is, pay attention to grammar, choice of words, sentence construction, and punctuation. Your selection should result in the most effective sentence—clear and precise, without awkwardness or ambiguity.

1. Kimberly wanted to meet with Mrs. Stone to review the material on the test, <u>but she did not have a free period</u>.

   (A) but she did not have a free period
   (B) but she does not have a free period
   (C) but she will not have a free period
   (D) but Mrs. Stone did not have a free period
   (E) but Mrs. Stone was not having a free period

2. <u>The students were told repeatedly by Mrs. Shaw</u> not to use the passive voice, but her advice went unheeded.

   (A) The students were told repeatedly by Mrs. Shaw
   (B) Repeatedly, the students were told by Mrs. Shaw
   (C) Mrs. Shaw told the students repeatedly
   (D) Mrs. Shaw, repeatedly telling the students
   (E) The students, repeatedly told by Mrs. Shaw

3. <u>Because he told the students to remain seated until the end of class</u>, Mr. Peterson was angry when they left before the bell rang.

   (A) Because he told the students to remain seated until the end of class
   (B) Telling the students to remain seated until the end of class
   (C) Because the students were told to remain seated until the end of class
   (D) He told the students to remain seated until the end of class, and as a result
   (E) After telling the students that they would remain seated until the end of class

GO ON TO THE NEXT PAGE

4. Requests for transcripts should be given <u>to the main office they will be processed within three days</u>.

   (A) to the main office they will be processed within three days
   (B) to the main office; they will be processed within three days
   (C) to the main office, they will be processed within three days
   (D) to the main office and within three days is when they will be processed
   (E) to the main office since they will be processed within three days

5. <u>After encountering a fierce thunderstorm near St. Louis, our trip was delayed by two hours</u>.

   (A) After encountering a fierce thunderstorm near St. Louis, the trip was delayed by two hours
   (B) Encountering a fierce thunderstorm near St. Louis, we took two hours longer than expected to complete the trip
   (C) A fierce thunderstorm encountered near St. Louis delayed us by two hours longer than we expected
   (D) Delayed by a fierce thunderstorm near St. Louis, our trip encountered a two hour delay
   (E) We encountered a fierce thunderstorm near St. Louis that delayed our trip by two hours

6. For people who commit their lives to community service, <u>helping others is more important</u> than being well paid.

   (A) helping others is more important
   (B) to be helpful to others is more important
   (C) there is more importance in helping others
   (D) helpfulness to others has more importance
   (E) help for others is more important

7. The highway bill had strong support, and <u>Congressman Smith did not believe that the House of Representatives would fail to approve it</u>.

   (A) Congressman Smith did not believe that the House of Representatives would fail to approve it
   (B) Congressman Smith had been convinced that the House of Representatives would approve it
   (C) Congressman Smith did not believe that the House of Representatives would approve it
   (D) Congressman Smith believed that the House of Representatives would approve it
   (E) Congressman Smith believed that the House of Representatives would not approve it

GO ON TO THE NEXT PAGE

8. <u>Catharine Beecher was less radical than other reformers of her time and she believed</u> that women should take a lead role in educating the young.

    (A) Catharine Beecher was less radical than other reformers of her time and she believed

    (B) Catharine Beecher had been less radical than other reformers of her time and she believed

    (C) Catharine Beecher was less radical than other reformers of her time, believing

    (D) Catharine Beecher disagreed with other reformers of her time and she believed

    (E) Catharine Beecher, less radical than other reformers of her time, believed

9. <u>The poetry of Cathy Song is a deft exploration of</u> themes such as the place of women in traditional Asian cultures and the dilemmas of being a "hyphenated American."

    (A) The poetry of Cathy Song is a deft exploration of

    (B) Cathy Song is a poet who is deft in exploring

    (C) The poetry of Cathy Song deftly explores

    (D) Cathy Song is deft in her exploration of

    (E) The poetry of deft Cathy Song explores

10. The more times people hear a story repeated, <u>the more likely we are to believe it is true</u>.

    (A) the more likely we are to believe it is true

    (B) the more likely they are to believe it is true

    (C) the more likely it is believed to be true

    (D) it is more likely to be believed as true

    (E) we are more likely to believe it is true

The Answers

1. (D) 2. (C) 3. (A) 4. (B) 5. (E) 6. (A) 7. (D) 8. (E). 9. (C). 10. (B). We wager you found these a bit easier than the Identifying Sentence Errors questions because hair-splitting grammar rules are not quite so important here. But you probably missed at least a couple of these, so here are the explanations.

The Explanations

1. When Your Antecedent Is Unclear

This question tries to trick you into looking for a tense error. But Kimberly wanted the meeting in the past and "did not have" is correct. The problem with the original sentence is an unclear antecedent of "she." Does "she" refer to Kimberly or Mrs. Stone? Response (E) clarifies that issue but with an incorrect progressive form. **Answer: (D).**

2. Don't Be Passive

Nothing is more crucial to improving sentences than eradicating passive voice. Passive voice weakens prose by burying the subject in a prepositional phrase or even editing it out. With passive voice, "we published the book in 2004" becomes "the book was published by us in 2004" or even simply "the book was published in 2004." Accurate, but hardly dynamic. There are occasions when the passive voice is acceptable, usually when the subject is unknown or unimportant. In this sentence, **(C)** is the only response that makes the sentence active while also making sense.

3. Being Direct with Directions

Nobody listens to poor Mr. Peterson. The facts are clear from the original sentence: Mr. Peterson told the students to remain and was angry when they left. Response (B) uses an incorrect present progressive form to explain the situation and response (C) uses the passive voice. Response (D) includes an extra phrase, as a result, that slows down the sentence, and response (E) features a misplaced use of the subjunctive. The original version is the best. **Answer: (A).**

4. When a Sentence Won't Quit

This sentence is a classic example of a run-on. It has two main clauses that express separate (if related) ideas. Response (C) makes the sentence into a comma splice, (E) creates a falsehood, and (D) is full of gobbledygook. The College Board says that it does not test spelling and punctuation, but semicolons are an exception. Use them to divide run-on sentences when the second half flows from the first. **Answer: (B).**

5. Stamp out Dangling Modifiers

Whenever a sentence begins with a clause that modifies a subject but does not name it, that subject must come immediately after the clause to avoid confusion. The trip didn't encounter a fierce thunderstorm—we did. "The trip was delayed" is a passive construction, adding to the woes in this sentence. The best fix is to say who was delayed—"we" were—and to describe what happened with the storm as directly as possible. **Answer: (E).**

6. Putting Participles to Work

Though you should always be suspicious of -ing forms, sometimes they are correct. In this case, helping others parallels being well paid and does a reasonable job of conveying the sentence's meaning. None of the other responses parallel being well paid, and (B), (C), and (D) are also more wordy than the original phrase. Response (E) makes "help" a noun and thereby creates uncertainty as to who is doing the helping. **Answer: (A).**

7. Don't Want No Double Negatives

This one includes a double negative, though not a blatant one such as, "We didn't get no beans for dinner." "Would fail to approve" is another way of saying "would not approve," but there is already a "not" earlier in the clause because the Congressman "did not believe that the House of Representatives would fail to approve it." In other words, he believed that the House would approve it. **Answer: (D).**

8. A Blast from the Past

In the immortal words of Henry David Thoreau, "Simplify, simplify." The first step is to consolidate the comparison of Catharine Beecher to other reformers in a separate clause set off by commas. By doing so, you can cut out a weak "to be" verb, a redundant pronoun, and an unnecessary conjunction. The correct response, **(E)**, is the shortest.

9. Watch Those Verbs

Vigorous verbs define good writing. Weaker material generally includes lots of "to be" verbs with nouns or adjectives to describe the action. In this sentence, the verb "explore" has been converted to "an exploration." In this question, and many others like it, you should covert the action word back to a verb and eliminate the extraneous "to be" verb. **Answer: (C).**

10. Convoluted Phrasing, Simple Answer

This question is a good example of how ETS likes the use grammatically correct but unorthodox phrasing to throw you off the track. Though it may take you a second to get the drift of the sentence, the solution is a simple matter of pronoun agreement. The third person "people" in the first clause must be matched by the third person "they" in the second. **Answer: (B).**

Keys to Success

1. Shorter is better. Picking the shortest answer to questions in this section is one of the most reliable strategies in this book. After reading the sentence, glance down and read the shortest answer first—even if that answer is shortest by only a hair. Then read the other responses to see if any of them beats it. The shortest answer won't always be correct, but use it as a measuring stick. If you must guess, always pick the shortest response. Be especially skeptical of the longest responses.

2. Watch for "to be" verb clutter. We're talking about forms like "is," "are," "was," "were," "has been," and "had been." These are sometimes necessary, but often they are a sign of passive voice. The play was written by me. (I wrote the play.) She has been told by the teacher. (The teacher told her.) The ball had been kicked by Mia Hamm. (Mia Hamm had kicked the ball.) Whenever possible, make sure the actor in the sentence is in front of the verb instead of hiding behind "by" at the end of the sentence.

3. Watch for -ing words at the beginning of sentences. These are often bad news. Be especially on guard for convoluted "to be" expressions, for example: "Being tired, I decided to take a nap." (I was tired and took a nap.) And those dangling modifiers can be a real headache: "Diving into the water, the rock hit my head." (I dove into the water and hit my head on the rock.) Not all -ing words are bad, but you'll often find more concise ways to make a point.

Improving Paragraphs

The difference between Improving Sentences and Improving Paragraphs boils down to this: Instead of only one sentence to improve, you now have ten to fifteen sentences. All of the errors you corrected in Improving Sentences are also fair game in Improving Paragraphs. But here, the emphasis is on the way sentences connect to one another.

Improving Paragraphs also has a lot in common with Passage-Based Reading. The material is presented in passages that are about two hundred words long—twice as long as the shortest reading passages but only a fourth as long as the longest ones. Most of what we say about Passage-Based Reading also applies here. Some students may choose to read the passage before answering the questions, others may skim the passage, and still others may dispense with reading and go straight to answering the questions. (See Chapter 5.)

The questions come in five categories:

Correcting Grammar Errors

The topics highlighted earlier get a workout here, including passive voice, run-on sentences, noun-pronoun agreement, dangling modifiers, and verb tense agreement. The questions typically ask you to correct an underlined portion of a sentence.

Paragraph Context

Many questions will ask you to revise a sentence to make it clearer in light of the paragraph context. For example, a pronoun might have an unclear antecedent, as in, "The workers lost their jobs after the enactment of stricter air quality regulations. This is unfortunate." If the passage is about recent trends in employment, you can correct the sentence to reflect the fact that the author means the job losses were unfortunate, while the enactment of stricter air quality regulations might or might not have been unfortunate.

Connecting Sentences

Passages often include simple sentences that can be combined to clarify the meaning of the passage or improve its flow. For instance, your task might be to combine the following two sentences: "The region is experiencing a prolonged drought. Dry conditions have made trees more vulnerable to beetle infestation." Answer: "A prolonged drought has made trees more vulnerable to beetle infestation."

Adding Sentences or Paragraphs

You may be asked to choose the most appropriate among five sentences that might be added to the passage, or to choose the best topic for a paragraph that might be added. To do so, you must understand the passage's tone and main idea and be able to identify other topics related to that idea.

Reading Comprehension

To make sure you understand the passage, ETS throws in an occasional question that has more to do with the meaning of the passage than fixing it. Such questions may deal with topics such as: Which sentence best states the main idea of the passage? What is the function of a particular sentence? What strategies has the author used to back up his/her opinion?

> "Taking timed practice tests and making educated guesses sort of go hand-in-hand. By taking mock SATs, I was able to get used to the answers that the test-makers were looking for, and was thus able to reason out answers on the actual test."
>
> —780V, 800M

If there is such a thing as an easy section of the SAT, this is it. The questions offer more context to get the answer than do Identifying Sentence Errors or Improving Sentences questions and are generally not as challenging as those in Critical Reading. You will encounter only one Improving Paragraphs passage per SAT, which will come at the end of the 25-minute Writing section. In the pages that follow, we give you two sample passages. Like the ones you will encounter all the real test, both are followed by six questions.

Directions: Each of the following passages is an early draft of an essay. Some parts of the passage need to be rewritten. Read the passage and select the best answers for the questions that follow. Some questions are about particular sentences or parts of sentences and ask you to improve sentence structure or word choice. Other questions ask you to consider organization and development. In choosing answers, follow the requirements of standard written English.

Questions 1–6 are based on the following passage.

(1) One of the most powerful storms ever to hit the U.S. mainland was Hurricane Camille, which roared ashore on August 17, 1969, near Port Christian, Mississippi. (2) Camille began as a tropical disturbance on August 9 in the Atlantic Ocean about 500 miles east of the Leeward Islands. (3) It reached hurricane strength on August 14, at which time its location was about 100 miles south of Cuba. (4) Turning north, the storm brushed past Cuba's western tip before emerging into the open waters of the Gulf of Mexico, quickly intensifying to a huge Category 5 storm on the Saffir-Simpson Hurricane Scale and began moving north-northwest at about 15 miles per hour.

(5) The eye of the storm hit the coast of Mississippi on the night of August 17. (6) Camille destroyed all weather instruments in its path, but its winds are estimated to be about 200 miles per hour at the time of landfall. (7) The most deadly aspect of Camille was its storm surge, estimated at 24 feet. (8) In the area of landfall, nearly 150 residents were killed. (9) In addition, 5,000 homes in the area were destroyed and 40,000 were damaged. (10) Camille's path of destruction continued north to St. Louis before the storm veered east to Virginia, where over 100 people were killed by flooding.

1. The tone of the passage is best described as

(A) skeptical
(B) sorrowful
(C) matter-of-fact
(D) sensational
(E) wistful

GO ON TO THE NEXT PAGE

2. Of the following, which is the best version of sentence 4 (reproduced below)?

Turning north, the storm brushed past Cuba's western tip before emerging into the open waters of the Gulf of Mexico, quickly intensifying to a huge Category 5 storm on the Saffir-Simpson Hurricane Scale and began moving north-northwest at about 15 miles per hour.

(A) (As it is now)
(B) Turning north, the storm brushed past Cuba's western tip before emerging into the open waters of the Gulf of Mexico. Following a quick intensification to a huge Category 5 storm on the Saffir-Simpson Hurricane Scale, it began moving north-northwest at about 15 miles per hour.
(C) Turning north, the storm brushed past Cuba's western tip before emerging into the open waters of the Gulf of Mexico. It quickly intensified to a huge Category 5 storm on the Saffir-Simpson Hurricane Scale and began moving north-northwest at about 15 miles per hour.
(D) The storm brushed past Cuba's western tip before emerging into the open waters of the Gulf of Mexico, turning north, and quickly intensifying to a huge Category 5 storm on the Saffir-Simpson Hurricane Scale and began moving north-northwest at about 15 miles per hour.
(E) Turning north, the storm brushed past Cuba's western tip before emerging into the open waters of the Gulf of Mexico. Quick intensification to a huge Category 5 storm on the Saffir-Simpson Hurricane Scale followed, and it began moving north-northwest at about 15 miles per hour.

3. In the context of the second paragraph, which of the following is the best revision of the underlined portion of sentence 6 (reproduced below).

Camille destroyed all weather instruments in its path, <u>but its winds are estimated to be about 200 miles per hour at the time of landfall</u>.

(A) (As it is now)
(B) but its winds were estimated to be about 200 miles per hour at the time of landfall.
(C) but its winds had been estimated to be about 200 miles per hour at the time of landfall.
(D) but its landfall winds had been estimated to be about 200 miles per hour at the time of landfall
(E) but its winds are estimated to have been about 200 miles per hour at the time of landfall.

4. To connect sentence 7 to the rest of the second paragraph, which is the best word or phrase to insert after "The most deadly aspect of Camille" (reproduced below)?

The most deadly aspect of Camille was its storm surge, estimated at 24 feet.

(A) , surely,
(B) , however,
(C) , by contrast,
(D) , therefore,
(E) , as a consequence,

GO ON TO THE NEXT PAGE

5. In context, which is the best way to revise and combine sentences 8 and 9 (reproduced below)?

In the area of landfall, nearly 150 residents were killed. In addition, 5,000 homes in the area were destroyed and 40,000 were damaged.

(A) In the area of landfall, nearly 150 residents were killed, 5,000 homes destroyed, and 40,000 homes damaged.

(B) In the area of landfall, nearly 150 residents were killed, 5,000 homes in the area were destroyed and 40,000 were damaged.

(C) In the area of landfall, nearly 150 residents were killed, while an additional 5,000 homes were destroyed and 40,000 damaged.

(D) In the area of landfall, nearly 150 residents were killed, and 5,000 and 40,000 homes were destroyed and damaged, respectively.

(E) In the area of landfall, nearly 150 residents were killed, and additionally, 5,000 homes in the area were destroyed and 40,000 were damaged.

6. Which of the following is the best revision of sentence 3 (reproduced below)?

It reached hurricane strength on August 14, at which time its location was about 100 miles south of Cuba.

(A) It reached hurricane strength on August 14, locating it about 100 miles south of Cuba.

(B) It reached hurricane strength on August 14, about 100 miles south of Cuba.

C) On August 14, it reached hurricane strength about 100 miles south of Cuba.

(D) On August 14, it reached hurricane strength when it was located 100 miles south of Cuba.

(E) It reached hurricane strength on August 14, maintaining a location about 100 miles south of Cuba.

The Answers

1. (C) 2. (C) 3. (E) 4. (B) 5. (A) 6. (C). There's nothing here you can't handle. Hurricanes are more interesting than ETS's typical fodder, but we think the questions are of about average difficulty.

The Explanations

1. Don't Be Tone Deaf

This is one of those questions designed to make sure you understand the whole passage. A quick read shows that the passage is crammed full of facts and does not express any emotions or judgments. We'd call that matter-of-fact. **Answer: (C).**

2. Coping with a (Sentence) Disaster

There are two problems with this sentence: It is a run-on, and it includes a verb ("began") that messes up the parallel structure of the clauses. You need to break this into two sentences, and (C) offers the most concise way of doing so. Answers (B) and (E) include awkward usage of "intensification," a verb masquerading as a noun. The strongest verb among the answer choices is "intensified." **Answer: (C).**

3. Tricky Tenses

Back to those aggravating tenses. You might have been tempted to choose (B), but this sentence suggests that the estimates of wind speed were made at the time of landfall. The estimates are actually being made today—and therefore should be in the present tense. That makes the present perfect "to have been" the only possible companion to the present "are estimated," and (E) is the correct response. Notice that the shorter-is-better rule does not apply in this case because answer (B) does not get the tense right. **Answer: (E).**

4. Smoothing the Transition

Sentence 7 says, "The most deadly aspect of Camille was its storm surge, estimated at 24 feet." Since the previous sentence focused on wind speed—and since most people envision hurricane winds as doing most of the destruction—it may come as a surprise that the storm surge was actually Camille's most deadly aspect. Of the possible answers, (B) best expresses the idea that the logic of sentence 7 runs counter to what most people probably believed after reading sentence 6. "However" is a better response than "by contrast" because sentences 6 and 7 do not present a contrast, but rather two facts that might not seem at a glance to go together. **Answer: (B).**

5. Concise Is Nice

This is one is a no-brainer. Apply your "shorter-is-better" rule and move on. (A) is correct, though a few people might be tripped up by the omission of "were" for the houses damaged and destroyed. In this instance, "were" is understood and it is not necessary to repeat. (B) is wrong because of the unnecessary repetition of "were" and "in the area." The words "additional" and "additionally" are not necessary—the latter is not even a real word. **Answer: (A).**

6. When Phrases Are out of Order

The awkwardness in this sentence comes from the fact that the action in the sentence, "reached hurricane strength," is separated from "about 100 miles south of Cuba," the place where it happened. The problem with response (B) is that "about 100 miles south of Cuba" does not modify "August 14." Solution: Move "August 14" to the beginning. **Answer: (C).**

Questions 7–12 are based on the following passage.

(1) Recreation in wilderness areas has increased dramatically in recent years, and as a result, the number of encounters between humans and bears has also been rising. (2) The thought of coming face to face with a bear may sound terrifying, but the vast majority of such situations pass without incident.

(3) Since bears generally try to avoid humans, make plenty of noise. (4) Many outfitter stores sell bear bells that can be strapped to a backpack. (5) Try to minimize food odors. (6) Store your food and garbage in air-tight containers. (7) Campers should never bring food into a tent. (8) If you encounter a bear while hiking, come to a stop and then back away slowly. (9) Look in the direction of the bear but do not make eye contact, which the bear might perceive as threatening. (10) Talk softly to let the bear know that you are human, and definitely not prey, but also not a threat. (11) Never consider running from a bear, as this may spark a chase instinct in an otherwise non-aggressive bear.

(12) Thousands of people encounter bears every year, but bear attacks are exceedingly rare. (13) You are far more likely to be injured in an automobile accident on the drive home than by a bear during an excursion into the outdoors.

7. Which of the following best states the main idea of the passage?
   (A) People should not be concerned about a bear attack in wilderness areas.
   (B) Though bear attacks are rare, people should take simple precautions when they are in bear country.
   (C) People should avoid wilderness areas where they are likely to encounter bears.
   (D) A few simple precautions can eliminate the danger of bear attacks in wilderness areas.
   (E) The frequency of bear attacks in wilderness areas is increasing rapidly.

GO ON TO THE NEXT PAGE

8. Which of the following would be the most suitable sentence to insert immediately before sentence 3?

   (A) Most people underestimate the dangers of bears in the back country.
   (B) Readers should not be concerned about encountering a bear in the back country.
   (C) Only outdoor experts should venture into bear country.
   (D) A few simple precautions can help maximize your safety in bear country.
   (E) Most people will encounter a bear at some time during their lives.

9. In context, which is the best way to revise and combine sentences 6 and 7 (reproduced below)?

   Store your food and garbage in air-tight containers. Campers should never bring food into a tent.

   (A) Store your food and garbage in air-tight containers; you should never bring food into a tent.
   (B) Food and garbage should be stored in air-tight containers, and food should never be brought into a tent.
   (C) Store your food and garbage in air-tight containers, and never bring food into a tent.
   (D) Store your food and garbage in air-tight containers, and campers should never bring food into a tent.
   (E) Store your food and garbage in air-tight containers, never bring food into a tent.

10. Inclusion of a paragraph on which of the following would most strengthen the passage?

   (A) the mating habits of bears
   (B) places where bear encounters are most likely
   (C) techniques used by bear hunters
   (D) the diet of bears
   (E) a comparison with bears with cougars

11. Which of the following best replaces the word "definitely" in sentence 10?

   (A) therefore
   (B) you are
   (C) unquestionably
   (D) usually
   (E) as a result

12. In the context of the passage, which of the following is the best revision of the underlined portion of sentence 11 (reproduced below)?

   Never consider running from a bear, as this may spark a chase instinct in an otherwise non-aggressive bear.

   (A) Always think twice before running from a bear,
   (B) Avoid running from a bear you encounter,
   (C) You should never consider running from a bear,
   (D) Running from a bear is not very wise,
   (E) Never run

GO ON TO THE NEXT PAGE

The Answers

7. (B) 8. (D) 9. (C) 10. (B) 11. (A) 12. (E). Our passage on bear attacks allows us to continue the disaster and mayhem theme (and hopefully keep you at least mildly entertained).

The Explanations

7. Getting the Main Idea

Like many others, this passage is not black and white. It doesn't tell you to forget about bear attacks and neither does it suggest that you should live in fear of them. The danger can never be eliminated but neither should it be overstated. **Answer: (B).**

8. That's An Insert

The second paragraph outlines strategies for minimizing the likelihood of encountering a bear, such as making plenty of noise and minimizing food odors, and strategies for lessening the likelihood of a violent confrontation if you do encounter a bear. Since both emphases fit nicely under the heading of safety, **(D)** is the correct answer.

9. Be Concise But Be Clear

We may have gotten a few of you on this one. Answer (A) is not correct because the two sentences express independent thoughts not appropriate for joining with a semicolon. (And besides, it includes an unnecessary "you should.") Answer (E) is the shortest of the bunch, but without a conjunction it is a comma splice. Response (B) is burdened with passive voice. Response (D) has an unnecessary "campers should" for an imperative sentence in which the subject (you) is understood. **Answer: (C).**

10. Strengthening the Sentence

The major theme of the passage is how to prepare for encounters with bears. Part of being prepared is knowing where you are likely to see one. **Answer (B)** is the only one that relates directly to encounters with bears. 'Nuff said.

11. Making the Logic Flow

Sentence 10 suggests that the reason people should talk softly when encountering a bear is "to let the bear know you are human." (The soft part relates to the idea that you are "not a threat.") A human by definition is not prey, and answer **(A)** is the response that best establishes the idea that "not prey" follows from "human."

12. Brevity Is the Soul of Wit

Repeat after us: Short is good, shorter is better, shortest is best. Responses (A) to (D) fiddle around before getting to the point. At first glance, you might be put off by the fact that (E) says merely "never run" as opposed to "never run from a bear." But look at the context again. The whole passage is about bears, and there is no ambiguity about what "never run" refers to. **Answer: (E).**

Keys to Success

1. Experiment with reading the passages vs. going straight to the questions. The passages in Improving Paragraphs are easier to skip around in than those in Passage-Based Reading. While reading comprehension passages are numbered at five-line intervals, every sentence in Improving Paragraphs is numbered. The language is generally easier to understand and the selections are relatively short. We think the case for going straight to the questions is at least as strong as in Passage-Based Reading. You decide for yourself.

2. Shorter is better—most of the time. After pounding away at shorter-is-better, perhaps we should remind you once again that ETS knows you know that shorter is better. Watch for short responses that omit key information or distort meanings, as in question 3. In the absence of errors like these, shorter is still definitely better.

3. Answer sentence-specific questions before answering comprehension questions. If you decide to dive straight into the questions before reading, skip comprehension questions such as 1 and 7 until you have answered the ones that focus on particular sentences. In the process of answering those, you will pick up more about broad issues such as the passage's main idea and tone.

HOW THE ESSAYS WILL BE SCORED

Below are the College Board's scoring guidelines for the essay. The essays will be graded holistically, meaning that the overall impression conveyed by the essay will be the basis of the score:

Score of 6
An essay in this category is *outstanding*, demonstrating clear and consistent mastery, although it may have a few minor errors. A typical essay:
- Effectively and insightfully develops a point of view on the topic and demonstrates outstanding critical thinking, using clearly appropriate examples, reasons, and other evidence to support its position
- Is well organized and clearly focused, demonstrating clear coherence and smooth progression of ideas
- Exhibits skillful use of language, using a varied, accurate, and apt vocabulary
- Demonstrates meaningful variety in sentence structure
- Is free of most errors in grammar, usage, and mechanics

Score of 5
An essay in this category is *effective*, demonstrating reasonably consistent mastery, although it will have occasional errors or lapses in quality. A typical essay:
- Effectively develops a point of view on the topic and demonstrates strong critical thinking, generally using appropriate examples, reasons, and other evidence to support its position
- Is well organized and focused, demonstrating coherence and progression of ideas
- Exhibits facility in the use of language, using appropriate vocabulary
- Demonstrates variety in sentence structure
- Is generally free of most errors in grammar, usage, and mechanics

Score of 4
An essay in this category is *competent*, demonstrating adequate mastery, although it will have lapses in quality. A typical essay:
- Develops a point of view on the topic and demonstrates competent critical thinking, using adequate examples, reasons, and other evidence to support its position

- Is generally organized and focused, demonstrating some coherence and progression of ideas
- Exhibits adequate but inconsistent facility in the use of language, using generally appropriate vocabulary
- Demonstrates some variety in sentence structure
- Has some errors in grammar, usage, and mechanics

Score of 3

An essay in this category is *inadequate*, but demonstrates developing mastery, and is marked by one or more of the following weaknesses:

- Develops a point of view on the topic, but may do so inconsistently, demonstrating some critical thinking, but using inadequate examples, reasons, or other evidence to support its position
- Is limited in its organization or focus, but may demonstrate some lapses in coherence progression of ideas
- Displays developing facility in the use of language, but sometimes uses weak vocabulary or inappropriate word choice
- Lacks variety or demonstrates problems in sentence structure
- Contains an accumulation of errors in grammar, usage, and mechanics

Score of 2

An essay in this category is *seriously limited*, demonstrating little mastery, and is flawed by one or more of the following weaknesses:

- Develops a point of view on the topic that is vague or seriously limited, demonstrating weak critical thinking, providing inappropriate or insufficient examples, reasons, or other evidence to support its position
- Is poorly organized and/or focused, or demonstrates serious problems with coherence or progression of ideas
- Displays very little facility in the use of language, using very limited vocabulary or incorrect word choice
- Demonstrates frequent problems in sentence structure
- Contains errors in grammar, usage, and mechanics so serious that meaning is somewhat obscured

Score of 1

An essay in this category is *fundamentally deficient*, demonstrating very little or no mastery, and is severely flawed by one or more of the following weaknesses:

- Develops no viable point of view on the topic, or provides little or no evidence to support its position
- Is disorganized or unfocused, resulting in a disjointed or incoherent essay
- Displays fundamental errors in vocabulary
- Demonstrates severe flaws in sentence structure
- Contains pervasive errors in grammar, usage, or mechanics that persistently interfere with meaning

CRITICAL READING

5

TOTAL TESTING TIME: 70 MINUTES

SECTIONS:

✔ 2 of 25 minutes
✔ 1 of 20 minutes

QUESTION TYPES:

✔ Sentence Completion
✔ Passage-Based Reading
✔ Paragraph-Length Reading

Both of the main types of Critical Reading questions, Sentence Completion and Passage-Based Reading, appeared in the old Verbal section. Budget most of your time for the Passage-Based Reading, where plowing through the passages is the main chore. The new wrinkle: Shorter paragraph-length passages are now also included. The biggest change? The dreaded analogies are axed.

Sentence Completion

Many students consider Sentence Completions to be the easiest kind of question on the SAT. Part of this has to do with the fact that these questions can be answered quickly. But statistically, there is a higher proportion of the hardest questions among the Sentence Completion than there is in the Passage-Based Reading. Why? Because the Sentence Completion questions place greater emphasis on vocabulary. If you don't know the words, you have little chance of getting the answers.

The College Board divides Sentence Completion questions into four types. Here are some relatively easy examples of each:

One-Blank Vocabulary-Based

1. The ------- countryside stretched out before her, cool and quiet in the morning mist.

    (A) raucous
    (B) placid
    (C) lively
    (D) jaded
    (E) disquieted

Two-Blank Vocabulary-Based

2. The dog sat forlornly beside the door; he had been ------- and ------- since his master left.

    (A) electrified . . content
    (B) excited . . bemused
    (C) morose . . listless
    (D) eager . . disappointed
    (E) dilatory . . joyous

One-Blank Logic-Based

3. Although most people tend to be resistant to change, they are also quick to ------- new technology when it proves useful in daily life.

    (A) embrace
    (B) eschew
    (C) enact
    (D) empower
    (E) dislike

Two-Blank Logic-Based

4. Because Peter ------- to finish his homework, the teacher ------- him in front of the class.

    (A) hastened . . ennobled
    (B) decided . . berated
    (C) neglected . . admonished
    (D) disdained . . circumscribed
    (E) elected . . alienated

For anyone who is curious, the answers are: **1. (B) 2. (C) 3. (A) 4. (C).** Got 'em all? Don't get too pleased with yourself. They get a wee bit harder as you go along.

The distinction between vocabulary- and logic-based questions is a fine one. Sometimes the hard part is knowing the words (vocabulary-based questions), and sometimes the hard part is following the analytical reasoning that dictates the answer (logic-based questions). So goes the theory anyway. In our informal review, we found that vocabulary-based questions were generally one-blank and logic questions were generally two-blank. As with all sections of the SAT except Reading Comprehension, the questions get harder as you go. The first three or four questions are generally easy, the next few get harder, and the last one is often a nasty vocabulary-based mind-bender.

The secret to solving the sentence completions may have as much to do with listening as thinking—listening, that is, to the little voice inside your head. "Say the problem to yourself without looking at the answers and often the right answer will pop into your head," says a Cornell admit who scored 710 V, 800 M. If you are lucky enough to have an epiphany of this sort, glance down to see if it is in the answer choices. If so, and you are doing a two-word question, see if the second word fits. If yes again, glance at the other choices, and if nothing seems equally plausible, blacken your oval and move on.

You come out ahead when you solve problems this way because a) you save time, and b) you don't get bogged down in the tricks that ETS has cooked up to throw you off track. But alas, many questions won't be so easy. Don't lose heart. If your initial read does not reveal the answer, look deeper and you'll see patterns that can offer important clues. These patterns are best described as tendencies rather than rules because there are always exceptions, but more often than not these patterns will lead you to pay dirt.

The majority of Sentence Completion questions share a common structure. They consist of two clauses connected by punctuation such as a comma, semicolon, or colon, or connected by linking words such as although, "but," "despite," "since," "that," and "whereas," to name a few. (If you want to get

WHEN THE CLAUSES CONTRADICT

A favorite tactic of ETS is to build sentences out of two clauses that express ideas or conditions that seemingly do not go together. To spot this kind of question, look for any and all of the following words and phrases: *although, but, despite, however, nevertheless, rather than, though, while, whereas, yet.* When you encounter one of these, the sentence will generally express a contrast or contradiction.

technical, these linking words are generally conjunctions or conjunctive adverbs.) In one-blank questions, or in two-blank questions where both blanks are in the same clause, the right answer is generally defined by its relationship to the most important phrase in the opposite clause—what we call "the key phrase."

Confused? Don't be. Look back at Question 1. A comma divides the sentence into two clauses. "Cool and quiet in the morning mist" is the key phrase that determines the correct response: placid. In Question 2, the key phrase is "forlornly," which has nearly the same meaning as the combination of "morose" and "listless." Problems like these, in which a colon, semicolon, or comma joins the two clauses—and in which there is no linking word—are the least complicated. In such problems, the correct answer generally has the same meaning as the key phrase, as in questions 1 and 2.

The presence of a linking word—either in the middle of the sentence or at the beginning—complicates the relationship between the key phrase and the answer. Look again at Question 3. The sentence begins with "although," a word used to explain how two conditions that seem contradictory can coexist. The key phrase is resistant to change, but the word "although" implies that you should look for an answer that means the opposite of "resist" or "resistant." Which response is most clearly the opposite of these two? The correct one: (A) embrace.

Most two-blank questions present a variation on this theme. Typically, these sentences have a blank in both clauses. The clauses are generally connected in the same way as in the one-blank questions, that is, by punctuation and/or by a linking word. The absence of a key phrase without a blank can be a challenge, but you may also find that having two blanks in different parts of the sentence can be an advantage because you have two chances to find the correct answer.

Go back to Question 4 on page 144. Begin with the word "because," a word that shows that the first blank will be the cause of what happens in the second. Next, plug in the pairs of words and see which one makes the most logical cause-and-effect sentence. Responses (A)

> "It's hard to prepare for the vocab just because the English dictionary is so dang long. We prepped in English class and I studied flashcards, but very few of those words actually showed up."
>
> —770 V, 800 M

and (D) are out because the second word in the pair does not make sense in the context of "teacher ------- him." The teacher could have berated him, but not because he decided to do his homework. Nor would the teacher have alienated him because he elected to finish his work. The correct answer is (C) neglected . . admonished.

For all we have said about patterns and tendencies, we should stress again that the best way to solve sentence completion problems is by ear. When in doubt, go with the response that sounds the most fluid and/or expresses the clearest logic.

Excluding the ungraded section, each SAT includes nineteen Sentence Completion questions. All three Critical Reading sections on each test begin with five to eight of them. See how you fare on the following ten questions, then consult the answers and explanations below. (No peeking.)

Directions: Each sentence below has one or two blanks, each blank indicating that something has been omitted. Beneath the sentence are five words or sets of words labeled A through E. Choose the word or set of words that, when inserted in a sentence, best fits the meaning of the sentence has a whole.

1. As big as the United States and Mexico combined, the continent of Antarctica is a ------- place, with little vegetation and temperatures that average about −60° Fahrenheit.

   (A) reflective
   (B) forbidding
   (C) awesome
   (D) predominate
   (E) dauntless

2. After tons of waste had been dumped at the landfill, a ------- smell emanated from the site.

   (A) lurid
   (B) doleful
   (C) putrid
   (D) turgid
   (E) despicable

3. Dorothy has been quietly effective since her promotion to plant manager; though ------- with her employees, she has already ------- productivity on the assembly line.

   (A) jovial . . promoted
   (B) strident . . momentous
   (C) direct . . enlarged
   (D) soft-spoken . . increased
   (E) scrupulous . . elongated

4. Many drivers ------- this road on their way through the county because its sharp curves and blind intersections make it -------.

   (A) bypass . . deleterious
   (B) dislike . . risky
   (C) encompass . . disjointed
   (D) enjoy . . engaging
   (E) avoid . . hazardous

5. In *Their Eyes Were Watching God*, Zora Neale Hurston makes ------- use of dialect to portray the ------- of African American Southerners in the 1930s.

   (A) excessive . . alienation
   (B) consistent . . foibles
   (C) innovative . . cadences
   (D) inappropriate . . speech
   (E) intemperate . . rage

6. Atmospheric pressure, a ------- measured by barometers, is an important ------- of developing weather systems.

   (A) mechanism . . effect
   (B) process . . agent
   (C) forecast . . precursor
   (D) phenomenon . . outgrowth
   (E) condition . . predictor

GO ON TO THE NEXT PAGE

7. The story of buried treasure on the island was -------, based as it was on unsubstantiated rumors.

(A) phlegmatic
(B) apocryphal
(C) uninformed
(D) distasteful
(E) unknown

8. While the lieutenant demanded that his men act -------, he also insisted that they not be ------- to danger.

(A) bravely . . intrepid
(B) affirmatively . . dubious
(C) courageously . . oblivious
(D) lively . . incredulous
(E) flatulently . . impertinent

9. Critics describe the new novel as -------, even -------; it excoriates the rich and powerful and sounds a call for the disempowered to mobilize.

(A) controversial . . offensive
(B) belligerent . . mocking
(C) salacious . . blasphemous
(D) iconoclastic . . revolutionary
(E) disturbing . . malevolent

10. Usually ------- to criticism, Mr. Smith showed surprising ------- at his negative reviews from the critics.

(A) impervious . . pique
(B) immune . . volubility
(C) hostile . . truculence
(D) disgruntled . . dismissiveness
(E) derisive . . rage

The Answers

Did you get all ten? Don't feel bad if you didn't; these are typical of the hardest ones you'll see. **The answers: 1. (B) 2. (C) 3. (D) 4. (E) 5. (C) 6. (E) 7. (B) 8. (C) 9. (D) 10. (A).**

The Explanations

1. A Forbidding Place

This problem is relatively easy, the kind that students should expect at the beginning of a section. The blank modifies "place," thereby eliminating "reflective," which applies to people, and "predominate," a verb that means "larger in number." "Dauntless," meaning "invulnerable to fear," is a distracter that calls to mind "daunting." The key phrase, which comes immediately after "------- place," is "with little vegetation" and "temperatures that average about –60° Fahrenheit." A place like that is forbidding and the answer is **(B)**.

2. What's That Smell?

Technically, this is a logic-based problem. The linking word after sets up a cause-and-effect relationship between "tons of waste" and "------- smell." You know that smell is nasty, but we've turbo-charged the problem with tough distracters. For instance, you might be tempted to choose "turgid," a word that sounds stinky but really means "bombastic" or "ostentatious." Likewise, "lurid" means "shocking" or "sensational" and is obviously inappropriate. These are diversions from the real answer, **(C) putrid**, the smell of stuff rotting.

3. Key Phrase Follow-Up

A sentence divided by a semicolon (or colon) virtually always consists of two clauses that express a similar meaning. The key phrase in this problem is "quietly effective." The first blank after the semicolon calls for a synonym of "quietly" while the second should be filled with a word that means "effective." Response (A) is typical of distracters that include words that convey some of the right meaning but don't quite fit. "Jovial" means "lighthearted," and if a form of "promote" were in the answer, the right choice would be "promoting" instead of "promoted" since her work is ongoing. The closest synonym to "quiet" or "quietly" among the answers is "soft-spoken," and "increased" also fits better than any of the other second words in the pairs. While her job of promoting productivity is continuing, it is appropriate to say that she has increased productivity since any measurement must be based on past results. **Answer: (D)**.

4. When a Distracter Is Response (A)

In problems, with two blanks, a common trick is to include a wrong answer in which the first word in the pair looks right. This is the case with "bypass . . deleterious." Often, a distracter such as this comes before the right answer so that students moving too quickly will pick it as the right answer and move on. Though "bypass" appears to be appropriate, "deleterious" connotes something that is harmful or negative in its nature. (A road is not deleterious in itself, but an accident can have a deleterious affect on one's health.) "Dislike . . risky" is another choice that might appear possible at first glance, but the timeframe of "on their way through the county" rules out this one because the dislike would not be limited to this period. **Answer: (E)**.

5. Feeling the Positive Vibes

Even if you've never heard of Zora Neale Hurston, you can guess that she is an African American woman because ETS takes every opportunity to write about people of color. We're glad that the bad old days of the white male SAT are over, but we also cannot fail to note that the test's statements about women and nonwhites are predictable and therefore can give you an advantage. (See Political Correctness and the SAT, page 19). Since virtually every reference to persons of either group is positive, you can solve some questions without knowing the meanings of every word. In this case, the first word in the pair is unlikely to be "excessive," "inappropriate," or "intemperate." Once you spot the most positive word among the five, "innovative," you can be fairly sure that (C) is the right choice even if you have no idea what "cadences" means. If you do know the word "cadences," you recognize it as the closest synonym for use of "dialect" among the second words in the pairs. "Speech" would also be a plausible answer were it not paired with "inappropriate." **Answer: (C)**.

6. A Different Kind of Pressure

The key phrase in this problem is "atmospheric pressure." The hard part is figuring out exactly what sort of thing atmospheric pressure really is. A mechanism? A process? A phenomenon? ETS hopes that you will pick one of these without thinking it through, but atmospheric pressure is actually a weather condition. Even if the first blank stumps you, think about the weather reports you see on TV and use a little logic. Barometers exist because they can help predict weather conditions. **Answer: (E)**.

7. Dealing With Fifty-Cent Words

This question is typical of the hardest vocabulary-based problems, the kind that generally comes at the end of a section. The key phrase is "unsubstantiated rumors." Let's suppose you don't know that "apocryphal"—the correct answer—means "of questionable or dubious authenticity." You do know the definition of "uninformed," "distasteful," and "unknown." None of them are an exact fit. Faced with the choice between a word they know that doesn't exactly fit and a word that they don't know, too many students choose the simpler word just because its definition is familiar. For many students, the best approach will be to guess between "apocryphal" and "phlegmatic" (meaning "unemotional"). **Answer: (B)**.

8. A Logical Contrast

Although the odds are remote that you'll see so much as one question with a military theme, we thought it would be nice to put at least one question in the book for the guys. Joined by the linking word "while," the two clauses express a contrast in the lieutenant's demands: his men should act ------- but not -------. "Bravely" is a perfectly acceptable possibility but is revealed as a distracter because "intrepid" ("fearless") does not fit the second blank. Answers (B) and (D) do not present a logical contrast, and if you don't know what "flatulently" means…er, look it up. "Courageously . . oblivious" captures the idea that the soldiers should be brave but not reckless. **Answer: (C)**.

9. Two Blanks, Heightening Intensity

The word "even" is your clue that the second blank will be an intensified version of the first. The semicolon is a tip-off that the first clause and the second will probably express similar ideas, and the entire second clause is the key phrase. "It excoriates the rich and powerful" parallels the first blank, while "sounds a call for the disempowered to mobilize" approximates the meaning of the second blank. "Controversial," "belligerent," "salacious," and "disturbing" are all plausible responses for the first blank, but none comes as close to "excoriates the rich and powerful" as does "iconoclastic." Even if you don't know the meaning of "iconoclastic," "a call for the disempowered to mobilize" is a perfect match for "revolutionary." **Answer: (D)**.

10. Saving the Toughest for Last

We have noted that in sentences divided by a comma without a linking word, the meaning of the second clause generally parallels that of the first. But there are exceptions. In this case, there is an implied linking word—"though"—that does not appear. By reading the first clause as Though "usually ------- to criticism," you can quickly gather that the second clause will present a contrast or contradiction. "Immune . . volubility" is a nasty distracter because "immune" is a logical choice and many students don't know the meaning of "volubility." Though it looks like "volatility," it actually means "fluency" or "articulateness." Scratch that one. Responses (C), (D), and (E) have some tantalizing words, but none present an adequate contrast. But "impervious to criticism" works nicely and "pique"—a relatively difficult word—is a synonym of "irritate." **Answer: (A)**.

SHOULD I CRAM VOCABULARY?

Probably not. Trying to cram word definitions a month or two before the test is one of the biggest time wasters in SAT prep. In the words of a 720 V, 690 M scorer, "I studied approximately 500+ SAT words in my English class and there were only three or four words that were the same. Instead of wasting all this time on learning words it would be more useful to practice problems." Says another student who got 630 V, 630 M, "I studied as many vocab words as Kaplan had to offer and saw only one of those words on the test." With the demise of the analogies, studying vocabulary will become an even more dubious proposition. The one possible exception is if you have a long period of time—like six months to a year—in which you can learn words gradually. Several students in our survey suggested making a vocab notebook in which you record words from reading or prep books. Leave about four lines between each word—enough space to write a definition and use the word in a sentence. You'll need to do 1,000 words—and preferably 2,000 or more—to have much hope of making an impact. If you're determined to build your word power, a better strategy may be to work on prefixes, suffixes, and word roots. These will help you figure out a word even if you've never seen it before.

Keys to Success

1. **Watch for distracters.** These get more ornery as the questions get harder. In two-word questions, the first word of the distracter looks suspiciously like the first word in the correct answer. And since the sneaky test-makers often put the distracter before the real answer, students unwittingly pick the distracter and blissfully move on without realizing their mistake. In a two-blank question, make sure that both words fit.

2. **Don't get stuck when you don't know the vocab.** You can waste valuable time puzzling over questions with incomprehensible vocabulary. Spare yourself. If you're stumped after your first reading of the question and don't know the definitions of two or more words, skip the question and come back later or make a guess. You may get the answer by puzzling it through

with the techniques in this chapter, but if you're at all in danger of running out time, your first priority should be questions where the main challenge is reasoning rather than vocabulary.

3. Choose the most precise words. If you're stuck between two equally plausible alternatives, the one that is more descriptive is generally right. In question 9 above, "controversial" may seem logical at first glance, but "iconoclastic," a more precise word, is the best choice. To go a step further, distracters are often simple words while right answers are often more precise (and difficult) words.

4. Near the end of a batch of Sentence Completion questions, pick the most obscure word. ETS loves to put a vocab zinger in the last question of a section—with words like "munificence," "obstreperous," and "synergistic," "calumny," to name a few we've seen. If you're at the end and torn between a word you don't know and a word you do know that doesn't sound exactly right, pick the former.

Passage-Based Reading

Passage-Based Reading is the black hole of the SAT. Too many students get sucked into them and are never seen or heard from again (at least, not with their sanity intact).

The passages look reasonably benign. All you need to do is read. Easy, right? But the passages are long and so booooorrring. As paragraph after paragraph drones on about the cultural differences between Tadzhikistan and Uzbekistan, or about the shrinking habitat of the Peruvian three-toed newt, students inevitably lose their way. Concentration drops. Anxiety increases. The clock ticks. And suddenly you've at the end of a paragraph—and don't remember anything about what you've just read. Panic city. Game over. Goodbye Harvard, hello Fitchburg State.

Well, maybe it won't be quite that bad. But Passage-Based Reading is an area where preparation can make a huge difference. Very few of the questions are exceptionally hard, at least when judged by the percentage of students who get them wrong. Students generally miss them because they get flustered by the process of reading the passage.

Passage-Based Reading is divided into two types of questions: the traditional passages of 500–850 words, which may consist of two paired passages, and new 100-word passages called Paragraph-Length Reading. Lest there be any confusion, the Passage-Based Reading used to be called Reading Comprehension, and most everyone still calls it that. (You'll see us do so every once in a while.)

The most important issue in Passage-Based Reading is straightforward: How will you manage your time between the questions and the passages? Will you read the passages first or go directly to the questions? Will you read the whole passage or just relevant portions?

The choice is especially crucial for the longer passages because they take gobs of time. Since reading speed and efficiency tend to go down after the first hundred words, the long passages will have a multiplied effect on your time. The Passage-Based Reading is not the hardest section on the SAT, but it is often the most stressful. "I was nervous, and it is very tough to concentrate on long passages when your mind is wandering and thinking about other things," says a student who scored 560 V, 650 M.

> "My advice is to take difficult English courses and read as many classics as you can, such as *Wuthering Heights* and *Great Expectations.*"
> —670 V, 700 M

All the other multiple-choice sections have a similar rhythm: You may be nervous at the beginning, but then you answer the easy questions at the front and settle down. Many students can complete the first half of a typical section well before time is half gone. No longer worried about finishing, students can relax a little as they tackle the tough problems that tend to be concentrated at the end of the section, or as they revisit questions they may have skipped.

Passage-Based Reading does not work that way—at least not if you read the passage before answering the questions. On a typical long passage, a student must read for five or ten minutes before blackening any ovals. Although reading is a crucial part of answering the questions, it doesn't feel like answering the questions. High-strung students are always worried about the clock, and if the number of questions they have answered is not keeping pace with the time, anxiety can take hold. For this reason, we recommend that slow readers and high-strung test-takers consider a method that gets them answering questions before too much time has elapsed. Some students may prefer to do all the reading passages first—even though they come after the Sentence Completion questions in the Critical Reading sections. Others may want to do only the paragraph-length passages first and save the long ones for last. We recommend that you experiment.

> "Approach the SAT as a series of problems to solve, not a test that will determine the rest of your life."
>
> —700 V, 760 M

Despite its stress-inducing format, the Passage-Based Reading does cut students one major break: Most questions refer only to particular lines in the passage, and those lines are noted. Some questions, called Vocabulary-in-Context, ask you to define a particular word. Others, called Literal Comprehension questions, ask you to explain what is meant by a particular line or lines. Both of these types can generally be answered without regard to the passage as a whole.

A third type of question, which the College Board calls Extended Reasoning, does refer to the whole passage. These questions can relate to the tone or point of view of the speaker, the main idea of the passage, or some other big-picture issue. The secret to the long passages is to comprehend the main characteristics of the passage well enough to get the extended reasoning questions while wasting as little time as possible reading portions of the passage that are not directly relevant to any of the questions.

In each version of the SAT, you will find five long passages. Three of them will stand alone and be followed, depending on their length, by five to thirteen questions. The other two will be paired and followed by twelve or thirteen questions.

In the pages that follow, we offer examples of 1.) a conventional long passage, 2.) a paired selection of long passages, and 3.) two paragraph-length passages.

Three Kinds of Passages

According to the College Board, every SAT includes at least one fictional passage, as well as nonfiction selections from the humanities, social sciences, and natural sciences. With such a vast array of possibilities, there is no way to predict the exact subjects you will see in the Reading Comprehension. Nor is there any point in trying. But by understanding the kind of reasoning in these sections, you can get a feel for the issues that are likely to be raised. Within the categories of long and paragraph-length passages, there are three basic types:

First Person and Fictional Passages. These include portions of diaries, memoirs, short stories, or novels. In compiling this book, we examined ten versions of the SAT administered between 1995 and 2002 that were published in the College Board's *10 Real SATs*. Of the thirteen long passages of this sort, a majority were devoted to the experiences of women and minorities. Included were narratives from a Chinese American, a Haitian American, a Japanese American, a Mexican American, and a scholar offering personal reflections on the Navajo tribe. A common theme: the difficulty of balancing full participation in American life with loyalty to one's roots. The Chinese American wrote of her frustration at seeing her immigrant mother humiliated by a white woman. The Haitian American girl wrote about how her immigrant mother pushed her to become a doctor. A female poet explored a similar theme—her effort to balance the conflicting demands of motherhood and writing. Often, the passages address customs that are likely to be undervalued or misunderstood by white culture. The Japanese American explained the nonverbal way that Japanese families communicate when arranging marriages.

Third Person/Academic Passages. A majority of both the long and paragraph-length selections fall into this category. Most are written by scholars who are defending a particular point of view on, say, Black American fiction and the Romantic literary tradition (to use a real example). There is no way to generalize about the topics except to say that they include a healthy number with a minority and/or female focus. In a sample taken from a recent edition of *10 Real SATs*, historical figures who were referenced included Joan of Arc, Jane Austen, Frederick Douglass, W. E. B. DuBois, Marcus Garvey, George Orwell, Pablo Picasso, and Mark Twain. Social scientific topics included an anthropologist's analysis of cultural differences in the United States and an essay about the role of fences in suburban culture. Scientific topics included radio astronomy, genetics, and plastic surgery. Not all of these passages are academic. One passage in a recent SAT was taken from an essay by an animal trainer about how dogs perceive the world. The third-person passages have innumerable themes, but there is at least one to keep in the back of your mind: myth vs. reality. The test-makers like to find passages that take a new look at familiar topics.

Paired Passages. These selections crop up occasionally among the long passages. Combined, the two essays are generally about 800 words long. They are usually third person/academic, though an occasional first person essay may appear. Your task is to establish a relationship between the passages. If one passage outlines a widely held historical theory, the other passage may attack that theory or revise it in light of new information. If one passage examines a big topic, the other may look at a particular facet of the issue. Sometimes, the passages focus on topics with common themes. An essay on Frederick Douglass was paired with an excerpt about literature written by nineteenth-century women, comparing the "imprisonment" of the female role in that era to slavery. Another passage, offering a largely positive analysis of the societal impact of broadcast media, references George Orwell and suggests that he was wrong in believing that mass media would become a tool of governmental oppression. A companion passage also suggests Orwell was wrong, but for a different reason—that he failed to see the possibility that mass media could perpetrate mass deception, even if the government were not in control of it. The paired passages are like puzzle pieces that do not always fit neatly together. Your job is to figure out how they connect.

> "I never read the questions before the passage because it breaks my concentration and prevents me from getting a full understanding of the passage."
>
> —800 V, 720 M

Long Passages: Example #1

Each passage below is followed by questions based on its content. Answer the questions on the basis of what is stated and implied in each passage and in any introductory material that may be provided.

Questions 1–10 are based on the following passage.

The following selection is from a biography of Betty Shabazz, a college professor and civil rights activist who was best-known as the wife of Malcolm X, the famed African American leader who was assassinated in 1965.

After her heartrending death in the summer of 1997, journalists and friends eulogized Betty as a phenomenon of resilience—as one who had con-
Line quered betrayal, violence, grief, and fear. "That
5 she survived at all is miraculous," Angelou said. "And she survived whole." But whether they served on the battlefield or by the hearth, none of the black-liberation struggle's veterans escaped undamaged. Nobody who drew close to Malcolm
10 and survived—and none drew closer than Betty— escaped the vortex of his death and life. "There are a lot of people who went back into the grave," said Jean Reynolds, one of Malcolm's former disciples, describing the despair that followed the
15 minister's 1965 slaying. "People lost their minds, committed suicide little by little every day."

In many ways, Betty not only survived in the post-assassination years, but thrived. She fought with quiet conscience for education and human-
20 rights causes, exhausting herself in far too many campaigns for dignity, often on behalf of black women and children. She was not an ideologue. She never lifted Malcolm's sword to slash white supremacy. She preferred to think of herself as a
25 moral booster for Black America. Some black nationalists dismissed her as a bourgeois integrationist. But throughout her life, her defiance against the power structure's disposal of her husband surfaced in the subtle shades of resistance.

30 She believed in womanpower, yet she never considered herself a "libber," and often sent young women home to boyfriends and husbands after dispensing earthly advice about communicating with men and choosing the right lipstick. She was
35 queenly and eruptive, aristocratic but touchable to the rootsy folk in Brooklyn or Harlem. She demanded respect and deference always, whether holding forth an international women's conference or bargain shopping. She was gracious and cantan-
40 kerous, soulful and uncouth, fantastically generous and nosy. She was almost always disgracefully late. And she could cuss like twenty men, a genius she discovered after fielding too many threatening phone calls from her husband's enemies in the
45 months before and after his death.

Betty was charming and coy, and knew just when and how to sling the javelins of her eyes. "That lady had the prettiest eyes," gushed a Harlem nationalist who had secretly served as her
50 bodyguard in the late 1960s on behalf of her domineering sister-in-law and rival, Ella Collins. "Yeah, I know that was Malcolm's wife," he said, "but I still flirted with her." Her femininity, one friend said, "just oozed. And she knew it. And she
55 enjoyed it." Betty was afflicted with neither fits of dullness nor brilliance. But she was divinely practical and sensible when discussing education, Malcolm, and other beloved topics. She saw through hypocrisy and pretension, and had no

60 compunction about telling it like it was. Few of
her comrades ever saw her crumble, not even
when the men began throwing fistfuls of dirt on
her husband's coffin. Royalty never weeps in the
streets. Besides, Malcolm had warned that the salt
65 in her tears would only embitter her.

To Niara Sudarkasa, a friend and former president of Lincoln University, the historically black
school in Pennsylvania, Betty was "a tireless trav-
eler and resolute voice on behalf of economic,
70 political, and social justice for the dispossessed
and downtrodden from Selma to Soweto." To an
academic colleague, she was a "rock steady"
homegirl. To a travel companion who helped
nudge her relationship with Coretta Scott King
75 from rivalry to tolerance to genuine affection, she
was "a flawed, lovely human being." To her eldest
daughter, she was a heroine who dwells "amongst
the spirit of women."

Yet the widow's life was also an epic tragedy. In
80 her latter twenty-five years, she shrugged off the
nostalgic "Mrs. Malcolm X" cape and clad herself
in a distinguished new identity. But she may never
have fully come to terms with the past. In the end,
she was no more indomitable than countless other
85 long-suffering black women whose names history
has ignored. She longed for the privilege of
fragility as often as they surely did, but there was
her children's survival to consider, and her own.
Only in recent years has African America begun to
90 properly recognize the women who stayed alive
and upright through the convulsions of the black-
liberation struggle. But to ignore the cost of their
endurance is no less than abuse.

1. The author's primary objective in the
   passage is

   (A) to undermine the idea that Betty was
       primarily a civil rights activist
   (B) to call attention to the resilience of Betty
       and women like her
   (C) to suggest that Betty was a more
       important figure than historians
       previously realized
   (D) to assert that Betty's career after the
       assassination was more important than
       her earlier work
   (E) to discredit the idea that Betty did not
       contribute to Malcolm X's career

2. The primary function of the first paragraph
   is to emphasize

   (A) the tragedy of Betty's death in 1997
   (B) the nobility of the black-liberation struggle
   (C) the importance of remembering
       Malcolm X
   (D) the unity of Malcolm X's followers
   (E) the pain felt by those in the black-
       liberation struggle

3. In line 11, "vortex" is a metaphorical reference that calls to mind

   (A) an argument between enemies
   (B) a battle between armies
   (C) a collision of vehicles
   (D) a whirling mass of water or air
   (E) a robbery at gun-point

GO ON TO THE NEXT PAGE ⟩

4. From lines 18-29, it may be inferred that in the years after the assassination, Betty

(A) was less radical than some black leaders
(B) was not an advocate for black rights
(C) changed her views on white supremacy
(D) became alienated from most black leaders
(E) urged black nationalists to be more vigilant

5. In lines 37-39, the phrase "whether holding forth at an international women's conference or bargain shopping" is intended to illustrate that Betty

(A) enjoyed speaking at international women's conferences
(B) showed impatience when she felt slighted
(C) had the same personal style in a variety of settings
(D) had an active life and many interests
(E) could be both gracious and cantankerous

6. The purpose of the sentence beginning in line 39 ("She was gracious…generous and nosy.") is to show that Betty had

(A) an unstable mind
(B) diverse personality traits
(C) common mood swings
(D) difficulty staying focused
(E) a cerebral approach to life

7. In line 60, "compunction" most nearly means

(A) compulsion
(B) candor
(C) disdain
(D) dislike
(E) regret

8. By stating in lines 86-87 that Betty "longed for the privilege of fragility," the author suggests that she

(A) disliked her image as a strong woman
(B) considered herself to be privileged
(C) thought that underprivileged people are fragile
(D) believed that she could not be fragile
(E) envied other long-suffering women

9. In context, "recognize" in line 90 most nearly means

(A) distinguish
(B) acquaint
(C) acknowledge
(D) welcome
(E) delight

10. Which of the following best describes the author's attitude toward Betty?

(A) skeptical
(B) dutiful
(C) admiring
(D) scrupulous
(E) noncommittal

The Answers

We'll wager that without the time pressure of taking a real SAT, you found these questions relatively manageable—at least compared to the Sentence Completions and some of the brutal grammar questions in Chapter 4. **The answers: 1. (B) 2. (E) 3. (D) 4. (A) 5. (C) 6. (B) 7. (E) 8. (D) 9. (C) 10. (C).**

The Explanations

1. Getting the Main Idea

Reading Comprehension questions often begin with an item asking you to identify something akin to the primary objective or main idea of the passage. These questions are generally on the easy side. Note that these questions typically ask for a response from the author's perspective rather than your perspective or someone else's. Your first job with any reading passage is to understand what the author intends to convey. In this one, the writer is at great pains to emphasize Betty's resilience in overcoming obstacles. **Answer: (B).**

2. Feeling Their Pain

This extending reasoning question asks you to relate the first paragraph to the passage as a whole. Response (A) is a distracter that plays on the fact that the first clause of the paragraph references Betty's death. But the point of the paragraph is to talk about Betty's struggles, and by extension the struggles of others in the black liberation movement. The emphasis is on pain endured by those in the movement rather than on their nobility, importance, or unity. **Answer: (E).**

3. A Challenging Metaphor

Among the changes in the New SAT is the addition of a few more literary terms such as "metaphor," "simile," "personification," etc. A metaphorical reference explains one concept or situation in terms of another to suggest similarity. (Similes do much the same thing using like or as.) The key to this question is knowing that a vortex is a whirlpool, or a whirling mass of air. **Answer: (D).**

4. Radicals and Moderates

Some of the most challenging Reading Comprehension questions require you to make inferences. In other words, you've got to find the right answer from hints or incomplete information in the passage. In this question, the second paragraph includes a number of clues to the correct response. In lines 23-24, the author refers to the fact that she fought with quiet conscience, and in line 29 the author notes Betty's subtle shades of resistance. Notable as well is the fact that Betty was accused of being a bourgeois integrationist by black nationalists. But most telling is the author's observation that Betty never lifted Malcolm's sword to slash white supremacy. The paragraph makes no reference to any change in her views, and the fact that Betty was out of step with some black nationalists does not mean that she was alienated from most black leaders. But Betty was clearly less radical than some black leaders. **Answer: (A)**.

5. Showing Betty's Style

This question is typical of those that require students to understand the function of a particular sentence or phrase. The relevant excerpt immediately follows "she demanded deference and respect always" and serves as a concrete illustration of the variety of settings in which she maintained this personal style. **Answer: (C)**.

6. Diverse Adjectives Make a Point

The sentence in question shows the diversity of Betty's personality traits. Such traits would not be inconsistent with mood swings or even with an unstable mind, but the passage does not suggest that either is present. **Answer: (B)**.

7. Compunction, Not Compulsion

This is a standard Vocabulary-in-Context question. "Compunction" means "remorse" or "regret." "Compulsion," a word that sounds like "compunction," is a none-too-subtle distracter. **Answer: (E)**.

8. A Different Kind of Privilege

This question is typical of the more difficult Extended Reasoning questions. "Longed for the privilege of fragility" is an oblique way of suggesting that Betty wished that she could let her guard down. But, according to the passage, because she had a central role in the black liberation struggle, she believed that she needed to stay strong and therefore did not have the privilege of fragility. This is not the same thing as her disliking her image as a strong woman; the passage does not describe Betty's opinion of her image. Responses (B) and (C) use "privileged" and "underprivileged" as distracters, and there is no suggestion that Betty envied other women. **Answer: (D)**.

9. Another Word with Two Meanings

A favorite stratagem of ETS is to build Vocabulary-in-Context questions around words that have more than one meaning. "Recognize" is not a hard word, but it has more than one definition, and synonyms are elusive. If you recognize a person, he or she is familiar and may be an acquaintance. But "recognize" can also mean "recognition" or "acknowledgment." The correct response becomes clear with a simple restatement of the relevant line. Instead of "begun to properly recognize," the passage could just as easily say "begun to grant proper recognition to." To recognize a person's achievements is also to acknowledge them. **Answer: (C)**.

10. A Positive Tone

Although the author acknowledges Betty's faults, his portrait is unquestionably admiring. **Answer: (C)**.

Questions 11–22 are based on the following passages.

The following passages discuss interactions between Native Americans and European settlers in the years preceding the American Revolution.

Passage 1

When the Puritans first landed in Massachusetts they discovered an Indian custom so curious they felt called upon to find a name for it. In 1767,
Line when Thomas Hutchinson wrote his history of
5 the colony, the term was already an old saying: "An Indian gift," he told his readers, "is a proverbial expression signifying a present for which an equivalent return is expected." We still use this, of course, and in an even broader sense. If I am so
10 uncivilized as to ask for the return of a gift I have given, they call me an "Indian giver."
Imagine a scene. The Englishman comes into the Indian lodge. He falls to admiring a clay pipe with feathers tied to the stem. The tribe passes this
15 pipe around among themselves as a ritual gift. It stays with a family for awhile, but sooner or later it is always given away again. So the Indian, as is only

polite among his people, responds to the white man's interest by saying, "That's just some stuff we
20 don't need. Please take it. It's a gift." The Englishman is tickled pink. What a nice thing to send back to the British Museum! He takes the pipe home and sets it on the mantelpiece. The next day another Indian happens to visit him and sees the gift
25 which was due to come into his lodge soon. He too is delighted. "Ah!" he says, "the gift!" and he sticks it in his pouch. In consternation the Englishman invents the phrase "Indian giver" to describe these people with such a low sense of private property.
30 The opposite of this term would be something like "white-man-keeper," or, as we say nowadays, "capitalist," that is, a person whose first reaction to property is to take it out of circulation, to put it in a warehouse or museum, or—more to the point for
35 capitalism—to lay it aside to be used for production.
The Indian giver (the original ones, at any rate) understood a cardinal property of the gift: whatever we are given should be given away again, not kept. Or, if it is kept, something of similar
40 value should move on in its stead, the way a billiard ball may stop when it sends another scurrying across the felt, the momentum transferred. You may hold on to a Christmas gift, but it will

cease to be a gift in the true sense unless you have
45 given something else away. When it is passed
along, the gift may be given back to the original
donor, but this is not essential. In fact, it is better
if the gift is not returned, but is given instead to
some new, third party. The only essential is this:
50 the gift must always move.

Passage 2

The obvious contrast between the British
treatment of Native American tribes and that of
the French is fertile territory for modern-day
revisionist critics. But the difference is due less to
55 any political or moral imperative than to mere
expediency. The French came to the New World
less as colonizers than as traders. The supply of
beaver pelts, the lifeblood of New France,
depended on the good offices of the Algonquin,
60 the Huron, and the Iroquois tribes. By the mid-
1700s, the number of French in North America
was scarcely more than 50,000 souls scattered in
far-flung outposts from Lake Superior to
Newfoundland. These settlements were over-
65 whelmingly male, and, human nature being what
it is, intermarriage with the native population was
the inevitable result.

The British experience included no such need
for interdependence. To be sure, most Anglo
70 colonies weathered a tenuous period soon after
their inception during which they gladly accepted
any aid proffered by the Indians. But wave upon
wave of emigrants bolstered their ranks, and, in
places where disease had ravaged the first settlers,
75 a second, hardier generation grew up to take their
place. While the French settlers included a pre-
ponderance of lone-wolf males who were drawn
to trading furs deep in Indian country, the Anglos
were more likely to arrive in family units, espe-
80 cially in the New England colonies. The result

was a stable, contiguous pattern of settlement that
quickly became self-sustaining.

Where the French developed a symbiotic relationship with the native tribes, the British colonies
85 had little use for them. Land, not pelts, was the
commodity the Anglo emigrants sought in the
New World, and the Indians were their primary
obstacle to taking it. Among the Virginia settlers,
the early years of uneasy coexistence with the
90 natives gave way to a policy of removal and/or
extermination, especially after the Indian uprising
of 1622. The New Englanders were somewhat
more conciliatory and experimented with the creation of "praying towns" to convert the Indians to
95 Christianity. But after the so-called King Philip's
War of 1675–76, the New Englanders, too, seemed
to subscribe to the adage coined two centuries later
that "the only good Indian is a dead Indian."

11. Passage 1 is best described as

(A) a response to a controversial question
(B) a parody of a humorous incident
(C) an explanation of a cultural difference
(D) a condemnation of an unjust situation
(E) an overview of an unfamiliar way of life

GO ON TO THE NEXT PAGE ▷

12. In Passage 1, the phrase "white-man-keeper" in line 31 serves to highlight the author's belief that

(A) the concept of Indian giver was a product of English perceptions
(B) early stereotypes of Native Americans were unfair
(C) English settlers were unlikely to exchange gifts with Native Americans
(D) English settlers were seeking to create a capitalist society
(E) the English were more generous than the Native Americans

13. In Passage 1, use of the phrase "Indian giver" in line 36 differs from the earlier usages in lines 11 and 28 because it refers to

(A) the fact that true gifts should be passed along to others
(B) the English custom of storing gifts in warehouses and museums
(C) the cardinal property of gift giving
(D) the English distaste for exchanging gifts with the Native Americans
(E) the Indian custom of gift giving rather than English perceptions of it

14. In contrast to the English, the Native Americans saw a "gift" as

(A) a possession rather than a trinket
(B) an acknowledgment rather than a sign
(C) a process rather than a thing
(D) an outcome rather than a cause
(E) a symbol rather than an item

15. In line 37, "property" most nearly means

(A) characteristic
(B) location
(C) possession
(D) design
(E) product

16. In Passage 2, the author attempts to

(A) compare two conflicting views
(B) undermine a universal belief
(C) explain a difference in outcomes
(D) revise an outdated theory
(E) form a new hypothesis

17. The author of Passage 2 uses the second sentence of the first paragraph to suggest that the differences in the way that French and British settlers treated the Native Americans were due to

(A) coincidence rather than intention
(B) design rather than expediency
(C) circumstance rather than principle
(D) experience rather than naïvete
(E) avoidance rather than desire

18. The author of Passage 2 cites the fact that the French came "less as colonizers than as traders" (line 57) in order to

(A) account for the nomadic lifestyle of the French settlers
(B) show that the French depended on the Native Americans
(C) highlight the French dependence on the trade in beaver pelts
(D) explain why the French were hostile to the Native Americans
(E) describe the French pattern of settlement in the Great Lakes region

GO ON TO THE NEXT PAGE

19. In line 81, "contiguous" most nearly means

(A) prosperous
(B) rational
(C) continuing
(D) adjacent
(E) amorphous

20. Which of the following best represents each author's approach to examining relations between the Native Americans and the European settlers?

	Passage 1	Passage 2
(A)	organized	moderate
(B)	analytical	detailed
(C)	cautious	controlled
(D)	anecdotal	comparative
(E)	methodical	scholarly

21. The author of Passage 1 might criticize Passage 2 because it

(A) glorifies the French at the expense of the British
(B) overlooks key details about the Virginia colony
(C) condones violence against the Native Americans
(D) places too much blame on the British settlers
(E) omits the point of view of Native Americans

22. Both passages are consistent with the idea that

(A) the British settlers had little understanding of the Native Americans
(B) the removal of the Native Americans from their lands could have been prevented
(C) the British settlers gave better treatment to the Native Americans than did the French
(D) more dialogue would have improved relations between the British and the Native Americans
(E) only a minority of the British settlers mistreated the Native Americans

The Answers

These questions are a bit harder than those in the first set of questions. The two-passage format is more complicated because you need to deal with two authors. Sometimes the two passages are in basic agreement, sometimes they conflict, and sometimes, as in this case, their relationship is harder to define. The only thing for sure is that they present some sort of contrast. Every edition of the old SAT included one set of questions dealing with two passages. It remains to be seen how frequently this format will appear on the new version. **The answers: 11. (C) 12. (A) 13. (E) 14. (C) 15. (A) 16. (C) 17. (C) 18. (B) 19. (D) 20. (D). 21. (E) 22. (A).**

The Explanations

11. Cross-Cultural Communication

This one is typical of Extended Reasoning questions that ask you to show an understanding of the passage beyond the particulars being discussed. The passage is about the English concept of Indian giver and how the English misunderstood the Native American custom. The difference was cultural; the English viewed gifts as private property while the Native Americans shared them. **Answer: (C)**.

12. A Statement Made for Effect

The phrase "white-man-keeper" gets our attention. Many people are familiar with the phrase "Indian giver," a term created by the English settlers that reflects their perception of a Native custom. White-man-keeper would be a logical Native American perspective on English customs, and the phrase carries extra force because most readers will never have considered such a concept. "White-man-keeper" highlights the fact that "Indian giver" reflects English cultural assumptions. **Answer: (A)**.

13. Same Phrase, Different Meaning

This question is tricky because the author's third use of the phrase "Indian giver" conveys a different meaning than the first two. Those in lines 11 and 28 refer to the English perception of the Native American practice. But the author intends the reference in line 36 to connote gift-giving as the Native Americans practiced it. The author's intentions are made clear by a parenthetical reference "(the original ones, at any rate)," which suggests that the Native Americans practiced a true form of gift-giving before their contact with the English. The rest of the paragraph goes on describe this true Indian giving, in contrast to the stereotype of Indian giving created by the English. **Answer: (E)**.

14. The Gift that Keeps on Giving

This question puts the spotlight on Native American gift-giving. The passage makes clear, in lines 43-50, that the giving or receiving of a particular item is not the essence of giving a gift. An item that is given must be of interest, but the essence is the process by which the gift, or a comparable item in its place, continues to be given and received. If the gift doesn't move, it ceases to be a gift. **Answer: (C)**.

15. Understanding Alternate Definitions

Like "recognize" in question 9 in the last section, "property" can have several meanings. "Property" can be a piece of real estate or a possession, but in this case "property" refers to a characteristic of a gift. **Answer: (A).**

16. Seeing the Main Objective

You might be tempted to choose (A) because the passage does describe two sequences of events that may be said to conflict, but it would not be accurate to call them "views." Instead, the author is intent on explaining why the experience of the British differed from that of the French. The British treatment of Native Americans differed from that of the French because their respective colonies developed differently (e.g., the French depended on trade with the Indians while the British did not). The passage shows how these differences led to different outcomes with respect to the Native Americans. **Answer: (C).**

17. Understanding Cause and Effect

The second sentence says that "the difference is due less to any political or moral imperative than to mere expediency." Response (B) includes the word "expediency" but wrongly states that design rather than expediency accounts for the difference. Response (A) is also a plausible choice, but coincidence is not the same thing as expediency. The British found it expedient to treat the Native Americans differently because of differing circumstances. While the French had incentives to interact with and depend upon the Native Americans, the British had none. **Answer: (C).**

18. How Trade Leads to Dependence

The fact that the French came as traders is crucial because it shows their dependence on the Native Americans. The tribes supplied the pelts that were the lifeblood of New France. Response (C) is incorrect because the real issue is not dependence on beaver pelts per se, but dependence on the tribes. In turn, this dependence caused the French to interact differently with the Native Americans. **Answer: (B).**

19. More Vocabulary in Context

This one is another straightforward vocab problem. Do you know what "contiguous" means? We try to trick you by playing on words with incorrect meanings that might seem logical. The settlements are stable and self-sustaining, so we give you "prosperous" and "rational." "Amorphous" sounds a bit like "contiguous" so we throw it in. But "contiguous" means "adjacent" or "touching." **Answer: (D).**

20. A Funky-Looking Pair Problem

Problems like this have appeared occasionally through the years, so we thought we should throw one in. Passage 1 is built around a single anecdote, the story of the pipe that is offered as a gift. Passage 2 compares the experience of the British with that of the French to explain differing interactions with the Native Americans. **Answer: (D).**

21. What the Authors Would Think

Some questions, typically near the end of a section, may ask you to infer what one author might think of another author's point of view. A major preoccupation of the author of Passage 1 is to describe how the English failed to see things from the Native American perspective. The second passage, however, does not include any mention of the native perspective. It is reasonable to infer that the author of Passage 1 might take exception to this fact. You might be tempted to choose (C), but the second passage does not condone the treatment of the Native Americans even if it does describe it in a matter-of-fact way. **Answer: (E).**

22. The trick to this question is to understand the meaning of "consistent with the idea." It does not mean that both passages must explicitly endorse the idea, but rather that they must merely be compatible with the idea. If you're stuck, try the process of elimination. Passage 2 seems to contradict response (B); Passage 2 states that the main objective of the British settlers, who came in overwhelming numbers, was to take land. The British did not treat the Native Americans better than the French treated them, and there is nothing in either passage to indicate that more dialogue between the sides would have changed anything. Neither passage suggests that only a minority of British settlers mistreated the Native Americans. However, both passages support the idea that the British settlers had little understanding of, and little incentive to understand, the Native Americans. **Answer: (A).**

Paragraph-Length Passages

Paragraph-Length Critical Reading is the only variety of passage that was new to the SAT in 2005. Every version of the SAT includes four paragraph-length passages, each about one hundred words long. These passages are typically paired, with one pair consisting of two passages on unrelated topics, and the other pair consisting of passages that address the same topic. Each of the unrelated passages is followed by two questions; the two passages that address the same topic are typically followed by four or five questions. Two examples follow.

"I paid for the [prep] course but I only went once. Instead, I used the practice books they gave me the first day.... If you are able to figure out the problem by reading the explanations in the back of the book, then the three hours every Sunday is useless.... They tried to teach us how the test-maker thinks. However, you can go to a bookstore and get the same advice."

—750 V, 700 M

Directions: Each passage below is followed by questions based on its content. Answer the questions on the basis of what is <u>stated</u> or <u>implied</u> in each passage and in any introductory material that may be provided.

Before 1900, ambient light was a non-issue. When our ancestors gazed at the heavens, they saw a profusion of bright stars and planets, as well as the
Line chalky outline of the Milky Way. Meteoroids
5 streaked across the sky on a regular basis, and the constellations fired the imagination of everyone from poets and philosophers to common folk. Today's urbanite knows little of the allure that the night sky once held. The phrase "catch a falling
10 star" has limited meaning for today's city dwellers; many have never even seen one.

1. From the passage, it is possible to infer that the "ambient light" described in line 1 is produced by

(A) bright stars and planets
(B) city lights
(C) meteoroids
(D) the Milky Way
(E) an extraterrestrial source

2. The passage implies that

(A) modern people are less interested in the night sky than were their ancestors
(B) meteoroids are less frequent today than in past centuries
(C) the phrase "catch a falling star" is not familiar to today's city dwellers
(D) ambient light has changed the look of the night sky
(E) the brightest stars and planets are in the Milky Way

History isn't usually the class that sends students bounding out of bed in the morning eager for another day of school. When Hollywood
Line wants to conjure the image of boredom at school,
5 history is the course that is chosen. And why not? History teachers everywhere have bought into the idea that they must cover all there is to know about any given era. As a result, they cram in as many facts as possible, and students spend their
10 time memorizing rather than thinking.

3. The rhetorical question "And why not?" (line 5) primarily serves to emphasize that

(A) most students do not work hard in history class
(B) history is a logical subject to illustrate boredom at school
(C) Hollywood ought to be more truthful in its portrayals of history
(D) many history teachers need to improve how they teach
(E) there is no good reason why history class should be boring

4. It may be inferred from the passage that the author believes that

(A) facts are not important to the study of history
(B) Hollywood should stop making fun of history classes
(C) history is inevitably a boring subject
(D) history teachers of past generations were more effective
(E) history classes should cover fewer facts

The Answers

1. (B) 2. (D) 3. (B) 4. (E)

The Explanations

1. What Is Ambient Light?

If you don't know what "ambient" ("enveloping") means, the most important clue for this question occurs in the references to urbanites and city dwellers in the last two sentences. Nighttime ambient light—that which is given off by man-made sources and dims the night sky—is much more prevalent in cities. The fact that ambient light was not an issue before 1900 is because electric lights (first invented in 1879) were not prevalent outdoors at night before that time. **Answer: (B).**

2. The Author's Main Point

The author uses the discussion of stars, planets, the Milky Way, and falling stars to illustrate how people today, especially those in cities, have a diminished ability to see the night sky. Response (C) may seem like a plausible choice, but the idea that "catch a falling star" has limited meaning to city dwellers does not necessarily imply that they are unfamiliar with the phrase. **Answer: (D).**

3. What Is a Rhetorical Question?

It is a device that accentuates emphasis. "And why not?" validates Hollywood's choice of history class to illustrate boredom by suggesting that there are no logical objections to doing so. **Answer: (B).**

4. What the Author Believes

The author is attacking the way that history is taught. The author suggests that history classes are boring because teachers have bought into the idea that they must cover all there is to know about any given era and therefore cram in as many facts as possible. This is not the same thing as suggesting that facts are not important. Rather, the passage simply implies that fewer facts should be covered. The idea that many students are bored by history class is consistent with the passage, but the author implies that more students would like history if it were taught better. **Answer: (E).**

Honing Your Strategy

We suggest that you develop a unique style for Passage-Based Reading. You may develop one approach for the long passages and a different style for the short ones, or you may approach both types the same way. Here are your options:

1. Read the passage and then answer the questions. Most people's first impulse is to do the straightforward thing and read the passage. Often, this is the *wrong* approach—especially on the long passages. Reading an 800-word passage end to end will give you an interesting (or not-so-interesting) taste of a subject, but the questions will deal with only a fraction of this information. "Never read the whole thing thoroughly—you'll be too pressed for time," declares a student who scored 680 V, 740 M. "Read the questions first and then look for the answers. Carefully reading the complete passage is a waste of time," says a Davidson-bound student with 680 V, 730 M. In a typical 800-word passage, one of the questions applies directly to less than half the lines. Vocabulary-in-Context and Literal Comprehension questions can be answered by going directly to the lines that are referenced. Extended Reasoning questions can be answered by reading strategic parts of the passage.

Students who should consider reading the longer passages in their entirety include those who are speedy readers and those whose train of thought will be disrupted by not reading everything. One 710 V scorer poured cold water on skimming. "My advice is to slow down and focus on the story," he says. We are more inclined to support this strategy on the

A KEY TO READING COMPREHENSION

"Reading comprehension questions have answers that are meant to confuse you," says a particularly insightful 790 Verbal scorer. "If you're trying to decide between two interpretations of a passage in your mind, it's quite likely that there will be answer choices that match each interpretation in every question. I would recommend that you don't let your personal opinions get in the way. Try to become the author and use his or her point of view."

shorter passages, where the potential drawbacks of reading the whole passage are much smaller. See what you think.

2. Skim the passage or read only part of it, then tackle the questions. This method will be most useful for the long passages. "A trick that works for me is reading the first and last paragraphs as well as the first sentence of each paragraph in between," says a 750 V, 720 M scorer. Another possibility is to read until you understand the writer's point of view and then skim the rest. We recommend that you experiment with the balance between reading, skimming, and skipping. If you feel yourself constantly referring back to the passage, you may need to read more thoroughly. One trick: If you find yourself getting interested in the passage, that may be a signal that you understand the basic idea and should skip farther down. Strange as it may sound, getting interested in the passage may distract you from your real goal, which is answering the questions.

> "I taught myself the hard questions. It really does help, even though it feels wrong after taking too many tests in school where I *had* to answer every question."
>
> —770 V, 680 M

3. Start by reading or skimming the questions, then read the passage, then answer the questions. There was a lively debate among our survey respondents as to whether reading the questions before the passage was helpful. "Reading the questions before the passage helps you read for what you need," says a 740 V, 710 M scorer. A Brown admit who scored 770 V, 750 M advises that reading the questions first is "really helpful when the selection is boring." A Princeton-bound student with 720 V, 670 M advises that after first reading the questions, students should read the passage, formulate answers to the questions as they read, and then compare their responses to the answers. Says a student who scored 640 V, 680 M, "The strategy I used was to read the questions and circle key words to look for, then go back and read the passage."

"I never read the questions before the passage because it breaks my concentration and prevents me from getting a full understanding of the passage," writes a student who scored 800 V, 720 M. A Princeton admit who scored 730 V, 770 M believes that reading the questions first "interrupts your understanding of the passage as a whole when you are watching out for specific information." A third student who scored 610 V, 690 M eschewed reading the questions first because he forgot them by the time he was into the passage.

MARKING THE PASSAGE

Most students are not in the habit of writing in their books. In school, students are often required to hand in their textbooks at the end of the year. Marking them up is a no-no. Not so for your SAT test booklet. We strongly recommend that you write in it. Make your pencil an extension of your brain and write as you go. You'll see your thoughts on paper—a boon for visual learners—and your ideas will still be on the page twenty minutes later if you skip the problem and come back. Using the booklet for math computations is a no-brainer, but writing there can also pay dividends in Reading Comprehension. Testifies one student who scored 730 V, 690 M, "The passages are so dry, dull, and uninteresting that it is easy to lose concentration. I had to force myself to stay concentrated by underlining parts of the passage that seemed important, and by so doing, I had a brief summary of the passage underlined."

If you do decide to read the questions first, are you going to "glance" at them, or are you going to read them thoroughly? A glance may only give you a hint of what is to come but will take less time. We recommend that you experiment with reading the questions quickly, and then more thoroughly, and see which works best for you. If you do the latter, you'll definitely want to mark the passage at the spots addressed by the questions. Some students, after marking the passage, may then choose to read only the lines they have marked while answering the questions, though this method will leave a few Extended Reasoning questions that must then be dealt with.

4. Start with the questions, then glance over to the passage and mark it at the spots that are addressed by particular questions. Then read the passage until those spots and answer each question before moving on in the passage. This method may work for students who have difficulty remembering the passage when they answer the questions. By going directly to the questions immediately after reading the relevant material, students can take the questions one at a time and then keep reading. This method may require students to skip questions that do not reference a particular line or lines. The downside is that students must jump back and forth between the passage and the questions.

5. Answer the questions without having first read the passage. Use the questions to guide your reading. For all students, this method is worth trying on the short passages. With only about ten lines to read, some students will find this an efficient way to pick out the answer. On the longer passages, a totally question-based approach may be helpful for slow readers or for those who have had difficulty with these kinds of questions. "I would suggest not reading the passage through, but looking for the context of the questions. By the end, you'll have read most if not all of it," advises one student who got a 750 Verbal but said she struggled with reading comprehension. "Most of the time, you don't need to read the passage to answer the questions," chirps another student who scored 610 V, 680 M. "I'm a slow reader. I just tried to answer as many questions as I could without reading the passage," says a student who managed a 690 V using this approach. The primary flaw in this method is that it gives students little basis for answering the Extended Reasoning questions that deal with the main themes of the passage. Students who generally run short of time in the Reading-Based Passages may use this method to guarantee themselves a good shot at getting the questions that focus on particular lines in the passage.

Each of the five approaches has its advantages, and we recommend that you try at least several of them as a way of figuring out which one best suits your learning style.

Finding the Point of View

It is easy to figure out someone's point of view when you know the person. Take your mom, for instance. You know she'll be angling for you to go to bed earlier, do your homework sooner, and clean your room now. No surprise there. You've lived with her seventeen years, you know her point of view, and you can guess what she is going to say about ten seconds before she opens her mouth.

The trick to the Passage-Based Reading is to figure out the point of view of someone you don't know—after only a few hundred words on a printed page. Nothing is more important than mastering this skill.

Weak readers read everything as if it were an encyclopedia entry. They may understand the words on the page, but they don't hear the author's voice. Who is the writer and why did he or she write the passage? What beliefs or assumptions underlie the passage? Who are the writer's allies? Adversaries? What idea(s) is the writer defending? Attacking? Most passages won't spell out the answers to questions like these, but savvy readers will find plenty of evidence.

In highlighting point of view, we include two additional concepts that are separate but closely related: tone and main idea. Tone is how the writer expresses himself: emotional, restrained, sarcastic, matter-of-fact, unequivocal, and circumspect are all examples of tone. And main idea? We won't insult your intelligence with an explanation of that, but suffice it to say that the main idea flows out of the writer's point of view.

Keys to Success

1. Don't overlook the introduction. Each long passage is preceded by one to five sentences of italicized text. Many students simply breeze past this material, but it can include crucial details. One student, who scored 620 V, 710 M, reports that she read the introduction and glanced immediately to the questions to see if she could answer any of them before proceeding to the passage itself. The introduction is especially important in paired passage questions because it will help you establish a relationship between the passages.

2. Practice, practice, practice. Only repetition will teach you the best way to approach Reading-Based Passages. It doesn't matter which strategy you choose—as long as you find one that is right for you. "Reading comprehension requires focus to be able to get through efficiently and effectively, and

IS IT POSSIBLE TO THINK TOO MUCH?

Many students think so. "Focus on the concrete," says a student who scored 710 V, 650 M. Adds a second, "I tend to overanalyze and so I can create links between any words and find multiple answers to every question. Don't read too in-depth in the passage—read it at a surface level." This student has a nifty 750 V to back up her advice.

focus will only come with practice," says a student who scored 710 V, 750 M. If you're uncertain how to approach the passages, our recommendation is to read until you get the point of view, then to skim the rest and to move to the questions. Whether you should read the questions before the passage depends on whether doing so breaks your concentration, and whether you can remember enough while reading the passage to do you any good. If you do decide to read the questions first, be sure to experiment with marking the passage.

3. Find answers that match the tone of the passage. If the passage about F. Scott Fitzgerald is written in high-minded academic prose, don't choose (C) Gatsby was a scumbag. The answer is much more likely to be (D) Gatsby was emblematic of a moral crisis in the America of the 1920s. Stay away from answers that use less specific language in favor of those that express ideas with precision.

4. Do the paired passages one at a time. In other words, read the first passage and/or do the questions related to it; then, read the second passage and/or do the questions related to it; and lastly, do the questions relevant to both passages. Reading both passages before answering any questions would likely cause confusion and back-tracking. By finishing your work on questions relevant only to the first passage before moving on to those about the second, you will make yourself better prepared to understand the second passage.

5. Remember that the answer may not be in the line referenced in the question. Suppose a question informs you that line 14 is the place where the author refers to "a dark shadow on my heart." If the question asks what this dark shadow might symbolize, you may not learn until line 19 whether the phrase is a reference to the death of her only child or a remembrance of her much-lamented pet guinea pig. If you use the questions to locate relevant lines in the passage, be prepared to read a little before and a little after the line number(s) quoted in the question.

6. When in doubt, focus tightly on the meaning of the passage. Even the best students get stuck on questions where more than one response seems right. Often, students delve beyond the obvious meaning of the passage or second-guess obvious answers. "I would recommend not reading too much into the questions and making sure you understand what the question is asking," writes a 1600 scorer bound for Princeton. Adds an 800 V, 770 M scorer, "Don't think so deeply—the test writer probably didn't." Keep in mind that, as the College Board itself says, answers to Reading Comprehension questions can be both true and wrong. The correct response is not necessarily the one that reflects circumstances in the outside world, but rather the one that expresses the appropriate response to the passage.

7. Experiment with doing the passages before the Sentence Completion problems. We could go either way on this one. We suspect that many students will get confidence from knocking off the Sentence Completion problems first. But some white-knuckle readers may want to go straight to the reading passages and then loop back to the Sentence Completion problems. Try it both ways and see what works for you.

8. Stay calm. The strategy that makes you feel the most relaxed is the one you should use. If it is any consolation, even the highest scorers get confused and frustrated by some of the Passage-Based Reading questions. Complains a 760 V scorer, "Questions such as 'What is the best title for this story?' are particularly frustrating; this is a matter of personal opinion.... It doesn't make sense that there is just one correct answer." Alas, making sense is not always the number one priority of the folks who make the SAT. A 700 V scorer swears that "it often seems like there are two right answers." Adds this student, "Sometimes being lucky is the best option."

> "Kaplan I would not recommend. What was taught in the classroom was the exact same thing printed in the Kaplan book I bought from the bookstore."
>
> —740 V, 690 M

MATH

6

TOTAL TESTING TIME: 70 MINUTES

SECTIONS:

✔ **2 of 25 minutes**

✔ **1 of 20 minutes**

QUESTION TYPES:

✔ **Standard Multiple Choice**

✔ **Student-Produced Response ("Grid-Ins")**

Since its revision in 2005, the SAT Math section has featured one addition and one subtraction. Topics normally taught in Algebra II have been added, and quantitative comparison questions have been subtracted. But the biggest change is that math now comprises only one-third of your SAT score instead of one-half. Poets, rejoice. Engineers, gnash your teeth.

Here's the good news about the Math SAT: It's easier than the Critical Reading. At least it was for the Class of 2003—which had an average score of 507 on what was then called the Verbal section, but scored a robust 519 on the Math. Average Math scores have gone up 16 points in the past decade, apparently because students are taking more demanding math courses. That leads to more good news: Most people agree that preparation often has a bigger impact in Math than in Critical Reading. Nobody can predict which vocabulary words may pop up in Critical Reading, but the math problems stay reasonably consistent from test to test.

That said, we'll wager that not many of you are aiming for a 519, or for that matter a 520, as your math score. Getting a 620 or 720 may take some doing, especially because students often have trouble finishing the Math section. Throw in all those nasty ETS tricks—especially near the end of each section—and the Math SAT can become a stress-inducing, teeth-grinding, have-an-accident-in-your-pants kind of experience. And that's on a good day.

We got an ear-full about it on our surveys. "My biggest enemy was the clock. I never finished any of the math sections," complains one student who nevertheless was able to eke out a 690. A 710 scorer bemoans the fact that he was "pressed for time" and therefore "skipped over vital information." Adds a 730 V, 720 M scorer with rare eloquence: "It sucks to miss a question because you are going too fast and say 2 + 3 = 6." Along with the complaints about time pressure came strong frustration that low-level math could be so difficult. "I take really high math [multi-variable calculus] and I still can't get an 800 on the math," fumes a second student who scored 690. This student and many others railed about questions that were misinterpreted, tricks that made them miss an otherwise easy problem, and simple bonehead mistakes. With high-scorers like these in such a lather, imagine how average students feel.

> "It sucks to miss a question because you are going too fast and say 2 + 3 = 6."
>
> —730 V, 720 M

It's Not about the Math

The fact that you may have gotten good grades in Algebra II and Geometry is a feather in your cap, but it doesn't guarantee that you'll get the score you want on the SAT Math. Relevant math skills are necessary but they're only part of the equation. Imagine if everybody who earned an A in ninth and tenth grade math courses were to get, say, a 700. The bell curve would be busted and ETS would have to go back to the drawing board. But that's exactly what would happen if the test were simply an assessment of geometry and algebra skills.

A sad irony about the SAT—and particularly the math—is that many students believe they have done extremely well immediately after taking the test, only to be disappointed later. This pattern, repeated over and over at high schools throughout the nation, is more proof that the math on the SAT Math is not the issue. When students do not understand a problem, they know their answer is wrong. On the SAT Math, students generally know how to do the problems and believe they have gotten them right, never suspecting that they have fallen for a well-disguised distracter.

But that is how the game is played. To create its desired mix of high scorers, low scorers, and medium scorers, ETS juices up many of the questions with unexpected twists and turns. Some have complicated directions intended to sow confusion; others steer students toward seemingly obvious answers that are wrong; still others add a final step to the calculations that many students forget to do. The ability to spot these head-fakes is what ETS and the College Board refer to as "math reasoning"—and what separates average scorers from high scorers. After laying its traps, the test-makers add insult to injury by "speeding" the Math Section to make sure that some students do not have time to finish and others can do so only by rushing—thereby falling into the aforementioned traps.

As you begin your preparation, remember the principles of SAT-taking we discussed in Chapter 3. Here is a reminder of the two biggies:

- Take timed practice tests. Have we mentioned that practice tests are important? The best way to build test-taking savvy is to get tricked a few times. Are you missing questions because of math concepts or because of the ETS two-step? Practice tests will show where your vulnerabilities are.
- Fine-tune your speed. Your goal should be to move as fast as you can without losing accuracy. Finish a 25-minute section in 20 minutes and see how you do. Experiment with various skipping strategies. Discover how speed can help you relax by taking the pressure off.

As with Critical Reading, it may be necessary to unlearn some strategies your teachers have taught you. For instance, many math teachers require students to show their work and take off points if students skip steps. But the

SAT test-makers are not interested in process—only the correct answer. It is absolutely crucial that you skip steps on the SAT to get the answer quickly, and you should write down only what helps you solve a problem. Are you one of those organized, meticulous students who prints every step in immaculate detail? If so, you may need lots of practice in forcing yourself to move faster, skip steps, and eyeball problems to figure out approximate answers.

Inside the Bag of Tricks

The following is an overview of the most common ways that the test-makers jerk your chain. The questions may seem easy in this context, but imagine encountering them in the middle of a headlong chase to finish the test before time is called.

Information Overload

Are you the kind of person who can remember a phone number without writing it down? Or are you the kind who forgets it while fumbling for a pen? The answer may mean a lot on the SAT. With its word problems full of zigzags and double-talk, the SAT puts enormous emphasis on what psychologists call "short-term working memory." Though the computations behind the problems may be easy, the written scenarios are often confusing. Here is an example:

A bread basket contains biscuits and muffins. There are half as many biscuits as muffins. The muffins are either blueberry or raisin, and three times as many muffins are blueberry as are raisin. If one piece of bread is to be drawn at random from the bread basket, what is the probability that the piece drawn will be a raisin muffin?

(A) $\frac{1}{12}$

(B) $\frac{1}{6}$

(C) $\frac{1}{4}$

(D) $\frac{2}{6}$

(E) $\frac{2}{3}$

Answer: (B). If you know a little probability, you can do the numbers easily: $\frac{2}{3} \times \frac{1}{4} = \frac{2}{12} = \frac{1}{6}$. The hard part is getting your brain around how to set it up. Because the problem does not reveal until the end what you are looking for—the probability of getting a raisin muffin—you'll need to read it at least twice. You'll need to translate "half" and "three times" to fractions, all the while keeping straight muffins vs. biscuits and blueberry muffins vs. raisin muffins. Half as many biscuits as muffins means that two of every three pieces of bread ($\frac{2}{3}$) are muffins. Three times as many blueberry muffins as raisin muffins means that one out of every four muffins ($\frac{1}{4}$) are raisin. The pro portion of bread that is muffins times the proportion of muffins that is raisin yields the probability that the piece selected will be both muffin and raisin. Hence, $\frac{2}{3} \times \frac{1}{4} = \frac{2}{12} = \frac{1}{6}$. The calculation is easy—not-so-easy are the reading, inference, and short-term memory to keep it all straight.

$\blacklozenge \blacklozenge \blacklozenge$

Tricky Sequences

The following is a simplified version of a time-honored SAT sucker punch. A Dartmouth professor we know calls this "the fence-post problem:"

> A farmer wants to build a fence that is 100 feet long using posts that are 10 feet apart. How many posts will the farmer need to complete the fence?
>
> (A) 9
> (B) 10
> (C) 11
> (D) 12
> (E)100

Did you say 10? That's the answer ETS and College Board want you to get, but the real answer is (C) 11. (You need 11 posts because one will go at the beginning of the fence and one at the end.) Even if you got it right in this example, would you get a question like this if it were buried midway through a 3 hour and 45 minute test with a little camouflage? Let's try a slightly harder variation on the theme:

The first number of a sequence is 4 and every number after the first is 4 more than the number immediately preceding it. What is the value of the 50th number?

(A) 196
(B) 200
(C) 202
(D) 204
(E) 208

Shame on anyone who chose 204. The sequence starts with four—just as if the counting by 4s had begun from 0—and the 50th term is 200. Answer: (B). Is the ability to get questions like this really "reasoning"? Or is it simply the ability to spot a dirty trick? Your opinion may depend on whether you got the question right.

Less-Than and Greater-Than Gamesmanship

Though this concept is easy, the test-makers like to engender confusion with less-than and greater-than. Consider the following:

What is the least possible integer for which 60 percent of that integer is greater than 6?

(A) 8
(B) 9
(C) 10
(D) 11
(E) 12

There are two possible screw-ups here. First, you could forget the fact that you are doing a less-than/greater-than problem and chose 10, the number that 60 percent of which is 6. You might also mess up by choosing 9, which is the greatest possible integer that 60 percent of which is less than 6. The tricky part is that the question begins with the phrase "least possible," yet the answer, 11, must be greater than the number (10) that 60 percent of which is 6. The test-makers know that when students are in a hurry, they tend to miss information in the second or third sentence of a question as they rush to answer it. By changing the focus from "least possible" to "greater than," they transform a relatively easy question into a relatively hard one.

◆ ◆ ◆

When the Solution Isn't the Answer

Some questions will ask for a solution that can only be found by computing the value of something else. There is no great secret to these except that sometimes students do the initial calculation and forget that they must perform one (or two) more operations before getting their answer.

For instance:

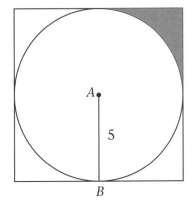

In the figure above, *AB* is the radius of the circle. What is the area of the shaded region?

(A) $100 - 25\pi$

(B) $25\pi - 100$

(C) $25 - \dfrac{25\pi}{4}$

(D) $5 - 20\pi$

(E) $25 - \dfrac{50\pi}{4}$

There's no way to figure out the area of the shaded region directly, but you can figure out the area of the non-shaped region and subtract. Since the radius of the circle is 5, you know that the area of the circle is 25π. Subtract that from the area of the square, 100, to get $100 - 25\pi$, the area of the four regions inside the square but outside the circle. But don't forget the last step. You must divide by four to get the area of the shaded region Answer: (C). There are harder variations of this kind of problem, but you'll get them so long as you remember what you're solving for.

The Deceptively Easy Problem

The test-makers love to stick these in at the end of sections to throw you for a loop. Check this out:

Points A and B are on line ℓ in the figure above. How many different points on line ℓ are half as far from Point A as from Point B?

(A) 4
(B) 3
(C) 2
(D) 1
(E) None

The answer is (C): 2. This problem rests on a paradox. Though there is only one point on line ℓ that is an equal distance from points A and B, there are two points that are half as far from A as from B. Most students will look to the left of point A for a point that is half the distance from A as it is from B, forgetting that there is a second point between A and B that is also half as far from A. This problem is a classic example of an end-of-the-section trick.

This Can't Be Right

The test-makers love to play on your insecurities. On a multistep problem, it is always unnerving to get to the second-to-last step and see a bizarre value. That's what they count on to mess you up. Like the following problem:

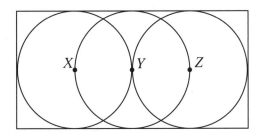

In the figure above, points X, Y, and Z are the centers of the three circles. If each circle has an area of 50, what is the area of the rectangle?

(A) $\dfrac{50}{\pi}$

(B) $50 - \dfrac{8}{\pi}$

(C) 50

(D) $\dfrac{200}{\pi}$

(E) $\dfrac{400}{\pi}$

In order to get this problem, you need to solve the formula for the area of a circle, πr^2, backwards to get the radius of the circle. You know that the base of the rectangle is $4r$ and the height is $2r$. But solving $50 = \pi r^2$ for r gives you a nasty $r = \sqrt{\dfrac{50}{\pi}}$ —not the sort of value you are expecting, especially since there are no square roots in the answer choices. The test-makers hope you will bail out here and try another approach. But stick to your guns. By multiplying the base × height, you get rid of the radicals $4\sqrt{\dfrac{50}{\pi}} \times 2\sqrt{\dfrac{50}{\pi}}$ and your answer is (E) $\dfrac{400}{\pi}$.

◆ ◆ ◆

Optical Illusions

When you're moving fast, your eye tends to slide over crucial information. See if you can get this little stinker:

If $m = \frac{1}{a}$ and $n = \frac{1}{b}$ and if $a = 5$ and $b = 6$, what is the value of $\frac{1}{m} \times \frac{1}{n}$?

(A) $\frac{1}{30}$

(B) $\frac{1}{6}$

(C) $\frac{1}{5}$

(D) 6

(E) 30

Answer: (E) 30. This problem rates at medium difficulty, though probably 95 percent of the students who take the test know how to get it. The tough part is the confused wording. Since m and n are defined in terms of a and b, the most logical wording for this question would be, "If $a = 5$ and $b = 6$ and $m = \frac{1}{a}$ and $n = \frac{1}{b}$, what is the value of $\frac{1}{m} \times \frac{1}{n}$?" But instead, the question defines m and n first, then a and b, and then doubles back to asking "what is the value of $\frac{1}{m} \times \frac{1}{n}$?" The obvious mistake, which many students will make, is to choose the answer that is equal to $\frac{1}{a} \times \frac{1}{b}$. Not coincidentally, that answer choice is (A)—the first one on the list. While distracters don't always appear in the (A) slot, they are particularly effective there because a student may move on without examining the other answers.

KNOCKING OFF THE RUST

Confidence is good on the SAT Math, but overconfidence can be a killer. That's why even math whiz kids may need a refresher on basic algebra and geometry. "I am in AP Calculus this year and I guess I just took knowing algebra for granted," says a student who was disappointed not to get his math score above 690. "I should have spent more time reviewing some of the algebra and geometry concepts I haven't had to deal with in a few years," moans a 640 M scorer. How do you find out if you're in the same boat? Take some practice tests and see what you miss.

Playing with Percentages

This one is the toughest problem of the bunch. It uses percentages, a topic from middle school math, but the challenge comes in the way the question is formulated:

> A car dealership normally charges $18,000 for a certain type of car. This price is 20 percent more than the amount it costs the dealership to get the car from the factory. At a clearance sale, the dealership decides to sell all cars for 20 percent less than its cost from the factory. How much does this type of car cost at the clearance sale?
>
> (A) $9,680
> (B) $11,340
> (C) $11,680
> (D) $12,000
> (E) $15,000

Did you say (C) $11,680? Oops. If you said (D) $12,000, bravo! This is a hard one, and it hinges on the fact that $18,000 is 20 percent more than another number. Therefore, you can't take 20 percent of $18,000—which most students do—but rather you must figure out what number plus 20 percent of itself equals $18,000. Hmm. You know you're looking for a round number. $16,000? That's $2,000 less than $18,000, but you know immediately that $2,000 is 20 percent of $10,000. Gotta be lower. How about...$15,000? Bingo. Twenty percent of 15 is 3 and 20 percent of $15,000 is $3,000. Subtract another 20 percent and your answer is $12,000.

Don't feel bad if you missed this one—many students will miss it.

When the Test-Makers Invent a Symbol

Talk about weird. Sometimes ETS goes off the deep end and says something like this: Let][be defined by A][B = BA^2. Every time you see an expression like 7][3, you know to translate it to 3(7^2). That in itself is not hard, but generally there is a second or third wrinkle to the problem that makes everything run together. Since you're dealing with a new concept, these are particularly brutal on short term memory. An example:

Let $W*X*Y*Z$ be defined for all numbers W, X, Y, and Z by $W*X*Y*Z = WY - XZ$. If $A = 5*3*4*2$, what is the value of $A*7*2*4$?

(A) −8
(B) 0
(C) 4
(D) 8
(E) 20

The answer to this question of medium difficulty is (B) 0. The only challenge is keeping the numbers straight in your head. By the formula $W*X*Y*Z$, $A = (5 \times 4) - (3 \times 2) = 14$. In turn, $14*7*2*4 = (14 \times 2) - (7 \times 4) = 0$. If this problem gives you trouble, you may have some issues with short-term memory. Even if you didn't have any trouble with the problem just now, you're more likely to space out and lose your train of thought under time pressure.

Taking the Pressure Off

Small wonder that so many downtrodden souls feel used and abused by the Math SAT. We'll wager that most readers know all the necessary formulas to solve the preceding questions. The traps are sneaky, but time pressure is what makes them work. If you're stressed, you'll get tricked. Relax and you won't be. Easier said than done? Sure. But there is one reliable way to take the pressure off: Move quickly so that you are not fighting the clock. We're not talking about a headlong scramble, but rather about developing strategies that allow you to move quickly while staying under control. The following strategies will help:

> "The most difficult part of the math section was knowing how to go about doing the problems. The actual computation was simple algebra and geometry."
>
> —800 V, 800 M

Eyeball and Estimate

Every good SAT-taker knows that half the time, you don't need to do any real calculations in order to get the right answer. By using round numbers, you can often estimate the answer in your head and then scan your choices for the right one. For example:

A chain of department stores must reduce its inventory of shirts, which totals 7,200. For a three-day period, the chain will offer a deep discount on all its shirts with the goal of selling between 15% and 16% of its shirts. Which of the following is a number of shirts that the chain could sell to satisfy that goal?

(A) 1,026
(B) 1,086
(C) 1,221
(D) 1,411
(E) 1,662

This question should take ten to twenty seconds. At a glance you know that 10% of 7,200 is 720. Add half of 720, or 360, to get 15% of 7,200. That number is 1,080 and the answer is (B) 1,086—the response that is closest to 1,080 while still being greater.

Another example:

Suppose that a jogger runs from her home to a park at a pace of 8 miles per hour, and then immediately returns home along the same route at a pace of 7 miles per hour. If the total time she spent was 1 hour, how many minutes did it take her to jog from her house to the park?

(A) 34
(B) 30
(C) 28
(D) 24
(E) 20

This one can be solved as a ratio and proportion problem but you should only need a few seconds to get it by eyeballing and estimating. Look at the answers. Since the jogger was going faster on her way to the park than she was on the way home, (A) and (B) are obviously wrong. You know you're looking for a number less than 30 but not a lot less. Response (D) 24 would mean that it took her 36 minutes on the way back. Common sense says that a one-eighth decrease in speed won't lead to a 50% increase in the amount of time needed to cover the distance. The answer must be closer to 30 minutes and therefore it is (C) 28. (If you're good, you realized that the ratio of time spent on the two distances, 32 minutes and 28 minutes, would be the same as the ratio of the speeds at which they were covered, 8 miles per hour and 7 miles per hour.)

◆ ◆ ◆

Plug In the Answers

Sometimes, the quickest way to answer a problem is not to try to solve it in the conventional way. With all the answers staring you in the face, an alternative is to plug them into the question and see which one works. Also called working backwards, plugging in should be a core strategy for just about everyone. Some problems are particularly suited to plugging in, such as the following:

> If y and z are different positive integers and $11y + 12z = 237$, what is the greatest possible value of z?
>
> (A) 11
> (B) 15
> (C) 17
> (D) 19
> (E) 21

There is more than one way to solve this problem, but here is ours: You're looking for the greatest possible value of z that fits the equation, so multiply the answer choices by 12, moving from largest to smallest. Your goal is to find the largest one that produces a product with 12 that, when subtracted from 237, yields a sum divisible by 11. You can see immediately that 21 can't be right because $12 \times 21 = 252$. Next, try $12 \times 19 = 228$. That's 9 less than 237—obviously can't be right. Next: $12 \times 17 = 204$. $237 - 204 = 33$. Divisible by 11? Yes—problem solved. Answer: (C). Some readers can probably see a few more shortcuts to getting this answer—the thought process moves faster than we can write it.

One final tip: If a problem has you stumped, go to the answers and plug in the middle value and see if you can solve it. Even if this answer does not prove to be the right one, you may be able to tell whether the correct answer is greater or less than the middle value, and thereby narrow the list of possible answers to two.

◆ ◆ ◆

Draw Pictures

On a test that puts enormous pressure on your short-term memory, jotted notes and drawings can be a big help. Drawing as you read takes only a few seconds, and you may be surprised at how much time you will save by not having to reread or double-check your facts. (Heed the immortal words of Mark Twain: "Slow down, I'm in a hurry.") Be as free as possible with your pencil, using your test book as your scratch paper. If drawing does not come naturally to you, take a practice test and force yourself to do so.

There are certain situations when drawing is crucial. Geometry problems are an obvious example. The test-makers will often draw pictures to go with problems, but sometimes they don't. So hear this: On any geometry problem without a picture, be sure to draw one yourself. The fact that there is no picture may be a sign of some hanky-panky that a picture will clearly expose.

Let's try an experiment. Answer the following question without a diagram:

> Four lines in the same plane intersect at point T. These lines form equal, non-overlapping angles. What is the measure of the angles?
>
> (A) 45°
> (B) 60°
> (C) 90°
> (D) 120°
> (E) 140°

Without a diagram, your answer is probably 90 degrees. Now draw a point with four lines running through it. See your mistake? Four lines make 8 angles. Answer: (A) 45°.

Diagrams can also help on information overload questions:

> The members of a certain health club have a choice of swimming or lifting weights. 54 of the members use the swimming pool and 47 members lift weights. If 13 of the members who use the swimming pool also lift weights, how many people are members of the health club?
>
> (A) 78
> (B) 88
> (C) 101
> (D) 113
> (E) 114

The only potential issue with this moderately easy problem is keeping the information straight. You might quickly jot a diagram to help you visualize the three categories of members and how they overlap. Answer: (B) 88.

Grinning through the Grid-ins

Though the majority of questions on the SAT Math are multiple-choice, some are not. The Grid-ins were created in 1994 to give hapless students even more to lose sleep over. ETS was already an expert trickster before Grid-ins were invented, but there was one problem. Though students might be fooled into computing a wrong answer, they could be saved from getting the problem wrong if their incorrect response did not appear in the answer choices. And even if it did, students sometimes realized their mistake upon seeing the correct answer in the list of possible responses.

The Grid-ins are nasty because you can get the wrong answer and never have a clue. Fortunately, Grid-ins comprise only a relatively small percent of the math questions on the SAT. The questions themselves look very much like standard multiple choice:

Suppose $a^2 + b^3 = 89$ and $a - b = 1$. If a and b are positive intengers, what is the value of $\frac{b}{a}$?

But instead of five multiple-choice responses to choose from, students are confronted with a rectangle on their answer sheets that looks like this:

Students are asked to "grid in" the correct ovals while inserting a decimal point or fraction line where appropriate. Students have the option of writing their answer in the top row of boxes but receive credit only if the ovals are filled in correctly. No questions have a negative answer.

But back to the equation at hand. At a glance, you know that b must be either 3 or 4 because 5^3 is equal to 125 and is too big. If b were 2, a would be 9, but that does not satisfy the $a - b = 1$ equation. If b were 3, a^2 would have to be 62—no good either. So b is 4, a is 5, $a - b = 1$, and $\frac{b}{a} = \frac{4}{5}$. The answer should be gridded in as follows:

or, you could also grid it in as:

Notice that this Grid-in problem has a subtle trick. In the two equations at the beginning of the problem, $a^2 + b^3 = 89$ and $a - b$, a precedes b. Yet the problem asks for $\frac{b}{a}$ as the answer. To further throw you off, $\frac{a}{b}$ is an improper fraction while $\frac{b}{a}$ is not. Therefore, flipping the fraction to $\frac{b}{a}$ converts it to a conventional fraction—the opposite of what would seem to be logical.

The Grid-in problems are a haven for tricks like these. Without the safety net of multiple-choice answers, you'll need to be extra careful not to be hoodwinked.

THE ART OF A GUESS

Distracters are a pain in the neck most of the time, but when you have no idea what the right answer is, they can be helpful. Since the correct answer is generally accompanied by at least one or two wrong answers that resemble it in one way or another, your best bet is to guess an answer that is similar to the other responses. Suppose you face a question with the following answers:

(A) 444
(B) 500
(C) 887
(D) 888
(E) 889

Without knowing the question, it is a good bet to eliminate (A) and (B) because they have the least in common with the other answers. Even if you pick randomly between (C), (D), and (E), your odds of answering correctly are now one in three rather than one in five. If you can eliminate two answers in a similar manner for every question that stumps you, the odds are good that you will raise your score. As a footnote, the responses above came from a question about an arithmetic sequence, and the answer was (E) 889.

Oh Yeah, the Math

Everybody has made a big deal about how the New SAT has added Algebra II. That's important news, but hold the phone. At least 80 percent of the test is still lower math that you learned for the first time in Algebra I, Geometry, or even before that. We won't waste your time with every topic that might appear on the test; you've studied it all in your previous math classes. But there are some topics that you should know without having to think twice. A quick refresher:

Prime Numbers

Memorize the first ten: 2, 3, 5, 7, 11, 13, 17, 19, 23, 29. The test-makers love to mess around with these.

Addition and Multiplication of Integers

Anybody can figure these out by thinking about it, but know them off the top of your head.

> Even + Even = Even
> Odd + Odd = Even
> Odd + Even = Odd
> Even × Even = Even
> Odd × Odd = Odd
> Odd × Even = Even
> Negative × Positive = Negative
> Negative × Negative = Positive

◆ ◆ ◆

Squares, Cubes, and Square Roots

Know the square of every whole number from 1 to 15:

$1^2 = 1$	$2^2 = 4$	$3^2 = 9$	$4^2 = 16$	$5^2 = 25$
$6^2 = 36$	$7^2 = 49$	$8^2 = 64$	$9^2 = 81$	$10^2 = 100$
$11^2 = 121$	$12^2 = 144$	$13^2 = 169$	$14^2 = 196$	$15^2 = 225$

Know the cube of every whole number from 1 to 5:

$$1^3 = 1 \qquad 2^3 = 8 \qquad 3^3 = 27$$
$$4^3 = 64 \qquad 5^3 = 125$$

Know the approximate value of the following square roots:

$$\sqrt{1} = 1$$
$$\sqrt{2} \approx 1.4$$
$$\sqrt{3} \approx 1.7$$
$$\sqrt{4} = 2$$
$$\sqrt{5} \approx 2.25$$

Don't forget that fractions squared or cubed are smaller than the original fraction, and negative numbers squared are positive while negative numbers cubed are negative.

Mean, Median, and Mode

The mean is the arithmetic average of a set of numbers, the median is the middle value of the set, and the mode is the value that is most often repeated within the set. Of these, mean or average is probably the most important. It is amazing how many confusing ways that the test-makers can devise to ask you to average a set of numbers.

Ratio and Proportion

Definitely review the intricacies of this concept, and know all of the ways to express ratios:

$$\frac{1}{4} = 1:4 = .25 = 25\% = \frac{25}{100}$$

The ability to convert word problems into ratios and back again is a crucial skill.

Exponents

Think you know what $a^2 + a^3$ is? It equals a^5, right? Think again. You can't simplify $a^2 + a^3$ unless you also know the value of a. The same goes for $a^3 - a^2$. The rules for exponents are as follows:

Add the exponents when multiplying:

$$a^3 \times a^2 = a^5$$

Subtract the exponents when dividing:

$$a^3 \div a^2 = a \text{ or } \frac{a^3}{a^2} = a$$

Multiply the exponents when raising to a power:

$$(a^3)^2 = a^6$$

◆ ◆ ◆

Probability and Combinations

Too many students have been stumped by the tiny bit of probability that appears on the SAT. There are two rules to know. First, when all possible outcomes are equally likely, the probability of a particular set of outcomes is equal to the number of those outcomes divided by the number of all possible outcomes. For instance, suppose 12 playing cards are placed face-down on a table. If three are diamonds and nine are spades, the likelihood of getting a diamond from a random draw is $\frac{3}{12}$ or $\frac{1}{4}$.

> **"The most challenging thing for me was just that I hadn't done any of this type of math since about seventh grade."**
>
> —800 V, 730 M

Combinations problems are a touch harder. For instance: In a cafeteria, children may choose one vegetable and one meat. The vegetables include corn, beans, peas, tomatoes, and lettuce. The meats include chicken, steak, beef, and fish. How many possible combinations of vegetables and meats can a child choose? All it takes is knowing the formula. Simply multiply the 5 vegetable choices times the 4 meat choices. $4 \times 5 = 20$ combinations.

◆ ◆ ◆

Triangles

No math topic is more important than triangles. You need to know their basic properties off the top of your head—regardless of whether relevant formulas and diagrams are printed in the front of the section. (You shouldn't waste time looking.) The first rule of triangles is that every single one of them contains three angles that measure a total of 180°. The second is that $a^2 + b^2 = c^2$. Here are some special triangles you should know:

Equilateral Triangle—all sides equal length

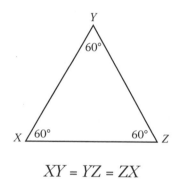

$$XY = YZ = ZX$$

Isosceles Triangle—two sides equal length

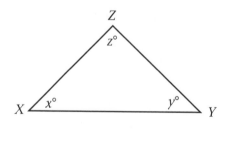

$$XZ = YZ, \angle X = \angle Y$$

Right Triangle—one angle of 90°

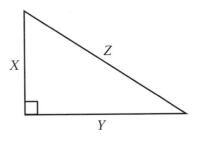

$$X^2 + Y^2 = Z^2$$

30°:60°:90° Right Triangle

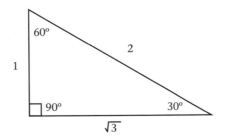

Ratio of sides: $1:\sqrt{3}:2$

45°:45°:90° Right Triangle

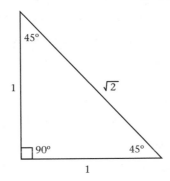

Ratio of sides: $1:1:\sqrt{2}$

3:4:5 Right Triangle

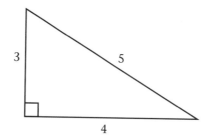

Ratio of sides: 3:4:5

Other common ratios: 5:12:13 and 7:24:25

◆ ◆ ◆

Perhaps the most important formula related to triangles: area = $\frac{1}{2}(bh)$ where b = base and h = height.

◆ ◆ ◆

KNOW YOUR CALCULATOR

Students have been allowed to use calculators on the SAT since 1994, but with the coming of the New SAT, calculators will take on added significance. College Board says that students will still be able to answer every question without a calculator, but common sense says that a calculator will be a big help for some. The most important rule: make sure your calculator has fresh batteries. If the screen goes blank after the third math problem, you're out of luck. Be familiar with all of your calculator's idiosyncrasies, including the location of the keys and their touch. Calculators have their own personalities; make sure you know yours well.

Parallel Lines

More common-sense rules to know cold:

$L1 \parallel L2$

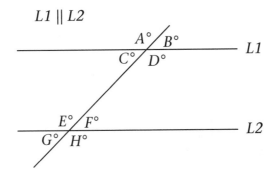

1) $A° = E° = D° = H°$
2) $B° = F° = G° = C°$

Any angle from 1) + Any angle from 2) = 180°

◆ ◆ ◆

And Finally

A few formulas related to circles that should be etched indelibly in your brain:

$$\pi r^2 = \text{area of a circle}$$
$$\pi d, \; 2\pi r = \text{circumference of a circle}$$
$$\pi r^2 h = \text{volume of a cylinder}$$

where $\pi \approx 3.14$, d = diameter, r = radius, h = height

Practice Problems

To help you brush up, try these practice problems. Solutions and explanations follow.

1. If p and r are different prime numbers greater than 2, then $(p \times r) + 2$ must be

   (A) an even integer
   (B) an odd integer
   (C) prime
   (D) divisible by 2
   (E) divisible by 3

2. If a and b are integers > 0 and $a \times b = 8a + 3$, which of the following must be true?

   I. a is even
   II. $a > b$
   III. $a + b$ is even

   (A) None
   (B) I only
   (C) II only
   (D) III only
   (E) I, II, and III

3. If a and b are positive integers, the expression $\dfrac{7a^{(b+3)}}{3a}$ is equal to which of the following?

   (A) $4a^{(b+3)}$

   (B) $7^{(b+3)}$

   (C) $21^{(b+4)}$

   (D) $\dfrac{7}{3}$

   (E) $\dfrac{7a^{(b+2)}}{3}$

4. In a supermarket, a can of beans costs one-fifth less than a jar of peaches. If the can of beans costs $2.00, how much does the jar of peaches cost?

   (A) $2.20
   (B) $2.40
   (C) $2.50
   (D) $2.60
   (E) $3.00

5. If a student scores 92 on each of her first three quizzes, and then gets grades of 86, 90, and 76 on subsequent quizzes, what is the average of her quiz grades?

   (A) 86
   (B) 88
   (C) 89
   (D) 90
   (E) 91

6. At a particular school, the day is divided into 7 periods. Students must take a class during exactly 6 of those periods and have study hall during their free period. All classes are offered during only 1 period. If students may choose from 5 different classes during each period, how many different schedules are possible?

   (A) 28
   (B) 35
   (C) 7^6
   (D) 7×5^6
   (E) 6×5^7

GO ON TO THE NEXT PAGE

7. On a flat surface, a man walks 30 feet, then turns at a 90° angle and walks 40 feet. He stops and digs a hole 20 feet deep. How many feet is the bottom of the hole from the spot where he started?

(A)   35
(B)   40
(C)   50
(D) $\sqrt{70}$
(E) $\sqrt{2900}$

---

8. The area of polygon ABCDEF is 15. If BC = CD, what is the area of the shaded region?

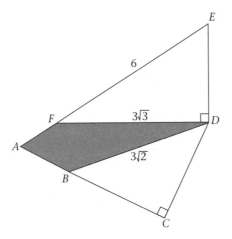

Note: Figure not drawn to scale

(A) $10.5 - 4.5\sqrt{3}$
(B) $15 - 4.5\sqrt{3}$
(C) $15 - 4.5\sqrt{2}$
(D) $12\sqrt{2}$
(E) $12 + 9\sqrt{3}$

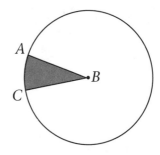

9. The circle above has a diameter of 12. If point B is at the center of the circle and the measure of ∠ABC is 30°, what is the area of the shaded region?

(A) 3π
(B) 12π
(C) 18π
(D) 24π
(E) 30π

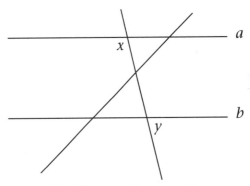

Note: Figure not drawn to scale

10. In the figure above, a∥b. If x = 100°, what is the value of y?

(A)   80
(B)   90
(C) 100
(D) 110
(E) 120

The Answers

1. (B) 2. (D) 3. (E) 4. (C) 5. (B) 6. (D) 7. (E) 8. (A) 9. (A) 10. (A).
We rate these questions medium to hard.

The Explanations

1. Priming the Pump

Prime numbers and even/odd counting come together in this one. You know that p and r are odd because all primes greater than 2 are odd. Their product must also be odd, as must $(p \times r) + 2$. The answer is **(B)**.

2. Understanding Even and Odd

This one is slightly harder than question 1. Since $8 \times$ any number will be even, $8a + 3$ must be odd. Therefore, $a \times b$ must also be odd and a and cannot be even. The proposition that $a > b$ is also false. For instance, if $a = 1$, $b = 11$. Since both a and b are odd, $a + b$ is even and **(D)** is correct.

3. The Agony of Exponents

The key on this one is simply that when you divide exponential expressions with the same base, the exponents are subtracted. The $\frac{7}{3}$ stays and $(b + 3) - 1 = b + 2$. **Answer: (E)**.

4. More Playing With Percentages

We thought you were due for another nasty ratio and proportion problem. The natural tendency is to compute one-fifth of $2.00—40—and make your answer $2.40. But the right way to solve is to say that $2.00 is $\frac{4}{5}$ of x. Therefore, multiply $2.00 by $\frac{5}{4}$ to get $2.50. **Answer: (C)**.

5. Weighing Weighted Averages

This moderately easy problem has a small wrinkle. If you compute the average of 92, 86, 90, and 76, you get (A) 86. But you're not that gullible (we hope). The student got a

92 on her first three quizzes, therefore the 92 must be counted three times to get the average of all 6 values—making the answer **(B)** 88.

6. The Right Combination

The students can take one of 5 classes during 7 periods, but one of those periods must be study hall. Disregarding the study halls, the students are picking from one of 5 classes for each of 6 periods, and 5^6 is the number of different schedules that are possible. Since students have 7 options for study hall, the answer is **(D)** 7×5^6.

7. A New Use for Right Triangles

Don't fret if you were stumped by this one—it may be the hardest of this bunch. To get it, you need to envision two perpendicular planes, one going along the ground and the other perpendicular to the ground. Each plane has a right triangle in it. The first has sides of 30 and 40 feet—and therefore you know that the hypotenuse is 50 feet because of the 3:4:5 rule. The side that is 50 feet is also the first side of a triangle perpendicular to the ground, which extends 20 feet down into the hole. Now that you know that two sides are 50 and 20, you can use the Pythagorean Theorem to compute the hypotenuse of the second triangle, which is also the distance from the bottom of the hole to the beginning point. Answer: **(E)** $\sqrt{2900}$.

8. Calculating Area by Inference

The two triangles in this figure are, respectively, a $1:\sqrt{3}:2$ right triangle and a $1:1:\sqrt{2}$ right triangle. Since $BD = 3\sqrt{2}$, both BC and $CD = 3$. By similar reasoning, $ED = 3$. Therefore, the area of BCD is $\frac{1}{2}(3 \times 3)$ while the area of DEF is $\frac{1}{2}(3 \times 3\sqrt{3})$. Subtracting these from 15 yields the answer, **(A)** $10.5 - 4.5\sqrt{3}$.

9. Circular Reasoning

A few easy calculations are all you need for this one. The question gives you the diameter of the circle, 12, which makes the area 36π.

With $360°$ in a circle, a $30°$ slice is $\frac{1}{12}$ th of the area. Answer: **(A)** 3π

10. Angles and Parallel Lines

This one is either hard or extremely easy. Since $\angle x$ and $\angle y$ are adjacent to the same line that cuts two parallel lines, $x° + y° = 180$. If $x = 100$, $y = 80$ and the answer is **(A)**.

The SAT's New Math

For all the hullabaloo about the addition of higher-level math, the truth is that only 15–20 percent of the math questions will cover new topics. You will have learned most of this material in your Algebra II class. And get this straight: The addition of new math will not necessarily make the test harder. On the old SAT, the math itself was never the issue; the test-makers were merely playing tricks with simple material. Expect more of the same on the New SAT, but the odds are good that the questions dealing with higher math will be more straightforward. Fewer mind games and more emphasis on the math is a good deal for students who work hard in school and know the formulas.

The following is an overview of the most significant new topics. We assume you have seen them in Geometry or Algebra II. If you're rusty, the following pages will jog your memory. But if you have difficulty following the examples— or if you have never encountered one or more of the topics—you may want to dust off your algebra textbook.

> "I felt unprepared to answer those bizarre probability questions."
>
> —760 V, 640 M

Algebraic Equations and Inequalities

This is a catch-all phrase that covers a lot of territory. In algebra, the goal is to solve for an unknown variable. Some equations have only one variable; others have several. With a one-variable equation, it is possible to solve for that variable, as in

$$8x - 5 = 27$$
$$8x = 32$$
$$x = 4$$

With two variables, the best you can do is to simplify the equation, or solve for one variable in terms of the other. For instance, you might encounter a question such as:

What is the y-intercept of the line determined by the equation: $4x - 4 = 3y + 3$?

(A)   7

(B)   –7

(C) $-\dfrac{7}{3}$

(D) $\dfrac{3}{7}$

(E) $\dfrac{1}{7}$

To solve this problem, you need to be familiar with the formula for a line: $y = mx + b$, where m is the slope of the line and b is the y-intercept. The long way to solve is to labor through the algebra until you get to $y = \dfrac{4}{3}x - \dfrac{7}{3}$. A quicker way is simply to subtract 3 from both sides to isolate the $3y$, then divide –7 by 3 to get the value for the intercept. Answer: (C).

In addition to this sort of problem—a "linear equation" in algebra jargon—you will also see equations that include exponential terms. A special case of these, quadratic equations, is discussed below.

One possibility would be an equation like this:

$$\frac{-4x(y^2 + 2) + 8x}{-xy^2}$$

(A)   –4

(B)   4

(C) $\dfrac{4}{xy^2}$

(D)   8

(E)   16

The key to this problem is to recognize that if you distribute $-4x$, you can create like terms that can be consolidated and dealt with. That is, if you multiply $-4x$ by all the terms inside the parentheses, you get

$$\frac{-4xy^2 - 8x + 8x}{-xy^2}$$

From there, you can get rid of the $8x$'s and divide to get your answer: (B) 4.

In addition to equations, you may also encounter inequalities that involve quantities that are less than, less than or equal to, greater than, or greater than or equal to (respectively, $<$, $\le$, $>$, and $\ge$) other quantities.

A variation on this theme is a domain and range problem such as the following:

If $f(x) = 6x^2 + 5$ for $-2 \le x \le 4$, then which of the following gives the range of f?

(A) $\{y: -12 \le y \le 20\}$
(B) $\{y: -29 \le y \le 20\}$
(C) $\{y: -8 \le y \le 9\}$
(D) $\{y: 4 \le y \le 20\}$
(E) $\{y: 29 \le y \le 101\}$

In case you have forgotten, the domain of a function is the set of values for which the function is defined, in this case $-2 \le x \le 4$. The range is the set of values that are the output—the value you must solve for. If you know how to do the problem, the computation is simple. Plug -2 and 4 into $6x^2 + 5$. Keep in mind that when you square -2, the product is 4 and not -4. Therefore, $6(-2)^2 + 5 = 29$ and $6(4)^2 + 5 = 101$. Answer: (E).

Radical Equations

For reasons not entirely clear to us, equations with roots in them are called "radical." (For good measure, the number under the root is called the "radicand.") But we digress. Like exponents, roots have their own special protocol. You can add them, as long as they have the same index (the little number that tells you the power of the root) and radicand. Thus,

$$3\sqrt{4} + 5\sqrt{4} = 8\sqrt{4}$$

and

$$7(\sqrt[5]{128}) - 5(\sqrt[5]{128}) = 2(\sqrt[5]{128})$$

By the same token, numbers under a radical sign with the same index can be multiplied and divided just like regular numbers. For instance,

$$\sqrt{9} \times \sqrt{5} = \sqrt{45}$$

$$\text{and}$$

$$\sqrt[3]{30} \div \sqrt[3]{6} = \sqrt[3]{5}$$

Quadratic Equations

A quadratic equation is defined by the fact that 1.) it consists of more than one term joined by a plus or minus sign 2.) it has only one variable and 3.) its largest exponent is 2. Quadratic equations are noteworthy because you can factor them in interesting ways. Factoring is the opposite operation of distributing. To factor an equation, you pull out a number, as in:

$$6x^2 + 8 = 2(3x^2 + 4)$$

Since 2 is a factor of both $6x^2$ and 8, it is possible to pull it out. (Whether you should distribute a number in or factor it out depends on what you are trying to do—both come in handy depending on the situation.)

But it does get harder. The "general form" of a quadratic equation is

$$ax^2 + bx + c = 0$$

$$\text{or to use numbers}$$

$$2x^2 + 10x + 12 = 0$$

For the purposes of the SAT, the most important kind of quadratic equations are the ones, like $2x^2 + 10x + 12$ that have factors that are integers. These can be put together and taken apart with relative ease. In other words:

$$2x^2 + 10x + 12 = (2x + 4)(x + 3)$$

Is this ringing a bell? Are you experiencing déjà vu Algebra II? You should be. If you can't factor a quadratic equation such as this by eyeballing it, get an algebra book and refresh your memory. You know that 2 × 2 will separate into $2x$ and x. To factor out the $10x$, you know that one of the integers plus 2 times the other integer equals 10; and lastly, you know that one integer times the other equals 12. The only integers that satisfy these criteria are 3 and 4, yielding $(2x + 4)(x + 3)$.

To put it back together, you can use the trusty FOIL method: multiply the First two terms ($2x$ and x), then multiply the Outside terms ($2x$ and 3); then multiply the Inside terms (x and 4); and finally, multiply the Last two terms (4 and 3). That spells FOIL and you're back to $2x^2 + 10x + 12$.

This allows you to do some amazing sleight-of-hand, such as the following:

$$\text{If } \frac{3x^2 + 15x + 18}{3x + 6} = 0$$

what is the value of x?

(A) 3
(B) –3
(C) 6
(D) –6
(E) –2

The first key to this question is to see the similarity between the numerator and the denominator of this expression. Whenever you have a denominator that looks like a factor of the numerator—in this case, the multiples of 3 are a dead giveaway—the odds are good that you can simplify the expression by factoring and canceling like terms. Think of it this way:

$$(3x + 6) \times (\underline{\hspace{1cm}}) = 3x^2 + 15x + 18$$

Can you figure this one out by looking? What number multiplied by 6 equals 18? Did you get $x + 3$? Ok, back to the original equation. Let's rewrite it this way:

$$\frac{(3x + 6)\,(x + 3)}{3x + 6} = 0$$

Now you've got it—simply cancel out the $(3x + 6)$'s to get $x + 3 = 0$. Answer: (B) –3.

Most of the quadratic equations that you will see on the SAT will be factorable in this way. As with special right triangles, there are a few special cases that are particularly likely to show up. Memorize these:

$$(x - y)^2 = x^2 - 2xy + y^2$$
$$(x + y)^2 = x^2 + 2xy + y^2$$
$$(x + y)(x - y) = x^2 - y^2$$

Some quadratic equations don't factor evenly, and to solve those you need a nasty-looking equation:

$$y = \frac{-b \pm \sqrt{b^2 - 4ac}}{2a}$$

This monstrosity is called the quadratic formula—you probably knew that already—and you should get reacquainted with it if your memory is fuzzy But in our experience, ETS favors the elegant simplicity of quadratic equations that factor to integers.

♦ ♦ ♦

Trigonometry as an "Alternative Method of Solution"

The prospect of trig on the SAT created a buzz, but the reality has been a lot less intimidating than the hype. Trig will appear only as an alternative method of solution for questions dealing with 30:60:90 triangles or 45:45:90 triangles. (See pages 203–204.) The odds are good that you'll be able to do everything in your head without resorting to trig, but you may want to remind yourself of a few basic concepts. Trigonometry describes the relationships between the sides of right triangles. These relationships are dictated by the measures of the angles. Sin 30° will always equal $\frac{1}{2}$ no matter what the length of each side. The values for the sine (sin), cosine (cos), and tangent (tan) of any angle are available from your calculator at the touch of a key. All you need to know is this:

$$\text{sine} = \frac{\text{opposite}}{\text{hypotenuse}} \qquad \text{cosine} = \frac{\text{adjacent}}{\text{hypotenuse}} \qquad \text{tangent} = \frac{\text{opposite}}{\text{adjacent}}$$

Here is what a problem might look like:

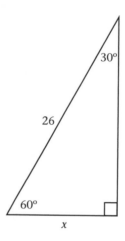

In the figure above, what is the value of x?

(A) 10
(B) 12
(C) 13
(D) 26
(E) 30

This problem can be solved in one of two ways. First, you can simply remember that the ratios of the sides of a 30:60:90 triangle are $1:\sqrt{3}:2$. Or, you can whip out your calculator and hit sin 30 or cos 60. Either way, the side of a 30:60:90 that is opposite the 30° angle is one-half as long as the side opposite the 90° angle. Answer: (C) 13.

♦ ♦ ♦

Negative and Fractional Exponents

The old SAT included only exponents that were positive integers. The new one will have a few extra twists. Consider an expression such as $4^{\frac{3}{4}}$. Pretty funky. With fractional exponents, you treat the top half like a regular exponent and then use the bottom number to take the root, i.e. $4^{\frac{3}{4}} = \sqrt[4]{4^3}$. From there, you get $\sqrt[4]{64} = 2$.

You may also see some negative exponents, such as 5^{-2}. Simply take the reciprocal, $\left(\frac{1}{5}\right)^2$, and solve.

Functions and Function Notation

The old SAT dealt with functions, but now you will be required to recognize and use proper notation. It isn't necessarily hard:

If $f(x) = 3(x) + 3^x$, you might be asked to solve for $f(4)$. Therefore, $f(4) = 3(4) + 3^4$. Answer: 93.

But things could also get more complicated. Suppose you face a question such as:

If $f(g(x)) = 8x + 4$

and $g(x) = 16x + 8$

which of the following is $f(x)$?

(A) 2

(B) $\frac{1}{4}$

(C) $\frac{1}{2}x$

(D) $2(8x + 4)$

(E) $2(g(x))$

In this problem, function f is a function of g. If $g(x) = 16x + 8$, and f turns $g(x)$ into $8x + 4$, what is $f(x)$?

You can tell by eye-balling it: $\frac{1}{2} \times (16x + 8) = 8x + 4$. Therefore, $f(x) = \frac{1}{2}$ x and the answer is (C).

Absolute value is another concept that you will see in combination with function notation or on its own. Can you compute $|f(x)|$ if $f(x) = x^3 - 3$ knowing that $x = -3$? Probably. You know that $-3^3 = -27$, and that $-27 - 3 = -30$. But the absolute value of a number is its distance from the origin—a positive value— and therefore the solution is 30.

The test may also include questions dealing with direct and inverse variation. When two variables show direct variation, if one increases then the other also increases. A function such as $f(x) = 10x$ is an example of direct variation. If x increases, so too does $f(x)$. An example of an inverse variation would be $f(x) = \dfrac{5}{x}$. As x gets larger, the value of $f(x)$ gets smaller.

To take it a step further, you also must be able to recognize the shape of functions—direct, inverse, and otherwise—in data that is modeled on real world situations. For instance, suppose you encounter the following:

Price of Candy Bars ($)	Number Sold (Per Day)
.50	100
.60	80
.70	65
.80	57
.90	52
1.00	50

A convenience store is considering how much to charge for candy bars. The chart above shows the number of candy bars per day that the store expects to sell at each price. If the price of the candy bars is plotted on the y axis and the number expected to be sold per day is plotted on the x axis, which of the following graphs most nearly reflects the shape of the curve?

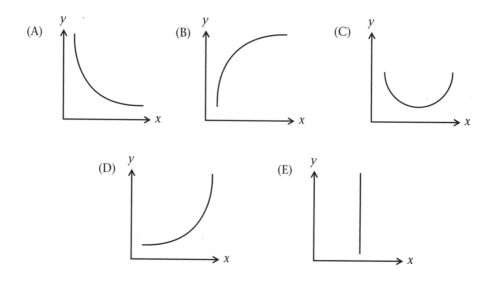

(A) (B) (C) (D) (E)

This question is a lot easier than it looks. From the data, you should immediately recognize an inverse relationship. When price goes up, the number sold goes down. To put it another way, when the x variable goes up, the y variable goes down—and vice versa. That means a curve that is downward sloping to the right. Answer: (A).

Geometry and Measurement

While algebra will account for most of the new math, the test will also include some harder geometry. First, there will be more geometric notation, as in:

$$\overleftrightarrow{AB} \rightarrow \text{line } AB$$

$$\overline{AB} \rightarrow \text{line segment } AB$$

$$\overrightarrow{AB} \rightarrow \text{ray from } A \text{ through } B$$

$$AB \rightarrow \text{distance between } A \text{ and } B$$

$$\overline{AB} \cong \overline{CD} \rightarrow \text{line segment } AB \text{ is congruent}$$
$$\text{to line segment } CD$$

Nothing too difficult there. You'll also need to know, as you may already, that a line tangent to a circle is perpendicular to a radius drawn to the point of contact, as below.

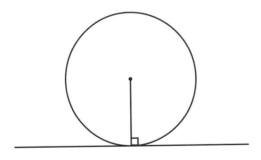

Perhaps the most significant additions to the geometry topics will be problems concerning the midpoint and distance formulas. Consider $\overline{AB}$. Suppose that A has coordinates (x_1, y_1) and B has coordinates (x_2, y_2). The midpoint of $\overline{AB}$ will have coordinates $(\frac{x_1 + x_2}{2}, \frac{y_1 + y_2}{2})$, and the distance AB will be $\sqrt{(x_1 - x_2)^2 + (y_1 - y_2)^2}$.

Our guess is that the midpoint formula won't cause your synapses to misfire, but the distance formula? Think $a^2 + b^2 = c^2$. In case your memory is shaky, that's the Pythagorean Theorem. When you find the distance between two points, all you're doing is finding the hypotenuse of a triangle. Let's do an example using a right triangle for simplicity. Suppose we need to find the distance of $\overline{PQ}$ that goes from point (1, 2) to point (4, 6):

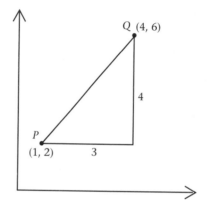

By plugging the coordinates of $\overline{PQ}$'s end points into the distance formula, we get

$$\sqrt{(4 - 1)^2 + (6 - 2)^2}$$

$$= \sqrt{3^2 + 4^2}$$

$$= \sqrt{25}$$

$$= 5$$

The difference between the values of the x coordinates (4 and 1) is 3, the length of the base. The difference between the values of the y coordinates (6 and 2) is 4, the length of the height. Using the distance formula, $3^2 + 4^2 = 25$, the square of the distance between the points. $\sqrt{25} = 5$ and there you have it.

We should hasten to add that the numbers rarely work out this cleanly—most square roots will be funky-looking decimals. But armed with your trusty calculator, you should not have a problem.

To help you get your juices going for the new math, on the next page are some sample problems with answers at the end.

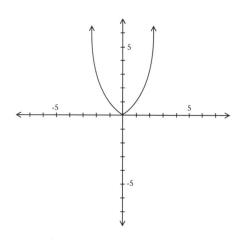

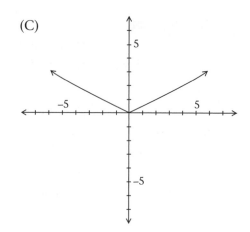

(C)

1. In the figure above, $f(x) = x^2$. Which of the following represents $f(x) = x^2 + 3$?

(A)

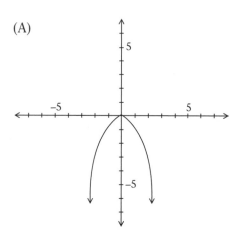

(D)

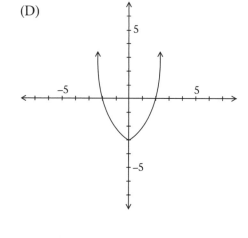

(B)

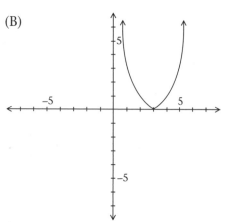

(E)

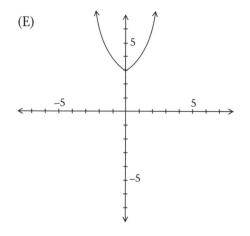

2. $\sqrt{12} \times 3\sqrt{12}$ = _____

   (A) $\sqrt{48}$
   (B) $4\sqrt{12}$
   (C) $3\sqrt{24}$
   (D) 36
   (E) 48

3. If $x - y = 4$

   and $x^2 - y^2 = 48$

   then which of the following is the value of y?

   (A) –8
   (B) –4
   (C) 2
   (D) 4
   (E) 8

4. $7^{-\frac{5}{2}}$ =

   (A) $-\sqrt{7^5}$

   (B) -14^5

   (C) $\dfrac{1}{\sqrt[5]{7^2}}$

   (D) $\dfrac{1}{\sqrt{7^5}}$

   (E) $7^{-\frac{2}{5}}$

5. Suppose that ABC is a right triangle that has two congruent angles. The side opposite the right angle, BC, measures 12 inches. Which of the following most nearly approximates the length of AB?

   (A)   6
   (B)   6.5
   (C)   8
   (D)   8.5
   (E) $2\sqrt{12}$

6. Suppose that the population of a particular city is projected to double every 7 years. If the city's population is currently 23,000, which of the following may be used to express the city's projected population after 12 years?

   (A) $23{,}000\ (2^{12})$
   (B) $46{,}000$
   (C) $23{,}000\ (2^{\frac{12}{7}})$
   (D) $552{,}000$
   (E) $23{,}000\ (7^2)$

GO ON TO THE NEXT PAGE

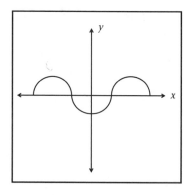

7. The figure above is the graph of $y = f(x)$. Which of the following is the graph of $|f(x)|$?

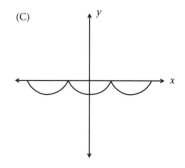

(C)

(A)

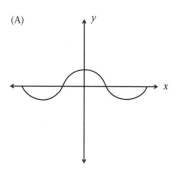

(D)

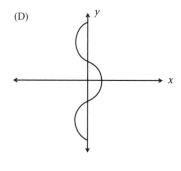

(B)

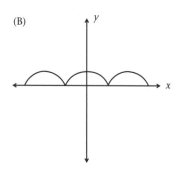

(E)

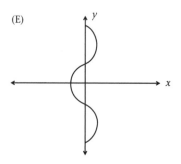

GO ON TO THE NEXT PAGE

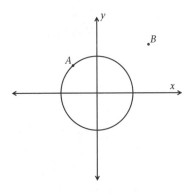

8. In the figure above, a circle that includes point A has its center at the origin. Point B is twice as far from the origin as point A. If the coordinates of point B are (6, 5), which of the following is the closest approximation of the circumference of the circle?

(A) 5π
(B) 6π
(C) 11π
(D) 30π
(E) $(\sqrt{61})\pi$

9. If $x^{-2} = \dfrac{9}{27(-2x-3)}$ then $x = ?$

(A) -3

(B) $\dfrac{1}{3}$

(C)   3

(D)   9

(E) 27

Number of books sold last week

	Book A	Book B	Book C
Store P	12	16	24
Store Q	16	20	20

Price of books

	Hardback	Paperback
Book A	$29	$16
Book B	$22	$12
Book C	$21	$9

10. Store P and Store Q are tracking the weekly sales of three best-selling books. Each of the books is available in both hardback and paperback. Both stores sell three times as many of the paperback editions of each book as they do of the hardback editions. What is the total cost of the hardback books sold at Store P last week?

(A) $150
(B) $175
(C) $301
(D) $394
(E) $903

The Answers

This batch of questions reflects the range of new topics that will appear in the math section. **The answers: 1. (E) 2. (D) 3. (D) 4. (D) 5. (D) 6. (C) 7. (B) 8. (E) 9. (A) 10. (C).** You may notice that questions 3–5 feature a run of three (D)'s in a row. We point this out because some so-called experts tell you to be leery of choosing the same letter three times in a row. Hogwash. Though it is true that strings of three are relatively unusual, you never know when you'll see one. Most versions of the SAT have several sequences of three in a row; we found one old SAT that had three such strings in a single verbal section. If you think you have the right answer, don't trouble yourself worrying if it happens to be the third (D) in a row. Focus on the content of the questions, not the pattern of letters on your answer sheet. Now that we've gotten that off our chests, here are the explanations.

The Explanations

1. Transformation

The main key to this problem is simply knowing that $f(x) = x^2$ means the same thing as $y = x^2$. The value of y gets big faster than the value of x because of the squaring, which yields the familiar u-shaped graph. Adding 3, or any new value that changes the graph of a function, is called a *transformation*. In this case, the transformation is to increase the value of y by 3 at every level of x. The answer choices include various nonsense along with the correct answer, **(E)**, which shows the function shifted up by 3.

2. Radical Thinking

This one is easy if you remember the rule for multiplying square roots. If the roots have the same index and radicand, as they do in this case, multiply them. $\sqrt{12} \times \sqrt{12} = 12$, and $3 \times 12 = 36$, **(D)**.

3. The Difference of Squares

This old chestnut is a special kind of quadratic equation known as the difference of squares. Any time you see $x^2 - y^2$, you can translate to $(x + y)(x - y)$.

$$\text{If } (x + y)(x - y) = 48$$
$$\text{and } (x - y) = 4,$$
$$\text{then } (x + y) = 12$$

There are quite a few combinations of numbers that would satisfy $(x - y) = 4$, but only one that will also satisfy $(x + y) = 12$. **Answer: (D).**

4. Exponents Get Messier

A negative, fractional exponent problem will tie you in knots if you can't remember the rules for solving—but it should be easy if you can. A negative exponent means that you put the term in the denominator rather than the numerator, as in

$$x^{-2} = \frac{1}{x^2}$$

With a fraction, you raise the number to the power of the numerator but put it under the root of the denominator, as in $x^{\frac{3}{4}} = \sqrt[4]{x^3}$. A negative, fractional exponent requires both of these operations. **Answer: (D).**

5. Right Triangle Reasoning

A little trig anyone? This problem features a right triangle with two congruent angles—making it a 45:45:90. You probably know that the sides of a triangle like this are in the ratio of $1:1:\sqrt{2}$. Hence, you could simply divide 12 (the length of the side opposite the 90° angle, and therefore the longest side) by $\sqrt{2}$ to get your answer. But the College Board and ETS want you to know that you can also use trig to solve this problem. You can use either Sine or Cosine. Let's take

$$\text{sine} = \frac{\text{opposite}}{\text{hypotenuse}}$$

The hypotenuse is 12 because it is opposite the biggest angle. So

$$\sin 45 = \frac{x}{12}$$

As the *sin* key on your calculator will tell you, *sin* 45 = .7071. Next, .7071(12) = 8.49. **Answer: (D).**

6. Population Explosion

The College Board and ETS say that the New SAT has more problems requiring students to apply numbers to real-world situations. This particular one is an example of an exponential sequence. We know that the initial population is 23,000, and that it will double every 7 years. After 7 years, the population will be 23,000(2). After 14 years, it will be 23,000(2^2). But the question asks for the population after 12 years. Here's a hint: $2 = 2^{\frac{7}{7}}$, and $2^2 = 2^{\frac{14}{7}}$. Got it now? The population after 12 years will be 23,000($2^{\frac{12}{7}}$). **Answer: (C).**

7. Absolute Value with a Twist

This question requires students to apply the concept of absolute value to a graph. As in question 1 above, the first key is to understand that $f(x)$ is the same thing as y. If we're taking $|f(x)|$, that means no y coordinate on the graph can be negative. For every point on the function where y has a negative value—that is, where the function dips below the x axis—we must flip it to make y positive. Let's say that a point on the function is (2,–1). Taking the absolute value of the function makes that point (2, 1). The correct answer is (B) because the middle part of the function has been flipped over the x axis, and all the values of y are ≥ 0. **Answer: (B).**

8. Going around in Circles

The formula for the circumference of a circle is πd where d is the circle's diameter. Since point A is on the circle, we know that the distance from A to the origin is the radius of the circle. Therefore, if point B is twice as far from the origin as point A, then the distance from point B to the origin is the circle's diameter. From here, the question boils down to applying the distance formula,

$$\sqrt{(x_1 - x_2)^2 + (y_1 - y_2)^2}$$

yielding $\sqrt{(6 - 0)^2 + (5 - 0)^2}$

or $\sqrt{61}$

Answer: (E), ($\sqrt{61}$)π.

9. A Quadratic Equation in Disguise

You should have recognized immediately that this problem is a scrambled quadratic equation. Your goal is to get everything on the same side of the equal marks so that you can factor it. First, remember that $x^{-2} = \dfrac{1}{x^2}$. Since both sides of the equation have more stuff on the bottom than the top, the easiest way to work is to flip both sides, yielding

$$x^2 = \frac{27(-2x - 3)}{9}$$

Next, divide 27 by 9 to get

$$x^2 = 3(-2x - 3)$$

From there, distribute the 3 to get

$$x^2 = -6x - 9$$

and then

$$x^2 + 6x + 9 = 0$$

Factoring yields $(x + 3)(x + 3) = 0$. **Answer: (A)** –3.

10. Digging through Data

The College Board calls this a "data interpretation" problem. The selection of data laid out in columns and rows is suggestive of matrix algebra, but all problems such as this can be solved with simple calculations. The question asks for the total cost of the hardbacks sold at Store P, and the crucial piece of information is that hardbacks account for $\dfrac{1}{4}$ of all sales. Therefore, the number of hardbacks sold at Store P is: Book A, 3; Book B, 4; and Book C, 6. Next multiply these by the price of the hardbacks:

$$3(\$29) + 4(\$22) + 6(\$21) = \$301$$

Answer: (C).

Keys to Success

1. Find Your Approach. We sympathize with the 590 M, 720 M scorer who writes, "Eventually I just didn't really know how to approach the SAT anymore because my teachers and my tutor would suggest contradicting methods." The moral: Don't fill your head with strategies from someone else. Our hope is that you will experiment with the approaches in this book, use those that work, and discard those that don't.

> "I think that practice makes the most dramatic effect on your score, but having a [private] tutor kept me disciplined and focused, which I could not have done on my own.... A good program has one central feature, which is practice."
>
> —770 V, 720 M

2. Balance Speed and Accuracy. A famous basketball coach once said, "Be quick, but don't hurry." Practice tests are where you should push your speed to the limit. It may seem uncomfortable at first, but that means you're stretching yourself. Once test day nears, your priority should shift to finding a comfortable groove where you can relax and be efficient.

3. Exercise Your Memory. Short-term memory is half the battle on the math SAT. You may feel hopelessly absent-minded—at the ripe old age of seventeen—but the fact is that you can improve your short-term memory with practice. Many students are simply not in the habit of focusing because they rarely read and always have distractions while studying. So…turn off the radio, get away from the TV, and really focus when you work. Practice doing problems in your head to build your capacity. If you're really serious, try memorizing strings of random numbers. If you work on your memory, it will improve.

4. Trust Yourself and Move On. Have you ever been on the verge of dropping a letter in a mail slot, only to find yourself ripping it open to double-check on something you meant to include? The chances are good that everything was there—but you just couldn't trust yourself. Some people are like that on the SAT, especially on the math. Trusting yourself is about more than merely saving time. It is a state of mind that says you are confident of success. So relax. Do your best and then move on.

THE FISKE SAT PRACTICE TESTS

7

THE FISKE SAT PRACTICE TESTS

Throughout this book, we have preached the importance of practicing for the SAT. We have also emphasized that there is no substitute for taking real SATs, like those available in the College Board's *Official SAT Study Guide*.

We offer the two tests that follow as a supplement to the real SATs. Think of these as SATs On Steroids. We guarantee that the following tests are the toughest SATs you'll find anywhere—harder vocabulary, trickier math, and the most esoteric hair-splitting possible in the reading comprehension.

Why a harder SAT? The goal is to build your capacity. When runners want to build their endurance, they train at high altitude where the air is thinner. Less oxygen means that the body works harder, which also makes it stronger. The same applies to taking the SAT. The more you work with the really tough questions, the better prepared you'll be.

If you're like most students, you can get a third to a half of the problems right on a real SAT without breaking a sweat. Realistically, there is a limit to how many times you need to practice cruising through these easy questions. Our version of the SAT includes fewer of the gimmes, and we have borrowed liberally from ETS's bag of dirty tricks. Whereas less than 10 percent of the questions on a typical SAT are considered "hard" by the College Board, more than a third of our questions would qualify as "hard." Most of the rest would be rated "medium."

These tests can be used in a variety of ways. Advanced students will probably want to take them on the clock. See how you do under extreme time pressure. Can you keep your head when time is running out? What are your strategies for budgeting your time?

Our tests will be particularly useful to those who want to hone their skipping and guessing strategies. For instance, take one test or section and mark every time you guess. Is there a pattern to the ones you get right and wrong? Compare your results when you guess immediately against your results when you skip a question and come back later. Mark the questions that you skip and return to, then count how many of those you got right. Does it really help to skip a question and come back, or are you better off guessing and moving on?

Students can also use our tests as an intensive diagnostic of their strengths and weaknesses. With more emphasis on the most challenging topics and questions, our tests are more likely to reveal areas for improvement than a typical SAT. Students in this category may want to give themselves extra time to finish because their emphasis will be less on speed than the content of the questions.

Once you have finished, take the time to score your test. Your score itself won't mean much, but learning how the test is scored can help you understand it better. If you do take one or both of the tests under timed conditions, and if you do compute your score, we would be very grateful if you could email us at editor@fiskeguide.com and tell us how you did. We're as curious as you may be about what constitutes a good score on our tests! We'll also appreciate any additional comments you have about the book.

You may notice that our SAT has only nine sections—and that our practice tests skip a section. It isn't a typo. For simplicity in scoring, we have omitted the unscored section, meaning that our SATs are only 3:20 minutes long versus 3:45 minutes for the real one.

Above all, no one should be intimidated by these tests. Nor should anyone expect to get a score on either of these that is comparable to an actual SAT score. Just keep reminding yourself: If you can handle these tests, the real SAT will be a piece of cake.

FISKE'S

SAT PRACTICE TEST

#1

SAT Reasoning Test™

Use a No. 2 pencil only. Be sure each mark is dark and completely fills the intended circle. Completely erase any errors or stray marks.

1 **Your Name:**
(Print)

Last   First   M.I.

I agree to the conditions on the back of the SAT®test book.

Signature: _____   Date ___ / ___ / ___

Home Address: _____
                    Number and Street   City   State   Zip Code

Center: _____
(Print)   City   State

2 **YOUR NAME**

Last Name (First 4 Letters) | First Init. | Mid Init.

3 **SOCIAL SECURITY NUMBER**

4 **DATE OF BIRTH**

MONTH	DAY	YEAR
○ Jan		
○ Feb		
○ Mar		
○ Apr		
○ May		
○ Jun		
○ Jul		
○ Aug		
○ Sep		
○ Oct		
○ Nov		
○ Dec		

5 **SEX**

○ Female   ○ Male

6 **REGISTRATION NUMBER**
(Copy from Admission Ticket.)

7 **TEST CENTER**
(Supplied by Test Center Supervisor.)

Important: Fill in items 8 and 9 exactly as shown on the back of the test book.

8 **FORM CODE**
(Copy and grid as on back of test book.)

9 **TEST FORM**
(Copy from back of test book.)

10 **TEST BOOK SERIAL NUMBER**
(Copy from front of test book.)

PRACTICE TEST #1

Begin your essay on this page. If you need more space, continue on the next page. Do not write outside of the essay box.

PRACTICE TEST #1

Start with number 1 for each new section. If a section has fewer questions than answer spaces, leave the extra answer spaces blank. Be sure to erase any errors or stray marks completely.

SECTION 2

1 (A)(B)(C)(D)(E) 11 (A)(B)(C)(D)(E) 21 (A)(B)(C)(D)(E) 31 (A)(B)(C)(D)(E)
2 (A)(B)(C)(D)(E) 12 (A)(B)(C)(D)(E) 22 (A)(B)(C)(D)(E) 32 (A)(B)(C)(D)(E)
3 (A)(B)(C)(D)(E) 13 (A)(B)(C)(D)(E) 23 (A)(B)(C)(D)(E) 33 (A)(B)(C)(D)(E)
4 (A)(B)(C)(D)(E) 14 (A)(B)(C)(D)(E) 24 (A)(B)(C)(D)(E) 34 (A)(B)(C)(D)(E)
5 (A)(B)(C)(D)(E) 15 (A)(B)(C)(D)(E) 25 (A)(B)(C)(D)(E) 35 (A)(B)(C)(D)(E)
6 (A)(B)(C)(D)(E) 16 (A)(B)(C)(D)(E) 26 (A)(B)(C)(D)(E) 36 (A)(B)(C)(D)(E)
7 (A)(B)(C)(D)(E) 17 (A)(B)(C)(D)(E) 27 (A)(B)(C)(D)(E) 37 (A)(B)(C)(D)(E)
8 (A)(B)(C)(D)(E) 18 (A)(B)(C)(D)(E) 28 (A)(B)(C)(D)(E) 38 (A)(B)(C)(D)(E)
9 (A)(B)(C)(D)(E) 19 (A)(B)(C)(D)(E) 29 (A)(B)(C)(D)(E) 39 (A)(B)(C)(D)(E)
10 (A)(B)(C)(D)(E) 20 (A)(B)(C)(D)(E) 30 (A)(B)(C)(D)(E) 40 (A)(B)(C)(D)(E)

SECTION 3

1 (A)(B)(C)(D)(E) 11 (A)(B)(C)(D)(E) 21 (A)(B)(C)(D)(E) 31 (A)(B)(C)(D)(E)
2 (A)(B)(C)(D)(E) 12 (A)(B)(C)(D)(E) 22 (A)(B)(C)(D)(E) 32 (A)(B)(C)(D)(E)
3 (A)(B)(C)(D)(E) 13 (A)(B)(C)(D)(E) 23 (A)(B)(C)(D)(E) 33 (A)(B)(C)(D)(E)
4 (A)(B)(C)(D)(E) 14 (A)(B)(C)(D)(E) 24 (A)(B)(C)(D)(E) 34 (A)(B)(C)(D)(E)
5 (A)(B)(C)(D)(E) 15 (A)(B)(C)(D)(E) 25 (A)(B)(C)(D)(E) 35 (A)(B)(C)(D)(E)
6 (A)(B)(C)(D)(E) 16 (A)(B)(C)(D)(E) 26 (A)(B)(C)(D)(E) 36 (A)(B)(C)(D)(E)
7 (A)(B)(C)(D)(E) 17 (A)(B)(C)(D)(E) 27 (A)(B)(C)(D)(E) 37 (A)(B)(C)(D)(E)
8 (A)(B)(C)(D)(E) 18 (A)(B)(C)(D)(E) 28 (A)(B)(C)(D)(E) 38 (A)(B)(C)(D)(E)
9 (A)(B)(C)(D)(E) 19 (A)(B)(C)(D)(E) 29 (A)(B)(C)(D)(E) 39 (A)(B)(C)(D)(E)
10 (A)(B)(C)(D)(E) 20 (A)(B)(C)(D)(E) 30 (A)(B)(C)(D)(E) 40 (A)(B)(C)(D)(E)

CAUTION Use the answer spaces in the grids below for Section 2 or Section 3 only if you are told to do so in your test book.

Student-Produced Responses ONLY ANSWERS ENTERED IN THE CIRCLES IN EACH GRID WILL BE SCORED. YOU WILL NOT RECEIVE CREDIT FOR ANYTHING WRITTEN IN THE BOXES ABOVE THE CIRCLES.

9   10   11   12   13

14   15   16   17   18

Start with number 1 for each new section. If a section has fewer questions than answer spaces, leave the extra answer spaces blank. Be sure to erase any errors or stray marks completely.

SECTION 4

1 (A)(B)(C)(D)(E)	11 (A)(B)(C)(D)(E)	21 (A)(B)(C)(D)(E)	31 (A)(B)(C)(D)(E)
2 (A)(B)(C)(D)(E)	12 (A)(B)(C)(D)(E)	22 (A)(B)(C)(D)(E)	32 (A)(B)(C)(D)(E)
3 (A)(B)(C)(D)(E)	13 (A)(B)(C)(D)(E)	23 (A)(B)(C)(D)(E)	33 (A)(B)(C)(D)(E)
4 (A)(B)(C)(D)(E)	14 (A)(B)(C)(D)(E)	24 (A)(B)(C)(D)(E)	34 (A)(B)(C)(D)(E)
5 (A)(B)(C)(D)(E)	15 (A)(B)(C)(D)(E)	25 (A)(B)(C)(D)(E)	35 (A)(B)(C)(D)(E)
6 (A)(B)(C)(D)(E)	16 (A)(B)(C)(D)(E)	26 (A)(B)(C)(D)(E)	36 (A)(B)(C)(D)(E)
7 (A)(B)(C)(D)(E)	17 (A)(B)(C)(D)(E)	27 (A)(B)(C)(D)(E)	37 (A)(B)(C)(D)(E)
8 (A)(B)(C)(D)(E)	18 (A)(B)(C)(D)(E)	28 (A)(B)(C)(D)(E)	38 (A)(B)(C)(D)(E)
9 (A)(B)(C)(D)(E)	19 (A)(B)(C)(D)(E)	29 (A)(B)(C)(D)(E)	39 (A)(B)(C)(D)(E)
10 (A)(B)(C)(D)(E)	20 (A)(B)(C)(D)(E)	30 (A)(B)(C)(D)(E)	40 (A)(B)(C)(D)(E)

SECTION 5

1 (A)(B)(C)(D)(E)	11 (A)(B)(C)(D)(E)	21 (A)(B)(C)(D)(E)	31 (A)(B)(C)(D)(E)
2 (A)(B)(C)(D)(E)	12 (A)(B)(C)(D)(E)	22 (A)(B)(C)(D)(E)	32 (A)(B)(C)(D)(E)
3 (A)(B)(C)(D)(E)	13 (A)(B)(C)(D)(E)	23 (A)(B)(C)(D)(E)	33 (A)(B)(C)(D)(E)
4 (A)(B)(C)(D)(E)	14 (A)(B)(C)(D)(E)	24 (A)(B)(C)(D)(E)	34 (A)(B)(C)(D)(E)
5 (A)(B)(C)(D)(E)	15 (A)(B)(C)(D)(E)	25 (A)(B)(C)(D)(E)	35 (A)(B)(C)(D)(E)
6 (A)(B)(C)(D)(E)	16 (A)(B)(C)(D)(E)	26 (A)(B)(C)(D)(E)	36 (A)(B)(C)(D)(E)
7 (A)(B)(C)(D)(E)	17 (A)(B)(C)(D)(E)	27 (A)(B)(C)(D)(E)	37 (A)(B)(C)(D)(E)
8 (A)(B)(C)(D)(E)	18 (A)(B)(C)(D)(E)	28 (A)(B)(C)(D)(E)	38 (A)(B)(C)(D)(E)
9 (A)(B)(C)(D)(E)	19 (A)(B)(C)(D)(E)	29 (A)(B)(C)(D)(E)	39 (A)(B)(C)(D)(E)
10 (A)(B)(C)(D)(E)	20 (A)(B)(C)(D)(E)	30 (A)(B)(C)(D)(E)	40 (A)(B)(C)(D)(E)

CAUTION Use the answer spaces in the grids below for Section 4 or Section 5 only if you are told to do so in your test book.

Student-Produced Responses ONLY ANSWERS ENTERED IN THE CIRCLES IN EACH GRID WILL BE SCORED. YOU WILL NOT RECEIVE CREDIT FOR ANYTHING WRITTEN IN THE BOXES ABOVE THE CIRCLES.

9   10   11   12   13

14   15   16   17   18

Start with number 1 for each new section. If a section has fewer questions than answer spaces, leave the extra answer spaces blank. Be sure to erase any errors or stray marks completely.

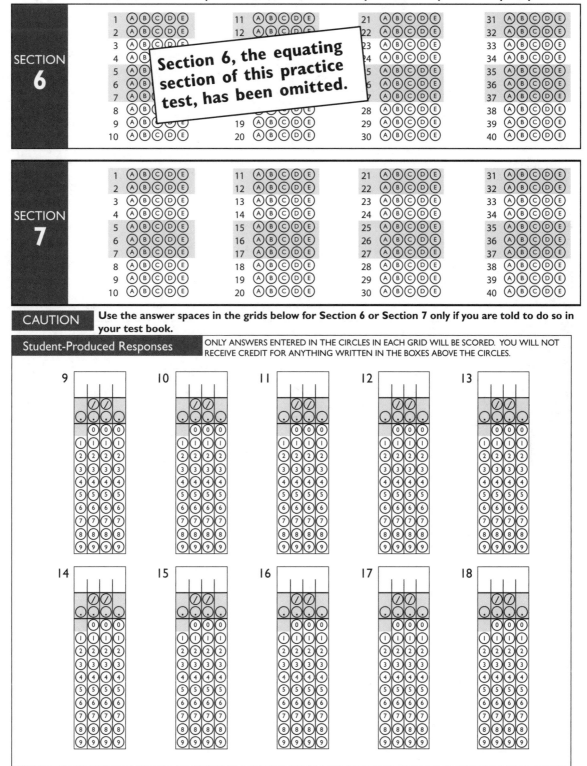

SECTION 6

Section 6, the equating section of this practice test, has been omitted.

SECTION 7

1 Ⓐ Ⓑ Ⓒ Ⓓ Ⓔ	11 Ⓐ Ⓑ Ⓒ Ⓓ Ⓔ	21 Ⓐ Ⓑ Ⓒ Ⓓ Ⓔ	31 Ⓐ Ⓑ Ⓒ Ⓓ Ⓔ
2 Ⓐ Ⓑ Ⓒ Ⓓ Ⓔ	12 Ⓐ Ⓑ Ⓒ Ⓓ Ⓔ	22 Ⓐ Ⓑ Ⓒ Ⓓ Ⓔ	32 Ⓐ Ⓑ Ⓒ Ⓓ Ⓔ
3 Ⓐ Ⓑ Ⓒ Ⓓ Ⓔ	13 Ⓐ Ⓑ Ⓒ Ⓓ Ⓔ	23 Ⓐ Ⓑ Ⓒ Ⓓ Ⓔ	33 Ⓐ Ⓑ Ⓒ Ⓓ Ⓔ
4 Ⓐ Ⓑ Ⓒ Ⓓ Ⓔ	14 Ⓐ Ⓑ Ⓒ Ⓓ Ⓔ	24 Ⓐ Ⓑ Ⓒ Ⓓ Ⓔ	34 Ⓐ Ⓑ Ⓒ Ⓓ Ⓔ
5 Ⓐ Ⓑ Ⓒ Ⓓ Ⓔ	15 Ⓐ Ⓑ Ⓒ Ⓓ Ⓔ	25 Ⓐ Ⓑ Ⓒ Ⓓ Ⓔ	35 Ⓐ Ⓑ Ⓒ Ⓓ Ⓔ
6 Ⓐ Ⓑ Ⓒ Ⓓ Ⓔ	16 Ⓐ Ⓑ Ⓒ Ⓓ Ⓔ	26 Ⓐ Ⓑ Ⓒ Ⓓ Ⓔ	36 Ⓐ Ⓑ Ⓒ Ⓓ Ⓔ
7 Ⓐ Ⓑ Ⓒ Ⓓ Ⓔ	17 Ⓐ Ⓑ Ⓒ Ⓓ Ⓔ	27 Ⓐ Ⓑ Ⓒ Ⓓ Ⓔ	37 Ⓐ Ⓑ Ⓒ Ⓓ Ⓔ
8 Ⓐ Ⓑ Ⓒ Ⓓ Ⓔ	18 Ⓐ Ⓑ Ⓒ Ⓓ Ⓔ	28 Ⓐ Ⓑ Ⓒ Ⓓ Ⓔ	38 Ⓐ Ⓑ Ⓒ Ⓓ Ⓔ
9 Ⓐ Ⓑ Ⓒ Ⓓ Ⓔ	19 Ⓐ Ⓑ Ⓒ Ⓓ Ⓔ	29 Ⓐ Ⓑ Ⓒ Ⓓ Ⓔ	39 Ⓐ Ⓑ Ⓒ Ⓓ Ⓔ
10 Ⓐ Ⓑ Ⓒ Ⓓ Ⓔ	20 Ⓐ Ⓑ Ⓒ Ⓓ Ⓔ	30 Ⓐ Ⓑ Ⓒ Ⓓ Ⓔ	40 Ⓐ Ⓑ Ⓒ Ⓓ Ⓔ

CAUTION **Use the answer spaces in the grids below for Section 6 or Section 7 only if you are told to do so in your test book.**

Student-Produced Responses

ONLY ANSWERS ENTERED IN THE CIRCLES IN EACH GRID WILL BE SCORED. YOU WILL NOT RECEIVE CREDIT FOR ANYTHING WRITTEN IN THE BOXES ABOVE THE CIRCLES.

9 10 11 12 13

14 15 16 17 18

PRACTICE TEST #1

Start with number 1 for each new section. If a section has fewer questions than answer spaces, leave the extra answer spaces blank. Be sure to erase any errors or stray marks completely.

SECTION 8

1	A B C D E	11	A B C D E	21	A B C D E	31	A B C D E
2	A B C D E	12	A B C D E	22	A B C D E	32	A B C D E
3	A B C D E	13	A B C D E	23	A B C D E	33	A B C D E
4	A B C D E	14	A B C D E	24	A B C D E	34	A B C D E
5	A B C D E	15	A B C D E	25	A B C D E	35	A B C D E
6	A B C D E	16	A B C D E	26	A B C D E	36	A B C D E
7	A B C D E	17	A B C D E	27	A B C D E	37	A B C D E
8	A B C D E	18	A B C D E	28	A B C D E	38	A B C D E
9	A B C D E	19	A B C D E	29	A B C D E	39	A B C D E
10	A B C D E	20	A B C D E	30	A B C D E	40	A B C D E

SECTION 9

1	A B C D E	11	A B C D E	21	A B C D E	31	A B C D E
2	A B C D E	12	A B C D E	22	A B C D E	32	A B C D E
3	A B C D E	13	A B C D E	23	A B C D E	33	A B C D E
4	A B C D E	14	A B C D E	24	A B C D E	34	A B C D E
5	A B C D E	15	A B C D E	25	A B C D E	35	A B C D E
6	A B C D E	16	A B C D E	26	A B C D E	36	A B C D E
7	A B C D E	17	A B C D E	27	A B C D E	37	A B C D E
8	A B C D E	18	A B C D E	28	A B C D E	38	A B C D E
9	A B C D E	19	A B C D E	29	A B C D E	39	A B C D E
10	A B C D E	20	A B C D E	30	A B C D E	40	A B C D E

SECTION 10

1	A B C D E	11	A B C D E	21	A B C D E	31	A B C D E
2	A B C D E	12	A B C D E	22	A B C D E	32	A B C D E
3	A B C D E	13	A B C D E	23	A B C D E	33	A B C D E
4	A B C D E	14	A B C D E	24	A B C D E	34	A B C D E
5	A B C D E	15	A B C D E	25	A B C D E	35	A B C D E
6	A B C D E	16	A B C D E	26	A B C D E	36	A B C D E
7	A B C D E	17	A B C D E	27	A B C D E	37	A B C D E
8	A B C D E	18	A B C D E	28	A B C D E	38	A B C D E
9	A B C D E	19	A B C D E	29	A B C D E	39	A B C D E
10	A B C D E	20	A B C D E	30	A B C D E	40	A B C D E

PRACTICE TEST #1

CERTIFICATION STATEMENT

Copy the statement below (do not print) and sign your name as you would an official document

I hereby agree to the conditions set forth online at www.collegeboard.com and/or in the Registration Bulletin and certify that I am the person whose name and address appears on this answer sheet.

_____

_____

_____

_____

Signature _____   Date _____

PRACTICE TEST #1

ESSAY
Time – 25 minutes

The essay gives you an opportunity to show how effectively you can develop and express ideas. You should, therefore, take care to develop your point of view, present your ideas logically and clearly, and use language precisely.

Your essay must be written on the lines provided on your answer sheet—you will receive no other paper on which to write. You will have enough space if you write on every line, avoid wide margins, and keep your handwriting to a reasonable size. Remember that people who are not familiar with your handwriting will read what you write. Try to write or print so that what you are writing is legible to those readers.

You will have twenty-five minutes to write an essay on the topic assigned below. DO NOT WRITE ON ANOTHER TOPIC. AN OFF-TOPIC ESSAY WILL RECEIVE A SCORE OF ZERO.

Think carefully about the issue presented in the following excerpt and the assignment below.

> We moderns rightly disparage war, but truth be told, there is nothing in the human experience outside of armed conflict that so consistently reveals the best of our species. The greatest heights of self-sacrifice, the deepest bonds of camaraderie, and the noblest dedication to a cause outside oneself; all are called forth in military service. Though only fools court the destruction of war, rising out of the maelstrom is the truest representation of human greatness.

Assignment: Does war call forth the most admirable human qualities? Plan and write an essay in which you develop your point of view on this issue. Support your position with reasoning and examples taken from your reading, studies, experience, or observations.

DO NOT WRITE YOUR ESSAY IN YOUR TEST BOOK. You will receive credit only for what you write on your answer sheet.

BEGIN WRITING YOUR ESSAY ON PAGE 2 OF THE ANSWER SHEET

**If you finish before time is called, you may check your work on this section only.
Do not turn to any other section in the test.**

SECTION 2
Time – 25 minutes
24 Questions

Turn to Section 2 (page 4) of your answer sheet to answer the questions in this section.

Directions: For each question in this section, select the best answer from among the choices given and fill in the corresponding circle on the answer sheet.

Each sentence below has one or two blanks, each blank indicating that something has been omitted. Beneath the sentence are five words or sets of words labeled A through E. Choose the word or set of words that, when inserted in the sentence, best fits the meaning of the sentence as a whole.

Example:

In the face of ------- evidence of the defendant's guilt, the jury voted ------- to convict him.

(A) mitigating . . grudgingly
(B) disagreeable . . parsimoniously
(C) unwelcome . . zealously
(D) derisive . . sternly
(E) overwhelming . . unanimously ⒶⒷⒸⒹ●

1. The town historian ------- the newspaper for covering the twentieth anniversary of an alleged UFO sighting while ------- to note the fiftieth anniversary of President Eisenhower's visit.

   (A) upbraided . . deigning
   (B) scolded . . failing
   (C) lauded . . hastening
   (D) piqued . . refusing
   (E) spurned . . deriding

2. For all her ------- talent, Sylvia Plath could not shake the ------- that ultimately drove her to commit suicide.

   (A) extraordinary . . reservations
   (B) honed . . sadness
   (C) considerable . . delirium
   (D) remarkable . . melancholy
   (E) estimable . . disintegration

3. Among the fiercest of the primates, the mandrill is notable for its ------- blue, purple, and scarlet facial markings.

   (A) discordant
   (B) distinguishable
   (C) emphatic
   (D) distinctive
   (E) dialectical

4. Due to his reputation for -------, Todd has no credibility among his peers.

   (A) inscrutability
   (B) disrepute
   (C) prevarication
   (D) incredulity
   (E) scrupulousness

GO ON TO THE NEXT PAGE

PRACTICE TEST #1

5. Only ------- drivers should attempt to ------- Black Mountain Road, which includes steep grades and dangerous hairpin curves.

(A) dedicated . . enjoin
(B) supercilious . . drive
(C) skilled . . encounter
(D) dynamic . . deride
(E) seasoned . . negotiate

The passages below are followed by questions based on their content; questions following a pair of related passages may also be based on the relationship between the paired passages. Answer the questions on the basis of what is <u>stated</u> or <u>implied</u> in the passages and in any introductory material that may be provided.

Questions 6-9 are based on the following passages.

Passage 1

Critics have spent years trying to link violent video content to violent behavior among children, but the proof has been elusive. From the
Line invention of talking movies to television and
5 now the computer, each new technology brings forth a hue and cry from those who declare that it is the end of civilization as we know it. But hasn't violence always been a part of human story-telling? Were William Shakespeare's
10 audiences incited to violence after watching a bloody production such as *Macbeth*? The video game industry has always been responsive to parental concerns, and its cooperation in creating the Entertainment Software Rating Board
15 (ESRB) is evidence of that commitment.

Passage 2

As a mother, I have no doubt of the connection between aggressive behavior and violent video games. I can always tell when my five-year-old, Josh, has spent too long in front of the
20 computer. His attention span is shorter, he is less responsive to me, and he is more likely to become agitated. I have noticed that the majority of our altercations occur on days when he has spent an hour or more on the computer. Last
25 month, I decided to limit his computer time to forty-five minutes per day, and to give him none at all when he has not finished his chores or has a play day scheduled with one of his friends. The result has been a more engaged, more cre-
30 ative child who actually enjoys playing with blocks or going outside to dig in the dirt.

6. The author of Passage 1 makes use of rhetorical questions (lines 7-11) to

(A) state a theory
(B) revise a thesis
(C) develop an argument
(D) return to a theme
(E) connect two arguments

7. Unlike the author of Passage 1, the author of Passage 2 makes use of

(A) scientific data
(B) historical research
(C) direct citation
(D) literary allusion
(E) first person voice

GO ON TO THE NEXT PAGE

8. Which of the following themes from
    Passage 2 might the author of Passage 1 be
    most likely to support?

    (A) parents should play a role in their
        children's use of video games
    (B) video games can cause children to be
        aggressive
    (C) video games can shorten a child's
        attention span
    (D) playing with blocks or going outside can
        provide better recreation than video
        games
    (E) children should avoid violent video
        games

9. Which best describes the relationship
    between Passage 2 and Passage 1?

    (A) Passage 2 describes a first-hand experi-
        ence that corroborates Passage 1
    (B) Passage 2 offers a point-by-point refuta-
        tion of Passage 1
    (C) Passage 2 supports the thrust of Passage
        1, though with a different emphasis
    (D) Passage 2 uses logical deduction to sup-
        port Passage 1
    (E) Passage 2 gives anecdotal evidence that
        refutes Passage 1

GO ON TO THE NEXT PAGE >

Questions 10-15 are based on the following passage.

The following passage was adapted from an essay titled "The Black Intellectual and the Sport of Prizefighting." Floyd Patterson was a professional boxer from 1952 to 1972.

Though he claims to love the sport of boxing, Patterson believes that the sport has alienated him from his wife and children, has made him vicious against his opponents (a viciousness he finds he
5 must have if he is to win and to counter the complaint expressed by Ingemar Johansson that Patterson "is too nice"), and has forced him to act out other people's hatred vicariously and publicly for money. Despite this, Patterson feels deeply
10 that being heavyweight champion of the world means a great deal. As he eloquently puts it:

> You've got to go on. You owe it to
> yourself, to the tradition of the title, to the
> public that sees the champion as somebody
15 special, to everything that must become
> sacred to you the first time you put gloves
> on your hands. You've got to believe in
> what you're doing or else nobody can
> believe that anything is worthwhile.

20 To Patterson, it is the duty of the champion, the black champion, to transcend the ugliness of the sport for his society; in this sense he reminds one of Gene Tunney, the last American heavyweight champion who seemed unsuited tempera-
25 mentally to be a boxer and obsessed with elevating the status of the sport. It is the black champion's burden and his honor. In this instance, of course, Patterson reminds us of Joe Louis. It is no coincidence, then, that Patterson
30 was champion during the late fifties, the era of the African American proving himself worthy of integration, the era of Sidney Poitier, who was the personification of black honor on the screen: the sort of honor that received, at one time, the
35 dubious recognition from whites that here (in their opinion) was a black who was white inside.

Whether Patterson was neurotically fishing for a compliment of that sort is not nearly as important as the fact that honor so painfully
40 bedeviled him, probably because being black and living in the modern world makes it so difficult to find frameworks for the display of it. If Patterson was disliked by the black intellectuals of the day, it is most likely because his position,
45 as he defined it in the sport of prizefighting, is so similar to their own: part of a tradition which they are unable to denounce but unable to embrace completely, torn by doubts not only about the nature of their ability but also about
50 the meaning of what they do in a society where their position is so precarious.

10. In lines 1-11, the author implies that Patterson

(A) has mixed feelings about his boxing career
(B) believes that being heavyweight champion was not worth the price
(C) wishes that he had chosen another profession
(D) believes that most boxers are vicious
(E) thinks that public opinion is overemphasized in the sport of boxing

11. In line 8, "vicariously" most nearly means

(A) through another person
(B) viciously and without remorse
(C) vigorously
(D) shunning publicity
(E) publicly and repentantly

12. In the quotation attributed to Patterson (lines 12-19), he suggests that

(A) only boxers who work hard and sacrifice have a chance to be heavyweight champion
(B) being a role model is the most important responsibility of a heavyweight champion
(C) only those who believe in themselves can be good enough boxers to be heavyweight champion
(D) the heavyweight champion should not be swayed by public opinion
(E) belief in oneself is the most important attribute necessary to become heavyweight champion

13. In lines 29-42, the author implies that

(A) Sydney Poitier was a better role model than Patterson
(B) Patterson's concern for honor caused him to be perceived as pandering to whites
(C) Patterson was excessively dependent on the opinions of whites
(D) Patterson believed that honor was more important than fishing for compliments from whites
(E) Patterson mistakenly believed that honor was more important than character

14. The primary purpose of the final sentence of the passage (lines 42-51) is to

(A) speculate as to whether black intellectuals disliked Patterson
(B) enumerate traits that Patterson shared with black intellectuals
(C) explain why Patterson was an intellectual at heart
(D) explain why black intellectuals disliked Patterson
(E) offer background on the tradition of which Patterson was a part

15. The author's attitude toward Patterson is best described as

(A) skeptical
(B) conciliatory
(C) praiseworthy
(D) sympathetic
(E) awed

PRACTICE TEST #1

GO ON TO THE NEXT PAGE

PRACTICE TEST #1

Questions 16-24 are based on the following passage.

The passage below is adapted from a short story written in 1983.

At his job, among his various other responsibilities, Marcovaldo had to water every morning the potted plant in the entrance hall. It
Line was one of those green houseplants with an
5 erect, thin stalk from which, on both sides, broad, long-stemmed, shiny leaves stick out: in other words, one of those plants that are so plant-shaped, with leaves so leaf-shaped, that they don't seem real. But still it was a plant,
10 and as such it suffered, because staying there, between the curtain and the umbrella stand, it lacked light, air, and dew. Every morning Marcovaldo discovered some baleful sign: the stem of one leaf drooped as if it could no
15 longer support the weight, another leaf was becoming spotted like the cheek of a child with measles, the tip of a third leaf was turning yellow; until, one or the other, plop!, was found on the floor. Meanwhile (what most wrung his
20 heart), the plant's stalk grew taller, taller, no longer making orderly fronds, but naked as a pole, with a clump at the top that made it resemble a palm tree.
      Marcovaldo cleared away the fallen leaves,
25 dusted the healthy ones, poured at the foot of the plant (slowly, so the pot wouldn't spill over and dirty the tiles) half a watering can of water, immediately absorbed by the earth in the pot. And to these simple actions he devoted an
30 attention he gave no other task of his, almost like the compassion felt for the troubles of a relative. And he sighed, whether for the plant

or himself: because in that lanky, yellowing bush within the company walls he recognized a
35 companion in misfortune.
      The plant (this was how it was called, simply, as if any more specific name were useless in a setting where it alone had to represent the vegetable kingdom) had become such a part of
40 Marcovaldo's life that it dominated his thoughts at every hour of the day and night. When he examined the gathering clouds in the sky, his gaze now was no longer that of a city dweller, wondering whether or not he should
45 wear his raincoat, but that of a farmer expecting from day to day the end of a drought. And the moment when he raised his head from his work and saw, against the light, beyond the little window of the warehouse, the curtain of
50 rain that had begun to fall, thick and silent, he would drop everything, run to the plant, take the pot in his arms, and set it outside in the courtyard.
      The plant, feeling the water run over its
55 leaves, seemed to expand, to offer the greatest possible surface to the drops, and in its joy it seemed to don its most brilliant green: or at least so Marcovaldo thought, as he lingered to observe it, forgetting to take shelter.
60   They stayed there in the courtyard, man and plant, facing each other, the man almost feeling plant sensations under the rain, the plant—no longer accustomed to the open air and to the phenomena of nature—amazed, much like a man
65 who finds himself suddenly drenched from head to foot, his clothes soaked. Marcovaldo, his nose in the air, sniffed the smell of the rain, a smell—for him—already of woods and fields, and he pursued with his mind some vague memories.
70 But among these memories there surfaced,

clearer and closer, that of the rheumatic aches
that afflicted him every year; and then, hastily,
he went back inside.

When working hours were over, the place
75 had to be locked up. Marcovaldo asked the
warehouse foreman: "Can I leave the plant outside there, in the courtyard?"

The foreman, Signor Viligelmo, was the kind
of man who avoided burdensome responsibili-
80 ties: "Are you crazy? What if somebody steals it?
Who'll answer for that?"

But Marcovaldo, seeing how much good the
rain did the plant, couldn't bring himself to put
it back inside: it would mean wasting that gift of
85 heaven. "I could keep it until tomorrow morning…" he suggested. "I'll load it on the rack of
my bike and take it home…that way it'll get as
much rain as possible."

Signor Viligelmo thought it over for a
90 moment, then concluded: "Then you're taking
the responsibility." And he gave his consent.

16. In the first paragraph (lines 1-23), the
author makes use of

(A) literary allusion
(B) first-person voice
(C) simile
(D) direct citation
(E) cognitive dissonance

17. The passage's detailed description of the
plant's infirmities serves primarily to
highlight

(A) that the plant is near death
(B) that the plant has been neglected
(C) the extent of Marcovaldo's attention to
the plant
(D) that the plant would be healthier
outdoors
(E) that Marcovaldo has no friends in the
warehouse other than the plant

18. In context, "baleful" (line 13) most nearly
means

(A) benevolent
(B) demoralizing
(C) disgruntling
(D) morbid
(E) ominous

19. The second paragraph (lines 24-35) implies
that Marcovaldo

(A) sees a reflection of himself in the
neglected plant
(B) resents having to care for the plant
(C) spends too much time caring for the plant
(D) resents others at his office who do not
take care of the plant
(E) leaves his work unfinished to care for
the plant

GO ON TO THE NEXT PAGE >

20. The use of personification in lines 60-66 serves to emphasize

(A) that plants and animals have similar biological needs
(B) the similarities between Marcavaldo and the plant
(C) that plants and humans need water
(D) that the plant is healthier after it gets water
(E) that the plant depends on Marcavaldo for its water

21. In line 64, "phenomena" most nearly means

(A) extraordinary
(B) diaspora
(C) phenomenal
(D) elements
(E) phylum

22. Marcavaldo's recollection of "the rheumatic aches that afflicted him" serves to emphasize

(A) the emptiness of Marcavaldo's life
(B) the flashbacks that haunt Marcavaldo
(C) the tenuousness of Marcavaldo's sanity
(D) Marcavaldo's repressed childhood memories
(E) Marcavaldo's inability to come to grips with his past

23. In context, the description of the foreman as a man who "avoided burdensome responsibilities" is best described as

(A) flattering
(B) mocking
(C) matter-of-fact
(D) elliptical
(E) hostile

24. Taken as a whole, the excerpt suggests that Marcavaldo

(A) is an expert at taking care of plants
(B) believes that plants are just as important as animals
(C) has little meaning in his life aside from the plant
(D) would be an excellent gardener
(E) has simmering hostility against the foreman

STOP

**If you finish before time is called, you may check your work on this section only.
Do not turn to any other section in the test.**

SECTION 3
Time – 25 minutes
18 Questions

Turn to Section 7 (page 6) of your answer sheet to answer the questions in this section.

Directions: For this section, solve each problem and decide which is the best of the choices given. Fill in the corresponding circle on the answer sheet. You may use any available space for scratch work.

Notes

1. The use of a calculator is permitted.

2. All numbers used are real numbers.

3. Figures that accompany problems in this test are intended to provide information useful in solving the problems. They are drawn as accurately as possible EXCEPT when it is stated in a specific problem that the figure is not drawn to scale. All figures lie in a plane unless otherwise indicated.

4. Unless otherwise specified, the domain of any function f is assumed to be the set of all real numbers x for which $f(x)$ is a real number.

Reference Information

$A = \pi r^2$
$C = 2\pi r$ $A = \ell w$ $A = \frac{1}{2}bh$ $V = \ell wh$ $V = \pi r^2 h$ $c^2 = a^2 + b^2$ Special Right Triangles

The number of degrees of arc in a circle is 360.
The sum of the measures in degrees of the angles of a triangle is 180.

---

1. In the xy coordinate system, if a line l passes through $(4, -1)$ and has a slope of $\frac{-3}{2}$, which of the following defines l?

(A) $y = -\frac{3}{2}x + 4$

(B) $y = -\frac{3}{2}x + 5$

(C) $y = -\frac{3}{2}x - 3$

(D) $-y = 5x + 7$

(E) $5y = -3x + 5$

2. A store sells rugs in three colors: maroon, gold, and orange. $\frac{3}{5}$ of the rugs are maroon. If there are half as many gold rugs in the store as maroon ones and 26 rugs are orange, how many rugs are in the store?

(A) 40
(B) 130
(C) 180
(D) 220
(E) 260

GO ON TO THE NEXT PAGE

3. A website asks users to create a four-digit access code using random combinations of the digits 0 to 9. If digits can be used only once, how many different access codes can be created?

(A) 5,040
(B) 5,240
(C) 50,420
(D) 52,400
(E) 99,990

4. Let the function f be defined by $f(x) = 3x + 2^x$. When $f(x) = 28$, what is the value of $4 - 3x$?

(A) −80
(B) −14
(C) −12
(D) −8
(E) 28

5. A rectangular sheet of paper measuring $8\frac{1}{2}$ inches by 11 inches is used to create a cylindrical tube. If no part of the sheet overlaps, which of the following is a possible value for the area, in square inches, of the base of the tube?

(A) $\dfrac{8.5}{\pi}$

(B) 4.25π

(C) $\dfrac{11}{2\pi^2}$

(D) $\dfrac{121}{4\pi}$

(E) $121\pi^2$

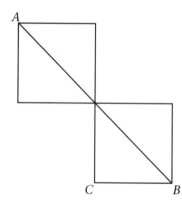

6. In the figure above, $\overline{AB}$ divides two squares into four right triangles. If $\overline{CB} = 4$, what is the length of $\overline{AB}$?

(A) 8
(B) $4\sqrt{2}$
(C) 16
(D) $8\sqrt{2}$
(E) 32

GO ON TO THE NEXT PAGE

7. If $y = x^{-3}$ and $0 < x < 1$, which of the following must be true?

    I. $y > x$
    II. $xy > 0$
    III. $y^2 > x^2$

    (A) I only
    (B) III only
    (C) I and II
    (D) II and III
    (E) I, II, and III

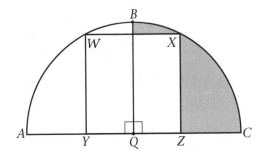

8. In the figure above, arc ABC is one half of a circle with center Q and radius 8. If each side of the square $WXYZ$ is also 8, then the area of the shaded region is

    (A) $64\pi - 64$
    (B) $64\pi - 32$
    (C) $32\pi - 32$
    (D) $32\pi - 16$
    (E) $16\pi - 32$

GO ON TO THE NEXT PAGE

Directions: For Student-Produced Response questions 9-18, use the grids at the bottom of the answer sheet page on which you have answered questions 1-8.

Each of the remaining 10 questions requires you to solve the problem and enter your answer by marking the circles in the special grid, as shown in the examples below. You may use any available space for scratchwork.

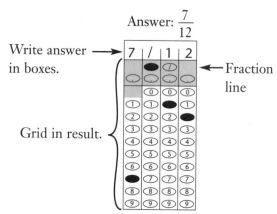

Answer: $\frac{7}{12}$

Write answer in boxes.

Fraction line

Grid in result.

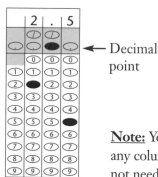

Answer: 2.5

Decimal point

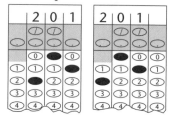

Answer: 201
Either position is correct.

Note: You may start your answers in any column, space permitting. Columns not needed should be left blank.

• Mark no more than one circle in any column.

• Because the answer sheet will be machine-scored, you will receive credit only if the circles are filled in correctly.

• Although not required, it is suggested that you write your answer in the boxes at the top of the columns to help you fill in the circles accurately.

• Some problems may have more than one correct answer. In such cases, grid only one answer.

• No question has a negative answer.

• **Mixed numbers** such as $3\frac{1}{2}$ must be gridded as 3.5 or $\frac{7}{2}$. (If 3 1 / 2 is gridded, it will be interpreted as $\frac{31}{2}$, not $3\frac{1}{2}$.)

• **Decimal Answers:** If you obtain a decimal answer with more digits than the grid can accommodate, it may be either rounded or truncated, but it must fill the entire grid. For example, if you obtain an answer such as 0.6666..., you should record your result as .666 or .667. A less accurate value such as .66 or .67 will be scored as incorrect.

Acceptable ways to grid $\frac{2}{3}$ are:

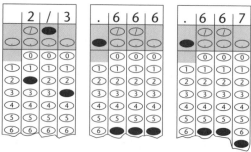

GO ON TO THE NEXT PAGE ⟶

9. Let $w\}\{x\}\{y\}\{z$ be defined as
$w\}\{x\}\{y\}\{z = x^y - w^z$ for all positive integers
w, x, y, and z. What is the value of
$6\}\{5\}\{4\}\{3$?

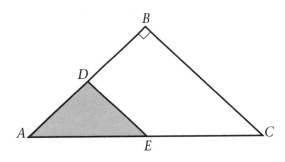

10. In the figure above, $\overline{DE} \parallel \overline{BC}$,
$\overline{AB} = \overline{BC} = 2$, and D is the midpoint of $\overline{AB}$.
If a point is chosen at random inside $\angle ABC$,
what is the probability that the point will be
in the shaded region?

GO ON TO THE NEXT PAGE

11. The product of $-2n$ and $4 - n$ is equal to 90. If n is a positive integer, what is the value of n?

12. A fruit stand displays 4 lemons, 3 limes, 3 oranges, and 2 tangerines. If two pieces of fruit are chosen at random, what are the odds of choosing 2 oranges?

13. On the number line above, there are 8 equal intervals between 0 and 1. What is the value of q?

GO ON TO THE NEXT PAGE

14. In the xy-coordinate plane, the distance between $(3,9)$ and $(x,14)$ is 13. If x is a positive integer, what is the value of x?

15. The average (arithmetic mean) of the high temperatures of x days is 52, and the average of the high temperatures of y days is 66. When the high temperatures of all days are combined, the average is 61. What is the value of $\frac{x}{y}$?

16. If $x^2 - y^2 = -24$ and $x + y = -4$, what is the value of $x - y$?

GO ON TO THE NEXT PAGE

17. If $x + 3y$ is equal to 150 percent of $4y$, what is the value of $\frac{y}{x}$?

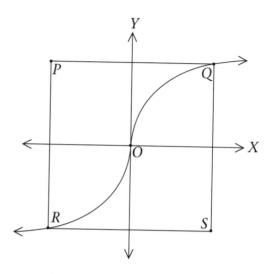

18. In the figure above, $PQRS$ is a square with area 16 centered on the origin. Points Q and R lie on the graph of $x = ky^3$, where k is a constant. What is the value of k?

GO ON TO THE NEXT PAGE

SECTION 4
Time – 25 minutes
35 Questions

Turn to Section 4 (page 5) of your answer sheet to answer the questions in this section.

Directions: For each question in this section, select the best answer from among the choices given and fill in the corresponding circle on the answer sheet.

The following sentences test correctness and effectiveness of expression. Part of each sentence or the entire sentence is underlined; beneath each sentence are five ways of phrasing the underlined material. Choice A repeats the original phrasing; the other four choices are different. If you think the original phrasing produces a better sentence than any of the alternatives, select choice A; if not, select one of the other choices.

In making your selection, follow requirements of standard written English; that is, pay attention to grammar, choice of words, sentence construction, and punctuation. Your selection should result in the most effective sentence—clear and precise, without awkwardness or ambiguity.

EXAMPLE:

In 1953, Ralph Ellison won the National Book Award for *Invisible Man* <u>and he was thirty-nine years old then</u>.

(A) and he was thirty-nine years old then
(B) with the age of thirty-nine years old
(C) upon arriving at thirty-nine
(D) at the time of reaching thirty-nine
(E) when he was thirty-nine years old

Ⓐ Ⓑ Ⓒ Ⓓ ●

1. <u>The representatives having come this far, they</u> were reluctant to leave without finishing their work.

(A) The representatives having come this far, they
(B) Having come this far, the representatives
(C) The representatives coming this far, they
(D) Coming this far, the representatives
(E) The representatives came this far, and they

2. <u>Weather patterns have changed for a variety of reasons</u> in the past two decades, and many of the causes are related to the impact of humans.

(A) Weather patterns have changed for a variety of reasons
(B) There is a variety of reasons why weather patterns have changed
(C) A variety of reasons are in existence for weather changes
(D) There are reasons for a variety of changes to weather patterns
(E) There are reasons why a variety of weather patterns have changed

GO ON TO THE NEXT PAGE

3. Many voters believe that both candidates are <u>corrupt, consequently, voter participation</u> in the election is likely to be low.

   (A) corrupt, consequently, voter participation
   (B) corrupt, voter participation
   (C) corrupt, therefore, voter participation
   (D) corrupt, and therefore people voting
   (E) corrupt; consequently, voter participation

4. <u>Ralph Abernathy, a prominent African American activist, whose role as an architect of the civil rights movement</u> was second only to that of Dr. Martin Luther King, Jr.

   (A) Ralph Abernathy, a prominent African American activist, whose role as an architect of the civil rights movement
   (B) Ralph Abernathy was a prominent African American activist whose role as an architect of the civil rights movement
   (C) Ralph Abernathy, who was a prominent African American activist and whose role as an architect of the civil rights movement
   (D) An African American with renown as an architect of the civil rights movement, Ralph Abernathy
   (E) An African American, Ralph Abernathy was an architect of the civil rights movement

5. Andrew Carnegie was at once ruthless in his business practices <u>but compassionate for his giving to charity</u>.

   (A) but compassionate for his giving to charity
   (B) although he was also compassionate for his giving to charity
   (C) and compassionate in his giving to charity
   (D) and he was compassionate for his giving to charity
   (E) and compassionate for charity

6. After walking all morning in the summer heat, the girls were as drenched as <u>if walking</u> through a rainstorm.

   (A) if walking
   (B) if having walked
   (C) if they had walked
   (D) if they were walking
   (E) if they would have walked

7. Lisa's mother told us that due to her illness, <u>she will not be able to attend the honor society banquet</u>.

   (A) she will not be able to attend the honor society banquet
   (B) she could not attend the honor society banquet
   (C) the decision was that she would not attend the honor society banquet
   (D) Lisa will not be able to attend the honor society banquet
   (E) the honor society banquet she will not attend

GO ON TO THE NEXT PAGE ⇒

8. Eero Saarinen ranks among the great architects of the twentieth century <u>being that his buildings are a combination of beauty and practicality</u>.

   (A) being that his buildings are a combination of beauty and practicality
   (B) considering that his buildings are a combination of beauty and practicality
   (C) due to the fact that his buildings have a combination of beauty and practicality
   (D) because his buildings are a combination of beauty and practicality
   (E) because his buildings combine beauty and practicality

9. <u>After the council announced that Marcie had been chosen as their leader</u>, everyone in attendance gave her a standing ovation.

   (A) After the council announced that Marcie had been chosen as their leader
   (B) After the council had announced that Marcie had been chosen as their leader
   (C) After the council announced that Marcie had been chosen as its leader
   (D) After the council decided to announce their new leader, Marcie
   (E) After the council announced that Marcie was chosen as its leader

10. Sally completed her medical degree last year, <u>and she has been working in a local hospital ever since</u>.

    (A) and she has been working in a local hospital ever since
    (B) ever since working in a local hospital
    (C) she has been working in a local hospital since then
    (D) and since then is working in a local hospital
    (E) since that time she has worked in a local hospital

11. Tim began sneezing uncontrollably during our <u>hike, being allergic to ragweed</u>.

    (A) hike, being allergic to ragweed
    (B) hike because he is allergic to ragweed
    (C) hike, due to being allergic to ragweed
    (D) hike with his allergy to ragweed
    (E) hike, he is allergic to ragweed

PRACTICE TEST #1

GO ON TO THE NEXT PAGE

The following sentences test your ability to recognize grammar and usage errors. Each sentence contains either a single error or no error at all. No sentence contains more than one error. The error, if there is one, is underlined and lettered. If the sentence contains an error, select the one underlined part that must be changed to make the sentence correct. If the sentence is correct, select choice E. In choosing answers, follow the requirements of standard written English.

EXAMPLE:

It is one thing <u>to hear</u> rumors that a
          A

colleague has a <u>fiery</u> temper, <u>for</u> it
          B   C

is quite another <u>to witness</u> an angry
          D

outburst with your own eyes. <u>No error</u>
          E

Ⓐ Ⓑ ● Ⓓ Ⓔ

12. Because the postal worker <u>was</u> not sure to
          A

<u>whom</u> the package <u>had been</u> addressed, she
 B   C

<u>put</u> it in the room for unclaimed freight.
 D

<u>No error</u>
   E

13. If Jane <u>were</u> to reach Atlanta in six hours,
      A

she <u>will arrive</u> at the wedding at least an
    B

hour early and <u>have</u> plenty of time <u>to eat</u> a
          C   D

quick lunch before the ceremony. <u>No error</u>
          E

14. The artist Romare Bearden <u>experimented</u>
          A

with a wide variety of <u>media</u> and artistic
          B

<u>styles</u>, but his work always <u>boar</u> testament
 C   D

to his African American identity. <u>No error</u>
          E

15. <u>For</u> the press conference, Senator Gandy
 A

<u>showed</u> his <u>sensitivity</u> to criticism when he
 B   C

<u>railed at</u> a reporter who challenged him.
 D

<u>No error</u>
   E

GO ON TO THE NEXT PAGE ⟶

16. The Ordovician Period, <u>which began</u>
                    A
approximately 490 million years ago, <u>was</u>
                                       B
<u>described</u> by shallow seas and <u>a rich variety</u>
   C   D
of marine invertebrates, <u>most notably</u> the
                              D
trilobite. <u>No error</u>
              E

17. The publisher has again <u>rejected</u> Dr.
                                   A
Johnson's manuscript, this time <u>asserting</u>
                                     B
that the changes he <u>makes</u> to the original
                        C
submission <u>are not</u> adequate. <u>No error</u>
               D   E

18. The blunder <u>had been</u> particularly devastating
                       A
for Mr. Jones, who was <u>deeply chagrined</u> by
                           B
the knowledge that he <u>could have</u> corrected it
                           C
if he <u>would have</u> known about it. <u>No error</u>
          D   E

19. Though nuclear scientist Wen Ho Lee

<u>had been</u> suspected of espionage, he <u>was</u>
   A   B
eventually cleared of all charges except <u>for</u>
                                              C
one count of improperly <u>copying</u> sensitive
                            D
data. <u>No error</u>
         E

20. Although Larry <u>found</u> his homework boring
                          A
at times, he knew that <u>completing</u> it was
                           B
essential <u>in</u> his goal <u>of</u> getting an A for
             C   D
the semester. <u>No error</u>
                   E

21. <u>Contradictory to</u> the position of his rival,
           A
Stevens <u>advocates</u> that the town cut its
            B
operating budget by six percent <u>during</u> the
                                     C
next three years to offset <u>an expected</u>
                               D
decline in tax revenue. <u>No error</u>
                            E

22. <u>Although</u> Peter and Tom were <u>strong</u>
           A   B
candidates with formidable <u>credentials</u>,
                               C
Cheryl firmly believed that she was the

<u>better</u> person for the job. <u>No error</u>
   D   E

GO ON TO THE NEXT PAGE

23. J.C.R. Licklider <u>would have been</u> among the
A
first to see the <u>potential of</u> the computer as
B
a tool for <u>communication</u>; as early as
C
1962, he <u>envisioned</u> a global network of
D
machines. <u>No error</u>
E

24. When Billy <u>sold</u> the bike to my brother
A
and <u>I</u>, we emptied our piggybanks, <u>pooled</u>
B   C
our resources, and split the <u>cost</u>. <u>No error</u>
D   E

25. No matter <u>what</u> the score, <u>everyone</u> on the
A   B
team always <u>believes</u> <u>they</u> can win. <u>No error</u>
C   D   E

26. <u>Beyond</u> the rolling plains of the American
A
heartland, the <u>majestic</u> outline of the Rocky
B
Mountains <u>loom</u> on the <u>distant</u> horizon.
C   D
<u>No error</u>
E

27. <u>Based on</u> the life of an Oglala Sioux medicine
A
man, *Black Elk Speaks* <u>is</u> one of the few books
B
that <u>chronicle</u> life in the Western United
C
States in the late 19th century <u>from a</u>
D
Native American perspective. <u>No error</u>
E

28. Her teacher said that Julie did a <u>good</u> job on
A
the test; she performed <u>well</u> on the science
B
section, even <u>better</u> on the math, and <u>best</u> of
C   D
all on the English. <u>No error</u>
E

29. <u>Having grown</u> weary of the constant
A
pressure <u>to produce</u> exemplary work,
B
Mark <u>was grateful</u> for three <u>restive</u> weeks
C   D
of vacation. <u>No error</u>
E

GO ON TO THE NEXT PAGE ⇒

> **Directions:** The following passage is an early draft of an essay. Some parts of the passage need to be rewritten.
>
> Read the passage and select the best answers for the questions that follow. Some questions are about particular sentences or parts of sentences and ask you to improve sentence structure or word choice. Other questions ask you to consider organization and development. In choosing answers, follow the requirements of standard written English.

Questions 30-35 are based on the following passage.

This essay was written in response to an assignment to choose the person from history whom you would most like to meet.

(1) If I could meet one person from history, I would choose Elizabeth Cady Stanton. (2) It is unknown to many people that Stanton was the foremost activist for women's rights from nineteenth century America, and perhaps the greatest of all time. (3) Because of her single-minded devotion to women's suffrage, Susan B. Anthony is the more famous of the two today. (4) Stanton was more important. (5) It was she who called, along with Lucretia Mott, the Seneca Falls Convention of 1848, and when the other delegates doubted that women should seek the vote, it was Stanton who rallied them. (6) The eloquence and rigor of her argumentation opened a number of new doors for women on countless fronts, including in particular the right to own property separate from their husbands and the right to divorce.
(7) Unlike Susan B. Anthony, she was unwilling to make alliances with segregationists who,

though they may have supported women's suffrage, did so while discriminating against black women. (8) Always true to her best self, Stanton campaigned until the end for equal rights for all women. (9) As a person, Anthony was gregarious and outgoing. (10) She loved to dance and enjoyed hosting friends in her home. (11) I would love to talk to Elizabeth Cady Stanton for an hour and tell her about the many accomplishments of women in the century since she died.

30. Which of the following is the most appropriate revision of sentence 2 (reproduced below)?

    It is unknown to many people that Stanton was the foremost activist for women's rights from nineteenth century America, and perhaps the greatest of all time.

    (A) Change "the foremost activist" to "foremost among activists"
    (B) Change "in nineteenth century America" to "of nineteenth century America"
    (C) Delete "to many people"
    (D) Change "perhaps the greatest of all time" to "perhaps the greatest activist of all time"
    (E) Change "It is unknown to many people" to "Many people do not know"

31. In context, which of the following is the best phrase to insert at the beginning of sentence 4?

    (A) At the time that she lived,
    (B) To spell it out,
    (C) In their time,
    (D) Without a doubt,
    (E) Looking at her contemporaries,

32. Sentence 5 in the passage does which of the following?

(A) introduces a new topic
(B) provides concrete evidence
(C) outlines a general theme
(D) presents a personal opinion
(E) links two contrasting views

33. In context, which of the following revisions would NOT improve sentence 6 (reproduced below)?

The eloquence and rigor of her argumentation opened a number of new doors for women on countless fronts, including in particular the right to own property separate from their husbands and the right to divorce.

(A) Change "argumentation" to "arguments"
(B) Change "separate from" to "independently of"
(C) Change "separate from their husbands" to "separate from their husband"
(D) Delete "a number of"
(E) Delete "in particular"

34. Which of the following would be the best sentence to insert at the beginning of the second paragraph?

(A) Stanton often eschewed political compromises.
(B) Stanton and Anthony did not always agree.
(C) Stanton was a dedicated activist.
(D) Stanton differed from Susan B. Anthony in many ways.
(E) No one questioned Stanton's morals.

35. In context, which is the best version of the underlined portions of sentences 9 and 10 (reproduced below)?

As a person, Anthony was gregarious and outgoing. She loved to dance and enjoyed hosting friends in her home.

(A) (as it is now)
(B) gregarious and outgoing, loving to dance
(C) gregarious and outgoing, she loved to dance
(D) gregarious and outgoing; she was a lover of dance
(E) gregarious and outgoing because she loved to dance

STOP

**If you finish before time is called, you may check your work on this section only.
Do not turn to any other section in the test.**

SECTION 5
Time – 25 minutes
24 Questions

Turn to Section 5 (page 5) of your answer sheet to answer the questions in this section.

Directions: For each question in this section, select the best answer from among the choices given and fill in the corresponding circle on the answer sheet.

Each sentence below has one or two blanks, each blank indicating that something has been omitted. Beneath the sentence are five words or sets of words labeled A through E. Choose the word or set of words that, when inserted in the sentence, best fits the meaning of the sentence as a whole.

Example:

In the face of ------- evidence of the defendant's guilt, the jury voted ------- to convict him.

(A) mitigating . . grudgingly
(B) disagreeable . . parsimoniously
(C) unwelcome . . zealously
(D) derisive . . sternly
(E) overwhelming . . unanimously

Ⓐ Ⓑ Ⓒ Ⓓ ●

1. Although known primarily for her Pulitzer prize–winning poetry, Gwendolyn Brooks also won critical ------- for her ------- novel, *Maud Martha*.

   (A) applause . . obstreperous
   (B) acclaim . . lone
   (C) notation . . unusual
   (D) respect . . cacophonous
   (E) discourse . . inimitable

2. The agent asked that we not reveal his name because he was traveling -------.

   (A) unanimously
   (B) stealthy
   (C) unidentified
   (D) incognito
   (E) concealed

3. Deeply embarrassed by the public -------, Representative Anderson promised to be more circumspect in future statements to the press.

   (A) censure
   (B) disgorging
   (C) entente
   (D) erudition
   (E) devolution

4. The ------- of John Quincy Adams was the most remarkable ------- of his career; he was first elected to the Senate in 1802 and was serving in the House of Representatives at the time of his death in 1848.

   (A) eloquence . . trait
   (B) appellation . . aspect
   (C) longevity . . facet
   (D) endurance . . development
   (E) originality . . effect

5. Although Sojourner Truth had no formal education, she was a ------- speaker whose homespun eloquence flowed spontaneously.

(A) doctrinaire
(B) facile
(C) dilatory
(D) decent
(E) redundant

6. Though the causes of global warming are still a source of -------, even skeptics ------- that the phenomenon is real.

(A) debate . . insist
(B) concern . . acknowledge
(C) contention . . concede
(D) unrest . . debate
(E) disagreement . . allege

7. Though seemingly insignificant, the fact that Mr. Peterson skipped a belt loop was ------- of his inattention to detail.

(A) functional
(B) a cause
(C) a downfall
(D) an indictment
(E) emblematic

8. Although his lecture inspired ------- looks, Mr. Begay assured the class that he was not trying to be -------.

(A) exasperated . . elusive
(B) astonished . . truculent
(C) quizzical . . cryptic
(D) ineluctable . . disbelieving
(E) daunted . . dense

GO ON TO THE NEXT PAGE

The passages below are followed by questions based on their content; questions following a pair of related passages may also be based on the relationship between the paired passages. Answer the questions on the basis of what is stated or implied in the passages and in any introductory material that may be provided.

Questions 9-10 are based on the following passage.

Aspergillus is a ubiquitous indoor mold and the major organism found on spoiling food. It causes inhalant allergies, and it can colonize
Line human airways and create a severe allergic asth-
5 matic condition that is called allergic bronchopulmonary aspergillosis. It is a hardy organism that can live in dry conditions; indeed, it has survived for thousands of years within Egyptian tombs. After the tombs were opened
10 by early pyramid explorers, the mold was responsible for infecting and killing them. In addition to causing allergy, aspergillus is a toxin-producing substance that can cause several forms of infectious disease.

9. In line 1, "ubiquitous" most nearly means

(A) harmful
(B) omnipresent
(C) deleterious
(D) parasitic
(E) microscopic

10. The two clauses of the third sentence (lines 6-9) are characterized, respectively, by

(A) statement and disclaimer
(B) rebuttal and analysis
(C) statement and query
(D) assertion and evidence
(E) hypothesis and theory

Questions 11-12 are based on the following passage.

The enormous expanse to the north and west of New Orleans, the key city that had been the paramount object of the Louisiana Purchase,
Line meant that thirteen new states would eventually
5 be created, in whole or in substantial part, from the eight hundred seventy-five thousand square miles that had been bought. The transformation of this territory into states would take most of the nineteenth century, but during that period,
10 there was little question that the people of the East were part of the process. Even those who never planned a trip to the West Coast thought of it as part of their country, and most would have fought to defend it.

11. In context, "paramount" (line 3) most nearly means

(A) largest
(B) controversial
(C) chief
(D) zenith
(E) magnanimous

GO ON TO THE NEXT PAGE

12. In the final two sentences of the passage, the author refutes the idea that

(A) the transformation of the Louisiana territory was slow and difficult

(B) the people of the East took no notice of the Louisiana Purchase

(C) Americans wanted to go to war over the Louisiana Purchase

(D) people from the East cared more about the Louisiana Purchase than those from the West

(E) people of the time did not want to plan trips to the West Coast

Questions 13-24 are based on the following passages.

Introduction:

The following passages discuss various facets of the legal system.

Passage 1

Once witnesses come to understand cross-examination as little more than a speech by the cross-examiner, the process is far less troubling.
Line They should also understand that the questions
5 will be asked so that they sound like statements. "You *did read* the contract before signing it, didn't you?" turns the question into a commentary. The witness immediately feels somewhat irrelevant, but if well prepared, the witness can hold his own.
10 As cross-examiners, we must be sure not to sound hostile or pedantic as we make these statement-questions. As everyone knows, when our spouse or partner asks questions in the form of statements, we fear we may be in for a long evening.
15 We may even object to being "interrogated."

When we prepare a witness, we may ask questions in a particular style to help them get used to a "lawyer" style. For example, a technique called the "loop back question" includes
20 the answer given in the prior question. "Now, you've said that the good showed up on Thursday. On that date, did you then…" By "looping back," we recast the previous statement in a way we like. If you live with a school-
25 teacher, you may be familiar with this form—it can sound suspiciously like a lecture.

But it is not just about question form; lawyers like to get into a rhythm of asking questions, trying to get the witness on cross-examination into
30 the habit of answering as expected. For example:
"You were the supervisor, weren't you?
"Yes."
"And you were responsible for staff hiring and termination, weren't you?"
35 "Yes."
"And you had the authority to hire and fire employees like Ms. Maldo"
"Yes."
And on and on as the witness gets used to
40 answering in the affirmative until we hope the questions give the cross-examiner what he or she is after. Simply put, if you say yes a lot, you may just continue to say yes even when you mean to say no.
45 "Then you knew Ms. Maldo was not religious when you terminated her employment, didn't you?"
If the "yes roll," works, we may get the yes we're after, even if the witness did not intend to
50 say yes. Repetition gets comfortable, for the lawyer anyway.

GO ON TO THE NEXT PAGE ➔

Passage 2

Lawyers have a duty to zealously represent their clients, with certain limitations. A lawyer cannot break the law to represent a client, and a
55 lawyer must avoid conflicts of interest. While a lawyer's attention may be divided among many clients, the interests of those clients must not be directly at odds with one another.

A conflict of interest occurs when someone's
60 loyalties are divided, or when personal circumstances make it impossible for that person to render an unbiased, objective opinion or to act in an objective manner. You have probably heard about doctors who will not operate on
65 family members. The doctors do not want to have to make life and death decisions for loved ones. If your spouse (parent, sibling, child) were on the operating table and the doctor's choices were amputation or likely death, would you want
70 to be the doctor making the decision? Could you? It is a difficult enough decision to make when you are not emotionally involved.

It is the same for lawyers. State bar associations articulate and enforce a code of ethical conduct
75 that prohibits conflict of interest. An attorney may be sued for malfeasance if he or she crosses these boundaries and renders an opinion that is not in the client's best interests due to a conflict of interest. The example dealing with doctors illustrated a
80 conflict of emotions. Other potential areas of conflict are social and business related. If, for instance, a lawyer serves on the board of a corporation with someone who is a party in a lawsuit, the lawyer should not agree to represent the individual or
85 entity who opposes that party.

Conflict of interest often occurs in cases of "dual representation," in which a lawyer represents two clients with incompatible interests in the same matter. Such dual representation is generally
90 either barred or discouraged by ethics rules. Suppose a lawyer represents a land developer who has filed suit to challenge a municipality's application of zoning laws. The lawyer should not, thereafter, agree to represent another client who
95 has offered testimony against the developer's project, and who may initiate legal action if the project is approved.

Lawyers owe their clients confidentiality and absolute loyalty. An attorney cannot be
100 absolutely loyal to one client if the attorney has other interests to serve.

13. The first four sentences of Passage 1 (lines 1-9) are intended to

(A) instruct witnesses about cross-examination
(B) place cross-examination in legal context
(C) downplay the significance of cross-examination
(D) list common mistakes in cross-examination
(E) tell lawyers how to prepare witnesses for cross-examination.

14. In the first paragraph, the author of Passage 1 suggests that witnesses may feel "somewhat irrelevant" (line 8) during cross-examination because

(A) the lawyer does not care how they respond
(B) they must respond to confusing questions
(C) they are not allowed to elaborate on their answers
(D) the lawyer uses the conversation to present a version of the facts
(E) the lawyer often spends most of the time conversing with the judge

15. In context, "pedantic" (line 11) most nearly means

(A) erudite
(B) scornful
(C) bookish
(D) intemperate
(E) soporific

16. According to Passage 1, the reason why lawyers ask "loop back" questions is to

(A) recast a previous response from the witness
(B) remind the witness of an answer given to a prior question
(C) use the power of suggestion to shape the witness's response
(D) rephrase a cross-examination that is going poorly
(E) focus jury attention on a previous response from the witness

17. The strategies for lawyers recounted in Passage 1 are best described as examples of

(A) nonchalance
(B) stultification
(C) subterfuge
(D) cloying
(E) destabilization

18. In lines 59-72, the author of Passage 2 makes use of

(A) metaphor
(B) personal narrative
(C) literary allusion
(D) aphorism
(E) analogy

19. In context, "articulate" (line 74) most nearly means

(A) inculcate
(B) outline
(C) declaim
(D) utter
(E) eloquent

20. In lines 81-85, the author of Passage 2 uses a hypothetical scenario to

(A) introduce a new idea
(B) offer implied evidence
(C) support a conclusion
(D) illustrate a concept
(E) make a deduction

PRACTICE TEST #1

GO ON TO THE NEXT PAGE

21. In lines 86-90, Passage 2 implies that dual representation is

(A) sometimes permissible
(B) always unacceptable
(C) rarely necessary
(D) frequently ignored
(E) often sanctioned

22. Passage 1 is unlike Passage 2 in that Passage 1

(A) addresses readers in the second-person
(B) explains an important legal principle
(C) outlines techniques that readers can use
(D) discusses the legality of particular actions
(E) describes what happens to those who act improperly

23. Both passages can be described as

(A) pompous
(B) theoretical
(C) confrontational
(D) deductive
(E) informational

24. Which of the following best describes the intended audience for each of the two passages?

(A) Passage 1 is intended for lawyers and Passage 2 is intended for prospective jurors
(B) Passage 1 is intended for a general audience and Passage 2 is intended for physicians
(C) Passage 1 is intended for lawyers and Passage 2 is intended for a general audience
(D) both passages are intended for lawyers
(E) both passages are intended for a general audience

STOP

**If you finish before time is called, you may check your work on this section only.
Do not turn to any other section in the test.**

SECTION 7
Time – 25 minutes
20 Questions

Directions: For this section, solve each problem and decide which is the best of the choices given. Fill in the corresponding circle on the answer sheet. You may use any available space for scratch work.

Notes

1. The use of a calculator is permitted.
2. All numbers used are real numbers.
3. Figures that accompany problems in this test are intended to provide information useful in solving the problems. They are drawn as accurately as possible EXCEPT when it is stated in a specific problem that the figure is not drawn to scale. All figures lie in a plane unless otherwise indicated.
4. Unless otherwise specified, the domain of any function f is assumed to be the set of all real numbers x for which $f(x)$ is a real number.

Reference Information

$A = \pi r^2$
$C = 2\pi r$
$A = lw$
$A = \frac{1}{2}bh$
$V = lwh$
$V = \pi r^2 h$
$c^2 = a^2 + b^2$ Special Right Triangles

The number of degrees of arc in a circle is 360.
The sum of the measures in degrees of the angles of a triangle is 180.

1. What is 3,549,674 rounded to the nearest thousand?

(A) 3,550,000
(B) 3,549,700
(C) 3,549,600
(D) 3,549,000
(E) 3,500,000

2. If a is an integer and 1 is the remainder when $2a^2 + 4$ is divided by 3, then a could be

(A) 4
(B) 5
(C) 6
(D) 7
(E) 8

GO ON TO THE NEXT PAGE

3. If $2 \leq x \leq 3$ and $5 \leq y \leq 7$, what is the greatest possible value of $\dfrac{4}{y-x}$?

   (A) $\dfrac{1}{3}$

   (B) $\dfrac{1}{2}$

   (C) 1

   (D) $\dfrac{3}{2}$

   (E) 2

4. If $y^2 + 17y + 52 = 0$, then the value of y could be

   (A) 4
   (B) 0
   (C) –2
   (D) –4
   (E) –17

5. A farmer is building a fence to create a rectangular pen. If the length of the pen is 16 and the distance diagonally across the pen from one corner to another is 20, what is the area of the pen?

   (A) 72
   (B) 96
   (C) 192
   (D) 288
   (E) 320

6. The figure above is a rectangle divided into four squares of equal size. If the perimeter of one of the squares is 2, then the perimeter of the rectangle is

   (A) 3
   (B) 4
   (C) 5
   (D) 10
   (E) 20

FEDERATED SHIRT COMPANY'S
MARCH SALES

	Tee Shirts	Knit Shirts	Total
Red	1600	1,800	
Blue	4,200		
Total	5,800		11,000

7. Federated Shirt Company manufactures only red and blue shirts, both of which are available as tee shirts or knit shirts. On the basis of the information in the table above, how many blue shirts did Federated Shirt Company manufacture in March?

   (A) 10,000
   (B) 7,600
   (C) 5,800
   (D) 4,200
   (E) 3,400

GO ON TO THE NEXT PAGE

8. A circle has radius r. If $2x$ is added to the diameter of the circle, by how much will the area of the circle increase?

(A) x^2
(B) $\pi(r + x)^2$
(C) $\pi(2rx + x^2)$
(D) $2rx + r^2$
(E) $r^2 + 2rx + x^2$

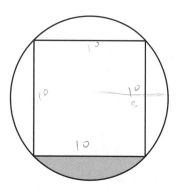

9. In the figure above, a square with sides of length 10 is inscribed in a circle. What is the area of the shaded portion of the figure?

(A) $\dfrac{25\pi}{2}$

(B) 50π

(C) $25\pi - 100$

(D) $50\pi - 100$

(E) $\dfrac{25\pi}{2} - 25$

10. A store increases the price of a bicycle by 20 percent. A week later, it lowers the price by 40 percent. The final price is what percentage of the original price?

(A) 52
(B) 72
(C) 80
(D) 82
(E) 90

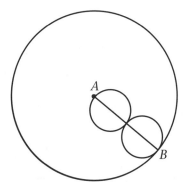

11. In the figure above, two circles are congruent, tangent, and bisected by the radius of a bigger circle, $\overline{AB}$. If the smaller circles each have a circumference of 6π, what is the area of the big circle?

(A) 12π
(B) 24π
(C) 48π
(D) 81π
(E) 144π

GO ON TO THE NEXT PAGE

12. In the figure above, $5AC = 2BC$. What is the ratio of $AC : BA$?

(A)   2:3
(B)   3:2
(C)   2:5
(D)   5:2
(E)   1:10

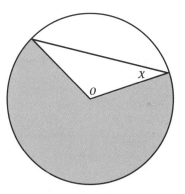

13. The circle O has a radius of 6. If the area of the shaded region is 24π, what is the value of x?

(A) 15
(B) 30
(C) 40
(D) 45
(E) 60

14. A triangle has one side that measures 6 inches and another side that measures 10 inches. Which of the following could be the area of the triangle in square inches?

    I. 24
    II. 30
    III. 60

(A) I only
(B) II only
(C) III only
(D) I and II only
(E) I, II, and III

15. A tree casts a shadow that is 48 feet long. A boy who is $4\frac{1}{2}$ feet tall is standing nearby and casts a shadow that is 6 feet long. How many feet tall is the tree?

(A) 24
(B) 32
(C) 36
(D) 54
(E) 64

PRACTICE TEST #1

GO ON TO THE NEXT PAGE

A	B
8	4
9	5
10	6
11	7

16. If y is a number from column A and z is a number from column B in the table above, how many different values are possible for $y - z$?

(A) 4
(B) 5
(C) 6
(D) 7
(E) 8

17. If x, y, and z are integers, and $xy = 24$, $xz = = -48$, and $yz = -72$, then $x + y + z$ could be

(A) −24
(B) 2
(C) 4
(D) 12
(E) 24

18. $27^{\frac{4}{3}} - 64^{\frac{5}{6}} =$

(A) −17
(B) −5
(C) 32
(D) 49
(E) 54

19. Let the function f be defined by $f(x) = 3x - 1$. If $\frac{4}{3} f(g^{\frac{1}{2}}) = 3$, then $g =$

(A) $\frac{2}{3}$

(B) $\frac{13}{2}$

(C) $\frac{144}{12}$

(D) $\frac{13}{144}$

(E) $\frac{169}{144}$

20. In the xy coordinate plane, which of the following could be described by $x = \frac{1}{2} y^2 - 4$?

(A)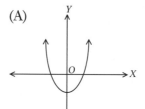

(B)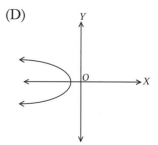

(C)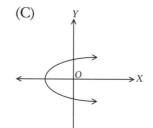

(D)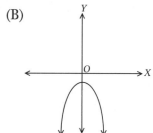

(E)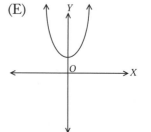

SECTION 8
Time – 20 minutes
19 Questions

Turn to Section 8 (page 7) of your answer sheet to answer the questions in this section.

Directions: For each question in this section, select the best answer from among the choices given and fill in the corresponding circle on the answer sheet.

Each sentence below has one or two blanks, each blank indicating that something has been omitted. Beneath the sentence are five words or sets of words labeled A through E. Choose the word or set of words that, when inserted in the sentence, best fits the meaning of the sentence as a whole.

Example:

In the face of ------- evidence of the defendant's guilt, the jury voted ------- to convict him.

(A) mitigating . . grudgingly
(B) disagreeable . . parsimoniously
(C) unwelcome . . zealously
(D) derisive . . sternly
(E) overwhelming . . unanimously

Ⓐ Ⓑ Ⓒ Ⓓ ●

1. Although ------- as a masterpiece today, Kate Chopin's *The Awakening* was ------- by contemporary critics because its heroine violated the standards of social acceptability for women of the 1890s.

(A) recognized . . lauded
(B) derided . . rejected
(C) hailed . . castigated
(D) described . . disentangled
(E) enumerated . . dismissed

2. John did his homework with -------, finishing every assignment in every class before 9:00 p.m.

(A) resurgence
(B) dynamism
(C) alacrity
(D) deliberation
(E) dutifulness

3. As she surveyed the layers of sediment deposited over millions of years, Julie reflected on the ------- nature of human life.

(A) ephemeral
(B) mystic
(C) amorphous
(D) incomprehensible
(E) grandiose

4. The worldwide influence of Woodrow Wilson reached its ------- in early 1919; scarcely six months later, his proposal for a League of Nations was foundering and he had suffered a debilitating stroke.

(A) nadir
(B) culmination
(C) conclusion
(D) denouement
(E) zenith

GO ON TO THE NEXT PAGE ⟶

5. Destruction of rainforest habitat has continued
------- in South America due to the relentless
------- of human settlement.

(A) escalating . . destruction
(B) accelerating . . continuance
(C) intermittently . . growth
(D) consistently . . interference
(E) unabated . . encroachment

6. The actor Ossie Davis was known for his
------- voice, a rich baritone that was
instantly recognizable.

(A) sonorous
(B) sonic
(C) desultory
(D) scrupulous
(E) syncopated

GO ON TO THE NEXT PAGE

PRACTICE TEST #1

The passage below is followed by questions based on its content. Answer the questions on the basis of what is <u>stated</u> or <u>implied</u> in the passage and in any introductory material that may be provided.

Questions 7-19 are based on the following passage.

The following passage is adapted from a short story written in 1958.

A thing finally happened which could almost have been predicted. Young people, even in West Vesey Place, will not submit forever to the prudent
Line counsel of their parents. Or some of them won't.
5 There was a boy named Ned Meriwether and his sister Emily Meriwether, who lived with their parents in West Vesey Place just one block away from the Dorsets' house. In November Ned and Emily were invited to the Dorsets' party, and because
10 they dreaded it they decided to play a trick on everyone concerned—even on themselves, as it turned out…They got up a plan for smuggling an uninvited guest into the Dorsets' party.

The parents of this Emily and Ned sensed
15 that their children were concealing something from them and suspected that the two were up to mischief of some kind. But they managed to deceive themselves with the thought that it was only natural for young people—"mere chil-
20 dren"—to be nervous about going to the Dorsets' house. And so instead of questioning them during the last hour before they left for the party, these sensible parents tried to do everything in their power to calm their two children.
25 The boy and the girl, seeing that this was the case, took advantage of it.

"You must not go down to the front door with us when we leave," the daughter insisted to her mother.

30 When, at eight o' clock, the lights of the automobile appeared in the street below, the brother and sister were still upstairs—watching from the bay window of the family sitting room. They kissed Mother and Daddy good-bye and
35 then they flew down the stairs and across the wide, carpeted entrance hall to a certain dark recess where a boy named Tom Bascomb was hidden. This boy was the uninvited guest whom Ned and Emily were going to smuggle into the
40 party. They had left the front door unlatched for Tom, and from the upstairs window just a few minutes ago they had watched him come across their front lawn. Now in the little recess of the hall there was a quick exchange of over-
45 coats and hats between Ned Meriwether and Tom Bascomb; for it was a feature of the plan that Tom should attend the party as Ned and that Ned should go as the uninvited guest.

The doorbell rang, and from his dark corner
50 Ned Meriwether whispered to his sister and to Tom, "Don't worry. I'll be at the Dorsets' in plenty of time."

Then, at a sign from Emily, Tom followed her to the entrance door and permitted her to
55 introduce him to old Mr. Dorset as her brother.

From the window of the upstairs sitting room the Meriwether parents watched Mr. Dorset and this boy and this girl walking across the lawn toward Mr. Dorset's peculiar looking car. A light
60 shone bravely and protectively from above the entrance of the house, and in its rays the parents were able to detect the strange angle at which Brother was carrying his head tonight and how his new fedora already seemed too small for him.

65 They even noticed that he seemed a bit taller
tonight.

"I hope it's all right," said the mother.

"What do you mean 'all right'?" the father
asked petulantly.

70 "I mean—," the mother began, and then she
hesitated. She did not want to mention that the
boy out there did not look like her own Ned. It
would have seemed to give away her feelings too
much. "I mean that I wonder if I should have

75 put Sister in that long dress at this age and let
her wear my cape. I'm afraid the cape is really
inappropriate. She's still young for that sort of
thing."

"Oh," said the father, "I thought you meant

80 something else."

"Whatever else did you think I meant,
Edwin?" the mother said, suddenly breathless.

"I thought you meant the business we've
discussed before," he said although this was of

85 course not what he had thought she meant. He
had thought she meant that the boy out there
did not look like their Ned. To him it had
seemed even that the boy's step was different
from Ned's. "The Dorsets' parties," he said,

90 "are not very nice affairs to be sending your
children to, Muriel. That's all I thought you
meant."

"But we can't keep them away," the mother
said defensively.

95 "Oh, it's just that they are growing up faster
than we realize," said the father, glancing at his
wife out of the corner of his eye.

By this time Mr. Dorset's car had pulled out
of sight, and from downstairs Muriel Meriwether

100 thought she heard another door closing. "What
was that?" she said, putting one hand on her
husband's.

"Don't be so jumpy," her husband said irritably, snatching away his hand. "It's the servants

105 closing up in the kitchen."

Both of them knew that the servants had
closed up in the kitchen long before this. Both
of them had heard quite distinctly the sound of
the side door closing as Ned went out. But they

110 went on talking in this fashion during most of
that evening.

7. The primary purpose of the first paragraph
(lines 1 to 13) is to

(A) evaluate the motivations of the main
characters

(B) provide details about the trick that Ned
and Emily are planning

(C) describe the setting in which the story
takes place

(D) give information necessary for understanding the story

(E) establish the fact that young people can
be irresponsible

8. The passage is narrated from the point of
view of

(A) Emily Meriwether

(B) Muriel Meriwether

(C) an observer who does not know the characters initially but who learns about
them during the course of the passage

(D) an observer who has only partial knowledge of the characters

(E) an observer who knows all about the
characters and their thoughts

GO ON TO THE NEXT PAGE ▷

9. In line 23, the author uses the word "sensible" in describing Mr. and Mrs. Meriwether to emphasize that they

    (A) understand that Ned and Emily are not being truthful
    (B) empathize with the nervousness that Ned and Emily show
    (C) should be able to see through Ned and Emily's ruse
    (D) understand that teenagers are rebellious
    (E) are uneasy about allowing Ned and Emily to attend the Dorsets' party

10. The Meriwethers believe that Ned and Emily are nervous about going to the Dorset's party, and the passage implies that Emily "took advantage of it" (line 26) by

    (A) insisting that her parents let her and Ned stay out until midnight
    (B) asking that her parents not come down to the door when she and Ned left
    (C) wearing her mother's cape to the Dorsets' party
    (D) dimming the lights in the downstairs hallway
    (E) asking that Tom Bascomb be allowed to go to the Dorsets' party

11. In line 43, "recess" most nearly means

    (A) secret room
    (B) spacious hall
    (C) quick break
    (D) steep staircase
    (E) secluded corner

12. In line 60, the description of the light as shining "bravely and protectively" serves to highlight the fact that

    (A) the light is strong and bright
    (B) Ned and Emily are leaving the safety of the house
    (C) Mr. and Mrs. Meriwether use the light to watch Ned and Emily
    (D) Mr. and Mrs. Meriwether should know that the boy is not Ned
    (E) Ned and Emily are nervous about leaving the house

13. The author's description of "the strange angle at which Brother was carrying his head tonight" (lines 62-63) suggests that

    (A) Ned feels awkward in his new fedora
    (B) the Meriwethers are worried about Ned's safety
    (C) Ned is nervous about going to the Dorset's party
    (D) the boy walking across the lawn is not Brother
    (E) Ned did not want his parents to see his face

14. After Mr. Dorset's car drives away, Muriel Meriwether is best described as

    (A) risible
    (B) laconic
    (C) sardonic
    (D) apprehensive
    (E) dyspeptic

PRACTICE TEST #1

15. In line 69, "petulantly" most nearly means

(A) anxiously
(B) phlegmatically
(C) irritably
(D) disinterestedly
(E) obnoxiously

16. In line 82, Mrs. Meriwether is "suddenly breathless" because she

(A) thinks her husband may confirm her suspicions that the boy was not Ned
(B) is angry with her husband for not saying what is on his mind
(C) is concerned that her husband also thinks that the cape is inappropriate for the party
(D) is worried about the safety of Ned and Emily at the party
(E) thinks that her husband is too distrustful of Ned and Emily

17. Mr. Meriwether implies that "the business we've discussed before" (lines 83-84) refers to

(A) the fact that Ned and Emily are growing up faster than the Meriwethers realize
(B) their suspicions that the boy who walked to the car with Emily was not Ned
(C) the appropriateness of Emily wearing Mrs. Meriwether's cape and coat
(D) the fact that the Dorsets' parties are not very nice affairs for their children
(E) Ned and Emily's tendency to rebel against authority

18. The passage reveals all of the following, directly or indirectly, except

(A) how Tom Bascomb secretly entered the Meriwether's house
(B) why Emily asks her parents not to go to the front door when Mr. Dorset arrives
(C) why the Meriwethers do not discuss their suspicions after Ned and Emily leave
(D) the identity of the boy who goes to Mr. Dorset's car with Emily
(E) what made the sound of a door closing after the Dorset's car drove out of sight

19. In the last paragraph (lines 106 to 111), the author suggests that the Meriwethers are

(A) inattentive to Ned and Emily
(B) distrustful of the Dorsets
(C) more controlling than most parents
(D) deceiving themselves
(E) distrustful of Ned and Emily

STOP

If you finish before time is called, you may check your work on this section only.

Do not turn to any other section in the test.

SECTION 9
Time – 20 minutes
16 Questions

Turn to Section 9 (page 7) of your answer sheet to answer the questions in this section.

Directions: For this section, solve each problem and decide which is the best of the choices given. Fill in the corresponding circle on the answer sheet. You may use any available space for scratch work.

Notes

1. The use of a calculator is permitted.

2. All numbers used are real numbers.

3. Figures that accompany problems in this test are intended to provide information useful in solving the problems. They are drawn as accurately as possible EXCEPT when it is stated in a specific problem that the figure is not drawn to scale. All figures lie in a plane unless otherwise indicated.

4. Unless otherwise specified, the domain of any function f is assumed to be the set of all real numbers x for which $f(x)$ is a real number.

Reference Information

      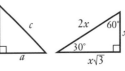

$A = \pi r^2$
$C = 2\pi r$
$A = \ell w$
$A = \frac{1}{2}bh$
$V = bh$
$V = \pi r^2 h$
$c^2 = a^2 + b^2$ Special Right Triangles

The number of degrees of arc in a circle is 360.
The sum of the measures in degrees of the angles of a triangle is 180.

1. A restaurant assigns a number to each customer. If numbers 48 through 202 have been waited on, how many customers have been served?

(A) 53
(B) 54
(C) 55
(D) 154
(E) 155

2. The sum of p consecutive positive integers is always an odd integer if p is a multiple of

(A) 3
(B) 4
(C) 5
(D) 6
(E) 7

GO ON TO THE NEXT PAGE

3. Let $\begin{array}{|cc|} a & b \\ c & d \end{array} = (ad)^2 - (cb)^2$ where a, b, c and $d,$ are integers. What is the value of $\begin{array}{|cc|} -3 & 8 \\ 2 & -5 \end{array}$

(A) –31
(B) –16
(C) 31
(D) 256
(E) 481

4. If $x \geq 0$, which of the following is the graph of $f(x) = 5 - x^2$

(A)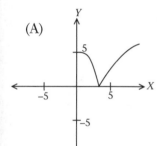

(B)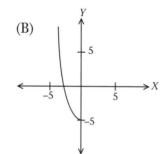

(C)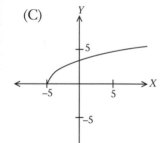

(D)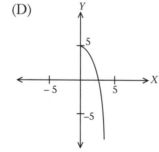

(E)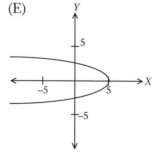

5. If $120\,(y - 4) = 240z$, which of the following gives the value of y in terms of z?

(A) $240z - 4$
(B) $\frac{1}{2} z - 2$
(C) $4 - \frac{z}{2}$
(D) $2z - 2$
(E) $2z + 4$

6. If the second and fourth digits are interchanged in each of the following numbers, which will yield the number with the greatest value?

(A) 62,345
(B) 62,346
(C) 63,346
(D) 63,436
(E) 64,246

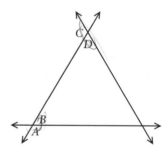

7. In the figure above, what is the sum of angles A, B, C, and D?

(A) 180
(B) 240
(C) 300
(D) 360
(E) 540

GO ON TO THE NEXT PAGE ⟩

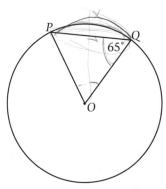

8. In the figure above, point O is the center of a circle. If $\angle PQO$ measures $65°$, what is the value in degrees of arc PQ?

(A) 40
(B) 50
(C) 60
(D) 65
(E) 80

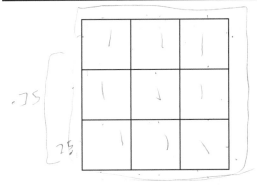

9. The figure above is a square divided into nine equal smaller squares. If the perimeter of one of the smaller squares is 1, then the perimeter of the large square is

(A)   2
(B) 2.25
(C) 2.5
(D)   3
(E) 4.5

10. Let the symbol $]q[$ represent the number of different pairs of positive integers whose product is q. For example, $]12[= 2$, since there are 2 different pairs of positive integers whose product is 12. What is the value of $]48[$?

(A)   5
(B)   6
(C)   8
(D) 10
(E) 12

11. A sequence of numbers begins with 0 and is described by $n, n + 4, \ldots$ What is the value of the 101st number in the sequence?

(A) 396
(B) 400
(C) 402
(D) 404
(E) 408

12. The area of circle A is 9π larger than the area of circle B. If the area of circle A is 25π, what is the radius of circle B?

(A) 2
(B) 4
(C) 5
(D) 6
(E) 9

GO ON TO THE NEXT PAGE

13. $(5^n)^{n-1} \times (5^{-n})^n =$

  (A) 5^{n-1}

  (B) 5

  (C) $\dfrac{1}{5}$

  (D) $\dfrac{1}{25}$

  (E) $\dfrac{1}{5^{n-1}}$

---

14. Let the function f be defined by $f(xy) = \dfrac{f(x)}{y}$.
If $f(150) = 3$, and if x and y are positive numbers, what is the value of $f(600)$?

  (A) $\dfrac{1}{4}$

  (B) $\dfrac{3}{4}$

  (C) 1

  (D) 2

  (E) 3

	Peter	George
Test 1	57	46
Test 2	51	53
Test 3	49	46
Test 4	53	54
Test 5	57	56

15. Peter and George took five tests, each with 60 questions. The table above shows the number of questions they answered correctly on each. After the fourth test, how many more correct answers had Peter given than George?

  (A)   8
  (B)   9
  (C) 10
  (D) 11
  (E) 12

---

16. If $\dfrac{a}{5} = a^2$, the value of a can be which of the following?

     I. $-\dfrac{1}{5}$

     II. 5^{-1}

     III. $\dfrac{1}{5}$

  (A) I only
  (B) II only
  (C) III only
  (D) I and II only
  (E) II and III only

STOP

**If you finish before time is called, you may check your work on this section only.
Do not turn to any other section in the test.**

PRACTICE TEST #1

SECTION 10
Time – 10 minutes
14 Questions

Turn to Section 10 (page 7) of your answer sheet to answer the questions in this section.

Directions: For each question in this section, select the best answer from among the choices given and fill in the corresponding circle on the answer sheet.

The following sentences test correctness and effectiveness of expression. Part of each sentence or the entire sentence is underlined; beneath each sentence are five ways of phrasing the underlined material. Choice A repeats the original phrasing; the other four choices are different. If you think the original phrasing produces a better sentence than any of the alternatives, select choice A; if not, select one of the other choices.

In making your selection, follow the requirements of standard written English; that is, pay attention to grammar, choice of words, sentence construction, and punctuation. Your selection should result in the most effective sentence—clear and precise, without awkwardness or ambiguity.

EXAMPLE:

In 1953, Ralph Ellison won the National Book Award for *Invisible Man* and he was thirty-nine years old then.

(A) and he was thirty-nine years old then
(B) the age of thirty-nine years old
(C) upon arriving at thirty-nine
(D) at the time of reaching thirty-nine
(E) when he was thirty-nine years old

Ⓐ Ⓑ Ⓒ Ⓓ ●

1. Having fluency in Japanese, Chinese, as well as Vietnamese, Ms. Huan is an ideal candidate for an assignment in east Asia.

(A) Having fluency in Japanese, Chinese, as well as Vietnamese
(B) Having fluency in Japanese, Chinese, and her knowledge of Vietnamese
(C) By being fluent in Japanese, Chinese, and also Vietnamese
(D) With her fluency in Japanese and Chinese, and also in Vietnamese
(E) Because of her fluency in Japanese, Chinese, and Vietnamese

GO ON TO THE NEXT PAGE

2. <u>Returning to his old elementary school as a young adult, the building seemed much smaller to George</u> than it did when he was a child.

    (A) Returning to his old elementary school as a young adult, the building seemed much smaller to George

    (B) After George returned to his old elementary school as a young adult, the building seemed much smaller

    (C) When George returned to his old elementary school as a young adult, the building seemed much smaller

    (D) Having returned to his old elementary school as a young adult, the building seemed much smaller to George

    (E) George returned to his old elementary school as a young adult, the building seemed much smaller

3. Ms. Turner chose Sheila as student of the <u>month for her work having been the best in the class</u>.

    (A) month for her work having been the best in the class

    (B) month; her work has been the best in the class

    (C) month, due to the fact being that her work had been the best in the class

    (D) month, having been the best in the class

    (E) month for her work that has been the best in the class

4. The job of a kindergarten teacher is every bit as challenging <u>as a lawyer</u>.

    (A) as a lawyer
    (B) like a lawyer's
    (C) like a lawyer
    (D) as that of a lawyer
    (E) such as a lawyer

5. Because Susan is a meticulous writer who does multiple drafts, <u>the changes suggested by her editor were, as usual, very minor</u>.

    (A) the changes suggested by her editor were, as usual, very minor

    (B) the changes usually suggested by her editor were very minor

    (C) the changes, as usual, suggested by her editor were very minor

    (D) the changes suggested by her editor were very minor, usually

    (E) as usual the changes suggested by her editor were very minor

6. If he is re-elected again, Representative Jackson <u>would have served</u> as a delegate in four different decades.

    (A) would have served
    (B) will have served
    (C) will serve
    (D) could have served
    (E) is serving

GO ON TO THE NEXT PAGE ⟩

7. The impact of antioxidants in preventing some forms of cancer <u>has been well documented</u>.

(A) has been well documented
(B) has been documented well
(C) is increasingly documented
(D) is being well documented
(E) have well been documented

8. Prior to 1960, many colleges did not admit African American <u>students, but today they can attend any college in the country</u>.

(A) students, but today they can attend any college in the country
(B) students whom today can attend any college in the country
(C) students, but today these students can attend any college in the country
(D) students; today, they are allowing these students to attend any college in the country
(E) students, that today are attending any college in the country

9. Not only was Frances Perkins the first woman to hold a cabinet position in the U. S. <u>government, in fact she was also</u> the longest-serving Secretary of Labor in the nation's history.

(A) government, in fact she was also
(B) government, she was also
(C) government; but in fact, she was also
(D) government, and she was also
(E) government, and also

10. John's mother is eager <u>that he participate</u> in the spring musical production this year.

(A) that he participate
(B) that he would participate
(C) that he can participate
(D) that he is participating
(E) that he participates

11. <u>Cape Town, enjoying a picturesque seaside location on the southwestern tip of the continent, is the capital of South Africa</u>.

(A) Cape Town, enjoying a picturesque seaside location on the southwestern tip of the continent, is the capital of South Africa
(B) Cape Town, which enjoys a picturesque seaside location on the southwestern tip of the continent, is the capital of South Africa.
(C) Cape Town, the capital of South Africa, enjoys a picturesque seaside location on the southwestern tip of the continent.
(D) Cape Town, the capital of South Africa, is a picturesque seaside location on the southwestern tip of the continent.
(E) Cape Town is the capital of South Africa, which enjoys a picturesque seaside location on the southwestern tip of the continent.

GO ON TO THE NEXT PAGE ➤

12. <u>By contrast to other genetically similar species</u>, reindeer can be domesticated.

   (A) By contrast to other genetically similar species
   (B) Contrasting with other genetically similar species
   (C) By contrast with other genetically similar species
   (D) In contrast to other genetically similar species
   (E) With other genetically similar species contrasted

13. Although Peter claims to be a scholar of Danish history, <u>he does not speak the language and has never set foot in Denmark.</u>

   (A) he does not speak Danish and has never set foot in Denmark
   (B) he is not a speaker of Danish and has never set foot in the country of Denmark
   (C) it is without speaking Danish or visiting Denmark
   (D) he does not speak the language and has never set foot there
   (E) he is not a Danish speaker nor ever set foot there

14. Writing under the pseudonym of "George Eliot," author Mary Ann Evans <u>enjoyed initial successfulness in convincing readers that she was a man</u>, though the astute Charles Dickens recognized immediately that she was actually a woman.

   (A) enjoyed initial successfulness in convincing readers that she was a man
   (B) succeeded in convincing readers, at least initially, that she was a man
   (C) had succeeded initially in convincing readers that she was a man
   (D) was successful, at least initially, by convincing readers that she was a man
   (E) initially succeeded in convincing readers that she was a man

STOP

If you finish before time is called, you may check your work on this section only. Do not turn to any other section in the test.

Practice Test 1 – Answer Key

Writing

Section 1

Essay Score: _____
(See pages 141-142
for the guidelines
for scoring the
essay.)

Section 4

(1) B	(10) A	(19) E	(28) E
(2) A	(11) B	(20) C	(29) D
(3) E	(12) E	(21) A	(30) E
(4) B	(13) B	(22) D	(31) C
(5) C	(14) D	(23) A	(32) B
(6) C	(15) A	(24) B	(33) C
(7) D	(16) B	(25) D	(34) A
(8) E	(17) C	(26) C	(35) A
(9) C	(18) D	(27) C	

_____
Number Correct

_____
Number Incorrect

Section 10

(1) E	(8) C
(2) C	(9) B
(3) B	(10) A
(4) D	(11) C
(5) A	(12) D
(6) B	(13) A
(7) A	(14) E

_____
Number Correct

_____
Number Incorrect

Critical Reading

Section 2

(1) B	(9) E	(17) C
(2) D	(10) A	(18) E
(3) D	(11) A	(19) A
(4) C	(12) B	(20) B
(5) E	(13) B	(21) D
(6) C	(14) D	(22) A
(7) E	(15) D	(23) B
(8) A	(16) C	(24) C

_____
Number Correct

_____
Number Incorrect

Section 5

(1) B	(9) B	(17) C
(2) D	(10) D	(18) E
(3) A	(11) C	(19) B
(4) C	(12) B	(20) D
(5) B	(13) E	(21) A
(6) C	(14) D	(22) C
(7) E	(15) C	(23) E
(8) C	(16) A	(24) C

_____
Number Correct

_____
Number Incorrect

Section 8

(1) C	(11) E
(2) C	(12) B
(3) A	(13) D
(4) E	(14) D
(5) E	(15) C
(6) A	(16) A
(7) D	(17) D
(8) E	(18) D
(9) C	(19) D
(10) B	

_____
Number Correct

_____
Number Incorrect

Math

Section 3

(1) B	**Student-Produced**
(2) E	**Response Questions**
(3) A	(9) 409
(4) D	(10) 1/4 or .250
(5) D	(11) 9
(6) D	(12) 1/22 or .045
(7) E	(13) 9/16 or .563
(8) E	(14) 15
	(15) 5/9 or .555
	(16) 6
	(17) 1/3 or .333
	(18) 1/4 or .250

_____
Number Correct

_____
Number Incorrect

Section 7

(1) A	(11) E
(2) C	(12) A
(3) E	(13) B
(4) D	(14) D
(5) C	(15) C
(6) C	(16) D
(7) B	(17) B
(8) C	(18) D
(9) E	(19) E
(10) B	(20) C

_____
Number Correct

_____
Number Incorrect

Section 9

(1) E	(9) D
(2) D	(10) A
(3) A	(11) B
(4) D	(12) B
(5) E	(13) C
(6) C	(14) B
(7) D	(15) D
(8) B	(16) E

_____
Number Correct

_____
Number Incorrect

Now the fun part: finding out your score. It could be ugly. On the bright side, we have no idea what a good score on this test is, and neither do you. The real SAT is a norm-referenced test—that is, the test is a reflection of how many students are expected to get each question right and wrong. In this way, College Board and ETS can calibrate the difficulty of each test. Since we don't have any norms to reference, your score on this test means *nothing*.

That said, we think you will appreciate going through the process of scoring to see how it works. Also, we would be curious to know what you got. If you do score your test—and we hope you will—write us at editor@fiskeguide.com and tell us what you got. Be sure to specify whether you took the test under timed conditions. Likewise, if you think you've spotted an error or a question that has two possible answers, let us know. If we agree, we'll print your name with our thanks in a future edition.

There is also the matter of grading your essay. We recommend that you ask parent(s) or friend(s). Get two of them to read the essay and use the scoring guidelines on pages 141-142. Both of your essay readers should grade the essay on the 1-6 scale outlined there.

The following five pages take you through the scoring process. On page 298, we offer a chart for converting your raw score into a scaled score. On page 299, another chart shows you how to combine your essay with your score on the Writing multiple-choice questions to get an overall Writing score.

Writing Score

Compute the number of multiple-choice questions you answered <u>correctly</u>:

Section 4, (Questions 1-35): _____

Section 10, (Questions 1-14): _____

Total: _____ **(1)**

Compute the number of multiple-choice questions you answered <u>incorrectly</u>:

Section 4, (Questions 1-35): _____

Section 10, (Questions 1-14): _____

Total: _____ multiplied by 0.25 = _____ **(2)**

(1) – (2) = _____, Writing Multiple-Choice Raw Score

<u>Round to the nearest whole number.</u>

Use the table on page 298 to find your Writing Multiple-Choice Scaled Score: _____

Writing Essay Score: Reader 1's Score: _____ + Reader 2's Score _____ = _____

With your Writing Multiple-Choice Raw Score and your Writing Essay Score, use the table on page 299 to find your Writing Composite Scaled Score: _____.

Critical Reading Score

Number of multiple-choice questions you answered <u>correctly</u>:

> Section 2, (Questions 1-24): _____
>
> Section 5, (Questions 1-24): _____
>
> Section 8, (Questions 1-19): _____
>
> **Total:** _____ **(1)**

Number of multiple-choice questions you answered <u>incorrectly</u>:

> Section 2, (Questions 1-24): _____
>
> Section 5, (Questions 1-24): _____
>
> Section 8, (Questions 1-19): _____
>
> **Total:** _____ multiplied by 0.25 = _____ **(2)**
>
> **(1) – (2) =** _____, Critical Reading Raw Score

Use the table on page 298 to find your Critical Reading Scaled Score: _____.

Math Score

Number of multiple-choice questions you answered correctly:

Section 3, (Questions 1-18): _____

Section 7, (Questions 1-20): _____

Section 9, (Questions 1-16): _____

Total: _____ **(1)**

Number of multiple-choice questions you answered <u>incorrectly</u>:

Section 3, (Questions 1-18): _____

Section 7, (Questions 1-20): _____

Section 9, (Questions 1-16): _____

Total: _____ multiplied by 0.25 = _____ **(2)**

(1) – (2) = _____, Math Raw Score

Use the table on page 298 to find your Math Scaled Score: _____.

Finally,

Writing Scaled Score _____ +

Critical Reading Scaled Score _____ +

Math Scaled Score _____ =

Your Combined Score _____

Raw Score	Critical Reading Scaled Score	Math Scaled Score	Writing Multiple-Choice Scaled Score*	Raw Score	Critical Reading Scaled Score	Math Scaled Score	Writing Multiple-Choice Scaled Score
67	800			31	510	550	60
66	800			30	510	540	58
65	800			29	500	530	57
64	780			28	490	520	56
63	760			27	490	520	55
62	750			26	480	510	54
61	740			25	480	500	53
60	730			24	470	490	52
59	710			23	460	480	51
58	700			22	460	480	50
57	690			21	450	470	49
56	680			20	440	460	48
55	670			19	440	450	47
54	660	800		18	430	450	46
53	650	800		17	420	440	45
52	650	780		16	420	430	44
51	640	760		15	410	420	44
50	630	740		14	400	410	43
49	620	720	80	13	400	410	42
48	620	700	80	12	390	400	41
47	610	680	80	11	380	390	40
46	600	670	79	10	370	380	39
45	600	660	78	9	360	370	38
44	590	650	76	8	350	360	38
43	590	640	74	7	340	350	37
42	580	630	73	6	330	340	36
41	570	630	71	5	320	330	35
40	570	620	70				
39	560	610	69				
38	550	600	67				
37	550	590	66				
36	540	580	65				
35	540	580	64				
34	530	570	63				
33	520	560	62				
32	520	550	61				

This table is for use only with the test in this booklet.

*The Writing multiple-choice score is reported on a 20-80 scale. Use the table on the opposite page to combine your Writing Multiple-Choice Raw Score with your Essay Raw Score to determine your Writing Scaled Score.

PRACTICE TEST #1

SAT Score Conversion Table for Writing Composite Scaled Score

Writing Multiple-Choice Raw Score	Essay Raw Score						
	6	7	8	9	10	11	12
49	760	780	800	800	800	800	800
48	760	780	800	800	800	800	800
47	750	770	780	800	800	800	800
46	730	760	770	780	800	800	800
45	720	740	750	770	780	800	800
44	700	720	740	760	770	780	800
43	690	710	720	740	750	770	780
42	680	700	710	730	740	760	770
41	660	680	700	720	730	750	760
40	650	670	690	710	720	740	750
39	640	660	680	700	710	730	740
38	630	650	670	690	700	720	730
37	620	640	660	680	690	710	720
36	610	630	650	670	680	700	710
35	600	620	640	660	670	690	700
34	590	610	630	650	660	680	690
33	580	600	620	640	650	670	680
32	570	590	610	630	640	660	670
31	560	580	600	620	630	650	660
30	560	580	590	610	620	640	650
29	550	570	580	600	610	630	640
28	540	560	570	590	600	620	630
27	530	550	560	580	590	610	620
26	520	540	550	570	590	600	610
25	510	530	540	560	580	600	610
24	500	520	540	560	570	590	600
23	490	510	530	550	560	580	590
22	480	500	520	540	550	570	580
21	480	500	510	530	540	560	570
20	470	490	500	520	530	550	560
19	460	480	490	510	530	550	560
18	450	470	490	510	520	540	550
17	440	460	480	500	510	530	540
16	440	460	470	490	500	520	530
15	430	450	460	480	500	520	530
14	420	440	460	480	490	510	520
13	420	440	450	470	480	500	510
12	410	430	440	460	470	490	500
11	400	420	440	460	470	490	500
10	390	410	430	450	460	480	490

This table is for use only with the test in this booklet.

The following are explanations of the answers for the problems. In the Writing and Critical Reading sections, we have bolded vocabulary words that you should make sure you understand. In the Writing and Critical Reading sections, we have tried to avoid overly technical explanations about grammar, parts of speech, etc. You don't need to know the grammar terms, but you should know a mistake when you see one.

TEST 1, SECTION 2 – CRITICAL READING

SENTENCE COMPLETIONS

Question 1. The best answer is (B). The question mentions two events, one that is significant (a visit from President Eisenhower) and one that is characterized as "alleged" and probably never happened. A town historian would likely be more interested in a presidential visit. Therefore, it would be logical for the historian to **scold** ("criticize") the paper if it failed to mention President Eisenhower's visit.

The best answer is NOT:

(A) because the reporter might have **upbraided** ("harshly criticized") the paper but **deign** ("to stoop" or "condescend to") is not appropriate.

(C) because **laud** means "to praise."

(D) because **piqued** ("to be provoked" or "aroused") describes a state of being rather than an action (such as "**scold**").

(E) because to **spurn** means "to reject or refuse" rather than "to criticize." The use of **derided** ("ridiculed") does not make sense.

Question 2. The best answer is (D) because famed author Sylvia Plath had talent that would be characterized favorably, and the fact that she committed suicide implies that she was **melancholy**.

The best answer is NOT:

(A) because although **extraordinary** fits, "reservations" does not have a logical connection to suicide.

(B) because **honed** is a verb that would be inappropriate for describing talent.

(C) because though "considerable" could be appropriate, it is was not "delirium" ("temporary state of mental confusion") that caused her suicide. Since "ultimately" implies that her condition was a long-term problem, "melancholy" is better choice.

(E) because though **estimable** ("deserving of respect") could be correct, disintegration is less a cause than a result. Melancholy can lead to both disintegration and suicide.

Question 3. The best answer is (D) because the mandrill's blue, purple, and scarlet facial markings are highly unusual and therefore **distinctive**.

The best answer is NOT:

(A) because there is no reason to believe that the mandrill's facial markings are **discordant** ("conflicting, disagreeable").

(B) because **distinguishable** is a general descriptor that is less appropriate than "distinctive" to describe the mandrill's unusual coloration.

(C) because **emphatic** ("forceful") generally applies to actions.

(E) because **dialectical** is a reference to a philosophical method.

Question 4. The best answer is (C) because Todd has no **credibility** and therefore has a reputation for "prevarication" ("concealing the truth").

The best answer is NOT:

(A) because **inscrutability** means "the quality of being unknowable."

(B) because **disrepute** means "loss of reputation."

(D) because **incredulity** means "the state of being doubtful."

(E) because **scrupulousness** means "honesty."

Question 5. The best answer is (E) because "seasoned," a synonym for "experienced," fits the first blank, and "negotiate," though it usually applies to people who are interacting, can also be used in connection with driving, as in "negotiate a curve."

The best answer is NOT:

(A) because **enjoin** means "to forbid."

(B) because **supercilious** means "proud" or "disdainful."

(C) because although "skilled" could fit the first blank, "attempt to encounter" is not a logical phrase in connection with a road. Any driver may encounter Black Mountain Road, but some may have difficulty with it.

(D) because "dynamic" is not a choice for the first blank and **deride** means "ridicule."

PASSAGE-BASED READING – Violent Video Games

Question 6. The best answer is **(C)** because the author of Passage 1 uses the two rhetorical questions to develop the idea that violence has always been part of entertainment with no obvious ill effects. Both rhetorical questions could easily be rephrased as statements to make this argument.

The best answer is NOT:

(A) because the purpose of the rhetorical questions is to develop an argument with specific evidence rather than to state a theory.

(B) because the rhetorical questions do not refer to any earlier thesis but are rather the initial statement of the author's point.

(D) because the rhetorical questions do not return to any theme.

(E) because the rhetorical questions make the only argument in the passage.

Question 7. The best answer is **(E)** because the author of Passage 2 uses the first person pronoun, I, and writes from personal experience.

The best answer is NOT:

(A) because Passage 2 does not contain any scientific data.

(B) because Passage 2 does not include historical research.

(C) because "direct citation" means "quoting another source directly."

(D) because Passage 2 does not **allude** ("refer to") any literary works.

Question 8. The best answer is **(A)** because Passage 1 refers to the fact that the video game industry, which the author possibly represents, has "always been responsive to parental concerns." This statement implies that concerns about children and video games play a significant role in the debate, and it also gives an implied endorsement of parents playing a role in choosing and/or monitoring video games used by their children.

The best answer is NOT:

(B) because the passage attempts to refute the idea that video games can cause children to be aggressive.

(C) because though Passage 1 talks only about violence and video games, the tone suggests that the author disagrees that video games necessarily have negative effects.

(D) because the author defends the video game industry and is therefore not likely to concede that other types of play provide better recreation.

(E) because the author argues against this view.

Question 9. The best answer is (E) because Passage 2 features a mother citing anecdotal evidence from her life that contradicts the views expressed in Passage 1.

The best answer is NOT:

(A) because Passage 2 does not **corroborate** ("support") Passage 1.

(B) because Passage 2 is not directed toward Passage 1 and offers only the personal experience of the author.

(C) because Passage 2 does not support the thrust ("main idea") of Passage 1.

(D) because Passage 2 uses personal anecdotes rather than logic.

PASSAGE-BASED READING – The Boxer

Question 10. The best answer is (A) because the passage cites Patterson's "love" of the sport of boxing but also his complaints about the violence of boxing and how it alienated him from his family.

The best answer is NOT:

(B) because the passage states that "being heavyweight champion of the world means a great deal" and never suggests that he does not think it is worth the price.

(C) because the passage does not suggest he wishes he had chosen another profession.

(D) because although the passage cites Patterson's belief that boxing "has made him vicious against his opponents," the passage does not address whether Patterson thought most boxers were vicious.

(E) because the passage does not address public opinion and the sport of boxing.

Question 11. The best answer is (A) because **vicariously** means "indirectly or through another person." In the passage, Patterson is portrayed as expressing the hatred of others through the sport of boxing.

The best answer is NOT:

(B) because although "vicariously" and "viciously" sound alike, their meanings are very different.

(C) because "vigorously" is not a synonym for "vicariously."

(D) because "shunning publicity" is not related to "vicariously."

(E) because "publicly and repentantly" is not related to "vicariously."

Question 12. The best answer is (B) because the quotation expresses Patterson's belief that "the public sees the champion as someone special," and that therefore the champion has an obligation to be a role model as champion and uphold "the tradition of the title."

The best answer is NOT:

(A) because the quotation does not compare boxing with other professions.

(C) because although the quotation from Patterson states that "you've got to believe in what you're doing," he is discussing the obligations of boxers outside the ring rather than their ability as boxers.

(D) because Patterson addresses not public opinion but the heavyweight champion's obligation to the public.

(E) because although Patterson addresses the obligations of a heavyweight champion, he does not discuss the attributes necessary to become heavyweight champion.

Question 13. The best answer is (B) because the passage makes an implied comparison between Patterson and Sydney Poitier, and then notes that the sort of honor portrayed by Poitier was sometimes perceived as "white on the inside." The passage states that blacks, like Patterson, found it "difficult to find frameworks" for the display of honor because such displays could be perceived as pandering to whites.

The best answer is NOT:

(A) because the passage does not evaluate Patterson relative to Poitier.

(C) because although the passage does suggest that Patterson may have been "neurotically fishing for compliments," it explains that Patterson's concept of honor was a motivation for his actions. The passage does not suggest that Patterson was "excessive" in seeking approval from whites.

(D) because although the passage suggests that honor was important to Patterson, it does not suggest that he had any awareness of "fishing for compliments from whites," and therefore does not suggest that he had any beliefs about it.

(E) because the passage does not discuss Patterson's views on honor versus character.

Question 14. The best answer is (D) because the last sentence begins with the proposition that "if black intellectuals disliked Patterson" and goes on to say that "it is most likely because" Patterson's position in society was in some ways similar to their own, about which they felt a degree of frustration.

The best answer is NOT:

(A) because the sentence uses the clause "if Patterson was disliked by the black intellectuals of the day" as a fact to be explained rather than as a conditional statement of a circumstance that might, or might not, have been true.

(B) because although the author does compare the situation of black intellectuals with that of Patterson, the purpose is to explain the attitude of black intellectuals toward Patterson rather than to enumerate traits that he shared with them.

(C) because although the passage does highlight Patterson's reflective nature, and by extension, his intellectual bent, it is not concerned with whether Patterson is an intellectual at heart and does not explain the source of his outlook on life.

(E) because while the passage comments in passing on Patterson's place in boxing history, particularly with respect to his attitude toward holding the heavyweight title, it does not devote significant attention to, or define, any tradition of which Patterson might have been a part.

Question 15. The best answer is (D) because the passage attempts to explain Patterson's mindset, and to suggest why Patterson acted as he did and was perceived as he was. The passage shows the extent to which Patterson was motivated by his concept of honor and doing what was best for the nation as heavyweight champion.

The best answer is NOT:

(A) because the passage shows why Patterson's actions were logical and understandable rather than approaching them with **skepticism** ("mistrust").

(B) because **conciliatory** ("willing to make concessions") applies to individuals or groups who have had conflict, or the potential for conflict, between them. The author of the passage does not have a relationship with Patterson but is analyzing him from afar.

(C) because although the author may believe that Patterson is praiseworthy in some respects, this does not mean that his attitude toward Patterson is praiseworthy (which would suggest that the author should be praised).

(E) because the author is not **awed** ("having a feeling of wonderment") by Patterson, but rather sees him realistically and analyzes him dispassionately ("impartially").

PASSAGE-BASED READING – The Plant

Question 16. The best answer is (C) because in the first paragraph of the passage, the author compares a leaf of the plant as "becoming spotted like the cheek of a child with the measles." Later, he describes the plant as "naked as a pole." Both of these are similes.

The best answer is NOT:

(A) because the paragraph does not allude ("make reference") to literature.

(B) because the passage does not use first person ("I") voice.

(D) because the passage does not cite another source directly.

(E) because the passage does not use "cognitive dissonance," an inconsistency between beliefs and actions that causes psychological conflict or anxiety.

Question 17. The best answer is (C) because in its detailed description of the plant's ailments, the "baleful" signs discovered by Marcovaldo, the passage illustrates how closely Marcovaldo examines the plant.

The best answer is NOT:

(A) because even though the plant has a variety of ailments, it is not necessarily near death.

(B) because although it is true that the plant has been neglected, this fact is less significant than Marcovaldo's care for and relationship to the plant.

(D) because the paragraph does not suggest that the plant would, or would not, be healthier in another location.

(E) because although Marcovaldo's obsessive attention to the plant does suggest that his life is deficient in other areas, the first paragraph makes no reference to others in the office and is not primarily concerned with Marcovaldo's personal life.

Question 18. The best answer is (E) because **baleful** means "portending misfortune" and is a synonym for **ominous**.

The best answer is NOT:

(A) because **benevolent** describes a person or entity dedicated to doing good.

(B) because **demoralizing** means "that which causes a loss of hope or enthusiasm." Baleful signs may be demoralizing, but not necessarily.

(C) because **disgruntling** describes a situation or circumstance that causes discontent.

(D) because **morbid** means "of or related to disease or death." "Morbid" is a relative of "baleful" but not a synonym.

Question 19. The best answer is (A) because the author notes in the second paragraph that Mercovaldo cared for the plant with "the compassion felt for the troubles of a relative" and also observes that Mercovaldo recognized the plant as "a companion in misfortune." The passage implies that the life of the plant parallels that of Mercovaldo.

The best answer is NOT:

(B) because Mercovaldo cares about the plant more than anything else in his life and does not resent doing so.

(C) because although Mercovaldo spends a large amount of time caring for the plant, there is no suggestion that he has other uses for his time or that he is wasting his time.

(D) because there is no reference in the relevant lines to others in the office or any implication that Mercovaldo feels resentment.

(E) because even though it is true that the plant depends on Mercovaldo, this fact is not a point that is significant or emphasized.

Question 20. The best answer is (B) because the personification in lines 60-66 reflects Mercovaldo's perspective on the plant as he brings it into the rain. The plant "seemed to don its most brilliant green: or at least so Mercovaldo who thought…" is a line that suggests that it is Mercovaldo who makes the plant into an almost human companion.

The best answer is NOT:

(A) because the story is not about plants and animals but about Mercovaldo's unusual relationship to a particular plant.

(C) because although it is true that the plant needs rain, the rain is a vehicle to show Mercovaldo's interaction with the plant and is not significant in itself.

(D) because while the plant does seem healthier after the rain, this fact is secondary to Mercovaldo's interactions with the plant.

(E) because although the plant does depend on Mercovaldo for water, this fact is not significant in itself.

Question 21. The best answer is (D) because the passage refers to "the **phenomena** of nature," which means the **elements** such as wind, rain, sun, etc.

The best answer is NOT:

(A) because **extraordinary** is a distracter that is a synonym for "phenomenal," not "phenomena."

(B) because **diaspora** refers to a body of people dispersed from their homeland to other places.

(C) because **phenomenal** ("unusual, incredible") is not a close synonym for "phenomena."

(E) because **phylum** is a category in the classification of languages or organisms.

Question 22. The best answer is (A) because the reference to "rheumatic aches," juxtaposed against the pleasant images of woods and fields, emphasizes the fact that Mercovaldo has been unable to enjoy simple pleasures such as the smell of rain in the outdoors. Mercovaldo, it seems, has been unable to find pleasure or meaning in this life.

The best answer is NOT:

(B) because there is no evidence that Mercovaldo is haunted by flashbacks. A seemingly pleasant image leads to a bad memory, but there is no indication that Mercovaldo is "haunted" by thoughts of this nature.

(C) because there is no suggestion that Mercovaldo's sanity is in doubt.

(D) because the emphasis is not on Mercovaldo's childhood memories, but on his inability to take pleasure in a simple thing like the smell of rain.

(E) because the aside about "rheumatic aches" does not extend to an evaluation of Mercovaldo's ability to come to grips with his past.

Question 23. The best answer is (B) because the reference to the foreman's avoidance of "burdensome responsibilities" is ironic. Most people would view putting a plant outside as a trivial matter, but the author mocks the foreman by highlighting that he is reluctant to take responsibility for anything, even a small matter such as this.

The best answer is NOT:

(A) because **flattering** means "favorable" and the reference is actually derogatory.

(C) because **matter-of-fact** does not reflect the ironic sense conveyed by the author.

(D) because **elliptical** means "characterized by few words" and "with a meaning that must be inferred."

(E) because **hostile** means "antagonistic."

Question 24. The best answer is (C) because throughout the passage, the author implies that Mercovaldo has nothing better to do than care for the plant.

The best answer is NOT:

(A) because although the passage describes Mercovaldo as devoting time and energy to taking care of the plant, it says nothing about his expertise in doing so.

(B) because although the passages suggests that Mercovaldo thinks the plant is important, it does not mention animals and does not suggest any relevant inferences.

(D) because the passage does not address whether Mercovaldo would be a good gardener.

(E) because the passage does not characterize Mercovaldo's attitude toward the foreman.

TEST 1, SECTION 3 – MATH

Question 1. The answer is (B). Given the coordinates $(4, -1)$, plug them into the equation $y = -\frac{3}{2}x + b$, the formula for a line. That yields $-1 = -\frac{12}{2} + b$. Therefore, $b = 5$ and the solution is $y = -\frac{3}{2}x + 5$.

Question 2. The answer is (E). This problem tests your ingenuity in setting up an equation. Do it in terms of the total number of rugs in the store. We'll call that number r. Therefore, $r = \frac{3}{5}r + \frac{3}{10}r + 26$. Got it? If the number of maroon rugs is $\frac{3}{5}r$ and the number of gold rugs is half that number, then the number of gold rugs must be $\frac{3}{10}r$. Add 26 for the orange, make $\frac{3}{5}$ into $\frac{6}{10}$, and combine like terms. $\frac{1}{10}r = 26$, and $r = 260$.

Question 3. The answer is (A). For the first digit, the person has ten choices. For the second digit, the person has nine choices. Then eight and seven for the final two. Therefore, $10 \times 9 \times 8 \times 7 = 5,040$.

Question 4. The answer is (D). This is a plug-in problem that asks you to eye-ball $28 = 3x + 2^x$ to figure out the value of x. You can draw a bead on x quickly. At a glance, you know that 1 and 2 are obviously too small and 5 is too big. You might try 3, but $x = 4$ gives you 28. Don't fall for the distracter, (E), but solve $4 - 3(4) = -8$.

Question 5. The answer is (D). Depending on which way you assume the paper is rolled up (the question does not specify), the circumference of the base of the tube will be either $8\frac{1}{2}$ inches or 11 inches. Because 11 is a whole number, go with it. Since the circumference equals πd, you know that

$$\pi d = 11$$
$$d = \frac{11}{\pi}$$
$$r = \frac{11}{2\pi}$$
$$\pi r^2 = \pi(\frac{11}{2\pi})^2$$
$$= \pi(\frac{121}{4\pi^2})$$
$$= \frac{121}{4\pi}$$

If $\frac{121}{4\pi}$ had not been among the answer choices, you could have looked for $\frac{(8.5)^2}{4\pi} = \frac{72.25}{4\pi}$. Given ETS's preference for round numbers, 11 is a better bet.

Question 6. The answer is (D). We know that the AB divides the squares into triangles with sides in the ratio of $1:1:\sqrt{2}$. If the length of CB is 4, then the length of AB is $4\sqrt{2} + 4\sqrt{2} = 8\sqrt{2}$.

Question 7. The answer is (E). All three choices are true. Since x is a fraction, and a negative exponent puts the fraction in the denominator, we would expect y to get larger as x is raised to a power. Since x is positive, y must also be positive and their product is greater than zero. Because multiplying fractions makes them get smaller, $y > x$ and therefore III is also true.

Question 8. The answer is (E). Since the radius of the circle is 8, the area of the semi-circle ABC is 32π and the area bounded by arc BC is 16π. Because the center of the circle is on one of the sides of $WXYZ$, Q must be the midpoint of $\overline{YZ}$. Therefore, the area of $DXQZ$ is 32 and the area of the shaded region is $16\pi - 32$.

MATH – STUDENT-PRODUCED RESPONSES

Question 9. The answer is 409. If $w\}\{x\}\{y\}\{z = x^y - w^z$, then $6\}\{5\}\{4\}\{3 = 5^4 - 6^3 = 625 - 216 = 409$.

Question 10. The answer is $\frac{1}{4}$ or .250. The object is to find the percentage of the big triangle ABC that is inside the smaller triangle ADE. Since $\overline{AB} = \overline{BC}$, you know that $\angle ABC$ has sides of $2:2:2\sqrt{2}$. You also know that its area is 2. Since $\overline{DE} \parallel \overline{BC}$, $\angle ADE$ is also a right triangle with area $\frac{1}{2}$. Therefore, the probability that the point will be inside the shaded region is $\frac{1}{4}$.

Question 11. The answer is 9. This one boils down to a relatively easy quadratic equation.

$$\text{If } (-2n)(4 - n) = 90$$

$$\text{Then } -8n + 2n^2 = 90$$

$$\text{And } -4n + n^2 = 45$$

From there

$$n^2 - 4n - 45 = 0$$

$$\text{And } (n - 9)(n + 5) = 0$$

$$\text{Since } n \text{ must be positive, } n = 9.$$

Question 12. The answer is $\frac{1}{22}$ or .045. When the first piece of fruit is chosen, the odds are 3 in 12 or $\frac{1}{4}$ that it will be an orange. For the second piece, the odds are 2 in 11. For the odds of both happening, the odds are

$$\frac{1}{4} \times \frac{2}{11} = \frac{2}{44} = \frac{1}{22} \text{ or } .045$$

Question 13. The answer is $\frac{9}{16}$ or .563. On the number line, $\sqrt{q}$ is three-quarters of the way between 0 and 1. Therefore, $\sqrt{q}$ = .75 or $\frac{3}{4}$, and q = $(.75)^2$ or $(\frac{3}{4})^2$.

Question 14. The answer is 15. If you're really good, you'll know immediately that 13 is the hypotenuse of a 5:12:13 right triangle, and that 12 must be the difference between the values of the *x*-coordinates. If you're not quite that good, then solve as follows:

$$\sqrt{(x-3)^2 + (9-14)^2} = 13$$

$$\sqrt{(x-3)^2 + 25} = 13$$

If you then square both sides, you get:

$$(x-3)^2 + 25 = 169$$

$$(x-3)^2 = 144$$

$$x = 15$$

Question 15. The answer is $\frac{5}{9}$ or .555. This problem may look hard, but it is a fairly simple issue of ratio and proportion. There is a difference of 14 between 52 and 66, and were *x* and *y* equal, the average high temperature would be right down the middle at 59. But instead, the average is 61, meaning that *y* is greater than *x*. How much greater? Looking again at the interval of 14, the numbers in *y* pull the average $\frac{9}{14}$ths of the way to 66. On the other hand, the numbers in *x* pull the average $\frac{5}{14}$ s of the way to 52. Since the average of 61 is pulled between 52 and 66 in proportion to weight of each average, (that is, the number of values that make up each), the value of $\frac{x}{y}$ is $\frac{5}{9}$, meaning that there are 5 days in *x* and 9 days in *y*.

Question 16. The answer is 6. Knowing how to factor makes this question a snap.

$$\text{If } x^2 - y^2 = -24, \text{ then}$$

$$(x-y)(x+y) = -24$$

If $x + y = -4$, then $x - y = 6$. Easy.

Question 17. The answer is $\frac{1}{3}$ or .333. If $x + 3y$ equals 150 percent of $4y$, that means

$$x + 3y = 6y$$

Therefore, $x = 3y$ and x is three times as big as y and $\frac{y}{x} = \frac{1}{3}$.

Question 18. The answer is $\frac{1}{4}$ or .250. Since the square $PQRS$ has area 16, each side is 4. Since it is centered on the origin, the coordinates of points R and Q are $(-2, -2)$ and $(2, 2)$, respectively. Plugging back in to $x = ky^3$, we get $2 = 8k$. Therefore, $k = \frac{1}{4}$.

TEST 1, SECTION 4 — WRITING

IMPROVING SENTENCES

Question 1. The best answer is (B) because this version places "the representatives" and "were reluctant" in a logical order and deletes the awkward participial phrase.

The best answer is NOT:

(A) because "having come this far" is an awkward participial phrase.

(C) because "coming this far" is an awkward participle that does not convey a meaning grammatically.

(D); ditto the explanation for (C).

(E) because to be grammatical, this version of the sentence would need to use the past perfect "had come."

Question 2. The best answer is (A) because the sentence conveys its meaning grammatically and concisely.

The best answer is NOT:

(B) because this formulation is wordy with an awkward beginning and a problem with subject-verb agreement.

(C) because this sentence uses a passive "to be" verb and "in existence" is an unnecessary phrase.

(D) because of the awkward and wordy "there are reasons" construction.

(E) because of the awkward and wordy "there are reasons" construction.

Question 3. The best answer is (E) because the sentence is a run-on and is correct when divided into two sentences.

The best answer is NOT:

(A) because the sentence is a run-on.

(B) because this version is a comma splice.

(C) because this version is also a run-on.

(D) because this version does not make grammatical sense.

Question 4. The best answer is (B) because this version is the most direct, concise, and grammatical formulation of the sentence.

The best answer is NOT:

(A) because this response has no verb and is not a sentence.

(C) because this sentence also has no verb.

(D) because "with renown" is not idiomatic.

(E) because this sentence is awkward for, among other things, placing "was an architect of the civil rights movement" before "second only to Martin Luther King, Jr."

Question 5. The best answer is (C) because the trick is knowing that "was at once" should be followed by "and" to join two traits that generally do not accompany one another.

The best answer is NOT:

(A) because "but" should be replaced by "and."

(B) because this response is wordy and "although" is redundant after "at once."

(D) because "compassionate in" is idiomatic rather than "compassionate for."

(E); ditto the problem with response (D).

Question 6. The best answer is (C) because the underlined clause calls for the past perfect tense to describe the fact that during the main action of the sentence, the girls looked as if they had been drenched in the past.

The best answer is NOT:

(A) because the girls were drenched by something that had happened in the past.

(B) because "if having walked" includes no subject and should be in the past perfect tense.

(D) because to indicate that the action had occurred in the past at the time of the main action of the sentence, the underlined clause should be in the past perfect tense rather than the past tense.

(E) because the subjunctive "would" is appropriate only for conditional events that might or might not happen depending on other events.

Question 7. The best answer is (D) because this response is the only one that clarifies the antecedent of "she." It is Lisa who will not be able to attend the honor banquet.

The best answer is NOT:

(A) because the antecedent of "she" is unclear.

(B) because the antecedent of "she" is unclear.

(C) because the sentence is wordy and the antecedent of "she" is unclear.

(E) because this response awkwardly places the object of the clause before the subject and verb. The antecedent of "she" is also unclear.

Question 8. The best answer is (E) because the sentence gives a concise explanation as to why Saarinen ranks among the great architects. Note the crispness of this sentence, with passive clutter such as "are a combination" replaced by the more vigorous "combine." Strong verbs eliminate the need for extraneous words.

The best answer is NOT:

(A) because this sentence includes a participle used inappropriately as a conjunction.

(B) because "considering" is also an inappropriate use of a conjunction.

(C) because although this sentence might be grammatically acceptable, it is wordy. "Due to the fact" is often unnecessary, as it is in this case.

(D) because although this sentence is better that (C), it is not as good as (E).

Question 9. The best answer is (C) because this version includes agreement between "the council" and "its."

The best answer is NOT:

(A) because "the council" is singular and "their" is plural.

(B) because the council's announcement is in the past, as distinguished from the choosing of Marcie as its leader, which is in the past perfect because it happened before the announcement.

(D) because this sentence includes an agreement error and awkward phrasing.

(E) because the choosing of Marcie should be referred to in the past perfect rather than the past.

Question 10. The best answer is (A) because the second clause follows logically from the first and the sentence has no extraneous words.

The best answer is NOT:

(B) because the sentence gives an incorrect impression of when Sally worked in the hospital.

(C) because this sentence is a comma splice.

(D) because the verb should be present perfect instead of the present progressive "is working."

(E) because this sentence is a comma splice.

Question 11. The best answer is (B) because this version correctly uses "because" as a subordinating conjunction.

The best answer is NOT:

(A) because this response incorrectly uses "being allergic to ragweed" to modify "Tim."

(C) because this version includes a wordy "due to being" construction.

(D) because "with" does not establish a relationship between the hike and Tim's sneezing.

(E) because this version is a comma splice.

CORRECTING SENTENCE ERRORS

Question 12. The best answer is (E) because this sentence correctly describes previous events in the past and past perfect tenses.

The best answer is NOT:

(A) because the past "was" is correct.

(B) because "whom" is the objective case of "who" and correct since the action of the sentence is done to "whom."

(C) because "had been" is correct in the past perfect tense.

(D) because "put" is correct in the past tense.

Question 13. The best answer is (B) because the correct usage is "would arrive," describing the event that would happen if Jane were to reach Atlanta in six hours.

The best answer is NOT:

(A) because "were" is a correct subjunctive usage.

(C) because "have" is a correct present tense usage.

(D) because "to eat" is a correct infinitive usage.

Question 14. The best answer is (D) because "boar" is a **homonym** (sounds the same, spelled differently) of "bore," the past tense of bear.

The best answer is NOT:

(A) because "experimented" is a correct past tense form.

(B) because "media" is a plural form of "medium." [Words with similar forms include **criterion** (s.)/**criteria** (pl.); and **phenomenon** (s.)/**phenomena** (pl.).]

(C) because "styles" is a correct plural form.

Question 15. The best answer is (A) because the correct preposition in this context is either "in" or "at."

The best answer is NOT:

(B) because "showed" is correct in the past tense.

(C) because "sensitivity" is correct when referring to the personal tendency to be offended.

(D) because **railed at** ("expressing criticisms in bitter language") is correct in this context.

Question 16. The best answer is (B) because no one was available to describe the Ordovician seas.

The best answer is NOT:

(A) because "which began" is a correct pronoun-verb usage in this context.

(C) because "a rich variety of" agrees with the singular "was" and is correct.

(D) because "most notably" is a correct adverb clause.

Question 17. The best answer is (C) because the changes were made in the past and use of the present "make" is incorrect.

The best answer is NOT:

(A) because "rejected" is a correct past tense usage.

(B) because "asserting" is a correct progressive usage.

(D) because "are not" is a correct present tense usage. You might be tempted to think that the correct usage is "were not," but "are not" is appropriate with the present perfect "has again rejected."

Question 18. The best answer is (D) because this version includes an incorrect use of the subjunctive. The phrase "if he had known" would be correct because the sentence describes a fact rather than a circumstance contingent on another circumstance.

The best answer is NOT:

(A) because the past perfect "had been" correctly places the blunder in the past at the time of the main action in the sentence.

(B) because deeply **chagrined** ("embarrassed") is an appropriate reaction to a blunder.

(C) because "could have" is a correct usage in combination with "had been particularly devastating."

Question 19. The best answer is (E) because the sentence is concise and correctly uses the past and past perfect tenses.

The best answer is NOT:

(A) because "had been" is a correct usage of the past perfect tense.

(B) because "was" is a correct usage of the past tense.

(C) because "for" is the correct preposition to use with "except."

(D) because "copying" is a correct gerund form that describes the action Lee was convicted of performing.

Question 20. The best answer is (C) because the correct preposition to use with "essential" is "for" rather than "in."

The best answer is NOT:

(A) because "found" is used correctly in the sense of "to experience" his homework.

(B) because "completing" is a gerund form that is correct.

(D) because the preposition "of" is used correctly with "goal."

Question 21. The best answer is (A) because the adjective "contradictory" is used incorrectly. The adverb "contrary" would be correct, as would "in contrast to."

The best answer is NOT:

(B) because "advocates" correctly uses the present tense to describe Stevens' position.

(C) because the preposition "during" is used correctly with "the next three years."

(D) because "expected" is used correctly as an adjective to describe "decline."

Question 22. The best answer is (D) because when comparing more than two, the superlative form of "good" is "best."

The best answer is NOT:

(A) because "although" is used correctly as a conjunction.

(B) because "strong" is an appropriate modifier of "competitor."

(C) because a strong competitor would have formidable "credentials."

Question 23. The best answer is (A) because the action occurs in the past; since Licklider envisioned a global network of machines, it is clear that he saw the potential of the computer. Therefore, the present perfect "would have been" is incorrect.

The best answer is NOT:

(B) because "potential of" is an idiom correctly used in this context.

(C) because "communication" is an appropriate modifier for "tool."

(D) because "envisioned" is an appropriate use of the past tense form of "envision."

Question 24. The best answer is (B) because "my brother and I" are the recipients of the action rather than the actors themselves and, as a result, the objective "me" is correct.

The best answer is NOT:

(A) because the past tense "sold" is consistent with the remainder of the sentence.

(C) because "pooled" accurately describes the boys' combining of their resources.

(D) because "cost," used as a noun in this instance, is correct.

Question 25. The best answer is (D) because the plural pronoun "they" does not agree with the singular noun "everyone."

The best answer is NOT:

(A) because "what" is a correct usage in relation to "no matter" and "score."

(B) because "everyone" is an appropriate pronoun for the team members.

(C) because the singular "believes" agrees with the singular "everyone."

Question 26. The best answer is (C) because the plural verb "loom" does not agree with the singular "majestic outline of the Rocky Mountains." The correct form would be "looms."

The best answer is NOT:

(A) because "beyond" is an appropriate preposition for the sentence.

(B) because "majestic" is a fitting adjective for the outline of the mountains.

(D) because "distant" aptly describes "the horizon."

Question 27. The best answer is (C) because the plural verb "chronicle" does not match the singular "Black Elk Speaks." If you are confused, eliminate the clutter between these two words and simply say, "*Black Elk Speaks* chronicles life in the Western United States..." The words between "speaks" and "chronicles" are simply there to confuse you.

The best answer is NOT:

(A) because "based on" begins a phrase that appropriately modifies *Black Elk Speaks*.

(B) because "is" agrees with the singular *Black Elk Speaks*.

(D) because "from a" begins an appropriate prepositional phrase modifying *Black Elk Speaks*.

Question 28. The best answer is (E) because the usages of "good," "better," "well," and "best" are correct. "Good" is an adjective that modifies a noun; "well," "better," and "best" are adverbs that modify verbs.

The best answer is NOT:

(A) because "good" correctly modifies "job."

(B) because "well" correctly modifies "performed."

(C) because "better" correctly compares Julie's performance on the science section with her performance on the math.

(D) because "best," the superlative form, correctly compares Julie's performance on the English portion of the test with that on the other two sections.

Question 29. The best answer is (D) because **restive** means "impatient" or "discontented." Do not confuse this word with "restful," which would be appropriate here.

The best answer is NOT:

(A) because although we have told you to be on your guard for "-ing" at the beginning of sentences, there are some cases when these are correct, or at least not incorrect. "Having grown" begins a clause that modifies "Mark," which must be the first word of the following clause to prevent "having…work" from being a dangling modifier.

(B) because "to produce" is an appropriate infinitive form after "constant pressure."

(C) because "was grateful" is a fitting past tense form of "grateful."

IMPROVING PARAGRAPHS – Elizabeth Cady Stanton Passage

Question 30. The best answer is (E) because substituting "many people do not know" removes the passive voice from this sentence.

The best answer is NOT:

(A) because "the foremost activist" is a crisper, more concise way of describing Stanton than the suggested revision.

(B) because "in" is a more appropriate preposition than "of" in this context.

(C) because many people do know about Stanton's role, even if many others do not.

(D) because "activist for women's rights" is understood in the second clause and therefore need not be repeated.

Question 31. The best answer is (C) because it is a logical extension of the preceding sentence, which notes that Anthony "is the more famous of the two today," suggesting that Anthony may not have been the more famous when Stanton and Anthony lived. "In their time" also echoes the statement in sentence 2 that Stanton was "the foremost activist for women's rights in the nineteenth century."

The best answer is NOT:

(A) because it is unclear whether "she" applies to Stanton or Anthony.

(B) because "to spell it out" adds nothing of value to the sentence.

(D) because "without a doubt" does not add meaningful content to the sentence.

(E) because "looking at her contemporaries" is a dangling clause that does not modify Stanton.

Question 32. The best answer is (B) because the fact that Elizabeth Cady Stanton called the Seneca Falls Convention is concrete evidence of her importance in the women's rights movement.

The best answer is NOT:

(A) because the sentence does not introduce a new topic but offers evidence to back up an existing one.

(C) because the sentence does not outline a general theme but offers concrete details.

(D) because the sentence cites historical facts, which, though they are used to back up an opinion, do not themselves constitute an opinion.

(E) because the sentence presents two pieces of evidence that support one view.

Question 33. The best answer is (C) because changing the reference to "separate from her husband" would cause disagreement between "women" (plural) and "husband" (singular) (assuming that they don't all share the same husband).

The best answer is NOT:

(A) because "argumentation," though technically acceptable, is less direct than "arguments."

(B) because "independently of" removes a parallelism problem. The initial sentence could also be made correct by "separately from their husbands" or "separate from that of their husbands."

(D) because "a number of" is unnecessary.

(E) because "in particular" is unnecessary.

Question 34. The best answer is (A) because **eschewed** means "shunned" and Stanton shunned political compromises such as making alliances with segregationists.

The best answer is NOT:

(B) because although it is true that Anthony and Stanton did not always agree, this fact is less important to the second paragraph than the fact that Stanton was not willing to compromise her beliefs.

(C) because the fact that Stanton was a dedicated activist is made clear throughout the passage and stating an obvious fact such as this at the beginning of the second paragraph would not improve the passage.

(D) because even though Stanton had some differences with Anthony, the passage is more about Stanton than a comparison of the two.

(E) because the passage says nothing about whether people questioned Stanton's morals.

Question 35. The best answer is (A) because the underlined portions of the two sentences convey their meanings clearly and do not have extraneous words.

The best answer is NOT:

(B) because this version is awkward and creates an issue of agreement between "loving" and "enjoyed."

(C) because this version is a comma splice.

(D) because the second clause in this version is convoluted. Were it simply "she loved to dance," this version would be comparable to (A) in effectiveness.

(E) because this version sets up a cause and effect relationship that is not in the original formulation.

TEST 1, SECTION 5 – CRITICAL READING

SENTENCE COMPLETIONS

Question 1. The best answer is (B) because "acclaim" follows logically from "critical," and since Brooks is known primarily for her novels, it is not a surprise that she published only one novel. But to make the case iron-clad, you must also use the process of elimination. This answer fits best.

The best answer is NOT:

(A) because although "applause" looks promising, **obstreperous** means "noisily obnoxious" and would not be applied to a book.

(C) because "critical notation" is awkward at best ("critical notice" would be acceptable), and "unusual," though possible, is not a particularly good descriptor.

(D) because even though "respect" seems possible in this context, **cacophonous** describes "an unpleasant or **discordant** sound."

(E) because **discourse**, though it denotes "verbal expression or conversation," does not have the positive connotations necessary to follow "won critical." **Inimitable**, likewise, could conceivably fit, though is not ideal because it does not relate to a term from the first clause.

Question 2. The best answer is (D) because **incognito** means "with one's identity concealed."

The best answer is NOT:

(A) because **unanimously** means "without dissent" and is not to be confused with **anonymously**, which means "with no name."

(B) because **stealthy**, an adjective, cannot modify "traveling." The adverb form, **stealthily**, which means "secretly," would be an acceptable choice, though it is not as good as "incognito."

(C) because a person can be **unidentified** only if his or her name is unknown. While it is possible for a person to travel with a concealed identity ("incognito"), it is not meaningful to speak of a person as traveling "unidentified."

(E) because although "concealed" means "hidden," the word does not make sense in this context without "identity."

Question 3. The best answer is (A) because the only choice that would be "deeply embarrassing" to a Representative is **censure**, a rebuke or expression of disapproval that, in the context of a legislative body, probably came from an official source.

The best answer is NOT:

(B) because a public **disgorging** would mean public vomiting. The word is a progressive verb form and not generally used as a noun.

(C) because **entente** is an agreement between two or more governments, as in the Triple Entente during World War I.

(D) because **erudition** means "extensive knowledge."

(E) because **devolution** means "the transfer of power or rights from higher to lower authority, especially in government."

Question 4. The best answer is (C) because the passage cites the span of 44 years during which John Quincy Adams served a congressman, senator, and president, thereby highlighting his **longevity**. In turn, Adams's longevity is an important **facet** or "aspect" of his career.

The best answer is NOT:

(A) because the passage has to do with Adams's length of service rather than his **eloquence**, though had he been eloquent (he wasn't), it would have been a "trait."

(B) because **appellation** means "name or title."

(D) because although John Quincy Adams showed considerable endurance, it would not make sense to speak of his endurance, a personality trait, as a "development."

(E) because although it could conceivably make sense to speak of John Quincy Adams' originality, such originality would be a cause and not an effect of his accomplishments.

Question 5. The best answer is (B) because **facile** ("fluent" or "effortless") is echoed by the question's key phrase, "flowed spontaneously." It helps to know that facile is often used to describe speaking or writing.

The best answer is NOT:

(A) because **doctrinaire** means "inflexibly attached to theories or doctrines."

(C) because **dilatory** means "slow or tending toward delay."

(D) because "decent" means "acceptable" and Truth was clearly a superb speaker.

(E) because **redundant** means "unnecessarily repetitive."

Question 6. The best answer is (C) because the sentence implies that there is a difference of opinion between those who believe global warming is a man-made problem and skeptics who question that theory. "Contention" and "concede" appropriately capture the differences of opinion, with "contention" applying to the causes of global warming and one side (the skeptics) conceding that global warming exists, but not necessarily with agreement about the causes.

The best answer is NOT:

(A) because although the causes of global warming could be a source of debate, the skeptics would not be the ones insisting that the phenomenon is real.

(B) because although the words seem to fit in the two blanks reasonably well, they don't establish a relationship that makes sense. The linking word "though" implies a contrast between the first and second clauses (as in "contention" versus "concede") that is not delivered by "concern" and "acknowledge."

(D) because the causes of global warming would not logically be a source of "unrest," and "debate" does not make a meaningful contrast with "unrest."

(E) because although the causes of global warming could be described as a source of disagreement, "allege" is not appropriate because skeptics are not the ones who would most vigorously assert that global warming is real.

Question 7. The best answer is (E) because **emblematic** ("symbolic") conveys the idea that the belt loop represents a larger truth about Mr. Peterson.

The best answer is NOT:

(A) because "functional" means "capable of performing."

(B) because skipping a belt loop would not logically be a cause of inattention to detail.

(C) because although "a downfall" is sometimes used in colloquial speech as a synonym for "flaw," it is not a grammatically correct usage. While it could be correct to state that "his downfall was inattention to detail," it would be incorrect to state that "inattention to detail was one of his downfalls."

(D) because while skipping a belt loop could be a sign or symptom of inattention to detail, it is not an indictment or judgment of that quality.

Question 8. The best answer is (C) because if Mr. Begay inspired quizzical looks, the students probably did not understand his meaning, and **cryptic** means "mysterious or incomprehensible."

The best answer is NOT:

(A) because although "exasperated" is a plausible response, "elusive" is typically used to describe physical movement rather than speech. Also, there is no obvious relationship between "exasperated" and "elusive" as there is with "quizzical" and "cryptic." That said, this is one of the toughest distracters on the test, and the meanings are probably closer than most you will see on the real SAT.

(B) because **truculent** means **pugnacious** or "confrontational" and does not form a meaningful relationship with "astonished."

(D) because **ineluctable** means "inevitable."

(E) because although the students could have been daunted by Mr. Begay, it would not be because he was **dense** ("dim-witted").

PASSAGE-BASED READING — Aspergillus

Question 9. The best answer is (B) because **ubiquitous** means **omnipresent** or "present everywhere."

The best answer is NOT:

(A) because "harmful" has no obvious relationship to "ubiquitous."

(C) because **deleterious** means "harmful."

(D) because **parasitic** means "living off another."

(E) because "microscopic" means "very small."

Question 10. The best answer is (D) because the first clause of the sentence is an assertion that Aspergillus is a hardy organism that can live in dry climates, and the second clause provides evidence of the fact that it has survived for thousands of years in Egyptian tombs.

The best answer is NOT:

(A) because the second clause is not a **disclaimer** ("denial of responsibility").

(B) because the first clause is not a **rebuttal** ("contrary argument") but a statement or assertion.

(C) because the second clause is not a **query** ("question").

(E) because the second clause is not a theory, but evidence that supports a statement or assertion.

PASSAGE-BASED READING – Louisiana Purchase

Question 11. The best answer is (C) because **paramount** means "most important," as does "chief." The answer is camouflaged, in classic ETS fashion, by the fact that most people associate "chief" with Native Americans.

The best answer is NOT:

(A) because "largest" refers to size rather than importance.

(B) because "controversial" means "marked by disagreement."

(D) because **zenith** means "highest point" or "culmination."

(E) because "magnanimous" means "unselfish and generous."

Question 12. The best answer is (B) because the sentences highlight the fact that even people who had never been to the West Coast "thought of it as part of their country, and would have fought to defend it."

The best answer is NOT:

(A) because the passage does not make reference to the idea that the transformation of the Louisiana Territory was either slow or difficult.

(C) because although the passage says that most Americans "would have fought to defend" the Western lands, the passage does not suggest that anyone wanted to go to war over it.

(D) because the passage does not suggest that anyone cared more about the Louisiana Territory than anyone else.

(E) because although the passage refers to people who did not plan trips to the West Coast, it does address the question of whether people wanted to plan such trips.

PASSAGE-BASED READING – The Legal System

Question 13. The best answer is (E) because the sentences describe how lawyers can help witnesses better understand the cross-examination process, noting that "if well-prepared, the witness can hold his own."

The best answer is NOT:

(A) because the sentences describe witnesses in the third person and analyze their behavior for the reader (lawyers). The intended audience of the essay becomes clear later when the passage refers lawyers as "we."

(B) because the sentences are concerned with how witnesses will react to cross-examination, not the legal context.

(C) because the sentences are dedicated to explaining cross-examination, not downplaying it.

(D) because the sentences describe how witnesses generally react to cross-examination but do not address mistakes.

Question 14. The best answer is (D) because the author says in the first sentence that cross-examination "is little more than a speech by the cross-examiner," and that the prevailing technique of cross-examination "turns the question into a commentary." The commentary offers a version of the facts that is favorable to the lawyer's client.

The best answer is NOT:

(A) because although the lawyer may be focused on giving a "speech" rather than having a genuine dialogue with the witness, it is inaccurate to suggest that the lawyer does not care how the witness responds.

(B) because the paragraph makes no mention of confusing questions.

(C) because even though it may be true that the lawyer will not allow witnesses to elaborate on their answers, this fact is not addressed in the first paragraph. When in doubt, always focus on material in the passage rather than what may or may not be true.

(E) because the paragraph makes no reference to the lawyer conversing with the judge.

Question 15. The best answer is (C) because **pedantic** and **bookish** are synonyms, though they do not express exactly the same meaning. They both imply that the subject has book knowledge but also carry a negative connotation of one-dimensional or obsessive concern with details, or with a display of learnedness.

The best answer is NOT:

(A) because although **erudite** is synonymous with "learned" or "scholarly," it does not carry the negative connotations of "bookish" and "pedantic." We do confess that this response could be interpreted by some readers as being correct, but this sort of hair-splitting characterizes the toughest problems.

(B) because **scornful** means "contemptuous."

(D) because **intemperate** means "hot-headed" or "immoderate."

(E) because **soporific** means "drowsy" or "inducing sleep."

Question 16. The best answer is (A) because the passage notes that the "loop back" method allows the lawyer to "recast the previous statement in a way we like."

The best answer is NOT:

(B) because the passage does not mention reminding the witness of a preceding response.

(C) because although a lawyer may use the power of suggestion, doing so is not mentioned in connection with the loop-back method.

(D) because the passage does not mention the scenario of a cross-examination going poorly.

(E) because although the loop back method may focus jury attention on a previous response, the purpose identified by the passage is "to recast the statement in a way we like."

Question 17. The best answer is (C) because the various techniques are aptly described as "a deceptive stratagem or technique," the definition of **subterfuge**.

The best answer is NOT:

(A) because "nonchalance" means "the quality of being unconcerned or indifferent."

(B) because **stultification** means "derision" or "ridicule."

(D) because **cloying** means "excessively sweet."

(E) because "destabilization" means "the act of making something less stable."

Question 18. The best answer is (E) because in the relevant lines, the author of Passage 2 makes an **analogy** between conflict of interest among lawyers and the issue of a doctor making a medical decision for a close relative.

The best answer is NOT:

(A) because a **metaphor** is a figure of speech in which the traits of one entity are used to represent another, as in "the diagnosis of cancer was a hammer blow." An analogy, by contrast, is a comparison of two situations that might be superficially dissimilar but show a common theme.

(B) because personal narrative (first person) is not used in the passage.

(C) because the passage does not **allude** to any works of literature.

(D) because an **aphorism** is a **pithy** statement of truth or opinion, as in "a penny saved is a penny earned."

Question 19. The best answer is (B) because state bar associations **articulate** or "spell out" a code of conduct. In other words, they outline it. This question plays on the fact that "articulate," used as a verb here, has a different meaning as an adjective. In the instance of "she is an articulate speaker," the word is a synonym for "eloquent."

The best answer is NOT:

(A) because **inculcate** means "to teach or place in the mind of another, generally through repetition."

(C) because **declaim** means "to recite formally, as in a speech."

(D) because "utter" means "to speak," and although the bar associations do articulate codes of conduct, they do not speak them orally.

(E) because "eloquent" is a synonym of other "articulate" and means "persuasive or facile in speech."

Question 20. The best answer is (D) because the author uses the hypothetical scenario, a doctor faced with the prospect of operating on a close relative, to illustrate the concept of conflict of interest.

The best answer is NOT:

(A) because the author discusses conflict of interest throughout the passage.

(B) because although we made up these questions, we are unsure what "implied evidence" is. Evidence is either real or not.

(C) because the author uses the scenario to illustrate conflict of interest, a concept that is not a "conclusion" but a state of affairs that unquestionably exists from time to time.

(E) because conflict of interest is not a deduction.

Question 21. The best answer is (A) because the relevant sentence includes "generally" and "discouraged" rather than a word like "prohibited," implying that dual representation can be permissible in some situations.

The best answer is NOT:

(B) because the relevant sentences include the phrase "generally either barred or discouraged."

(C) because the sentence does not suggest that dual representation is ever "necessary."

(D) because the sentence does not state that dual representation is ignored, frequently or not, though the sentence does imply that it may be permissible.

(E) because the sentence does not suggest that dual representation is often **sanctioned** ("approved"), though the passage leaves open the possibility that it may occasionally be so.

Question 22. The best answer is (C) because while Passage 2 discusses ways in which lawyers may violate ethical or legal standards, Passage 1 discusses particular actions that can make lawyers effective.

The best answer is NOT:

(A) because Passage 2, not Passage 1, addresses readers in the second person.

(B) because both passages, and especially Passage 2, explain important legal principles.

(D) because Passage 2, more so than Passage 1, discusses the legality of particular actions.

(E) because Passage 2 discusses circumstances in which lawyers can be sued.

Question 23. The best answer is (E) because the purpose of both passages is to impart information to the reader.

The best answer is NOT:

(A) because the tone of both passages is conversational rather than **pompous** ("self-important").

(B) because although both passages address principles of behavior, both are practical and concrete, rather than theoretical, in their presentation.

(C) because neither passage is **confrontational** ("argumentative").

(E) because neither passage uses **deductive** reasoning, which means "drawing a conclusion by reason or logic."

Question 24. The best answer is (C) because the first passage addresses lawyers as "we" and is written to instruct them, while the second passage discusses the actions of lawyers and is relevant to lawyers, or anyone who might use a lawyer, and is therefore intended for a general audience.

The best answer is NOT:

(A) because Passage 2 is not addressed to prospective jurors.

(B) because Passage 1 is not intended for a general audience and Passage 2 is not intended for physicians.

(D) because Passage 2 is relevant to people who are not lawyers but want to evaluate the behavior of lawyers.

(E) because the primary purpose of Passage 1 is to instruct lawyers on how to question witnesses.

TEST 1, SECTION 7 – MATH

Question 1. The answer is (A). The thousands place is the fourth digit, and 3,549,674 rounded to the nearest thousand is 3,550,000.

Question 2. The answer is (C). If a is 6, then $2a^2 + 4 = 76$, and $76 \div 3 = 25$ with a remainder of 1.

Question 3. The answer is (E). With $y - x$ in the denominator, the expression $\frac{4}{y - x}$ has its largest value when y is as small as possible and x as big as possible, in this case $x = 3$ and $y = 5$. Therefore, $\frac{4}{2} = 2$.

Question 4. The answer is (D). In sizing this one up, you should see immediately that y must be negative to make the entire expression equal zero. That leaves three possible answers. But -17 is impossible because y^2 and $17y$ would cancel, leaving 52. Next up, -2 does not work because it leaves the expression positive. Therefore, by process of elimination (or because the numbers work), the answer is -4.

Question 5. The answer is (C). To avoid wasting a lot of time, you must see that a length of 16 and a diagonal of 20 make this pen a combination of two 3:4:5 right triangles. In this case, the ratio is 12:16:20. If you figure this out, you get $12 \times 16 = 192$ very fast.

Question 6. The answer is (C). This is one for which a diagram really helps. If the perimeter of one of the squares is 2, that means each side is $\frac{1}{2}$. Simply count how many sides there are (10) to get the perimeter of 5.

Question 7. The answer is (B). Since the number of tee shirts is 5,800, you know the number of knit shirts is 5,200 (for a total of 11,000). That means $5,200 - 1,800 = 3,400$ blue knit shirts. Add that to 4,200 blue tee shirts for a total of 7,600 blue shirts.

Question 8. The answer is (C). In order to get this one, remember that if the diameter increases by $2x$, the radius increases by only x. Therefore, the radius is now $r + x$ and

$$\text{area} = \pi(r + x)^2$$
$$= \pi(r^2 + 2rx + x^2)$$
$$= \pi r^2 + \pi(2rx + x^2)$$

Since πr^2 was the original area, the answer is $\pi(2rx + x^2)$.

Question 9. The answer is (E). If the sides of the square are 10, a diagonal across the square, which is also the diameter of the circle, must be $10\sqrt{2}$. From there,

$$\text{area} = \pi r^2 = \pi(5\sqrt{2})^2$$
$$= \pi(25 \times 2)$$
$$= 50\pi$$

Since the area of the square is 100, the area of the regions not in the square is $50\pi - 100$. But since only one of them is shaded, the answer is $\dfrac{50\pi - 100}{4}$ or $\dfrac{25\pi}{2} - 25$.

Question 10. The answer is (B). There are several ways to do this, but we suggest assuming that the original price of the bike is $100. The 20 percent increase makes the price $120. Next, divide 120 by .4 to get 48. Finally, $120 - 48 = 72$, and the final price is 72 percent of the original price.

Question 11. The answer is (E). This problem comes together quickly. If the small circles have a circumference of 6π, their diameter is 6, and the radius of the big circle is 12. Therefore, $\pi r^2 = 144\pi$

Question 12. The answer is (A). Since $5\,\overline{AC} = 2\,\overline{BC}, \overline{AC}$ is $\dfrac{2}{5}$ of $\overline{BC}$. If $\overline{BC} - \overline{AC} = \overline{BA}$, that means $\overline{BA} = \dfrac{3}{5}$. Therefore, the answer is 2:3.

Question 13. The answer is (B). The area of the circle $O = \pi(6)^2 = 36\pi$. If the area of the shaded region is 24π, then the shaded area is $\dfrac{2}{3}$ of the circle with 240° of arc. Therefore, the angle of the triangle with its vertex at point o is 120°. Since the two sides of the triangle adjacent to the 120° angle are radii of the circle, they are of equal length and therefore the angles opposite them are of equal size. With 180° in a triangle, each must be 30°.

Question 14. The answer is (D). This mildly tricky question requires you to understand that the sides 6 and 10 can either be the base and the height of the triangle, or the height and the hypotenuse. Response II is obviously correct since $\dfrac{1}{2}(6 \times 10) = 30$. But those with sharp eyes will note that 6 and 10 can be the length of two sides of a special right triangle with the third side of 8. The area of this triangle would be 24.

Question 15. The answer is (C). This problem may look for a minute like geometry, but it is really ratio and proportion. If a boy who is $4\frac{1}{2}$ feet tall casts a shadow that is 6 feet tall, the boy is $\frac{3}{4}$ as tall as the shadow is long. Therefore, if the tree casts a shadow 48 feet long, the tree must be $\frac{3}{4}$ as tall as the shadow is long, or 36 feet tall.

Question 16. The answer is (D). In this problem, the key is understanding that 3 of the 4 possible sums overlap for each value of y. In other words, if y is 8, the possible values of $y - z$ are 4, 3, 2, and 1. If y is 9, the values of $y - z$ are 5, 4, 3, and 2. If y is 10, the values are 6, 5, 4, and 3. And if y is 11, the values are 7, 6, 5, and 4. Therefore, 7 different values are possible.

Question 17. The answer is (B). This question has round numbers with obvious factors, and the task is to sort through them to find the values of x, y, and z. If $xy = 24$, you might assume that x and y are positive (thereby ensuring that z is negative). In this scenario, the most likely values for x and y are 6 and 4. If x is 6, z would be -12, which would also satisfy $yz = -72$. So, $x + y + z = 6 + 4 + -12 = -2$. Oops. The calculations are right but the solution is not an answer choice. The trick, which might not occur to some students, is that x and y can also be -6 and -4 to satisfy $xy = 24$. That necessarily would make $z = 12$, and therefore $x + y + z = -6 + -4 + 12 = 2$.

Question 18. The answer is (D). The key to this problem is understanding that fractional exponents are roots, and that numbers like 27 and 64 are really 3 and 2 raised to a power. In this case,

$$27^{\frac{4}{3}} = \left(\sqrt[3]{27}\right)^4$$
$$= (3)^4$$
$$= 81$$
$$\text{and } 64^{\frac{5}{6}} = \left(\sqrt[6]{64}\right)^5$$
$$= \left(\sqrt[6]{2}\right)^5$$
$$= (2)^5$$
$$= 32$$

Therefore, $81 - 32 = 49$

Question 19. The answer is (E). There's a long way and a short way to solve this problem. For the long way, substitute $f(x)$ into the main formula:

If $\frac{4}{3} f(g^{\frac{1}{2}}) = 3$

and $(g^{\frac{1}{2}}) = (\sqrt{g}\,)$

then $\frac{4}{3}(3\sqrt{g} - 1) = 3$. From there, it is a matter of isolating g:

$4\sqrt{g} - \frac{4}{3} = 3$

$4\sqrt{g} = \frac{13}{3}$

$\sqrt{g} = \frac{13}{12}$

$g = \frac{169}{144}$

And the short way Since g is a root and there are no roots in answer choices, you know that the solution for g must be a value squared. Response (E) is the only choice in which both the numerator and denominator are squares of whole numbers.

Question 20. The answer is (C). Problems like this may look involved, but all they require is a little know-how. Process of elimination always works well. One easy way to start is to find the x- or y-intercept. If $y = 0$, what is the value of x? In this case, -4 is the only x-intercept, meaning that you can immediately eliminate responses (A), (B), and (E). Response (D) also includes a negative x-intercept, but the values of x get smaller fast as the absolute value of y gets bigger. Is that true of $x = \frac{1}{2}y^2 - 4$? Not at all. As the absolute value of y increases, x increases exponentially, meaning that the curve must open facing the right as in response (C).

TEST 1, SECTION 8 – CRITICAL READING

Question 1. The best answer is (C) because "although" sets up a contrast between the first and second clause, and the latter strongly suggests criticism because the heroines "violated the standards of social acceptability." The pair including **hailed** ("lauded") and **castigated** ("strongly criticized") best fulfills this meaning.

The best answer is NOT:

(A) because the critics of the 1890s would not **laud** ("praise") the novel for violating the standards of social acceptability.

(B) because **derided** ("belittled") and "rejected" do not establish an appropriate contrast between the two clauses.

(D) because **disentangled** ("free from entanglement") does not make sense as an action by contemporary critics

(E) because **enumerate** means "to count or list" rather than "to be included" and therefore does not make sense with "as a masterpiece."

Question 2. The best answer is (C) because **alacrity** means "cheerful eagerness."

The best answer is NOT:

(A) because **resurgence** means "renewal of energy or capacity."

(B) because **dynamism** means "a mechanism responsible for motion or development."

(D) because **deliberation** means "the act of considering or weighing" or "judiciousness."

(E) because **dutifulness** means "obedience."

Question 3. The best answer is (A) because as Julie is compared to the span of millions of years, the length of a human life is short, and therefore, **ephemeral** ("fleeting").

The best answer is NOT:

(B) because **mystic** means "mysterious" or "having to do with religious or spiritual **imponderables**."

(C) because **amorphous** means "lacking obvious form."

(D) because although the span of millions of years may be beyond human comprehension, the span of a human life would not therefore be incomprehensible.

(E) because **grandiose** means "characterized by grandeur or **pomposity**."

Question 4. The best answer is (E) because "scarcely" implies a contrast between the first and second clause with a short amount of time intervening between Wilson's "worldwide influence" and the "foundering" of his League of Nations. It can be inferred that Wilson's "debilitating stroke" drastically decreased his worldwide influence, and that his influence was at its **zenith**, or "highest point," scarcely six months before.

The best answer is NOT:

(A) because **nadir** means "lowest point."

(B) because "culmination" means "climax."

(C) because "conclusion" means "end" or "final part."

(D) because **denouement** means "solution."

Question 5. The best answer is (E) because **unabated** is a synonym for "relentlessly" and **encroachment** (a movement into a previously occupied space, usually unwelcome) accurately describes the destruction of rainforest habitat.

The best answer is NOT:

(A) because although "has continued escalating" is passable, "relentless destruction of human settlement" literally means that human settlement is being destroyed. (A better usage in the context would be "relentless destructiveness.")

(B) because although "accelerating" would be acceptable in the first blank, "relentless continuance" is a redundant phrase that does not effectively describe the destruction of rainforest habitat.

(C) because **intermittently** ("occasionally" or "from time to time") is not consistent with "relentless."

(D) because although some readers might consider this response acceptable, "continued consistently" is awkward and wordy. ("Consist" implies "continued.") In the second clause, "interference of human settlement" is passable, though "interference from human settlement" would be better, and in any case, "interference" is not a particularly effective way to describe the destruction of the rainforest.

Question 6. The best answer is (A) because sonorous means "a rich, resonant speaking voice."

The best answer is NOT:

(B) because **sonic** means "of or pertaining to sound" but does not suggest a quality of sound.

(C) because **desultory** means "inconsistent."

(D) because **scrupulous** means "honest."

(E) because **syncopated** means "rhythmic."

PASSAGE-BASED READING – The Meriwethers

Question 7. The best answer is (D) because the first paragraph explains the identities of the characters and the nature of the anecdote that follows.

The best answer is NOT:

(A) because while the first paragraph alludes to the motivations of the young people in the passage, it does not evaluate those motivations.

(B) because although the first paragraph devotes one sentence to describing the trick that Ned and Emily are planning, the primary purpose of the passage is to give information necessary to understand the trick as it unfolds.

(C) because the main purpose of the paragraph is to tell about the characters and their relationship to one another. Though the setting is mentioned, it is secondary to the characters.

(E) because although the passage begins with the fact that young people "will not submit forever to the prudent counsel of their parents," an evaluation of young people is not one of the main purposes of the passage.

Question 8. The best answer is (E) because the narrator often talks about the thoughts and motivations of the characters, even motivations of which the characters themselves are unaware.

The best answer is NOT:

(A) because Emily Meriwether is not the narrator.

(B) because Muriel Meriwether is not the narrator.

(C) because the narrator shows complete knowledge of the characters from the beginning of the passage.

(D) because the narrator has complete knowledge of the characters and their motivations.

Question 9. The best answer is (C) because the inclusion of the word "sensible" serves to highlight the fact that the Meriwethers are not being sensible in this case. The phrase could be read as "these *otherwise* sensible parents." The narrator lingers on the self-deception of the Meriwethers because their behavior is not sensible and implies that they should be able to see through the ruse.

The best answer is NOT:

(A) because although the Meriwethers have misgivings, they do not understand that Ned and Emily are not telling the truth.

(B) because Ned and Emily do not feel nervousness in the way the Meriwethers think they do.

(D) because this portion of the passage is about Ned and Emily, not about teenagers in general.

(E) because while it is true that the Meriwethers are uneasy, "sensible" relates to their self-deception.

Question 10. The best answer is (B) because Emily asks her parents not to come to the door so that they can allow Tom Bascomb to walk out in place of Ned.

The best answer is NOT:

(A) because Emily does not ask her parents for permission to stay out after midnight.

(C) because although Emily wore her mother's cape to the party, this was not related to the fact that Emily **feigned** ("faked") nervousness.

(D) because Emily did not dim the lights in the downstairs hallway.

(E) because Emily did not ask that Tom Bascomb be allowed to go to the Dorsets' party.

Question 11. The best answer is (E) because the passage uses **recess** in reference to the hallway to refer to a corner that was Tom's hiding place.

The best answer is NOT:

(A) because a recess in the hallway is not the same as a secret room.

(B) because the recess is a place in the hallway, not the hallway itself.

(C) because a quick break, like a school's recess period, is not the meaning of "recess" in the passage.

(D) because the secluded corner of the hallway is across the carpeted entrance hall from the stairs.

Question 12. The best answer is (B) because "bravely and protectively" reinforces the fact that home is a safe place, and that the rebellious teens are leaving its protection.

The best answer is NOT:

(A) because the fact that the light is "strong and bright" is not the same as that it is "brave and protective."

(C) because though the Meriwethers use the light to watch Ned and Emily, "brave and protective" has nothing to do with this fact.

(D) because characterizing the light as "brave and protective" is not related to the boy's identity.

(E) because there is no evidence that Ned and Emily are nervous about leaving the house.

Question 13. The best answer is (D) because the narrator implies that the Meriwethers have noticed that the boy does not look like Ned and have doubts about whether it is him.

The best answer is NOT:

(A) because the passage does not say whether Ned feels awkward in the **fedora** (a felt hat with a creased crown popular in the 1940s, 50s, and 60s).

(B) because the strange angle that "Brother" is carrying his head has no relation to whether the Meriwethers might be worried about Ned's safety.

(C) because there is no evidence that Ned is nervous about going to the Dorsets' party.

(E) because the reader knows that the boy in the fedora is not Ned.

Question 14. The best answer is (D) because Muriel Meriwether makes statements such as, "I hope it's all right," and frets about whether Emily should have worn the cape.

The best answer is NOT:

(A) because **risible** means "comical."

(B) because **laconic** means **terse** or "using few words."

(C) because **sardonic** means "ironic" or **wry**.

(E) **dyspeptic** means "in a bad humor as if suffering from indigestion."

Question 15. The best answer is (C) because **petulantly** is a synonym of "irritably."

The best answer is NOT:

(A) because "anxiously" means "with worry"

(B) because **phlegmatically** means "showing no emotion."

(D) because **disinterestedly** means "with a lack of interest" or "without personal gain."

(E) because although a petulant person can be obnoxious, the latter means "offensive" rather than "irritable." "Obnoxiously" means "offensively" or "objectionably."

Question 16. The best answer is (A) because Muriel Meriwether becomes "suddenly breathless" when Mr. Meriwether says, "I thought you meant something else." The paragraph implies that the "something else" is the fact that "the boy out there did not look like her own Ned."

The best answer is NOT:

(B) because Mrs. Meriwether is not angry but jumpy and nervous.

(C) because the passage implies that Mrs. Meriwether's statement about the cape was not really what was on her mind.

(D) because Mrs. Meriwether's anxiety is focused less on the party than on the circumstances surrounding Ned and Emily's departure.

(E) because the passage does not reference any judgments of Mrs. Meriwether about her husband.

Question 17. The best answer is (D) because even though Mr. Meriwether did not really think that his wife was referring to "the business we've discussed before," his later reference to the Dorsets' parties as "not very nice affairs to be sending your children to" implies that this was, in fact, "the business we've discussed before."

The best answer is NOT:

(A) because the passage does not make any comments about Ned and Emily maturing or doing so "faster than the meriwethers realize."

(B) because although Mr. Meriwether is suspicious, he makes the statement about "the business we've discussed before" to avoid talking about his suspicions.

(C) because in response to Mrs. Meriwether's comment about the cape, Mr. Meriwether says, "I thought you meant something else."

(D) because the Meriwethers do not discuss any tendency toward rebellion on the part of Ned and Emily.

Question 18. The best answer is (D) because the Meriwethers both have doubts about whether the boy was really Ned, but neither articulates those doubts.

The best answer is NOT:

(A) because the passage notes that the Ned and Emily "had left the front door unlatched for Tom."

(B) because the reason Emily does not want her parents to go to the front door is that Tom is hiding near there.

(C) because Tom, after hiding in the hallway, goes to the party with Emily in Ned's place.

(E) because the passage notes in the last paragraph that the sound was made when Ned went out.

Question 19. The best answer is (D) because the passage suggests that the Meriwethers are aware that something is amiss but are unwilling to confront or express their misgivings.

The best answer is NOT:

(A) because the passage does not suggest that the Meriwethers are inattentive to Ned and Emily.

(B) because the passage does not suggest that the Meriwethers are distrustful of the Dorsets.

(C) because the passage does not hint in any way that the Meriwethers are controlling.

(E) because although the Dorsets have vague suspicions about the circumstances in this instance, they are not distrustful of Ned and Emily. Indeed, their trust is part of why they overlook obvious evidence of Ned and Emily's mischief.

TEST 1, SECTION 9 – MATH

Question 1. The answer is (E). There's nothing like an ETS counting scam to start off a section. What could be easier than counting from 48 through 202, right? Maybe. Keep in mind that you need to count 48, 49, and 50, before you count 152 more to get through 202. The answer is 155.

Question 2. The answer is (D). You can get this one. The key is to avoid spending too much time on it. For occasions like this, it pays to know your odds and evens backwards and forwards. The question asks how long a sequence of consecutive numbers must be in order that, no matter which numbers are chosen, the sum of the numbers will always be odd. What sort of numbers, when summed, always make an odd number? Even numbers can never do so. The only way to make an odd sum from a sequence of numbers is to have an odd number of odd numbers. How many consecutive numbers must a sequence have in order to guarantee an odd number of odds? It can't be 3, 5, or 7 numbers long because sometimes these sequences will be made up of an odd number of odds and an even number of evens, but sometimes vice versa. A sequence of four numbers is no good because it will always have an even number of odds and an even number of evens. That leaves 6, and multiples of 6, which will always have three odd numbers and three even numbers, or multiples thereof.

Question 3. The answer is (A). All you need to do for this one is keep your numbers straight:

$$(-3 \times -5)^2 - (2 \times 8)^2 = 225 - 256$$
$$= -31$$

Question 4. The answer is (D). When graphing a problem with x greater than or equal to zero, you know immediately that the function will be confined to half the xy plane—the question is, which half? Since we know that x can never be negative, the function will not intersect the left side of the graph, thereby eliminating (B), (C), and (E). By making $x = 0$, we know that when $x = 0$, $y = 5$. We also know that as x gets bigger, y gets smaller very fast. That leaves us with our answer, response (D).

Question 5. The answer is (E). The game is to isolate y on one side of the equal marks.

$$\text{If } 120\,(y - 4) = 240z$$

$$\text{Then } 120y - 480 = 240z$$

$$120y = 240z + 480$$

$$y = \frac{240z + 480}{120}$$

$$y = 2z + 4$$

Question 6. The answer is (C). Since the first digit in all five numbers is the same and the second will be replaced by the fourth, your first key is the fourth digit. That eliminates (D). Your next key is the third digit. That eliminates (E). Next, look at the second digit, which will become the fourth. Eliminate (A) and (B), leaving (C).

Question 7. The answer is (D). We can't include too many this easy in a test that is supposed to be hard. You can tell at a glance that angles A and B are supplementary, and that C and D are also supplementary. Hence, $180 + 180 = 360$.

Question 8. The answer is (B). Since you know that angle PQO measures 65 degrees, you also know that angle QPO is 65. Why? Because since their opposite sides are radii of the circle, they are of equal length, and hence the angles are congruent. That makes $POQ = 50$ degrees, which means that arc PQ is also 50.

Question 9. The answer is (D). If the perimeter of the small squares is 1, that means the length of one side is .25. There are 12 of these sides on the outside of the big square, meaning that the circumference of the big square is 3.

Question 10. The answer is (A). The pairs are: 1×48, 2×24, 3×16, 4×12, and 6×8.

Question 11. The answer is (B). Since the sequence starts with 0 rather than 4, the 100th term is 396 and the 101st is 400.

Question 12. The answer is (B). It helps to know that the difference between 5^2 and 4^2 is 9. In this case, the area of circle A is 25π, meaning that its radius must be 5. For a circle 9π smaller, the radius must be 4. Even if you did not know this, you know that Circle B is smaller, and therefore only responses (A) and (B) could be correct. A quick plug-in would determine which one.

Question 13. The answer is (C). The only difference between the two expressions in this equation is that the second one has one more n outside the parentheses. Since the exponent $-n$ pushes the second term to the denominator, we have

$$(5^n)^{n-1} \times (5^{-n})^n = \frac{(5^n)^{n-1}}{(5^n)^n} = \frac{1}{5}$$

Question 14. The answer is (B). Understand that $600 = 150 \times 4$. Therefore,

$$f(150 \times 4) = \frac{f(150)}{4} = \frac{3}{4}$$

Question 15. The answer is (D). One way to do this question is add the scores for Peter on the first four tests and then do the same for George. Most students will simply eyeball the running total of the difference. After Test 1, Peter has answered 11 more correctly. His lead then drops to 9, climbs to 12, and then drops back to 11 after the fourth test.

Question 16. The answer is (E). Choice I is not correct. If $a = \frac{1}{5}$, then $\frac{a}{5} = a^2$ because when the problem is inverted and multiplied, the values are $\frac{1}{5} \times \frac{1}{5}$. However, $-\frac{1}{5}$ does not satisfy this condition because $\frac{1}{5} \times -\frac{1}{5}$ does not equal $(\frac{1}{5})^2$. Since $5^{-1} = \frac{1}{5}$ response II is also correct.

TEST 1, SECTION 10 — WRITING

IMPROVING SENTENCES

Question 1. The best answer is (E) because it establishes a concise causal relationship between the two clauses of the sentence. Ms. Huan is an ideal candidate because of her fluency in the three languages.

The best answer is NOT:

(A) because "as well as" is an unnecessary phrase that adds to the wordiness of the sentence. "Having" is also marginal because it does not define the relationship between Ms. Huan's linguistic fluency and the fact that she is an outstanding candidate.

(B) because this response is even wordier than (A).

(C) because "by being fluent" is an awkward construction that is neither logical nor grammatical when paired with "is an ideal candidate."

(D) because although this response is acceptable in most respects, "and also in" is an unnecessary phrase.

Question 2. The best answer is (C) because it fixes a dangling modifier with a logical initial clause that links George and his old school.

The best answer is NOT:

(A) because in this response, the first clause is a dangling modifier. "George," the subject whom the clause modifies, does not immediately follow as the first word of the next clause.

(B) because the building seems smaller during, not after, the time when George returned.

(D) because this response incorrectly uses the present perfect tense and the first clause is a dangling modifier.

(E) because without a conjunction to link the clauses, the sentence does not make sense.

Question 3. The best answer is (B) because the semicolon correctly separates the two clauses, which could stand alone as simple sentences but are joined by the semicolon to accentuate their cause-and-effect relationship.

The best answer is NOT:

(A) because the prepositional clause "for her work" does not mesh with the state-of-being phrase "having been the best in the class." A phrase such as "for her work that was the best in the class" is technically correct but awkward.

(C) because this response has a wordy "due to the fact" and an unnecessary use of the past perfect "had been."

(D) because the second clause lacks a subject for "having been the best in the class."

(E) because this response is technically correct but includes two unnecessary words, "for" and "that," which make it inferior to (B).

Question 4. The best answer is (D) because, notwithstanding the fact that shorter is usually better, the rule of **parallelism** dictates that the sentence compare the job of a kindergarten teacher with the job ("that") of being a lawyer.

The best answer is NOT:

(A) because the job of a kindergarten teacher is not being compared to a lawyer, but to his or her job.

(B) because the expression should be "as challenging as" rather than "as challenging like."

(C) because "like a lawyer" makes an incorrect idiom and does not satisfy the rule of parallelism.

(E) because this response garbles the grammar and meaning of the sentence.

Question 5. The best answer is (A) because the sentence concisely establishes a relationship between Susan's meticulousness and the fact that her editor's changes are usually minor. As a side note, this sentence shows an acceptable use of the passive voice. Since Susan's writing is the focus of the sentence, "the changes" are more important than "the editor," and use of the passive voice puts the spotlight on the changes.

The best answer is NOT:

(B) because referring to "changes usually suggested" does not make sense because each piece of writing would require changes that, even if usually minor, would not be identical from instance to instance.

(C) because "as usual" is misplaced between "changes" and "suggested."

(D) because "usually" is poorly placed and should be used to refer to action across many instances rather than merely the action in this particular instance.

(E) because "as usual" is misplaced before "the changes suggested by her editor."

Question 6. The best answer is (B) because the sentence describes a future circumstance which, if it prevails, will cause a particular outcome. In this case, Representative Jackson "will have served as a delegate in four different decades."

The best answer is NOT:

(A) because although the sentence describes an "if...then" situation, the indicative construction in the first clause should be followed by an indicative in the second.

(C) because the future perfect rather than the future tense should be used to signify that, in the future, a condition will have been satisfied in the past continuing into the present.

(D) because "could have" incorrectly implies that Representative Jackson will not have served in four different decades.

(E) because the present progressive is incorrect.

Question 7. The best answer is (A) because "has been well documented" correctly uses the present perfect to describe action that took place in the past and continues into the present.

The best answer is NOT:

(B) because the predicate adjective "well documented" is correct with the modifier "well" preceding "documented."

(C) because the present "is" is not appropriate for action that took place in the past.

(D) because the present progressive "is being" is incorrect for action that took place in the past.

(E) because "have been" is incorrect for a sentence using the third person singular.

Question 8. The best answer is (C) because since the first clause has two collective nouns, "colleges" and "students," the second clause should include a clarification as to which of these two is the subject. The phrase "these students" is necessary to clarify the subject.

The best answer is NOT:

(A) because the antecedent to "they" is initially unclear, causing confusion to the reader.

(B) because the use of "whom" is incorrect because the students are the subject of the second clause (and therefore should be referred to as "who"), and also because "who" can be read (incorrectly) to refer to the same individuals who were not admitted in the 1960s.

(D) because this response is unnecessarily wordy and the antecedent to "they" is initially unclear.

(E) because this response has an incorrect pronoun ("that" instead of "who") and implies that the students of the 1960s are the same ones attending today.

Question 9. The best answer is (B) because "not only" implies that the main idea of the first clause will be followed by another that "also" applies, and in cases such as this, no linking word is necessary in the middle of the sentence.

The best answer is NOT:

(A) because "in fact" is redundant after "not only."

(C) because "but" is not necessary after "not only."

(D) because "not only" makes "and" incorrect.

(E) because "not only…and" is incorrect, with or without "she."

Question 10. The best answer is (A) because this question is an especially nasty instance of the subjunctive mood that you might not see—but we decided to zing you with it anyway. Remember, the subjunctive is used in conditional situations to describe what would, could, should, ought, or might be. In the third person singular, the present subjunctive drops the "s" on most regular verbs, as is in "Lord help us," and in this case, "eager that he participate."

The best answer is NOT:

(B) because in the absence of an "if…then" statement, "would" is not appropriate.

(C) because the issue is not that he "can" but whether he will.

(D) because the present progressive is not appropriate for an anticipated action.

(E) because the present tense is not appropriate for this hoped-for condition.

Question 11. The best answer is (C) because this response places "the capital of South Africa" next to "Cape Town" (as an "appositive") and converts the modifier "enjoying" into the action verb "enjoy."

The best answer is NOT:

(A) because the main clause of this response is an awkward modifying phrase followed by a "to be" verb.

(B) because this response includes a minor modification ("enjoying" to "which enjoys") that does not improve the sentence.

(D) because this response says that Cape Town "is" a seaside location rather than the more appropriate "has" or "enjoys" a seaside location.

(E) because "which enjoys" applies to Cape Town, not "the capital of South Africa." The phrase "and enjoys" would be acceptable instead.

Question 12. The best answer is (D) because "in contrast to" is the relevant idiom for this sentence.

The best answer is NOT:

(A) because although "by contrast" can be correct in comparing two entities, if "to" is used, the proper phase is "in contrast to."

(B) because although "contrasting" can be used as an adjective, it is inferior to "in contrast to" if placed at the beginning of a modifying clause.

(C) because "by contrast with" is an incorrect variation of "in contrast to."

(E) because it is hard to figure out exactly what this response means.

Question 13. The best answer is (A) because the sentence adequately expresses that Peter's claim of being a scholar of Danish culture is undermined because he does not speak the language and has not been to Denmark.

The best answer is NOT:

(B) because "is not a speaker of" is a wordy construction and "the country of" is unnecessary in this context.

(C) because the passive "it is" construction does not improve the sentence.

(D) because "there" does not have an obvious antecedent. Even though the reader could gather that the sentence is talking about Denmark, the reference to Danish history is not an adequate antecedent for "there."

(E) because "nor ever" is incorrect without "has he."

Question 14. The best answer is (E) because this response concisely conveys the idea that Evans initially succeeded in convincing readers that she was a man.

The best answer is NOT:

(A) because this response is unnecessarily wordy.

(B) because the narrative of this response is unnecessarily delayed by "at least initially."

(C) because this response unnecessarily uses the past perfect and places "initially" after "succeeded," a less fluid phrase than "initially succeeded."

(D) because this response is wordy and includes an incorrect preposition ("by").

FISKE'S
SAT PRACTICE TEST
#2

SAT Reasoning Test™

Use a No. 2 pencil only. Be sure each mark is dark and completely fills the intended circle. Completely erase any errors or stray marks.

1 Your Name:
(Print)

Last   First   M.I.

I agree to the conditions on the back of the SAT®test book.

Signature: _____   Date ___ / ___ / ___

Home Address: _____

Center: _____
(Print)   City   State

Number and Street   City   State   Zip Code

2 YOUR NAME

Last Name (First 4 Letters) | First Init. | Mid Init.

3 SOCIAL SECURITY NUMBER

5 SEX

◯ Female   ◯ Male

6 REGISTRATION NUMBER
(Copy from Admission Ticket.)

4 DATE OF BIRTH

MONTH | DAY | YEAR

Jan
Feb
Mar
Apr
May
Jun
Jul
Aug
Sep
Oct
Nov
Dec

7 TEST CENTER
(Supplied by Test Center Supervisor.)

Important: Fill in items 8 and 9 exactly as shown on the back of the test book.

8 FORM CODE
(Copy and grid as on back of test book.)

9 TEST FORM
(Copy from back of test book.)

10 TEST BOOK SERIAL NUMBER
(Copy from front of test book.)

PRACTICE TEST #2

Page 1

Begin your essay on this page. If you need more space, continue on the next page. Do not write outside of the essay box.

Start with number 1 for each new section. If a section has fewer questions than answer spaces, leave the extra answer spaces blank. Be sure to erase any errors or stray marks completely.

SECTION 2

1 (A)(B)(C)(D)(E)	11 (A)(B)(C)(D)(E)	21 (A)(B)(C)(D)(E)	31 (A)(B)(C)(D)(E)
2 (A)(B)(C)(D)(E)	12 (A)(B)(C)(D)(E)	22 (A)(B)(C)(D)(E)	32 (A)(B)(C)(D)(E)
3 (A)(B)(C)(D)(E)	13 (A)(B)(C)(D)(E)	23 (A)(B)(C)(D)(E)	33 (A)(B)(C)(D)(E)
4 (A)(B)(C)(D)(E)	14 (A)(B)(C)(D)(E)	24 (A)(B)(C)(D)(E)	34 (A)(B)(C)(D)(E)
5 (A)(B)(C)(D)(E)	15 (A)(B)(C)(D)(E)	25 (A)(B)(C)(D)(E)	35 (A)(B)(C)(D)(E)
6 (A)(B)(C)(D)(E)	16 (A)(B)(C)(D)(E)	26 (A)(B)(C)(D)(E)	36 (A)(B)(C)(D)(E)
7 (A)(B)(C)(D)(E)	17 (A)(B)(C)(D)(E)	27 (A)(B)(C)(D)(E)	37 (A)(B)(C)(D)(E)
8 (A)(B)(C)(D)(E)	18 (A)(B)(C)(D)(E)	28 (A)(B)(C)(D)(E)	38 (A)(B)(C)(D)(E)
9 (A)(B)(C)(D)(E)	19 (A)(B)(C)(D)(E)	29 (A)(B)(C)(D)(E)	39 (A)(B)(C)(D)(E)
10 (A)(B)(C)(D)(E)	20 (A)(B)(C)(D)(E)	30 (A)(B)(C)(D)(E)	40 (A)(B)(C)(D)(E)

SECTION 3

1 (A)(B)(C)(D)(E)	11 (A)(B)(C)(D)(E)	21 (A)(B)(C)(D)(E)	31 (A)(B)(C)(D)(E)
2 (A)(B)(C)(D)(E)	12 (A)(B)(C)(D)(E)	22 (A)(B)(C)(D)(E)	32 (A)(B)(C)(D)(E)
3 (A)(B)(C)(D)(E)	13 (A)(B)(C)(D)(E)	23 (A)(B)(C)(D)(E)	33 (A)(B)(C)(D)(E)
4 (A)(B)(C)(D)(E)	14 (A)(B)(C)(D)(E)	24 (A)(B)(C)(D)(E)	34 (A)(B)(C)(D)(E)
5 (A)(B)(C)(D)(E)	15 (A)(B)(C)(D)(E)	25 (A)(B)(C)(D)(E)	35 (A)(B)(C)(D)(E)
6 (A)(B)(C)(D)(E)	16 (A)(B)(C)(D)(E)	26 (A)(B)(C)(D)(E)	36 (A)(B)(C)(D)(E)
7 (A)(B)(C)(D)(E)	17 (A)(B)(C)(D)(E)	27 (A)(B)(C)(D)(E)	37 (A)(B)(C)(D)(E)
8 (A)(B)(C)(D)(E)	18 (A)(B)(C)(D)(E)	28 (A)(B)(C)(D)(E)	38 (A)(B)(C)(D)(E)
9 (A)(B)(C)(D)(E)	19 (A)(B)(C)(D)(E)	29 (A)(B)(C)(D)(E)	39 (A)(B)(C)(D)(E)
10 (A)(B)(C)(D)(E)	20 (A)(B)(C)(D)(E)	30 (A)(B)(C)(D)(E)	40 (A)(B)(C)(D)(E)

CAUTION Use the answer spaces in the grids below for Section 2 or Section 3 only if you are told to do so in your test book.

Student-Produced Responses ONLY ANSWERS ENTERED IN THE CIRCLES IN EACH GRID WILL BE SCORED. YOU WILL NOT RECEIVE CREDIT FOR ANYTHING WRITTEN IN THE BOXES ABOVE THE CIRCLES.

9 10 11 12 13

14 15 16 17 18

Start with number 1 for each new section. If a section has fewer questions than answer spaces, leave the extra answer spaces blank. Be sure to erase any errors or stray marks completely.

SECTION 4

1	A B C D E	11	A B C D E	21	A B C D E	31	A B C D E
2	A B C D E	12	A B C D E	22	A B C D E	32	A B C D E
3	A B C D E	13	A B C D E	23	A B C D E	33	A B C D E
4	A B C D E	14	A B C D E	24	A B C D E	34	A B C D E
5	A B C D E	15	A B C D E	25	A B C D E	35	A B C D E
6	A B C D E	16	A B C D E	26	A B C D E	36	A B C D E
7	A B C D E	17	A B C D E	27	A B C D E	37	A B C D E
8	A B C D E	18	A B C D E	28	A B C D E	38	A B C D E
9	A B C D E	19	A B C D E	29	A B C D E	39	A B C D E
10	A B C D E	20	A B C D E	30	A B C D E	40	A B C D E

SECTION 5

1	A B C D E	11	A B C D E	21	A B C D E	31	A B C D E
2	A B C D E	12	A B C D E	22	A B C D E	32	A B C D E
3	A B C D E	13	A B C D E	23	A B C D E	33	A B C D E
4	A B C D E	14	A B C D E	24	A B C D E	34	A B C D E
5	A B C D E	15	A B C D E	25	A B C D E	35	A B C D E
6	A B C D E	16	A B C D E	26	A B C D E	36	A B C D E
7	A B C D E	17	A B C D E	27	A B C D E	37	A B C D E
8	A B C D E	18	A B C D E	28	A B C D E	38	A B C D E
9	A B C D E	19	A B C D E	29	A B C D E	39	A B C D E
10	A B C D E	20	A B C D E	30	A B C D E	40	A B C D E

CAUTION Use the answer spaces in the grids below for Section 4 or Section 5 only if you are told to do so in your test book.

Student-Produced Responses

ONLY ANSWERS ENTERED IN THE CIRCLES IN EACH GRID WILL BE SCORED. YOU WILL NOT RECEIVE CREDIT FOR ANYTHING WRITTEN IN THE BOXES ABOVE THE CIRCLES.

9 10 11 12 13

14 15 16 17 18

Start with number 1 for each new section. If a section has fewer questions than answer spaces, leave the extra answer spaces blank. Be sure to erase any errors or stray marks completely.

SECTION 6

1 (A)(B)(C)(D)(E)	11 (A)(B)(C)(D)(E)	21 (A)(B)(C)(D)(E)	31 (A)(B)(C)(D)(E)
2 (A)(B)(C)(D)(E)	12 (A)(B)(C)(D)(E)	22 (A)(B)(C)(D)(E)	32 (A)(B)(C)(D)(E)
3 (A)(B)(C)(D)(E)	13 (A)(B)(C)(D)(E)	23 (A)(B)(C)(D)(E)	33 (A)(B)(C)(D)(E)
4 (A)(B)(C)(D)(E)	14 (A)(B)(C)(D)(E)	24 (A)(B)(C)(D)(E)	34 (A)(B)(C)(D)(E)
5 (A)(B)(C)(D)(E)	15 (A)(B)(C)(D)(E)	25 (A)(B)(C)(D)(E)	35 (A)(B)(C)(D)(E)
6 (A)(B)(C)(D)(E)	16 (A)(B)(C)(D)(E)	26 (A)(B)(C)(D)(E)	36 (A)(B)(C)(D)(E)
7 (A)(B)(C)(D)(E)	17 (A)(B)(C)(D)(E)	27 (A)(B)(C)(D)(E)	37 (A)(B)(C)(D)(E)
8 (A)(B)(C)(D)(E)	18 (A)(B)(C)(D)(E)	28 (A)(B)(C)(D)(E)	38 (A)(B)(C)(D)(E)
9 (A)(B)(C)(D)(E)	19 (A)(B)(C)(D)(E)	29 (A)(B)(C)(D)(E)	39 (A)(B)(C)(D)(E)
10 (A)(B)(C)(D)(E)	20 (A)(B)(C)(D)(E)	30 (A)(B)(C)(D)(E)	40 (A)(B)(C)(D)(E)

SECTION 7

1 (A)(B)(C)(D)(E)	11 (A)(B)(C)(D)(E)	21 (A)(B)(C)(D)(E)	31 (A)(B)(C)(D)(E)
2 (A)(B)(C)(D)(E)	12 (A)(B)(C)(D)(E)	22	32 (A)(B)(C)(D)(E)
3 (A)(B)(C)(D)(E)	13		33 (A)(B)(C)(D)(E)
4 (A)(B)(C)(D)(E)			34 (A)(B)(C)(D)(E)
5 (A)(B)(C)(D)(E)			35 (A)(B)(C)(D)(E)
6 (A)(B)(C)(D)(E)			36 (A)(B)(C)(D)(E)
7 (A)(B)(C)(D)(E)			37 (A)(B)(C)(D)(E)
8 (A)(B)(C)(D)(E)		28	38 (A)(B)(C)(D)(E)
9 (A)(B)(C)(D)(E)	19 (A)(B)(C)(D)(E)	29 (A)(B)(C)(D)(E)	39 (A)(B)(C)(D)(E)
10 (A)(B)(C)(D)(E)	20 (A)(B)(C)(D)(E)	30 (A)(B)(C)(D)(E)	40 (A)(B)(C)(D)(E)

Section 7, the equating section of this practice test, has been omitted.

CAUTION Use the answer spaces in the grids below for Section 6 or Section 7 only if you are told to do so in your test book.

Student-Produced Responses ONLY ANSWERS ENTERED IN THE CIRCLES IN EACH GRID WILL BE SCORED. YOU WILL NOT RECEIVE CREDIT FOR ANYTHING WRITTEN IN THE BOXES ABOVE THE CIRCLES.

9   10   11   12   13

14   15   16   17   18

Start with number 1 for each new section. If a section has fewer questions than answer spaces, leave the extra answer spaces blank. Be sure to erase any errors or stray marks completely.

SECTION 8

1	Ⓐ Ⓑ Ⓒ Ⓓ Ⓔ	11	Ⓐ Ⓑ Ⓒ Ⓓ Ⓔ	21	Ⓐ Ⓑ Ⓒ Ⓓ Ⓔ	31	Ⓐ Ⓑ Ⓒ Ⓓ Ⓔ
2	Ⓐ Ⓑ Ⓒ Ⓓ Ⓔ	12	Ⓐ Ⓑ Ⓒ Ⓓ Ⓔ	22	Ⓐ Ⓑ Ⓒ Ⓓ Ⓔ	32	Ⓐ Ⓑ Ⓒ Ⓓ Ⓔ
3	Ⓐ Ⓑ Ⓒ Ⓓ Ⓔ	13	Ⓐ Ⓑ Ⓒ Ⓓ Ⓔ	23	Ⓐ Ⓑ Ⓒ Ⓓ Ⓔ	33	Ⓐ Ⓑ Ⓒ Ⓓ Ⓔ
4	Ⓐ Ⓑ Ⓒ Ⓓ Ⓔ	14	Ⓐ Ⓑ Ⓒ Ⓓ Ⓔ	24	Ⓐ Ⓑ Ⓒ Ⓓ Ⓔ	34	Ⓐ Ⓑ Ⓒ Ⓓ Ⓔ
5	Ⓐ Ⓑ Ⓒ Ⓓ Ⓔ	15	Ⓐ Ⓑ Ⓒ Ⓓ Ⓔ	25	Ⓐ Ⓑ Ⓒ Ⓓ Ⓔ	35	Ⓐ Ⓑ Ⓒ Ⓓ Ⓔ
6	Ⓐ Ⓑ Ⓒ Ⓓ Ⓔ	16	Ⓐ Ⓑ Ⓒ Ⓓ Ⓔ	26	Ⓐ Ⓑ Ⓒ Ⓓ Ⓔ	36	Ⓐ Ⓑ Ⓒ Ⓓ Ⓔ
7	Ⓐ Ⓑ Ⓒ Ⓓ Ⓔ	17	Ⓐ Ⓑ Ⓒ Ⓓ Ⓔ	27	Ⓐ Ⓑ Ⓒ Ⓓ Ⓔ	37	Ⓐ Ⓑ Ⓒ Ⓓ Ⓔ
8	Ⓐ Ⓑ Ⓒ Ⓓ Ⓔ	18	Ⓐ Ⓑ Ⓒ Ⓓ Ⓔ	28	Ⓐ Ⓑ Ⓒ Ⓓ Ⓔ	38	Ⓐ Ⓑ Ⓒ Ⓓ Ⓔ
9	Ⓐ Ⓑ Ⓒ Ⓓ Ⓔ	19	Ⓐ Ⓑ Ⓒ Ⓓ Ⓔ	29	Ⓐ Ⓑ Ⓒ Ⓓ Ⓔ	39	Ⓐ Ⓑ Ⓒ Ⓓ Ⓔ
10	Ⓐ Ⓑ Ⓒ Ⓓ Ⓔ	20	Ⓐ Ⓑ Ⓒ Ⓓ Ⓔ	30	Ⓐ Ⓑ Ⓒ Ⓓ Ⓔ	40	Ⓐ Ⓑ Ⓒ Ⓓ Ⓔ

SECTION 9

1	Ⓐ Ⓑ Ⓒ Ⓓ Ⓔ	11	Ⓐ Ⓑ Ⓒ Ⓓ Ⓔ	21	Ⓐ Ⓑ Ⓒ Ⓓ Ⓔ	31	Ⓐ Ⓑ Ⓒ Ⓓ Ⓔ
2	Ⓐ Ⓑ Ⓒ Ⓓ Ⓔ	12	Ⓐ Ⓑ Ⓒ Ⓓ Ⓔ	22	Ⓐ Ⓑ Ⓒ Ⓓ Ⓔ	32	Ⓐ Ⓑ Ⓒ Ⓓ Ⓔ
3	Ⓐ Ⓑ Ⓒ Ⓓ Ⓔ	13	Ⓐ Ⓑ Ⓒ Ⓓ Ⓔ	23	Ⓐ Ⓑ Ⓒ Ⓓ Ⓔ	33	Ⓐ Ⓑ Ⓒ Ⓓ Ⓔ
4	Ⓐ Ⓑ Ⓒ Ⓓ Ⓔ	14	Ⓐ Ⓑ Ⓒ Ⓓ Ⓔ	24	Ⓐ Ⓑ Ⓒ Ⓓ Ⓔ	34	Ⓐ Ⓑ Ⓒ Ⓓ Ⓔ
5	Ⓐ Ⓑ Ⓒ Ⓓ Ⓔ	15	Ⓐ Ⓑ Ⓒ Ⓓ Ⓔ	25	Ⓐ Ⓑ Ⓒ Ⓓ Ⓔ	35	Ⓐ Ⓑ Ⓒ Ⓓ Ⓔ
6	Ⓐ Ⓑ Ⓒ Ⓓ Ⓔ	16	Ⓐ Ⓑ Ⓒ Ⓓ Ⓔ	26	Ⓐ Ⓑ Ⓒ Ⓓ Ⓔ	36	Ⓐ Ⓑ Ⓒ Ⓓ Ⓔ
7	Ⓐ Ⓑ Ⓒ Ⓓ Ⓔ	17	Ⓐ Ⓑ Ⓒ Ⓓ Ⓔ	27	Ⓐ Ⓑ Ⓒ Ⓓ Ⓔ	37	Ⓐ Ⓑ Ⓒ Ⓓ Ⓔ
8	Ⓐ Ⓑ Ⓒ Ⓓ Ⓔ	18	Ⓐ Ⓑ Ⓒ Ⓓ Ⓔ	28	Ⓐ Ⓑ Ⓒ Ⓓ Ⓔ	38	Ⓐ Ⓑ Ⓒ Ⓓ Ⓔ
9	Ⓐ Ⓑ Ⓒ Ⓓ Ⓔ	19	Ⓐ Ⓑ Ⓒ Ⓓ Ⓔ	29	Ⓐ Ⓑ Ⓒ Ⓓ Ⓔ	39	Ⓐ Ⓑ Ⓒ Ⓓ Ⓔ
10	Ⓐ Ⓑ Ⓒ Ⓓ Ⓔ	20	Ⓐ Ⓑ Ⓒ Ⓓ Ⓔ	30	Ⓐ Ⓑ Ⓒ Ⓓ Ⓔ	40	Ⓐ Ⓑ Ⓒ Ⓓ Ⓔ

SECTION 10

1	Ⓐ Ⓑ Ⓒ Ⓓ Ⓔ	11	Ⓐ Ⓑ Ⓒ Ⓓ Ⓔ	21	Ⓐ Ⓑ Ⓒ Ⓓ Ⓔ	31	Ⓐ Ⓑ Ⓒ Ⓓ Ⓔ
2	Ⓐ Ⓑ Ⓒ Ⓓ Ⓔ	12	Ⓐ Ⓑ Ⓒ Ⓓ Ⓔ	22	Ⓐ Ⓑ Ⓒ Ⓓ Ⓔ	32	Ⓐ Ⓑ Ⓒ Ⓓ Ⓔ
3	Ⓐ Ⓑ Ⓒ Ⓓ Ⓔ	13	Ⓐ Ⓑ Ⓒ Ⓓ Ⓔ	23	Ⓐ Ⓑ Ⓒ Ⓓ Ⓔ	33	Ⓐ Ⓑ Ⓒ Ⓓ Ⓔ
4	Ⓐ Ⓑ Ⓒ Ⓓ Ⓔ	14	Ⓐ Ⓑ Ⓒ Ⓓ Ⓔ	24	Ⓐ Ⓑ Ⓒ Ⓓ Ⓔ	34	Ⓐ Ⓑ Ⓒ Ⓓ Ⓔ
5	Ⓐ Ⓑ Ⓒ Ⓓ Ⓔ	15	Ⓐ Ⓑ Ⓒ Ⓓ Ⓔ	25	Ⓐ Ⓑ Ⓒ Ⓓ Ⓔ	35	Ⓐ Ⓑ Ⓒ Ⓓ Ⓔ
6	Ⓐ Ⓑ Ⓒ Ⓓ Ⓔ	16	Ⓐ Ⓑ Ⓒ Ⓓ Ⓔ	26	Ⓐ Ⓑ Ⓒ Ⓓ Ⓔ	36	Ⓐ Ⓑ Ⓒ Ⓓ Ⓔ
7	Ⓐ Ⓑ Ⓒ Ⓓ Ⓔ	17	Ⓐ Ⓑ Ⓒ Ⓓ Ⓔ	27	Ⓐ Ⓑ Ⓒ Ⓓ Ⓔ	37	Ⓐ Ⓑ Ⓒ Ⓓ Ⓔ
8	Ⓐ Ⓑ Ⓒ Ⓓ Ⓔ	18	Ⓐ Ⓑ Ⓒ Ⓓ Ⓔ	28	Ⓐ Ⓑ Ⓒ Ⓓ Ⓔ	38	Ⓐ Ⓑ Ⓒ Ⓓ Ⓔ
9	Ⓐ Ⓑ Ⓒ Ⓓ Ⓔ	19	Ⓐ Ⓑ Ⓒ Ⓓ Ⓔ	29	Ⓐ Ⓑ Ⓒ Ⓓ Ⓔ	39	Ⓐ Ⓑ Ⓒ Ⓓ Ⓔ
10	Ⓐ Ⓑ Ⓒ Ⓓ Ⓔ	20	Ⓐ Ⓑ Ⓒ Ⓓ Ⓔ	30	Ⓐ Ⓑ Ⓒ Ⓓ Ⓔ	40	Ⓐ Ⓑ Ⓒ Ⓓ Ⓔ

CERTIFICATION STATEMENT

Copy the statement below (do not print) and sign your name as you would an official document

I hereby agree to the conditions set forth online at www.collegeboard.com and/or in the Registration Bulletin and certify that I am the person whose name and address appears on this answer sheet.

_____

_____

_____

_____

Signature _____   Date _____

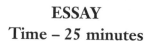
ESSAY
Time – 25 minutes

The essay gives you an opportunity to show how effectively you can develop and express ideas. You should, therefore, take care to develop your point of view, present your ideas logically and clearly, and use language precisely.

Your essay must be written on the lines provided on your answer sheet—you will receive no other paper on which to write. You will have enough space if you write on every line, avoid wide margins, and keep your handwriting to a reasonable size. Remember that people who are not familiar with your handwriting will read what you write. Try to write or print so that what you are writing is legible to those readers.

You will have twenty-five minutes to write an essay on the topic assigned below. DO NOT WRITE ON ANOTHER TOPIC. AN OFF-TOPIC ESSAY WILL RECEIVE A SCORE OF ZERO.

Think carefully about the issue presented in the following excerpt and the assignment below.

> The true history of an age cannot be written in the present tense. Contemporary observers cannot possibly understand the time in which they live as well as those who survey it from afar. Only when the principals have long since passed from the stage—and new ones risen to take their places—can the historian fix a clear-eyed gaze upon the scene and sort out its real significance.

Assignment: Do historians understand the past better than those who live through it? Plan and write an essay in which you develop your point of view on this issue. Support your position with reasoning and examples taken from your reading, studies, experience, or observations.

DO NOT WRITE YOUR ESSAY IN YOUR TEST BOOK. You will receive credit only for what you write on your answer sheet.

BEGIN WRITING YOUR ESSAY ON PAGE 2 OF THE ANSWER SHEET

**If you finish before time is called, you may check your work on this section only.
Do not turn to any other section in the test.**

SECTION 2
Time – 25 minutes
18 Questions

Turn to Section 2 (page 4) of your answer sheet to answer the questions in this section.

Directions: For this section, solve each problem and decide which is the best of the choices given. Fill in the corresponding circle on the answer sheet. You may use any available space for scratch work.

Notes

1. The use of a calculator is permitted.

2. All numbers used are real numbers.

3. Figures that accompany problems in this test are intended to provide information useful in solving the problems. They are drawn as accurately as possible EXCEPT when it is stated in a specific problem that the figure is not drawn to scale. All figures lie in a plane unless otherwise indicated.

4. Unless otherwise specified, the domain of any function f is assumed to be the set of all real numbers x for which $f(x)$ is a real number.

Reference Information

$A = \pi r^2$
$C = 2\pi r$
$A = lw$
$A = \frac{1}{2}bh$
$V = lwh$
$V = \pi r^2 h$
$c^2 = a^2 + b^2$
Special Right Triangles

The number of degrees of arc in a circle is 360.
The sum of the measures in degrees of the angles of a triangle is 180.

1. Of the following, which number is the greatest?

(A) 0.04
(B) 0.38
(C) 0.384
(D) 0.3084
(E) 0.3784

2. A farmer divides a fence into 60 segments of equal length, each bounded by a post on both sides. If he later decides to take down half the fence, how many posts must he leave standing?

(A) 15
(B) 29
(C) 30
(D) 31
(E) 60

GO ON TO THE NEXT PAGE

3. If $f(x) = 3x + 4$, then $f(9) =$

   (A) 7
   (B) 16
   (C) 23
   (D) 27
   (E) 31

5. A certain right triangle has one side that is twice as long as another of its sides. If the lengths of these two sides are 18 and 36, what is the <u>perimeter</u> of the triangle?

   (A) 54
   (B) $72\sqrt{3}$
   (C) $72\sqrt{2}$
   (D) $54 + 18\sqrt{3}$
   (E) $\sqrt{3}$

| $x^2 + 3$ | 3x + 3 | 4x + 6 |

Note: Figure not drawn to scale

4. In the figure above, a line segment has been divided into three smaller segments, and the length of each segment is described by the accompanying equations. If the combined length of all three segments is 72, what is the length of the middle segment?

   (A) 12
   (B) 18
   (C) 26
   (D) 28
   (E) 32

6. An organization invests $18,000 in stocks and bonds. The stocks pay 7 percent, the bonds pay 6 percent, and the amount earned from the two is $1,150. How much did the organization invest in bonds?

   (A) $7,000
   (B) $8,000
   (C) $10,000
   (D) $11,000
   (E) $12,000

GO ON TO THE NEXT PAGE

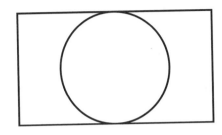

7. In the figure above, two sides of a rectangle are tangent to a circle. If the length of the rectangle is 7 and the area is 35, what is the circumference of the circle?

(A) π
(B) 2.5π
(C) 5π
(D) 7π
(E) 35π

8. Which of the following is the graph of $f(x) = -2(\sqrt{x^2 + 9}) + 9$?

(A)

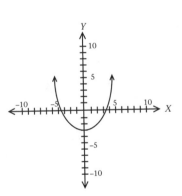

(B)

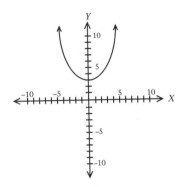

(C)

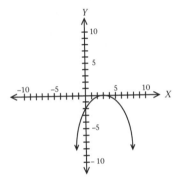

(D)

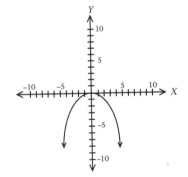

(E)

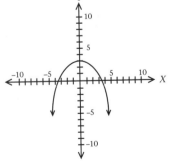

Directions: For Student-Produced Response questions 9-18, use the grids at the bottom of the answer sheet page on which you have answered questions 1-8.

Each of the remaining 10 questions requires you to solve the problem and enter your answer by marking the circles in the special grid, as shown in the examples below. You may use any available space for scratchwork.

Answer: $\frac{7}{12}$

Write answer in boxes.

Grid in result.

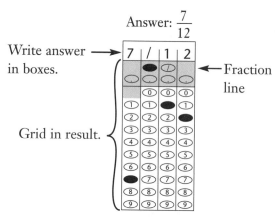

← Fraction line

Answer: 2.5

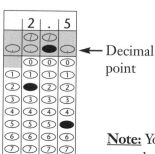

← Decimal point

Answer: 201
Either position is correct.

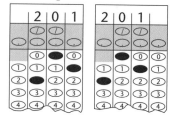

Note: You may start your answers in any column, space permitting. Columns not needed should be left blank.

- Mark no more than one circle in any column.

- Because the answer sheet will be machine-scored, you will receive credit only if the circles are filled in correctly.

- Although not required, it is suggested that you write your answer in the boxes at the top of the columns to help you fill in the circles accurately.

- Some problems may have more than one correct answer. In such cases, grid only one answer.

- No question has a negative answer.

- **Mixed numbers** such as $3\frac{1}{2}$ must be gridded as 3.5 or $\frac{7}{2}$. (If [3 1 / 2] is gridded, it will be interpreted as $\frac{31}{2}$, not $3\frac{1}{2}$.)

- **Decimal Answers:** If you obtain a decimal answer with more digits than the grid can accommodate, it may be either rounded or truncated, but it must fill the entire grid. For example, if you obtain an answer such as 0.6666..., you should record your result as .666 or .667. A less accurate value such as .66 or .67 will be scored as incorrect.

Acceptable ways to grid $\frac{2}{3}$ are:

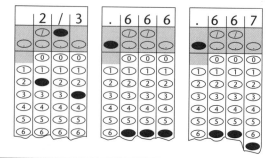

Candidate	Number of Votes
Jones	78
Li	112
Davis	96
Peterson	y
Olson	z

9. In a town with 540 eligible voters, 4 candi-
    dates were running for the position of
    mayor. If everyone voted for exactly one
    candidate and the distribution of votes is
    given in the table above, what is the maxi-
    mum possible value of z?

10. If $f(n) = (n + 8)(n - 3)(n - 12)$, how many
    positive integers satisfy $f(n) < 0$?

GO ON TO THE NEXT PAGE

11. In a rectangular coordinate system, a circle is tangent to the *y* axis at a point with coordinates (0, 5). If another point on the circle is (10, 5), what is the radius of the circle?

13. A menu includes 6 entrees, 4 vegetables, and 3 deserts. If the diners get chicken, one of the six entree choices, they must also have potatoes as their vegetable. How many combinations of entrees, vegetables, and deserts are possible?

12. Assume *x* and *y* are positive integers. If $x^2 + 12x + 35 = 48$ and $y^2 + 7y + 12 = 30$, what is the value of $x + y$?

GO ON TO THE NEXT PAGE

14. Let f be defined by

$f(y) = \left(2\sqrt[3]{y} + 3\sqrt[3]{y} \right) y^{\frac{2}{3}}$. If $y = 6$, what is the value of $f(4)$?

15. Let the function q be defined by

$q(x) = \dfrac{7 + x^2}{9}$. If $q(3p) = 16$, what is the value of p?

16. In the xy-coordinate plane, the distance between $(8, 4)$ and $(x, 11)$ is 8. What is one possible value of x?

GO ON TO THE NEXT PAGE

$k, -3k$

17. The first term in the sequence above is k, and each term after the first is -3 times the preceding term. If the first term is 2, what is the median of the first five terms?

DISTANCE IN MILES FROM ELMWOOD	
Parsonville	12
Rockdale	10
Jones City	18
Fairmont	8
Davistown	x

18. The table above shows the distance in miles that separates the town of Elmwood from five other towns. What is the value of x that would make the mean of the five numbers exactly two times the median?

GO ON TO THE NEXT PAGE

SECTION 3
Time – 25 minutes
35 Questions

Directions: For each question in this section, select the best answer from among the choices given and fill in the corresponding circle on the answer sheet.

The following sentences test correctness and effectiveness of expression. Part of each sentence or the entire sentence is underlined; beneath each sentence are five ways of phrasing the underlined material. Choice A repeats the original phrasing; the other four choices are different. If you think the original phrasing produces a better sentence than any of the alternatives, select choice A; if not, select one of the other choices.

In making your selection, follow the requirements of standard written English; that is, pay attention to grammar, choice of words, sentence construction, and punctuation. Your selection should result in the most effective sentence—clear and precise, without awkwardness or ambiguity.

EXAMPLE:

In 1953, Ralph Ellison won the National Book Award for *Invisible Man* <u>and he was thirty-nine years old then</u>.

(A) and he was thirty-nine years old then
(B) with the age of thirty-nine years old
(C) upon arriving at thirty-nine
(D) at the time of reaching thirty-nine
(E) when he was thirty-nine years old

(A) (B) (C) (D) ●

1. <u>Our menus were placed on the table by the waiter, and then he went to the kitchen to check on the day's specials</u>.

(A) Our menus were placed on the table by the waiter, and then he went to the kitchen to check on the day's specials
(B) The waiter, after having placed our menus on the table, went to the kitchen to check on the day's specials
(C) After our menus were placed on the table, the waiter went to the kitchen to check on the day's specials
(D) The waiter placed our menus on the table and went to the kitchen to check on the day's specials
(E) Prior to going to the kitchen to check on the day's specials, the waiter places our menus on the table

GO ON TO THE NEXT PAGE

2. Sheila Johnston has been a real estate agent in the city <u>for more than thirty years, she has earned a reputation</u> for integrity and prompt customer service.

   (A) for more than thirty years, she has earned a reputation
   (B) for more than thirty years and has earned a reputation
   (C) for more than thirty years, having earned a reputation
   (D) for more than thirty years, and as a result she has earned a reputation
   (E) for more than thirty years, thereby earning a reputation

3. The facts of the case were in doubt, but Detective Stephens <u>did not disbelieve the suspect's alibi</u> even when a witness gave a conflicting account.

   (A) did not disbelieve the suspect's alibi
   (B) was disbelieving of the suspect's alibi
   (C) did not believe the suspect's alibi
   (D) believed the suspect's alibi
   (E) had belief in the suspect's alibi

4. With Franklin Chang-Diaz, <u>with a flight on seven space missions, is one of NASA's most experienced astronauts</u>.

   (A) with a flight on seven space missions, is one of NASA's most experienced astronauts.
   (B) flying on seven space missions, is one of NASA's most experienced astronauts.
   (C) who has flown on seven space missions, is one of NASA's most experienced astronauts.
   (D) having been a flier on seven space missions, is one of NASA's most experienced astronauts.
   (E) having been one of NASA's most experienced astronauts, has flown on seven space missions.

5. <u>If Josh would have known that his car had an oil leak</u>, he would have taken it to be repaired rather than risk a potentially catastrophic breakdown.

   (A) If Josh would have known that his car had an oil leak
   (B) Would that Josh had known that his car had an oil leak
   (C) If Josh were to know that his car had an oil leak
   (D) If Josh knew that his car had an oil leak
   (E) If Josh had known that his car had an oil leak

GO ON TO THE NEXT PAGE

6. Prominent ears and a bushy tail, the latter generally held low, <u>give the coyote a distinctive profile</u>.

    (A) give the coyote a distinctive profile
    (B) gives the coyote a distinctive profile
    (C) are distinctive indicators of the coyote
    (D) give the coyote a profile that can be easily seen
    (E) is what makes the coyote distinctive

7. <u>The political career of Juan Domingo Peron had an unusual quality</u>, in part because eighteen years elapsed between his terms as president of Argentina.

    (A) The political career of Juan Domingo Peron had an unusual quality
    (B) Juan Domingo Peron, who had an unusual political career
    (C) The political career of Juan Domingo Peron was unusual
    (D) Juan Domingo Peron had an unusual political career
    (E) An unusual political career developed for Juan Domingo Peron,

8. <u>Once thought to be an ideal substitute for saturated fats, scientists have recently proven that partially hydrogenated oil increases</u> bad cholesterol and decreases good cholesterol.

    (A) Once thought to be an ideal substitute for saturated fats, scientists have recently proven that partially hydrogenated oil increases
    (B) Once thought to be an ideal substitute for saturated fats, partially hydrogenated oil has been recently proven by scientists to increase
    (C) Scientists have recently proven that partially hydrogenated oil, once thought to be an ideal substitute for saturated fats, increases
    (D) Scientists have recently proven that, once thought to be an ideal substitute for saturated fats, partially hydrogenated oil increases
    (E) Partially hydrogenated oil, once thought to be an ideal substitute for saturated fats, has recently been proven to increase

GO ON TO THE NEXT PAGE

9. Sarah spent hours on her paper for English, <u>but it was not her best work, although</u> she thought she deserved an A.

(A) but it was not her best work, although
(B) because it was not her best work, although
(C) and considering that it was not her best work,
(D) and although it was not her best work,
(E) but it was not her best work, although

10. <u>Whether it be for an hour or a minute</u>, no one should be forced to wait in line when there are idle employees in the vicinity.

(A) Whether it be for an hour or a minute
(B) Whether it was for an hour or a minute
(C) If for an hour or a minute
(D) Though only an hour or a minute
(E) Whether the amount of time is for an hour or a minute

11. <u>Critics may argue whether Flip Wilson or Redd Foxx was the best comedian</u>, but each was an important influence on popular culture in the 1970s.

(A) Critics may argue whether Flip Wilson or Redd Foxx was the best comedian
(B) Critics argue whether Flip Wilson or Redd Foxx was the best comedian
(C) Critics are arguing whether Flip Wilson or Redd Fox was the best comedian
(D) Critics may argue whether Flip Wilson or Redd Foxx was the better comedian
(E) Though Critics may argue whether Flip Wilson or Redd Foxx was the best comedian

GO ON TO THE NEXT PAGE

The following sentences test your ability to recognize grammar and usage errors. Each sentence contains either a single error or no error at all. No sentence contains more than one error. The error, if there is one, is underlined and lettered. If the sentence contains an error, select the one underlined part that must be changed to make the sentence correct. If the sentence is correct, select choice E. In choosing answers, follow the requirements of standard written English.

EXAMPLE:

It is one thing <u>to hear</u> rumors that a colleague
            A

has a <u>fiery</u> temper, <u>for</u> it is quite
      B   C

another <u>to witness</u> an angry outburst with
         D

your own eyes. <u>No error</u>
          E

12. If Peter <u>had</u> told Rodney to stay in the left
        A

lane, <u>he</u> might have <u>avoided</u> the accident that
     B   C

<u>happened</u> moments later. <u>No error</u>
   D   E

13. Although the price tag for the trip was

<u>steep</u>, everyone agreed that <u>paying for</u>
  A   B

<u>your</u> own ticket <u>was</u> the right thing to do.
  C   D

<u>No error</u>
  E

14. If Lucy <u>were</u> to go on the trip to the
       A

Grand Canyon, she <u>would</u> need to bring
            B

her own provisions, <u>including</u> a tent, a
             C

good pair of boots, <u>and</u> some warm socks.
              D

<u>No error</u>
  E

15. <u>Exculpatory</u> evidence aside, the jury
    A

<u>interpreted</u> the defendant's refusal
   B

<u>to testify</u> on his own behalf as a <u>taciturn</u>
  C   D

admission of guilt. <u>No error</u>
            E

GO ON TO THE NEXT PAGE ⟩

16. In response to our <u>cajoling</u>, Susan gave the
                              A

check to Kim and <u>me</u>, saying that we <u>ought</u>
                        B   C

to deposit it soon, <u>preferably</u> by the end of
                              D

the day. <u>No error</u>
                  E

17. Although hiking <u>through</u> the woods was
                              A

fun, <u>it was</u> also tiring, and we were happy
        B

<u>arriving</u> back at the bus for a <u>leisurely</u> ride
C   D

home. <u>No error</u>
            E

18. So <u>indelible</u> was the memory of
              A

Abraham Lincoln's assassination that

people <u>would have remembered</u> for the
              B

rest of their lives where they <u>were</u> and

what they <u>were doing</u> when they <u>heard</u>
                  C   D

the news. <u>No error</u>
                  E

19. The ability <u>to juggle</u> many different tasks
                        A

<u>are</u> essential for those <u>with aspirations</u>
B   C

<u>of working</u> in the hospitality industry.
        D
<u>No error</u>
      E

20. If Frank <u>was</u> not available, the only person
                    A

who <u>could</u> make a final decision in such
        B

matters was Elle, and she <u>is</u> inevitably
                                      C

reluctant <u>to do</u> so. <u>No error</u>
                  D   E

21. The nation's oldest <u>continuously</u> inhabited
                                    A

village, Acoma Pueblo, <u>sits</u> high on a
                                    B

rocky bluff in western New Mexico and

<u>offers</u> stunning views of the <u>surrounding</u>
C   D

countryside. <u>No error</u>
                      E

GO ON TO THE NEXT PAGE ⟩

22. Though some historians <u>scoff</u> at the name,
                          A

    "Harlem Renaissance" is the <u>moniker</u> most
                                    B

    often <u>applying</u> to the <u>flowering</u> of African
            C   D

    American culture that occurred in New

    York City in the 1920s. <u>No error</u>
                                 E

23. The driving instructor <u>warned</u> her pupil to
                            A

    go <u>slow</u> as she <u>entered</u> an intersection that
        B   C

    only a week earlier <u>had been</u> the scene of a
                            D

    fatal accident. <u>No error</u>
                        E

24. If the pilot <u>had been</u> alerted that there
                    A

    <u>was</u> a problem with the plane's rudder,
     B

    she <u>could take</u> countermeasures that
            C

    <u>would have</u> prevented the crash. <u>No error</u>
        D   E

25. As he <u>peaked</u> around the corner and <u>through</u>
            A   B

    the bushes, Billy <u>could</u> barely <u>make out</u> the
                        C   D

    shape of his father's car. <u>No error</u>
                                    E

26. The rules <u>of usage</u> for <u>comas</u> <u>are</u> a source
                A   B   C

    of great <u>consternation</u> for many students
                D

    of writing. <u>No error</u>
                    E

27. Shannon and Rosie have <u>comparable</u>
                            A

    grades in all their classes, <u>but</u> Shannon is
                                    B

    <u>the best</u> writer and Rosie <u>the abler</u>
        C   D

    mathematician. <u>No error</u>
                        E

GO ON TO THE NEXT PAGE ▷

28. The race <u>was close</u>, but for Susan
              A

<u>to have overtaken</u> Mary, she <u>would</u>
      B   C

<u>have had to</u> run the last lap in sixty-six
    D

seconds or less. <u>No error</u>
             E

29. <u>To combat</u> the spread of germs, the pool's
     A

lifeguards <u>monitor</u> the level of chlorine in
         B

the water and <u>require</u> everyone to take a
         C

shower before <u>they</u> enter. <u>No error</u>
        D   E

Directions: The following passage is an early draft of an essay. Some parts of the passage need to be rewritten.

Read the passage and select the best answers for the questions that follow. Some questions are about particular sentences or parts of sentences and ask you to improve sentence structure or word choice. Other questions ask you to consider organization and development. In choosing answers, follow the requirements of standard written English.

Questions 30-35 are based on the following passage.

(1) I miss Billy. **(2)** I miss his sly sense of humor, and the knack he had for making me laugh at things that were a normal part of my day. **(3)** In ninth grade, Billy sat next to me in Geometry and Biology. **(4)** We used to make a game of trying to see if we could get the Biology teacher, Mr. Paul, off on a tangent. **(5)** The goal was to get him talking about things that did not have much to do with what was going on in class. **(6)** We had no purpose other than to waste class time.

(7) Billy was a master at asking, with what seemed like sincere curiosity, "Mr. Paul, what did you do this weekend?" **(8)** Mr. Paul was such a talker that all we needed to do was give him a little prompting and he was off to the races. **(9)** We timed how long we could keep Mr. Paul off the subject. **(10)** Our record was sixteen minutes. **(11)** We learned more than we ever wanted to know about his wife, his baby girl, his golden retriever named Duff, and how Mr. Paul always knows when it is going to rain because his knee started popping.

(12) Billy and I had big plans to go to college together and then start our own business. **(13)** That is, until his family decided to move to Philadelphia. **(14)** Having friends move away is a part of life. **(15)** I just wish it had been somebody other than Billy.

30. In context, what is the best way to deal with sentence 5 (reproduced below)?

The goal was to get him talking about things that did not have much to do with what was going on in class.

(A) Delete it
(B) Move it to after sentence 6
(C) Move it to after sentence 7
(D) Change "the" to "our"
(E) Clarify with an additional sentence

31. Which is the best version of the underlined portion of sentence 4 (reproduced below)?

We used to make a game of trying to see if we could get the Biology teacher, Mr. Paul, off on a tangent.

(A) (As it is now)
(B) to try to see if we could get
(C) of seeing if we could get
(D) of getting if we could
(E) of trying to get

GO ON TO THE NEXT PAGE

32. Which of the following is the best version of the underlined portion of sentences 9 and 10 (reproduced below)?

We timed how long we could keep Mr. Paul off the subject. Our record was sixteen minutes.

(A) off the subject, and our record was
(B) off the subject, which was
(C) off the subject; our record was
(D) off the subject, with a record of
(E) off the subject, our record was

33. Which of the following ways to revise the underlined portion of sentence 11 (reproduced below) most effectively links the sentence to the rest of the second paragraph?

We learned more than we ever wanted to know about his wife, his baby girl, his golden retriever named Duff, and how Mr. Paul always knows when it is going to rain because his knee started popping.

(A) Because we learned more
(B) Due to the time we spent in his class, we learned more
(C) From a year in his class, we learned more
(D) In this class, we learned more
(E) After the class, we knew more

34. Which is the best version of the underlined portion of sentence 11 (reproduced below)?

We learned more than we ever wanted to know about his wife, his baby girl, his golden retriever named Duff, and how Mr. Paul always knows when it is going to rain because his knee started popping.

(A) (As it is now)
(B) because his knee had started popping
(C) because the popping starts in his knee
(D) because of popping in his knee
(E) because his knee starts popping

35. Which of the following is the best sentence to insert before sentence 12?

(A) We will always remember those days in Mr. Paul's class.
(B) My friendship with Billy continued to deepen through the end of tenth grade.
(C) Billy and I never had so much fun as when we were laughing at Mr. Paul.
(D) Billy and I were not mean kids, but we did like to laugh.
(E) Kidding aside, we liked Mr. Paul.

STOP

**If you finish before time is called, you may check your work on this section only.
Do not turn to any other section in the test.**

SECTION 4
Time – 25 minutes
24 Questions

Turn to Section 4 (page 5) of your answer sheet to answer the questions in this section.

Directions: For each question in this section, select the best answer from among the choices given and fill in the corresponding circle on the answer sheet.

Each sentence below has one or two blanks, each blank indicating that something has been omitted. Beneath the sentence are five words or sets of words labeled A through E. Choose the word or set of words that, when inserted in the sentence, <u>best</u> fits the meaning of the sentence as a whole.

Example:

In the face of ------- evidence of the defendant's guilt, the jury voted ------- to convict him.

(A) mitigating . . grudgingly
(B) disagreeable . . parsimoniously
(C) unwelcome . . zealously
(D) derisive . . sternly
(E) overwhelming . . unanimously

Ⓐ Ⓑ Ⓒ Ⓓ ●

---

1. Gnassingbe Eyadema was a ------- in the political landscape of western Africa, ------- as president of Togo for more than thirty-five years.

   (A) figure . . overseeing
   (B) dominator . . presiding
   (C) player . . certifying
   (D) fixture . . serving
   (E) leader . . chosen

2. Tom felt the cool of a spring -------, blowing gently against his cheeks and forehead.

   (A) zephyr
   (B) gale
   (C) torrent
   (D) maelstrom
   (E) wisp

3. Peter was eager to ------- himself with his new supervisor, but he succeeded only in appearing -------.

   (A) acquaint . . oblivious
   (B) aspire . . noncommittal
   (C) introduce . . truculent
   (D) ingratiate . . obsequious
   (E) align . . jovial

GO ON TO THE NEXT PAGE ▷

 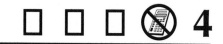
4. Until the landmark trial of John Peter Zenger in 1735, citizens could be charged with ------- if they criticized the government, even when those criticisms were truthful.

(A) noncompliance
(B) maliciousness
(C) interlocution
(D) interdiction
(E) sedition

5. After the sudden death of his wife, Mr. Agbo often seemed -------, and at times deeply -------.

(A) pensive . . incandescent
(B) incapacitated . . troubled
(C) emphatic . . overwrought
(D) wistful . . despondent
(E) distended . . enthralled

6. He claimed to welcome opinions that differed from his own, but it was an ------- to his ------- vanity that anyone would dare to disagree with him.

(A) impediment . . immodest
(B) irritant . . noisome
(C) affront . . overweening
(D) elixir . . iconoclastic
(E) tribute . . unyielding

7. To avoid revealing that they were in cahoots, Steve and George exchanged a ------- glance when no one was looking.

(A) furtive
(B) guilty
(C) disjointed
(D) procrastinating
(E) cloaked

8. In her declining years, Ms. Smith's ------- demeanor was in sharp contrast to her outgoing, vivacious personality as a young woman.

(A) disingenuous
(B) iridescent
(C) phlegmatic
(D) immaculate
(E) destitute

GO ON TO THE NEXT PAGE

The passages below are followed by questions based on their content; questions following a pair of related passages may also be based on the relationship between the paired passages. Answer the questions on the basis of what is <u>stated</u> or <u>implied</u> in the passages and in any introductory material that may be provided.

Questions 9-10 are based on the following passage.

Perhaps the greatest interpreter of the gospel music tradition was Mahalia Jackson. Born in a poor neighborhood of New Orleans in 1911,
Line Jackson made her singing debut at the age of
5   four in the Plymouth Rock Baptist Church Children's Choir. In her late teens, she worked as a maid while singing at church services and funerals. Her career took off in the late 1930s when she began her collaboration with storied
10   composer Thomas A. Dorsey. Jackson was known for her impassioned performances that brought heightened energy and sensuality to gospel. Though strongly influenced by Bessy Smith, Jackson was unwavering in her refusal to
15   sing the blues, famously rejecting Louis Armstrong's invitation to join his band.

9. In context, "storied" (line 9) most nearly means

(A) competent
(B) creative
(C) consistent
(D) celebrated
(E) concomitant

10. In lines 13-16, the author implies which of the following?

(A) Bessy Smith was a more versatile singer than Jackson
(B) Bessy Smith was in Louis Armstrong's band
(C) Louis Armstrong liked Jackson's singing better than Smith's
(D) Bessy Smith was a blues singer
(E) Jackson secretly wanted to sing the blues

Questions 11-12 are based on the following passage.

Measuring about five miles by three miles, Eigg has the most varied landscape of the small isles off Scotland's west coast. A high plateau
Line makes up the backbone of the island, which gives
5   way to secluded valleys, open fields, and finally, the craggy shoreline. Eigg's most striking geological feature is the Sgurr of Eigg, a massive basalt ridge that thrusts more than 1,300 feet above sea level. Sedimentary rocks from the
10   Jurassic Period are exposed on the island's north shore, with ammonites the most abundant species. Also at the north end of the island is the so-called Singing Sands, a beach of finely ground quartz that makes a high-pitched squeaking
15   noise under foot.

11. The passage is primarily concerned with the island's

(A) climate
(B) vegetation
(C) topography
(D) atmosphere
(E) location

GO ON TO THE NEXT PAGE

12. In the last sentence (lines 12-15), the author implies that "Singing Sands"

(A) is an inappropriate name for the beach
(B) is not a pleasant beach
(C) is within one hundred feet of the Jurassic fossil bed
(D) is named for the high-pitched squeaking noise made by the quartz
(E) is the best beach on the island

Questions 13-24 are based on the following passages.

The following passages discuss Thomas Jefferson and two of his policy initiatives as they related to African Americans and Native Americans.

Passage 1

In 1784, after the treaty with Britain was formalized, Jefferson prepared a plan for the governance of present and future territories. It divided the territory then held by the new nation into fourteen future states, ten of them north of the Ohio, and authorized the settlers to establish a provisional government adopting "the constitution and laws of any one of the original states." Each new territory could thus choose to be a free or slave territory.

Jefferson addressed the issue of slavery as follows:

After the year 1800, there shall be neither slavery nor involuntary servitude in any of the said states, otherwise than in punishment of crimes, whereof the party shall have been convicted to have been personally guilty.

This was not the first time that Jefferson had weighed in with a plan to curtail or abolish slavery. Eight years earlier, in the same month that he drafted the Declaration of Independence, Jefferson submitted to influential friends in Virginia a draft proposal for that state's constitution. It included the following language under the heading "Slaves:"

"No person hereafter coming into this country shall be held within the same in slavery under any pretext." This provision was consistent with Virginia's opposition to the importation of slaves, but it was not Jefferson's position in 1784 when drafting a plan for the territories. There, he permitted slavery to continue with respect to all slaves, imported or otherwise, for another sixteen years.

In later years, critics have dwelled on the sixteen-year delay, suggesting that such an interval would have been time enough for slavery to become established in the territories. But the delay was clearly calculated to placate strong opposition among Jefferson's fellow Southerners. The proposal also required that the new states created in the territories be bound by the Articles of Confederation. Those articles permitted slave owners to take their property into other states without losing it. Thus the states would have been prohibited from fully abolishing slavery even within their own borders. If adopted, Jefferson's proposal would have created a conflict in the year 1800 with the Articles of Confederation, which permitted the free movement of property. Jefferson's antislavery amendment applied to all present and future territory.

Conveniently for Jefferson, this was one contradiction between his stated ideals and political

reality that he would never be forced to reconcile. The proposal fell one state short of adoption. Massachusetts, Connecticut, Rhode Island, New
60 Hampshire, New York, and Pennsylvania supported it; Maryland, South Carolina, and Virginia voted against it. North Carolina was divided. Its defeat meant that slavery continued to be lawful in all of the territory west of the then-thirteen states.

Passage 2

65 Jefferson's status as the icon of equality is hardly consistent with his attitude toward native peoples. Professor Anthony F. C. Wallace, University of Pennsylvania anthropologist, goes so far as to paint Jefferson as "the planner of
70 cultural genocide." He believes Jefferson's deeply controlling temperament, his conviction that he knew what was best for everybody, was the reason he could have presided over policies such as he advocated in the following letter to a
75 friend, in which he made a harsh program of extinction sound like beneficence:

I believe the business of hunting insufficient to furnish clothing and subsistence to the Indians. The promotion of
80 Agriculture, therefore, and household manufacture are essential in their preservation, and I am disposed to aid and encourage it liberally. This will enable them to live on much smaller portions of
85 land....While they are learning to do better on less land, our increasing numbers will call for more land.

President Jefferson put these thoughts into action. In 1803, at the time of his exceptional
90 achievement in expanding the nation via the

Louisiana Purchase, he made a plan that resulted in a dramatic shrinkage of the land area held by the large Kaskaskias tribe that lived in a village along the Mississippi River about sixty
95 miles south of St. Louis. The tribal chief, Jean-Batiste du Coigne, had met Jefferson twenty years earlier and named his infant son after Governor Jefferson, as he was known at the time. Now Jefferson suggested to one of his
100 operatives that a spy be sent into du Coigne's village to learn facts that would help them arrange a deal whereby they would take all the tribe's lands and give them a reservation of just 350 acres. In return, the United States promised
105 to protect the Kaskaskias from other tribes, grant them a $1,000 annuity, and pay the expenses of a priest who would give them seven years of basic schooling. For du Coigne himself, a special house and the use of one hundred
110 acres was given as a reward for approving this larcenous exchange.

13. In line 7, "provisional" most nearly means

(A) temporary
(B) legitimate
(C) tentative
(D) legal
(E) legislative

GO ON TO THE NEXT PAGE ➔

14. As described in Passage 1, Jefferson's plan for slavery in the territories differed from his earlier proposal for the state of Virginia because it

(A) applied only to the importation of slaves
(B) was speedily enacted
(C) allowed importation of slaves to continue for sixteen years
(D) defined slavery as involuntary servitude
(E) sparked widespread public opposition

15. The critics mentioned in the fourth paragraph of Passage 1 probably believe that Jefferson

(A) miscalculated the level of opposition from Southerners
(B) was not politically adroit enough to win enactment of his proposal
(C) should not have required new states created from the territories to be bound by the Articles of Confederation
(D) was too hasty in his efforts to abolish slavery
(E) was not sufficiently committed to abolishing slavery

16. As described in lines 42-52, the provision in the Articles of Confederation that permitted the "free movement of property" was incompatible with Jefferson's proposal for the territories because

(A) the territories would not be free states
(B) Jefferson had not envisioned the movement of property
(C) Jefferson wanted to limit the rights of property owners
(D) slaves were property
(E) no one planned to bring slaves into the territories

17. In Passage 1, the first sentence of the fifth paragraph (lines 55-57) implies that Jefferson's ideals

(A) were sometimes in conflict with one another
(B) did not always represent his true beliefs
(C) were unpopular among most Americans
(D) were not always consistent with political reality
(E) created frustration among the true advocates of abolition

18. In line 76 of Passage 2, "beneficence" most nearly means

(A) deservedly
(B) charity
(C) enticing
(D) beneficial
(E) artifice

GO ON TO THE NEXT PAGE

19. In describing the views of Professor Anthony F. C. Wallace, the author of Passage 2 implies that

(A) she disagrees with some of Wallace's views but endorses others
(B) she finds Wallace's views distasteful but agrees with them nevertheless
(C) she agrees with the essence of Wallace's views, though she may hold a less extreme position
(D) she disagrees with the essence of Wallace's views but acknowledges an element of truth in some of them
(E) she believes that Wallace's views, though inflammatory, should be given a fair hearing

20. Passage 2 suggests that Jefferson's ultimate goal in promoting agriculture among the Native Americans was to

(A) improve their ability to provide clothing and subsistence
(B) make more land available for development by the United States
(C) show them the most efficient agricultural techniques
(D) ensure that they developed more unified communities
(E) end their reliance on hunting as a means of subsistence

21. The author of Passage 2 recounts Jefferson's meeting with tribal chief Jean-Batiste du Coigne, and the fact that du Coigne named his son after Jefferson in order to

(A) highlight Jefferson's duplicity in his later dealings with du Coigne
(B) cast doubt on the possibility that Jefferson would cheat du Coigne
(C) suggest that Jefferson's relationship with du Coigne was a close one
(D) imply that Jefferson's relationship with du Coigne had soured
(E) emphasize Jefferson's complicity with du Coigne in the Kaskaskias land deal

22. In context, "larcenous" (line 111) most nearly means

(A) clandestine
(B) illicit
(C) laconic
(D) criminal
(E) scrupulous

GO ON TO THE NEXT PAGE

23. In comparison with that in Passage 1, the portrayal of Jefferson in Passage 2 can best be described as

(A) pejorative
(B) admiring
(C) aphoristic
(D) oxymoronic
(E) didactic

24. One element of Jefferson's worldview addressed in Passage 2 but not in Passage 1 is his

(A) belief in the inevitability of human progress
(B) preference for compromise rather than confrontation
(C) vision of the United States as a global empire
(D) reaction to those who criticized American expansionism
(E) attitude toward the lifestyle of another culture

STOP

**If you finish before time is called, you may check your work on this section only.
Do not turn to any other section in the test.**

PRACTICE TEST #2

SECTION 5
Time – 25 minutes
20 Questions

Turn to Section 5 (page 5) of your answer sheet to answer the questions in this section.

Directions: For this section, solve each problem and decide which is the best of the choices given. Fill in the corresponding circle on the answer sheet. You may use any available space for scratch work.

Notes

1. The use of a calculator is permitted.

2. All numbers used are real numbers.

3. Figures that accompany problems in this test are intended to provide information useful in solving the problems. They are drawn as accurately as possible EXCEPT when it is stated in a specific problem that the figure is not drawn to scale. All figures lie in a plane unless otherwise indicated.

4. Unless otherwise specified, the domain of any function f is assumed to be the set of all real numbers x for which $f(x)$ is a real number.

Reference Information

$A = \pi r^2$
$C = 2\pi r$
$A = lw$
$A = \frac{1}{2}bh$
$V = lwh$
$V = \pi r^2 h$
$c^2 = a^2 + b^2$
Special Right Triangles

The number of degrees of arc in a circle is 360.
The sum of the measures in degrees of the angles of a triangle is 180.

---

1. A hotel includes meeting rooms of two sizes. The combined area of the 14 rooms of one size is x square feet and the combined area of the 7 rooms of the other size is also x square feet. In terms of x, what is the area, in square feet, of each of the larger rooms?

   (A) $2x$

   (B) $\dfrac{1}{2x}$

   (C) $7x - 14$

   (D) $\dfrac{x}{7}$

   (E) $\dfrac{x}{14}$

2. In the arithmetic sequence $y + 6$, 12, y, $y - 3$, what is the value of y?

   (A) 6
   (B) 9
   (C) 12
   (D) 15
   (E) 18

GO ON TO THE NEXT PAGE

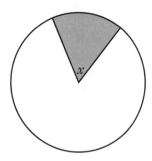

3. In the figure above, the vertex of angle x is the center of the circle. If $x = 60°$ and the circumference of the circle is 12π, what is the area of the shaded sector?

(A) 6π
(B) 9π
(C) 12π
(D) 24π
(E) 36π

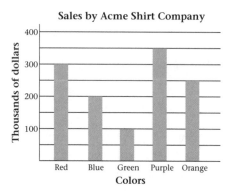

4. The graph above shows the Acme Shirt Company's sales revenue from shirts of various colors. What percentage of the total is from red?

(A) 20
(B) 25
(C) 30
(D) 35
(E) 40

5. A parcel of land is divided into 64 smaller lots. If the original piece of land is square, and if the 64 lots are also square, how many of the lots border outside the parcel?

(A) 16
(B) 24
(C) 28
(D) 32
(E) 48

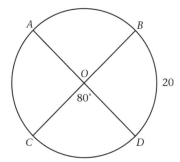

6. In the figure above, $\overline{AD}$ and $\overline{CB}$ pass through the center of a circle O. If the length of arc BD is 20, what is the circumference of the circle?

(A) 72
(B) 80
(C) 84
(D) 90
(E) 96

GO ON TO THE NEXT PAGE

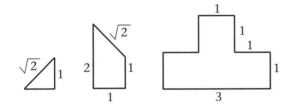

7. The figures above represent three pieces of a puzzle. Which of the following figures could be made from the three pieces without overlapping or cutting them?

I.
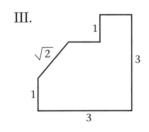

II.
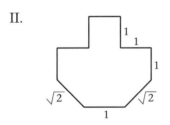

III.
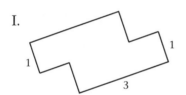

(A) I only
(B) II only
(C) I and II only
(D) II and III only
(E) I, II, and III

8. If the degree measures of the angles of a triangle are in the ratio 10:12:14, what is the difference in degrees between the measure of the largest angle and the measure of the smallest?

(A) 10°
(B) 20°
(C) 30°
(D) 40°
(E) 50°

9. If $x^{\frac{6}{7}} > x^{\frac{7}{6}}$, the value of x could be

(A) 0

(B) $\dfrac{1}{6}$

(C) $\dfrac{7}{6}$

(D) 6

(E) $\sqrt[7]{6}$

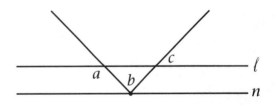

10. In the figure above, if $\ell \parallel n$, what is the value of b in terms of a and c

(A) $a + c$
(B) $a - c$
(C) $180 - c$
(D) $180 - a - c$
(E) $180 - a + c$

GO ON TO THE NEXT PAGE

11. If $=(\frac{q}{q-2})(\frac{1}{q-1})(\frac{q}{q+1})=\frac{8}{p}$ for positive integers p and q, what is the value of p?

(A) 8
(B) 12
(C) 15
(D) 16
(E) 20

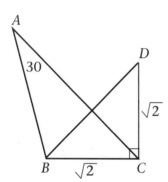

12. $\triangle ABC$ shares two verticies with $\triangle BCD$. If $\overline{AC} \perp \overline{BD}$, what is the length of $\overline{AB}$?

(A) 1
(B) $\sqrt{3}$
(C) $\sqrt{2}$
(D) $\sqrt{3} - \sqrt{2}$
(E) 2

13. Six distinct points lie on a circle. How many line segments can be drawn connecting two of the points?

(A) 3
(B) 6
(C) 12
(D) 15
(E) 18

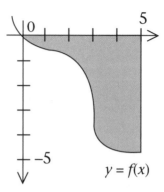

$y = f(x)$

14. The shaded region in the figure above is bounded by the x-axis, the line $x = 5$, and the graph of $y = f(x)$. If the point (p, q) lies in the shaded region, which of the following must be true?

    I. $p \le |q + 5|$
    II. $p \le |q| + 5$
    III. $|p| \le q$

(A) I only
(B) II only
(C) I and II only
(D) II and III only
(E) I, II, and III

GO ON TO THE NEXT PAGE

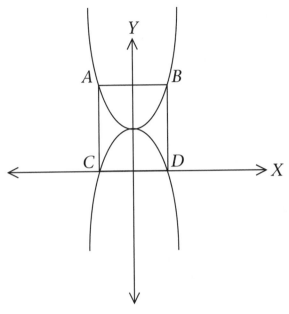

Note: Figure not drawn to scale

15. The figure above shows the graphs of $y = q + x^2$ and $y = q - x^2$. If these functions intersect the vertices of rectangle $ABCD$ as shown, and if the length of $\overline{CD}$ is equal to 8, what is the value of q?

(A) 2
(B) 4
(C) 8
(D) 16
(E) 32

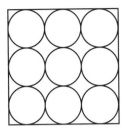

16. The figure above includes 9 congruent circles that are tangent to each other and to the square. If the total area of the 9 circles is 225π, what is the area of the square?

(A) 45π
(B) 90π
(C) 450
(D) 675π
(E) 900

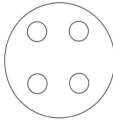

Note: Figure not drawn to scale

17. In the figure above, a circle with diameter 10 includes four smaller circles with diameter 1. What is the probability that a point chosen at random from inside the larger circle will NOT be inside one of the smaller circles?

(A) $\dfrac{1}{100}$

(B) $\dfrac{1}{25}$

(C) $\dfrac{9}{10}$

(D) $\dfrac{99}{100}$

(E) $\dfrac{24}{25}$

18. If the function g is defined by $g(x) = x^2 + bx - c$, where b and c are positive constants, which of the following could be the graph of g?

(A)

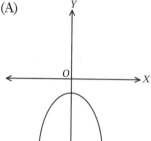

(B)

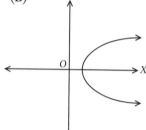

(C)

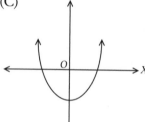

(D)

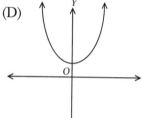

(E)

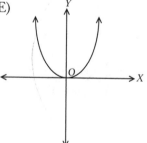

19. If one side of a cube has an area of 1, what is the distance from any vertex to the center of the cube?

(A) $\dfrac{\sqrt{2}}{2}$

(B) $\dfrac{\sqrt{3}}{2}$

(C) $\sqrt{3}$

(D) 2

(E) $2\sqrt{3}$

20. The function f is defined by $f(x) = x^2$. If y is an integer, the value of $f(x)$ CANNOT end in which of the following digits?

(A) 9
(B) 8
(C) 6
(D) 5
(E) 4

GO ON TO THE NEXT PAGE

SECTION 6
Time – 25 minutes
24 Questions

Turn to Section 6 (page 6) of your answer sheet to answer the questions in this section.

Directions: For each question in this section, select the best answer from among the choices given and fill in the corresponding circle on the answer sheet.

Each sentence below has one or two blanks, each blank indicating that something has been omitted. Beneath the sentence are five words or sets of words labeled A through E. Choose the word or set of words that, when inserted in the sentence, best fits the meaning of the sentence as a whole.

Example:

In the face of ------- evidence of the defendant's guilt, the jury voted ------- to convict him.

(A) mitigating . . grudgingly
(B) disagreeable . . parsimoniously
(C) unwelcome . . zealously
(D) derisive . . sternly
(E) overwhelming . . unanimously

Ⓐ Ⓑ Ⓒ Ⓓ ●

1. Born to a family of humble means in rural South Carolina, Althea Gibson overcame racial discrimination to become the ------- female tennis player of the late 1950s.

(A) redoubtable
(B) pre-eminent
(C) multifarious
(D) idealized
(E) intrepid

2. For the neophyte philosophy student, Ludwig Wittgenstein's *Tractatus Logico-Philosophicus* is so ------- as to be -------.

(A) elementary . . inaccessible
(B) cryptic . . irrelevant
(C) byzantine . . incomprehensible
(D) onerous . . debilitating
(E) inconclusive . . impenetrable

3. Representative Peterson ------- himself with his ------- speech; thereafter, many of his colleagues were openly contemptuous.

(A) castigated . . ineffectual
(B) eviscerated . . egregious
(C) denuded . . intemperate
(D) fulminated . . angry
(E) stultified . . incoherent

GO ON TO THE NEXT PAGE

4. Although the accused man had spent eight months in a psychiatric ward, the judge saw no reason to question his mental -------.

   (A) acuity
   (B) mind
   (C) derangement
   (D) attitude
   (E) perception

5. Marcy expected her coach to be upset by the team's lackluster play, but she was nevertheless surprised by his ------- tirade.

   (A) jocular
   (B) nuanced
   (C) enigmatic
   (D) apoplectic
   (E) mendacious

GO ON TO THE NEXT PAGE

The passages below are followed by questions based on their content; questions following a pair of related passages may also be based on the relationship between the paired passages. Answer the questions on the basis of what is stated or implied in the passages and in any introductory material that may be provided.

Questions 6-9 are based on the following passages.

Passage 1

Environmental tobacco smoke can be deadly; the Environmental Protection Agency has identified it as a class A carcinogen, meaning that it
Line is known to cause cancer in humans. The EPA
5 reviewed all the scientific evidence and concluded that the non-smoking spouse's risk of developing lung cancer is significantly increased by exposure to environmental tobacco smoke. Significantly, the combustion end of the ciga-
10 rette produces much higher concentrations of known chemical irritants and cancer-causing agents than the inhaled end. Even when a smoker is down the hall or one another floor, the smoke and its many toxins permeate the air.
15 Environmental tobacco smoke causes about three thousand deaths per year in non-smokers.

Passage 2

By the 1970s, the tobacco industry knew that the debate over environmental tobacco smoke (ETS) would have enormous implications. It was
20 one thing for smokers to endanger their own health and quite another for them to harm innocent bystanders. The industry desperately clung to the idea that smokers and non-smokers could get along with common sense and courtesy,
25 thereby framing the issue as one of etiquette rather than science. But by the mid-1980s, there was mounting evidence of a small but significant increase in respiratory disease among non-smokers, especially spouses, with long-term exposure
30 to ETS. Universities and hospitals were the first to curtail or eliminate smoking, followed by government, and then the private sector. By 2000, smoking had been virtually eliminated in indoor public places.

6. Both passages express the view that environmental tobacco smoke

   (A) ought to be curtailed or eliminated
   (B) should be regulated by the government
   (C) is a matter of courtesy and etiquette
   (D) can cause lung disease
   (E) is present in most public places

7. Which of the following aspects of environmental tobacco smoke is cited in Passage 1 but not in Passage 2?

   (A) the fact that it causes disease
   (B) a reason why it is harmful
   (C) scientific evidence of its dangers
   (D) its impact on non-smoking spouses
   (E) why efforts have been made to limit exposure to it

GO ON TO THE NEXT PAGE

8. Passage 2 implies that the debate over environmental tobacco smoke would have "enormous implications" because

(A) proof that environmental tobacco smoke is harmful to non-smokers would cause smoking to be made illegal

(B) many smokers would quit if they knew that their smoking was harmful to others

(C) limiting environmental tobacco would now be viewed as a matter of common sense and courtesy

(D) smoking had previously been perceived as harmful only to the smoker and not to innocent bystanders

(E) few people before 1990 believed that environmental tobacco smoke was harmful to non-smokers

9. Unlike Passage 1, Passage 2 portrays the issue of smoking in indoor public places, and whether or not it should be allowed, as partly a function of

(A) scientific reasoning
(B) personal opinion
(C) individual responsibility
(D) common sense and courtesy
(E) public perception

Questions 10-15 are based on the following passage.

This passage describes a legal case and facts relevant to it. In the passage, in vitro *means "outside the womb."*

Mary Sue Easterly and Junior Davis were married in 1980, and for nine years they tried to have a baby. During one of their many *in vitro*
Line attempts, several eggs were taken from Mary
5 Sue's ovaries to be fertilized with Junior's sperm. Then they were frozen for possible use by the couple in the future. But the strain of the procedures, when added to the couple's other problems, led to the end of the marriage. After the
10 couple filed for divorce, the frozen embryos became the subject of years of litigation.

Both Mary Sue and Junior sought "custody" of the embryos in *Davis v. Davis*, as the case was known, with both Mary Sue and Junior asserting
15 that the embryos were "part of me." Mary Sue argued further that she would like to have children without Junior and that he had effectively consented to fatherhood when he agreed to allow his sperm to fertilize the eggs. But Junior Davis
20 argued that the embryos should be destroyed because he did not want his children to be raised in a broken home. After Mary Sue remarried, she again sought "custody" of the embryos, this time so that she might donate them to an infertile cou-
25 ple, she argued. Junior Davis again opposed, contending that he should not be forced to become a father against his will to children he did not know.

The trial judge awarded the embryos to Mary Sue, arguing that they were not frozen fertilized
30 eggs, but rather "children *in vitro*." Thus, it was in the "best interests of the children *in vitro* to

have a chance at life," the judge reasoned. Junior
Davis appealed, and one year later an intermedi-
ate court awarded joint custody to Mary Sue and
35 Junior Davis. Mary Sue appealed to the
Tennessee Supreme Court, arguing that she
would donate the embryos to a childless couple.
　　Junior Davis reiterated that he should not
be made to be a father against his will in a
40 reversal of the arguments used in *Roe v. Wade*.
Junior Davis asked for custody of the embryos
so that he might destroy them. In the end, the
Tennessee Supreme Court held that "the right
of procreation is a vital part of the individual's
45 right to privacy." Therefore, Junior Davis's
interest in not becoming a parent outweighed
Mary Sue's interest in gaining possession of the
embryos to donate to another couple.
　　Though it is not a United States Supreme
50 Court case, *Davis v. Davis* has generally become
the standard for reviewing the rights of individuals "not to become" parents against their will.

10. In context, "effectively" (line 17) implies
that

(A) Junior's actions amounted to consent even
if he did not explicitly give such consent
(B) Junior consented and then denied that he
had done so
(C) Junior's consent was given under duress
therefore was not legally binding
(D) Junior's consent was effective at the
time, but not necessarily in the future
(E) Junior's consent was voluntary and therefore binding in perpetuity

11. The second and third sentences of the second
paragraph (lines 15-22) are characterized,
respectively, by

(A) assertion and disclaimer
(B) rebuttal and analysis
(C) statement and query
(D) argument and counter-argument
(E) hypothesis and theory

12. In lines 28-30, the judge's finding that the
fertilized eggs were actually "children *in
vitro*" was significant because

(A) the embryos were the property of Mary
Sue
(B) Junior had claimed that they were not
children
(C) children have legal rights that embryos
do not
(D) lower courts had not recognized them as
children
(E) the finding could not be overturned on
appeal

13. As used in line 44, "procreation" most
nearly means

(A) creation
(B) misconception
(C) reproduction
(D) incantation
(E) misogyny

GO ON TO THE NEXT PAGE

14. The primary purpose of the last sentence of the fourth paragraph (lines 45-48) is to

(A) explain why Junior's argument was superior to Mary Sue's

(B) explain why Junior Davis continued to pursue the case

(C) establish the relevancy of the Tennessee Supreme Court

(D) discuss the impact of the decision in *Davis v. Davis*

(E) explain the reasoning of the Tennessee Supreme Court

15. The primary purpose of the passage is to

(A) review a case that established a legal precedent

(B) explain the significance of *in vitro* fertilization

(C) tell the story of Mary Sue and Junior Davis

(D) show a potential pitfall of divorce

(E) explore why a divorced couple entered a custody battle

Questions 16-24 are based on the following passage.

In this passage, poet W. H. Auden discusses the life and work of fellow poet W. B. Yeats.

I shall not attempt in this paper to answer such questions as, "How good a poet is Yeats? Which are his best poems and why?"—that is
Line the job of better critics than I and of posterity—
5 but rather to consider him as a predecessor whose importance no one will or can deny, to raise, that is to say, such questions as, "What were the problems which faced Yeats as a poet compared with ours? How far do they overlap?
10 How far are they different? In so far as they are different, what can we learn from the way in which Yeats dealt with his world, and about how to deal with our own?"

Let me begin with the element in his work
15 which seems most foreign to us, his cosmology, his concern with the occult. Here, I think, is a curious fact. In most cases, when a major author influences a beginner, that influence extends to his matter, to his opinions as well as to his man-
20 ner—think of Hardy, or Eliot, or D. H. Lawrence; yet, though there is scarcely a lyric written today in which the influence of his style and rhythm is not detectable, one whole side of Yeats, the side summed up in the *Vision*, has left
25 virtually no trace.

However diverse our fundamental beliefs may be, the reaction of most of us to all that occult is, I fancy, the same: how on earth, we wonder, could a man of Yeats's gifts take such
30 nonsense seriously? I have a further bewilderment, which may be due to my English upbringing, one of snobbery. How *could* Yeats,

with his great aesthetic appreciation of aristoc-
racy, ancestral houses, ceremonious tradition,
35 take up something so essentially lower-middle
class—or should I say Southern Californian—
so ineluctably associated with suburban villas
and clearly unattractive faces? A. E. Housman's
pessimistic stoicism seems to me nonsense too,
40 but at least it is a kind of nonsense that can be
believed by a gentleman—but mediums, spells,
the Mysterious Orient—*how* embarrassing.

    In fact, of course, it is to Yeats's credit, and an
example to me, that he ignored such considera-
45 tions, nor, granted that his worldview was false,
can we claim credit for rejecting what we have
no temptation to accept, nor deny that the
poetry he wrote involving it is very good. What
we should consider, then, is firstly, why Celtic
50 mythology in his earlier phases, and occult symbolism in his later, should have attracted Yeats
when they fail to attract us; secondly, what are
the comparable kinds of beliefs to which we are
drawn and why; thirdly, what is the relation
55 between myth, belief, and poetry?

16. The primary purpose of the passage is to

(A) draw attention to Yeats's belief in the
occult
(B) explain why Yeats is a better poet than
most people believe
(C) explain why it is fruitless to try to inter-
pret Yeats's poetry
(D) argue that more time must be spent on
interpreting Yeats's poetry
(E) suggest an approach for interpreting
Yeats and his poetry

17. The author uses rhetorical questions in
(lines 7-13) to

(A) begin an interrogation
(B) state a conclusion
(C) dispute an argument
(D) offer examples
(E) outline a thesis

18. The author uses "cosmology" (line 15) to
refer to Yeats's

(A) fascination with stars and the heavens
(B) belief that the cosmos has hidden
meaning
(C) beliefs about how the universe works
(D) ability to understand the cosmos
(E) preoccupation with surface appearances

19. The "curious fact" noted by the author in
line 17 is that

(A) Yeats's writing style has been very
influential, but not his concern with
the occult
(B) Yeats is more influential than Hardy,
Eliot, or D. H. Lawrence
(C) Yeats's influence extends to his matter as
well as his rhythm
(D) even the aspects of Yeats that seem foreign to readers have been influential
(E) Yeats's concern with the occult is bewil-
dering to most readers

GO ON TO THE NEXT PAGE ➤

20. The author uses italics for the word "could" (line 32) to emphasize

(A) the silliness of Yeats's preoccupation with the occult
(B) the reaction of most readers to Yeats's preoccupation with the occult
(C) the fact that Yeats identifies with the lower-middle class
(D) the irony of Yeats's belief in the occult in light of his skills as a writer
(E) the negative reaction of Yeats's contemporaries to his preoccupation with the occult

21. By inserting "or should I say Southern Californian" (line 36), the author uses

(A) a stereotype to evoke an image
(B) a metaphor to illustrate an argument
(C) an aside to provide an example
(D) a simile to highlight similarities
(E) an analogy to create dissonance

22. In line 37, "ineluctably" most nearly means

(A) unavoidably
(B) indelibly
(C) inscrutably
(D) frequently
(E) periodically

23. The phrase "and an example to me" (lines 43-44) is used by the author to highlight

(A) reasons why Yeats's belief in the occult should not be taken seriously
(B) the author's embarrassment over Yeats's preoccupation with "mediums, spells, and the Mysterious Orient"
(C) the suggestion that the author should reconsider his own impulse to Yeats's preoccupation with the occult
(D) the extent to which Yeats's worldview was provocative and interesting
(E) that Yeats was right to ignore questions about his preoccupation with the occult

24. In the final paragraph, the author suggests that readers of Yeats should not "claim credit for rejecting what we have no temptation to accept," but should instead

(A) consider the possibility that Yeats's worldview is accurate
(B) learn more about occult symbolism and Celtic mythology in 17th century Ireland
(C) keep in mind that Yeats dealt with occult symbolism only in his earlier phases
(D) change their system of belief to make it more like that of Yeats
(E) reflect on myths in their own lives that are comparable to those that Yeats believed

STOP

If you finish before time is called, you may check your work on this section only.
Do not turn to any other section in the test.

SECTION 8
Time – 25 minutes
16 Questions

Turn to Section 8 (page 7) of your answer sheet to answer the questions in this section.

Directions: For this section, solve each problem and decide which is the best of the choices given. Fill in the corresponding circle on the answer sheet. You may use any available space for scratch work.

Notes

1. The use of a calculator is permitted.

2. All numbers used are real numbers.

3. Figures that accompany problems in this test are intended to provide information useful in solving the problems. They are drawn as accurately as possible EXCEPT when it is stated in a specific problem that the figure is not drawn to scale. All figures lie in a plane unless otherwise indicated.

4. Unless otherwise specified, the domain of any function f is assumed to be the set of all real numbers x for which $f(x)$ is a real number.

Reference Information

$A = \pi r^2$
$C = 2\pi r$
$\qquad A = \ell w \qquad A = \frac{1}{2}bh \qquad V = \ell wh \qquad V = \pi r^2 h \qquad c^2 = a^2 + b^2 \quad$ Special Right Triangles

The number of degrees of arc in a circle is 360.
The sum of the measures in degrees of the angles of a triangle is 180.

1. A sporting goods store offers 2 free boxes of ping-pong balls to every customer who purchases 3 boxes of ping-pong balls. What is the amount of the percentage discount that the store offers per box?

(A) 50
(B) 40
(C) 30
(D) 20
(E) 10

2. If $f(x) = 3x^2$ and $g(x) = (3x)^2$, then $f(5) - g(5) =$

(A) −150
(B) 0
(C) 75
(D) 150
(E) 300

GO ON TO THE NEXT PAGE

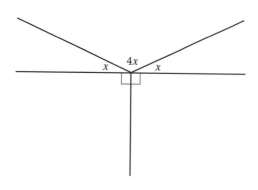

3. In the figure above, what is the value of *x* in degrees?

(A) 30
(B) 40
(C) 45
(D) 50
(E) 60

4. At Ridgecrest High School, 52 students are in the marching band, 34 are on the yearbook staff, and 28 in the debate club. If 9 students participate in all 3 organizations, and another 17 students participate in 2 of the 3, what is the total number of students in the 3 clubs?

(A) 69
(B) 79
(C) 88
(D) 97
(E) 114

5. Jenna and Ellen plan to paint a fence. Jenna could paint the fence alone in exactly 6 hours. Ellen could paint it alone in exactly 9 hours. Working together, how many minutes will it take Jenna and Ellen to paint the fence?

(A) 154
(B) 196
(C) 200
(D) 208
(E) 216

6. Joe and Marty sold candy bars to raise money for a school trip. Joe sold $30 more candy bars than Marty. Their combined sales were $330. How much were Marty's sales?

(A) $110
(B) $150
(C) $180
(D) $230
(E) $300

7. An airplane flies directly into the wind for four hours and travels 1,200 miles. The return trip takes three hours. Assuming that the speed of the wind and the thrust of the plane are constant throughout the flight, and that every mile-per-hour of headwind or tailwind causes an equivalent change in the air speed of the plane, how many miles per hour is the wind blowing?

(A) 30
(B) 40
(C) 50
(D) 100
(E) 200

GO ON TO THE NEXT PAGE

8. If $a - 12 = 10 - a$, then $a =$

(A) −12
(B) −2
(C) 10
(D) 11
(E) 12

---

9. A shoe costs six times more than a pair of socks and $12 more than double the price of the pair of socks. How much does the shoe cost?

(A) $12.00
(B) $18.00
(C) $24.00
(D) $36.00
(E) $48.00

---

10. If $*y*$ is defined by the equation $*y* = \sqrt{\dfrac{y}{4}}$, for all whole numbers y, which of the following equals 2?

(A) $*2*$
(B) $*4*$
(C) $*8*$
(D) $*16*$
(E) $*64*$

11. If $x^5 = 5$ and $x^4 = \dfrac{4}{y}$, what is the value of x in terms of y?

(A) $\dfrac{5y}{4}$

(B) $\dfrac{4y}{5}$

(C) $\dfrac{2y}{4}$

(D) $5y$

(E) $5 - \dfrac{4}{y}$

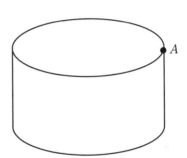

<u>Note</u>: Figure not drawn to scale

12. In the figure above, the volume of the cylinder is 54π and its height is 6. What is the length of the longest line segment that can be drawn from A to another point on the surface of the cylinder?

(A)   9
(B) −12
(C)   15
(D) $6\sqrt{2}$
(E) $9\sqrt{3}$

GO ON TO THE NEXT PAGE

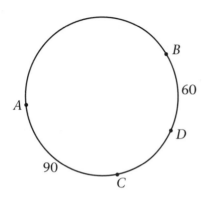

13. In the figure above, arc $AC = 90°$ and arc $BD = 60°$. If arc $AB = 2(\text{arc } CD)$, what is the measure of arc CD in degrees?

(A) 35
(B) 70
(C) 140
(D) 160
(E) 210

14. If a and b are positive and $4a^2b^{-2} = 64a$, what is a^{-1} in terms of b?

(A) $256a^2b^{-2}$

(B) $\dfrac{1}{4^3a\sqrt{b^2}}$

(C) $\dfrac{1}{16b^2}$

(D) $\dfrac{a}{4^2 b^2}$

(E) $\dfrac{4}{\sqrt{b^2}}$

15. If a is an integer greater than 1 and if $b = a - \dfrac{1}{a}$, which of the following must be true?

    I. $a > b$
    II. $a - b < 1$
    III. $ab < a^2$

(A) I only
(B) III only
(C) I and III only
(D) I and III only
(E) I, II, and III

16. At 3:00 p.m. on December 21, a tree casts a shadow 40 feet long, and a treasure chest is buried 30 feet below the tip of the shadow. Assuming that the ground is flat, how far is the treasure chest from the base of the tree?

(A) 20 feet
(B) 30 feet
(C) 40 feet
(D) 50 feet
(E) 60 feet

GO ON TO THE NEXT PAGE

SECTION 9
Time – 20 minutes
19 Questions

Directions: For each question in this section, select the best answer from among the choices given and fill in the corresponding circle on the answer sheet.

Each sentence below has one or two blanks, each blank indicating that something has been omitted. Beneath the sentence are five words or sets of words labeled A through E. Choose the word or set of words that, when inserted in the sentence, <u>best</u> fits the meaning of the sentence as a whole.

Example:

In the face of ------- evidence of the defendant's guilt, the jury voted ------- to convict him.

(A) mitigating . . grudgingly
(B) disagreeable . . parsimoniously
(C) unwelcome . . zealously
(D) derisive . . sternly
(E) overwhelming . . unanimously

1. Although Earnest Hemingway's writing style was direct and concrete, it was not without -------.

(A) brevity
(B) lucidity
(C) gravity
(D) subtlety
(E) veracity

2. The governor ------- so often on his highly-touted tax reform initiative that his aides began to doubt his -------.

(A) declaimed . . pulchritude
(B) wavered . . dogmatism
(C) expounded . . passion
(D) vacillated . . conviction
(E) proselytized . . candor

3. Shirley Chisholm did not have a realistic chance of winning the presidency in 1972, but she ran a ------- campaign.

(A) quixotic
(B) quiet
(C) obliging
(D) spirited
(E) disjointed

4. Support for the proposal was overwhelming; only George -------.

(A) consented
(B) demurred
(C) assented
(D) denied
(E) disengaged

GO ON TO THE NEXT PAGE

5. Navigating the obstacle course required considerable -------; only the most ------- contestants could do so successfully.

   (A) skill . . shiftless
   (B) introspection . . nimble
   (C) self-actualization . . zealous
   (D) industriousness . . grounded
   (E) finesse . . adroit

6. Although unquestionably competent, Mr. Franklin is a difficult colleague because he is ------- to advice and ------- of other people's opinions.

   (A) impervious . . dismissive
   (B) impertinent . . laudatory
   (C) contemptuous . . disrespectful
   (D) impregnable . . disliking
   (E) histrionic . . distrustful

GO ON TO THE NEXT PAGE ⟩

The passage below is followed by questions based on its content. Answer the questions on the basis of what is stated or implied in the passage and in any introductory material that may be provided.

Questions 7-19 are based on the following passage.

The following passage is adapted from a book on the history of the women's rights movement. "Rosie" is a reference to Rosie the Riveter, a fictitious character created to represent the women who took jobs in the nation's factories while men were fighting in World War II.

By the mid-1940s, women had a new image. Rosie and her minions had given women confidence, muscle, a patriotic soul, and a role in the
Line working world at a time of worldwide need.
5 With the blessing and praise of the highest American authorities, women were urged to go forth and rivet, build, and stand in the shoes of their missing men. But only figuratively.

"Women's difference was deliberately
10 enhanced in the new definition of female identity," one prominent feminist suggests. "Translated into a male sphere of machinery and military accoutrements, glamour distinguished wartime women and the temporary sac-
15 rifice of service to country superceded their underlying maternal dedication. Propaganda did…shift gender norms by defining female virtue through public activity. Working-class women appeared in a new visual idiom of
20 power and skill, no longer simply the helpless victims of exploitation portrayed in the photography of the Progressive Era."

But with working mothers leaving home, even in pursuit of such praiseworthy service, the
25 issue of child care—often thought of as a "contemporary problem"—would become a matter of public debate as early as the 1940s. By 1944, a significant number of married women were now working outside of the home, which translated
30 for many into an urgent need for child care. In addition to attempting to balance the needs of wartime America, women who chose to go to work were still largely responsible for the care of their children.

35 This usually meant that in addition to cooking, cleaning, and nursing children after a day's work in the factories, women were also charged with the responsibility of securing private child care arrangements. And though their service
40 was to the nation, the critics were everywhere. When women missed work because they could not find baby-sitters, they faced criticism for contributing to high rates of "absenteeism" at a time when America needed every hand. At the
45 same time, social scientists—at times spouting the language of their own agendas—warned of a post-war generation "of juvenile delinquents" and "latchkey" childhoods.

Local governments were urged to undertake
50 efforts to help women as the debate over who should ultimately be responsible for solving the problem got underway. And although women drew support from some government officials—notably General Louis McSherry, who urged
55 that "adequate facilities for the care of children of working mothers" be made a priority—authorities of many child advocacy programs frequently argued in response that it was in the best interests of the children to have their
60 mothers home.

These differences not withstanding, in 1943, federal funds were finally approved for use in establishing child care centers. But even with the addition of federal funds, the number of children served by these centers was miniscule when compared to the number of working mothers and the number of children estimated to be left at home each morning. Rowbotham suggests that only about 140,000 children across the United States were being served by child care centers during the latter years of World War II.

But even so, "wartime circumstances did…affect popular assumptions and indirectly contributed to new patterns of daily life," Rowbotham says. "Can women in the war industry be good mothers?" asked psychiatrist Dr. Leslie Hohman in 1942. She went on to advocate a "schedule" of household tasks and shared child care between partners so that both parents could spend engaged time with their children in "companionship." Suddenly women's time was of social significance.

There were new opportunities and entrepreneurial hopes that pushed progress forward. Pre-prepared, commercially created, and frozen food companies—once suppliers to the military—began offering their wares for sale to the public. The intention, marketers argued, was to help harried women save time. Though these new efforts would pay off better later, the optimism underlying this effort bordered on the fantastic. As late as 1941, a full third of all American households still relied upon wood or coal for heat or to cook food, and many women were still fetching it from outside.

And yet, there were other more positive changes as well. Prior to the swell of married women into the nation's workforce, critics voiced fears "that the war would…change women's expectations." It did. With a new understanding of their worth, many women and women's advocacy clubs and groups began to feel that the time was right to renew discussion of long dormant issues of equality. Thus, the questions of "equal pay for equal work" and the passage of an Equal Rights Amendment were put back on the table.

7. The sentence "but only figuratively" (line 8) implies that

(A) most people of the time did not support the women's rights movement even if they said they did
(B) though many people endorsed the symbolism of women helping with the war effort, there was less support for the reality of women in the working world
(C) Rosie the Riveter was a myth created by those who wanted to glorify working women
(D) the "highest American authorities" were actually trying to prevent women from taking jobs in factories
(E) Rosie the Riveter was a poor image for American women

GO ON TO THE NEXT PAGE >

PRACTICE TEST #2

8. The passage quotes an author who suggests that "women's difference was deliberately enhanced in the new definition of female identity" in order to

(A) show that women were actually superior to men in many industrial jobs

(B) show that women could work in industrial jobs and still be glamorous

(C) maintain traditional attitudes toward women and emphasize that their new roles were temporary

(D) highlight that women were unique individuals and capable of taking on new roles

(E) debunk the myth that men and women have innate differences

9. In line 13, "accoutrements" most nearly means

(A) arraignments

(B) denouements

(C) verisimilitudes

(D) battlements

(E) implements

10. The author suggests that an impediment to securing government support for child care was the fact that some authorities

(A) doubted whether child care was cost-effective

(B) argued that such child care would be an unwarranted expansion of government

(C) believed that women should stay home with their children

(D) supported the idea of both parents taking care of the children

(E) doubted that the government possessed adequate facilities to get involved

11. The last two sentences of the fourth paragraph (lines 41-48) suggest that working mothers were

(A) counseled to quit their jobs and resume child care

(B) criticized when they went to work and when they stayed home with children

(C) more satisfied when they stayed home with children than from working

(D) frequently burdened with low-paying jobs that did not offer a livable wage

(E) reluctant to quit their jobs because of financial issues

12. It can be inferred from the passage that the author believes most of the criticism directed toward working mothers in the 1940s was

(A) vitriolic

(B) lackadaisical

(C) pragmatic

(D) unfair

(E) dilatory

GO ON TO THE NEXT PAGE

13. Of the total number of working mothers during World War II, the percentage who were served by child care centers was

(A) significant
(B) large
(C) proportional
(D) moderate
(E) tiny

14. In lines 82-83, the author suggests that "women's time was of social significance" due to

(A) the need for women to devote themselves fully to factory work
(B) the fact that women needed additional training for work in the factories
(C) the demands on women's time for both factory work and child care
(D) the belief that men should take on more of the responsibility for child care
(E) the idea that women were less suited to physically demanding work than men

15. In context, "fantastic" (lines 92-93) most nearly means

(A) incomprehensible
(B) delusional
(C) extraordinary
(D) supernatural
(E) ephemeral

16. In lines 93-96, the author implies that the makers of pre-prepared and frozen foods did not have the degree of success in the early 1940s that they would later enjoy because

(A) the country had not developed a taste for such foods
(B) most women were too busy with child care to shop for such foods
(C) many women had a bias against using pre-prepared foods
(D) pre-prepared foods were not available in many communities
(E) many homes did not have the technology to make use of such foods

17. The author implies that the overall impact of the changes in the role of women that occurred in the 1940s was

(A) indeterminate
(B) largely favorable
(C) largely unfavorable
(D) deleterious
(E) insignificant

GO ON TO THE NEXT PAGE ⟩

18. In the final paragraph (lines 97-108), the author implies that women's experience in the workforce during the 1940s

  (A) encouraged them to renew the push for equal rights
  (B) changed their understanding of women's advocacy groups
  (C) created expectations that could not be met until decades later
  (D) created fears that women's expectations would not change
  (E) undermined later initiatives for equal rights

19. The passage is best characterized as

  (A) a summary of societal trends in the 1940s
  (B) an explanation of why women felt confined in the 1940s
  (C) a comparison of the role of women in society before World War II versus their role after the war
  (D) an examination of one phase in the evolution of the role of women in society
  (E) an argument in favor of equal rights for women

STOP

If you finish before time is called, you may check your work on this section only.
Do not turn to any other section in the test.

SECTION 10
Time – 10 minutes
14 Questions

Turn to Section 10 (page 7) of your answer sheet to answer the questions in this section.

Directions: For each question in this section, select the best answer from among the choices given and fill in the corresponding circle on the answer sheet.

The following sentences test correctness and effectiveness of expression. Part of each sentence or the entire sentence is underlined; beneath each sentence are five ways of phrasing the underlined material. Choice A repeats the original phrasing; the other four choices are different. If you think the original phrasing produces a better sentence than any of the alternatives, select choice A; if not, select one of the other choices.

In making your selection, follow the requirements of standard written English; that is, pay attention to grammar, choice of words, sentence construction, and punctuation. Your selection should result in the most effective sentence—clear and precise, without awkwardness or ambiguity.

EXAMPLE:

In 1953, Ralph Ellison won the National Book Award for *Invisible Man* <u>and he was thirty-nine years old then</u>.

(A) and he was thirty-nine years old then
(B) with the age of thirty-nine years old
(C) upon arriving at thirty-nine
(D) at the time of reaching thirty-nine
(E) when he was thirty-nine years old

Ⓐ Ⓑ Ⓒ Ⓓ ●

1. <u>Only those that have renewed their memberships</u> in the past six months will be allowed to attend the festivities on opening night.

(A) Only those that have renewed their memberships
(B) Only you that have renewed your memberships
(C) Only if you have renewed your membership
(D) Only those who have renewed their memberships
(E) Only those who have renewed their membership

2. <u>The rain, which was torrential, lasted for four days</u>, an interminable length of time for backpackers huddled in a tent.

(A) The rain, which was torrential, lasted for four days
(B) The rain, torrential as it was, lasted for four days
(C) The four-day rain came down torrentially and lasted
(D) The rain was torrential and lasted for four days
(E) The torrential rain lasted for four days

3. In addition to providing a habitat for the endangered koala bear, eucalyptus trees yield medicinal oil from their leaves.

   (A) In addition to providing a habitat
   (B) While a provider of a habitat
   (C) Providing a habitat
   (D) In addition to being a provider of a habitat
   (E) As a habitat provider

4. Cats are able to move stealthily across uneven terrain and can therefore draw near to their prey before pouncing.

   (A) and can therefore draw near to their prey before pouncing
   (B) therefore pouncing on their prey after drawing near
   (C) so that before pouncing they draw near to their prey
   (D) so, therefore, they can pounce on their prey after drawing near
   (E) and therefore have the ability to pounce after drawing near their prey

5. During the 1980s, the inflation rate slowed significantly, while continuing to remain low in the 1990s.

   (A) significantly, while continuing to remain low
   (B) significantly, and it continued to be low
   (C) significantly and remained low
   (D) significantly and then continued lowering
   (E) significantly, continuing low

6. After Margaret Thatcher's successful management of the Falklands War, her approval rating among the British public was, not surprisingly, quite high.

   (A) her approval rating among the British public was, not surprisingly, quite high
   (B) this raised, not surprisingly, her approval rating among the British public
   (C) not to anyone's surprise her approval rating among the British public was quite high
   (D) her high approval rating among the British public was not to anyone's surprise
   (E) her approval rating among the British public, being very high, was not surprising

7. Juan Domingo Peron had an unusual political career, eighteen years elapsed between his terms as president of Argentina.

   (A) career, eighteen
   (B) career, not in the least because
   (C) career after eighteen
   (D) career, most notably because eighteen
   (E) career, with eighteen

8. With his name meaning "the old master," Lao-tse lived more than 2,500 years ago and is revered as the founder of Taoism.

   (A) His name meaning "the old master," Lao-tse
   (B) Lao-tse, whose name means "the old master,"
   (C) With a name that has the meaning of "the old master," Lao-tse
   (D) "The old master," meaning Lao-tse,
   (E) Lao-tse, who was "the old master,"

9. Increasing numbers of Hispanic and African American students are entering <u>diverse professions as</u> medicine, law, accounting, and engineering.

   (A) diverse professions as
   (B) professions of such diversity as
   (C) a diversity of professions like
   (D) professions as diverse as
   (E) professional areas that are diverse as

10. <u>If we were to compare the number of immigrants from Spain with Poland</u> between 1900 and 1920, we would find that the latter far outnumbered the former.

   (A) If we were to compare the number of immigrants from Spain with Poland
   (B) If we compared the number of immigrants from Spain with Poland
   (C) Had we compared the number of immigrants from Spain with Poland
   (D) Were we to compare the number of immigrants from Spain with Poland
   (E) If we were to compare the number of immigrants from Spain with those from Poland

11. The pituitary gland, <u>influencing on growth and metabolism</u>, is located at the base of the brain in vertebrate species.

   (A) influencing on growth and metabolism
   (B) an influence in growth and metabolism
   (C) which influences growth and metabolism
   (D) where growth and metabolism is influenced
   (E) a growth and metabolism influence

12. <u>After getting soaked by the thunderstorm,</u> the skies cleared and we walked for several more hours.

   (A) After getting soaked by the thunderstorm
   (B) After the thunderstorm soaked us
   (C) When we were soaked by the thunderstorm
   (D) Although we were soaked by the thunderstorm
   (E) After the soaking of the thunderstorm

13. The puffin, <u>which is characterized by a distinctive, vertically flattened bill,</u> inhabits coastal regions in northern latitudes.

   (A) which is characterized by a distinctive, vertically flattened bill
   (B) which has a distinctively vertical, flattened bill
   (C) has a distinctive, vertically flattened bill
   (D) with its distinctive, vertically flattened bill
   (E) distinctively with its vertically flattened bill

14. Garments made of synthetic fabrics are generally more appropriate for camping <u>than cotton, which absorbs water</u> and can chill the skin.

   (A) than cotton, which absorbs water
   (B) than those made of cotton, which absorbs water
   (C) than fabric made of cotton, which absorbs water
   (D) than cotton, which water absorbs into
   (E) than water-absorbing cotton, which

STOP
If you finish before time is called, you may check your work on this section only.
Do not turn to any other section in the test.

Practice Test 2 – Answer Key

Writing

Section 1

Essay Score: _____
(See pages 141-142 for the guide-lines for scoring the essay.)

Section 3

(1) D	(10) A	(19) B	(28) E
(2) B	(11) D	(20) A	(29) D
(3) D	(12) B	(21) E	(30) A
(4) C	(13) C	(22) C	(31) E
(5) E	(14) E	(23) B	(32) C
(6) A	(15) D	(24) C	(33) C
(7) D	(16) E	(25) A	(34) E
(8) C	(17) C	(26) B	(35) B
(9) D	(18) B	(27) C	

_____ Number Correct

_____ Number Incorrect

Section 10

(1) D	(8) B
(2) E	(9) D
(3) A	(10) E
(4) A	(11) C
(5) C	(12) B
(6) A	(13) D
(7) D	(14) B

_____ Number Correct

_____ Number Incorrect

Critical Reading

Section 4

(1) D	(9) D	(17) D
(2) A	(10) D	(18) B
(3) D	(11) C	(19) C
(4) E	(12) D	(20) B
(5) D	(13) A	(21) A
(6) C	(14) C	(22) D
(7) A	(15) E	(23) A
(8) C	(16) D	(24) E

_____ Number Correct

_____ Number Incorrect

Section 6

(1) B	(9) E	(17) D
(2) C	(10) A	(18) C
(3) E	(11) D	(19) A
(4) A	(12) C	(20) B
(5) D	(13) C	(21) A
(6) D	(14) E	(22) A
(7) B	(15) A	(23) C
(8) D	(16) E	(24) E

_____ Number Correct

_____ Number Incorrect

Section 9

(1) D	(11) B
(2) D	(12) D
(3) D	(13) E
(4) B	(14) C
(5) E	(15) B
(6) A	(16) E
(7) B	(17) B
(8) C	(18) A
(9) E	(19) D
(10) C	

_____ Number Correct

_____ Number Incorrect

Math

Section 2

(1) C
(2) D
(3) E
(4) B
(5) D
(6) D
(7) C
(8) E

Student-Produced
Response Questions

(9) 254
(10) 8
(11) 5
(12) 3
(13) 63
(14) 30
(15) 3.90
(16) 3 or 13
(17) 2
(18) 72

Section 5

(1) D   (11) C
(2) B   (12) E
(3) A   (13) D
(4) B   (14) B
(5) C   (15) D
(6) A   (16) E
(7) C   (17) E
(8) D   (18) C
(9) B   (19) B
(10) B   (20) B

Section 8

(1) B   (9) B
(2) A   (10) D
(3) A   (11) A
(4) B   (12) D
(5) E   (13) B
(6) B   (14) C
(7) C   (15) E
(8) D   (16) D

_____
Number Correct

_____
Number Correct

_____
Number Correct

_____
Number Incorrect

_____
Number Incorrect

_____
Number Incorrect

As with Test 1, we have no idea what a good score is. The real SAT is a norm-referenced test—that is, questions are used based on how many students are expected to get them right and wrong. In this way, College Board and ETS can calibrate the difficulty of each test. Since we don't have any norms for our practice tests, your score means *nothing*.

That said, we think you will benefit from going through the scoring process to see how it works. We would also be intrigued to know what you got. If you do score your test—and we hope you will—write us at editor@fiskeguide.com and tell us what you got. Be sure to specify whether you took the test under timed conditions.

There is also the matter of grading your essay. We recommend that you choose two parent(s) or friend(s). Ask them to read the scoring guidelines on pages 141-142 and evaluate your essay accordingly. Both should grade your essay on the 1-6 scale outlined there.

The following chart takes you through the scoring process. On page 416, we offer a chart for converting your raw score into a scaled score. On page 417, another chart shows you how to combine your essay with your score on the Writing multiple-choice questions to get an overall Writing score.

Writing Score

Compute the number of multiple-choice questions you answered <u>correctly</u>:

Section 3, (Questions 1-35): _____

Section 10, (Questions 1-14): _____

Total: _____ **(1)**

Compute the number of multiple-choice questions you answered <u>incorrectly</u>:

Section 4, (Questions 1-35): _____

Section 10, (Questions 1-14): _____

Total: _____ multiplied by 0.25 = _____ **(2)**

(1) – (2) = _____, Writing Multiple-Choice Raw Score

<u>Round to the nearest whole number.</u>

Use the table on page 416 to find your Writing Multiple-Choice Scaled Score: _____

Writing Essay Score: Reader 1's Score: _____ + Reader 2's Score _____ = _____

With your Writing Multiple-Choice Raw Score and your Writing Essay Score, use the table on page 417 to find your Writing Composite Scaled Score: _____.

Critical Reading Score

Number of multiple-choice questions you answered <u>correctly</u>:

Section 2, (Questions 1-24): _____

Section 5, (Questions 1-24): _____

Section 8, (Questions 1-19): _____

Total: _____ **(1)**

Number of multiple-choice questions you answered <u>incorrectly</u>:

Section 2, (Questions 1-24): _____

Section 5, (Questions 1-24): _____

Section 8, (Questions 1-19): _____

Total: _____ multiplied by 0.25 = _____ **(2)**

(1) – (2) = _____, Critical Reading Raw Score

Use the table on page 416 to find your Critical Reading Scaled Score: _____.

Math Score

Number of multiple-choice questions you answered correctly:

Section 3, (Questions 1-18): _____

Section 7, (Questions 1-20): _____

Section 9, (Questions 1-16): _____

Total: _____ **(1)**

Number of multiple-choice questions you answered <u>incorrectly</u>:

Section 3, (Questions 1-18): _____

Section 7, (Questions 1-20): _____

Section 9, (Questions 1-16): _____

Total: _____ multiplied by 0.25 = _____ **(2)**

(1) – (2) = _____, Math Raw Score

Use the table on page 416 to find your Math Scaled Score: _____.

Finally,

Writing Scaled Score _____ +

Critical Reading Scaled Score _____ +

Math Scaled Score _____ =

Your Combined Score _____

SAT Score Conversion Table

Raw Score	Critical Reading Scaled Score	Math Scaled Score	Writing Multiple-Choice Scaled Score*	Raw Score	Critical Reading Scaled Score	Math Scaled Score	Writing Multiple-Choice Scaled Score
67	800			31	510	550	60
66	800			30	510	540	58
65	800			29	500	530	57
64	780			28	490	520	56
63	760			27	490	520	55
62	750			26	480	510	54
61	740			25	480	500	53
60	730			24	470	490	52
59	710			23	460	480	51
58	700			22	460	480	50
57	690			21	450	470	49
56	680			20	440	460	48
55	670			19	440	450	47
54	660	800		18	430	450	46
53	650	800		17	420	440	45
52	650	780		16	420	430	44
51	640	760		15	410	420	44
50	630	740		14	400	410	43
49	620	720	80	13	400	410	42
48	620	700	80	12	390	400	41
47	610	680	80	11	380	390	40
46	600	670	79	10	370	380	39
45	600	660	78	9	360	370	38
44	590	650	76	8	350	360	38
43	590	640	74	7	340	350	37
42	580	630	73	6	330	340	36
41	570	630	71	5	320	330	35
40	570	620	70				
39	560	610	69				
38	550	600	67				
37	550	590	66				
36	540	580	65				
35	540	580	64				
34	530	570	63				
33	520	560	62				
32	520	550	61				

This table is for use only with the test in this booklet.

*The Writing multiple-choice score is reported on a 20-80 scale. Use the table on the opposite page to combine your Writing Multiple-Choice Raw Score with your Essay Raw Score to determine your Writing Scaled Score.

PRACTICE TEST #2

Writing Multiple-Choice Raw Score	Essay Raw Score						
	6	7	8	9	10	11	12
49	760	780	800	800	800	800	800
48	760	780	800	800	800	800	800
47	750	770	780	800	800	800	800
46	730	760	770	780	800	800	800
45	720	740	750	770	780	800	800
44	700	720	740	760	770	780	800
43	690	710	720	740	750	770	780
42	680	700	710	730	740	760	770
41	660	680	700	720	730	750	760
40	650	670	690	710	720	740	750
39	640	660	680	700	710	730	740
38	630	650	670	690	700	720	730
37	620	640	660	680	690	710	720
36	610	630	650	670	680	700	710
35	600	620	640	660	670	690	700
34	590	610	630	650	660	680	690
33	580	600	620	640	650	670	680
32	570	590	610	630	640	660	670
31	560	580	600	620	630	650	660
30	560	580	590	610	620	640	650
29	550	570	580	600	610	630	640
28	540	560	570	590	600	620	630
27	530	550	560	580	590	610	620
26	520	540	550	570	590	600	610
25	510	530	540	560	580	600	610
24	500	520	540	560	570	590	600
23	490	510	530	550	560	580	590
22	480	500	520	540	550	570	580
21	480	500	510	530	540	560	570
20	470	490	500	520	530	550	560
19	460	480	490	510	530	550	560
18	450	470	490	510	520	540	550
17	440	460	480	500	510	530	540
16	440	460	470	490	500	520	530
15	430	450	460	480	500	520	530
14	420	440	460	480	490	510	520
13	420	440	450	470	480	500	510
12	410	430	440	460	470	490	500
11	400	420	440	460	470	490	500
10	390	410	430	450	460	410	490

This table is for use only with the test in this booklet.

The Solutions

The following are explanations of the answers to the problems in Practice Test 2. In the Writing and Critical Reading sections, we have bolded vocabulary words that you should make sure you understand. Also in the Writing and Critical Reading sections, we have tried to avoid overly technical explanations about grammar, parts of speech, etc. You don't need to know the technical grammar terms; you simply need to know a mistake when you see one.

TEST 2, SECTION 2 – MATH

Question 1. The answer is (C). Response (A), the first distracter, is actually the smallest of the numbers because the 4 is in the hundredths place. Response (C) is .004 greater than Response (B).

Question 2. The answer is (D). This question is a variation on the pesky fence-post problem. If the fence has 60 segments of equal length, there must be 61 posts, including one at the end of the 60th segment. If he takes down half the fence, he must leave 31 posts standing.

Question 3. The answer is (E). This is straightforward function notation question: $f(9) = 3(9) + 4 = 31$.

Question 4. The answer is (B). The trick to this problem is finding the value of x. Combining the lengths of the three segments gives you

$$x^2 + 7x + 12 = 72$$

From there,

$$x^2 + 7x - 60 = 0$$

And

$$(x + 12)(x - 5) = 0$$

Finally,

$$3(5) + 3 = 18$$

Question 5. The answer is (D). If the hypotenuse of a right triangle is twice as long as another side, it must be a 30:60:90 right triangle with sides in the ratio of $1 : \sqrt{3} : 2$. If the lengths of the first two sides are 18 and 36, the length of the third side must be $18\sqrt{3}$. The sum of the three is $54 + 18\sqrt{3}$.

Question 6. The answer is (D). This problem is a classic illustration of the importance of short cuts. If you were to set up an equation to solve this problem, you would get

$$.06(18,000 - x) + .07(18,000 - y) = 1,150$$

We dare say that every reader is capable of doing this one by finding an equation for either x or y and then plugging it back in to solve for the other variable. Forget that. Instead, multiply $18,000 \times .06$ to get 1,080. Then punch in $18,000 \times .07 = 1,260$. Since the total amount of interest, 1,150, is closer to 1,080 than to 1,260, you know immediately that more money was invested at 6 percent than at 7 percent, thereby eliminating (A) and (B) as possible choices. Next, you can eliminate (E) at a glance if you realize that $12,000 is two-thirds of the total invested, but that 1,150 is less than two-thirds of the way toward 1,080 from 1,260. Now you're down to (C) and (D). Try (C): $10,000 \times .06 = 600$ and $8,000 \times .07 = 560$. But since $600 + 560 = 1,160$, this can't be the answer. Therefore, (D) is your choice by process of elimination. Don't take time to check that (D) is really the answer. Trust yourself and move on.

Question 7. The answer is (C). The circumference of a circle is equal to the diameter multiplied by π. If the area of the rectangle is 35 and the length is 7, the width must be 5, which is also the value of the circle's diameter. Therefore, the circumference is 5π.

Question 8. The answer is (E). Don't be put off by the yucky equation. The first move in graphing questions such as this is to find the y-intercept. In this case, if you make $x = 0$, your equation for $f(x)$ says that $y = 3$. You're already down to (B) and (E) as the only possible answers. Next, determine what happens to y as x gets larger. If $x < 4$, then $y > 0$. Since $\sqrt{x^2 + 9}$ is multiplied by a negative number, $f(x)$ must get smaller as x gets bigger, making (E) your only choice.

MATH – STUDENT-PRODUCED RESPONSES

Question 9. The answer is 254. The total received by Jones, Li, and Davis is 286, leaving a total of 254 possible votes for Olson. Some students may assume that Peterson had to get at least one vote, which would make 253 the greatest possible total, but Peterson could have gotten zero.

Question 10. The answer is 8. When three integers are multiplied, the product is negative if one of the three is negative, or if all three are negative. But if n is a positive integer, $n + 8$ cannot be negative. Therefore, positive integers must be found that make $(n - 12) < 0$ while making $(n - 3) > 0$. Among positive integers, 4, 5, 6, 7, 8, 9, 10, and 11 are the only ones that fill this bill. There are eight—count 'em.

Question 11. The answer is 5. If a circle is tangent to the y axis at $(0,5)$, and another point on the circle is $(10, 5)$, then the diameter of the circle is 10. (For students who have difficulty visualizing this scenario, a quick drawing would probably make it clear.) If the diameter is 10, the radius must be 5.

Question 12. The answer is 3. This problem features two quadratic equations that are easy to factor. First, deal with

$$x^2 + 12x + 35 = 48$$

Subtracting 48 gives you:

$$x^2 + 12x - 13 = 0$$

From there:

$$(x + 13)(x - 1) = 0$$

Since x must be positive, $x = 1$.

For $y^2 + 7y + 12 = 30$, do the same thing:

$$y^2 + 7y - 18 = 0$$

Then,

$$(y + 9)(y - 2) = 0$$

$$y = 2$$

Finally, $1 + 2 = 3$

Question 13. The answer is 63. In a straightforward combination problem, you merely multiply the number of choices in each category to get the total number of possible combinations, in this case $6 \times 4 \times 3 = 72$. The wrinkle in this one is the part about people being required to have potatoes if they order chicken. Without this restriction, there would 12 possible combinations with chicken as the entree: $1 \times 4 \times 3 = 12$. But in this case, the number is $1 \times 1 \times 3 = 3$. Therefore, the chicken and potatoes requirement eliminates nine possible combinations, yielding 63 as the answer.

Question 14. The answer is 30. This one depends on the fact that when multiplying, add the exponents.

The expression

$$(2\sqrt[3]{y} + 3\sqrt[3]{y}\,)y^{\frac{2}{3}}$$

Can be rewritten as

$$(2y^{\frac{1}{3}} + 3y^{\frac{1}{3}})\,y^{\frac{2}{3}}$$

Distributing $y^{\frac{2}{3}}$ yields

$$2y + 3y$$

If $y = 6$, $f(y) = 30$.

Question 15. The answer is 3.90. Inserting $3p$ into $q(x) = \dfrac{7 + x^2}{9}$ yields:

$$q(p) = \frac{7 + (3p)^2}{9} = 16$$

And then $7 + 9p^2 = 144$

And finally $9p^2 = 137$

From there, divide by 9 to get $p^2 = 15.2$. Your trusty square-root button will give you $p = 3.90$.

Question 16. The answer is 3 or 13. This question requires a straightforward application of the distance formula, which is

$$\text{distance} = \sqrt{(x_2 - x_1)^2 + (y_2 - y_1)^2}$$

In this case, $8 = \sqrt{(x - 8)^2 + (11 - 4)^2} = \sqrt{(x - 8)^2 + 49}$

From here, note that the expression under the radical sign must equal 64, meaning that $(x - 8)^2 = 25$. Therefore, $x = 3$ or 13.

Question 17. The answer is 2. Students can figure out this problem in a snap by noting that the sequence will include alternating positive and negative terms of increasing absolute value—meaning that 2 will always be the median of the sequence for any number of odd terms. The first five terms of the sequence are 2, –6, 18, –54, and 162.

Question 18. The answer is 72. The mean of a set of numbers is the average, and the median is the value of the middle number. In this problem, 12 will be the median because the value of x must be great in order to pull the average up to twice the medium, or 24. Since the mean of a set of values is their sum divided by the number of those values, we can get the value of the sum by multiplying the mean (24) by the number of terms (5) to get 120. In turn, 120 minus the sum of the first four terms, 48, yields the value of x, 72.

TEST 2, SECTION 3 – WRITING

Improving Sentences

Question 1. The best answer is (D) because this response is the most active and concise version of the sentence.

The best answer is NOT:
(A) because this response includes unnecessary use of the passive voice that detracts from the vigor of the sentence.

(B) because this response includes an unnecessary participial phrase that is awkwardly constructed.

(C) because although this response is slightly more fluid than (A), it includes unnecessary use of the passive voice in the first phrase.

(E) because this response includes an awkward reversal of the order of the clauses and an incorrect usage of the present tense in the second clause.

Question 2. The best answer is (B) because this response correctly omits a second reference to Sheila Johnston (who is understood to be the subject). The response directly conveys the related facts that Sheila Johnston has served for thirty years and that she has earned a reputation, though it does not imply that the latter is caused by the former.

The best answer is NOT:

(A) because this response is a "comma splice," meaning that the two clauses should be joined by a conjunction or separated into two sentences.

(C) because this response inappropriately suggests that the reason Sheila Johnston's reputation for integrity is the reason why she has been an agent for more than thirty years.

(D) because this response incorrectly states that her reputation is the result of her thirty years experience.

(E) because this response also incorrectly states that Johnston has earned her reputation because of her thirty years of service.

Question 3. The best response is (D) because it fixes the double negative "did not disbelieve" with a more appropriate phrase.

The best answer is NOT:

(A) because we don't want no double negatives.

(B) because "was disbelieving" awkwardly turns the active verb "disbelieve" into a noun and the passive verb "to be."

(C) because this response misstates the detective's views. He *did* believe the suspect.

(E) because this response also **emasculates** the verb "believe" by turning it into a noun.

Question 4. The best answer is (C) because this response includes the most direct appositive clause describing Franklin Chang-Diaz.

The best answer is NOT:

(A) because "with a flight" is a passive way of saying that Chang-Diaz "has flown."

(B) because "flying" is an incorrect use of the present tense. The present perfect form "having flown" would be more appropriate though still somewhat awkward.

(D) because "having been a flier" is wordy and passive.

(E) because "having been" incorrectly applies the past perfect tense to the fact that Chang-Diaz is an experienced astronaut, a fact that is true in the present.

Question 5. The best answer is (E) because the first clause calls for the past perfect indicative: if one thing <u>had</u> been done, another would or might have taken place.

The best answer is NOT:

(A) because the "if" clause states a condition that preceded what Josh would have done and therefore requires the past perfect tense.

(B) because "would that," at best, is an archaic, seldom-used construction not appropriate in this context.

(C) because the past subjunctive "were to know" calls for the present tense "would take" in the second clause rather than the existing present perfect "would have taken."

(D) because the past tense form "knew" does not denote a condition that precedes "would have taken."

Question 6. The best answer is (A) because the compound subject, "prominent ears and a bushy tail," requires a plural verb, "give."

The best answer is NOT:

(B) because the singular "gives" is incorrect.

(C) because the physical features of the coyote are not "indicators."

(D) because this response is grammatically correct but wordy.

(E) because this response incorrectly uses the singular "is."

Question 7. The best answer is (D) because this response concisely and actively conveys that Peron had an unusual political career.

The best answer is NOT:

(A) because "had an unusual quality" is unnecessarily wordy.

(B) because the phrase "who had an usual political career" does not form a sentence with the second clause.

(C) because this response has an unnecessary use of the passive voice.

(E) because the logical order of the clause has been reversed and the clause inappropriately makes Peron's political career the subject.

Question 8. The best answer is (C) because this response conveys the relevant information about partially hydrogenated oil with an appropriate modifying clause.

The best answer is NOT:

(A) because the first clause in this sentence is a dangling modifier. In order for this sentence to be correct, "partially hydrogenated oil" must immediately follow the first clause.

(B) because this response contains an unnecessary use of the passive voice.

(D) because "partially hydrogenated oil" should precede rather than follow the modifying clause that begins with "once thought."

(E) because the people who did the action—the scientists—have been edited out by use of the passive voice.

Question 9. The best answer is (D) because this response eliminates the unnecessary conjunction "but" while retaining the more appropriate "although." The conjunction "and" is also necessary because the first clause of the sentence, and the second and third ones together, express separate thoughts and could stand alone as complete sentences.

The best answer is NOT:

(A) because "but" does not set up an appropriate contrast with the final clause of the sentence.

(B) because the clause that begins with "because" establishes an incorrect relationship with the first clause.

(C) because this response implies that she thought she deserved an A because it was not her best work.

(E) because "although" is better placed before "it was not her best work" to establish an appropriate context for the second and third clauses. Beginning the second clause with "but" makes necessary the use of two conjunctions when one will do.

Question 10. The best answer is (A) because this response correctly uses the present subjunctive "be" in a conditional statement.

The best answer is NOT:

(B) because this response incorrectly uses the past tense in the first clause.

(C) because "whether" is the best word for communicating a circumstance that will happen if either of two outcomes prevail. "If" applies when one possible condition will create a circumstance (if…then).

(D) because "though" is not an appropriate substitute for "whether." This response also omits the necessary preposition "for."

(E) because a conditional clause introduced by "whether" calls for the present subjunctive rather than the present indicative.

Question 11. The best answer is (D) because when comparing two entities, the comparative "better" is correct instead of the superlative "best."

The best answer is NOT:

(A) because "better" rather than "best" is correct in this context.

(B) because in addition to the fact that "best" is correct, "may argue" is better than "argue" because the statement is hypothetical.

(C) because the present progressive is inappropriate in this context and "best" is incorrect.

(E) because "though" is redundant with "but."

IDENTIFYING SENTENCE ERRORS

Question 12. The best answer is (B) because the antecedent of "he" is unclear. The word in this blank should be either "Peter" or "Rodney."

The best answer is NOT:

(A) because the past "had" is correct.

(C) because he might have "avoided" is correct.

(D) because "happened" is a correct use of the past tense.

Question 13. The best answer is (C) because the pronoun "your" does not agree with "everyone." The correct pronoun, the third person singular, is "his or her."

The best answer is NOT:

(A) because "steep" can be a synonym for "expensive."

(B) because "paying for" is an acceptable gerund (verb used as a noun).

(D) because the past tense is correct in this context.

Question 14. The best answer is (E) because this response correctly expresses a conditional "if...then" statement by using the subjunctive.

The best answer is NOT:

(A) because since the subjunctive is called for in a conditional statement such as this, "were" is correct.

(B) because "would" is correct in describing what would happen if she were to go.

(C) because "including" is an appropriate word for enumerating the provisions that Lucy would need to bring.

(D) because "and" is appropriate in this context.

Question 15. The best answer is (D) because this response misuses **taciturn**, a word that describes a person who is quiet, in place of "tacit," which refers to an unspoken understanding or agreement.

The best answer is NOT:

(A) because **exculpatory** (that which **exonerates,** or "removes from blame") is correctly used in this context.

(B) because "interpreted" is a correct past tense usage of "interpret."

(C) because "to testify" is a correct infinitive usage.

Question 16. The best answer is (E) because the sentence correctly describes the process by which the check was received and the advice Susan gave.

The best answer is NOT:

(A) because **cajoling** is a progressive form of "cajole," which means "to urge with gentle appeals."

(B) because the objective "me" is correct, rather than "I." "Susan and me" is the indirect object of the action rather than the subject that does the action.

(C) because "ought to" is a correct auxiliary verb form when combined with "to deposit."

(D) because "preferably" appropriately modifies "ought to deposit."

Question 17. The best answer is (C) because "arriving" is an incorrect use of a participle instead of the correct infinitive form "to arrive."

The best answer is NOT:

(A) because "through" is a correct usage.

(B) because "it was" correctly links to the predicate adjective "tiring."

(D) because "leisurely" is a correct adverb form.

Question 18. The best answer is (B) because at the time when Abraham Lincoln was assassinated, the people "would remember for the rest of their lives" (present and future) rather than "would have remembered" (past continuing into the present).

The best answer is NOT:

(A) because **indelible** ("permanent," "unforgettable") is used correctly.

(C) because "were doing" is a correct usage of the past progressive form of "do."

(D) because the past tense "heard" is correct in this context.

Question 19. The best answer is (B) because "the ability" is the singular subject of the sentence, and therefore the verb should also be the singular "is" rather than "are."

The best answer is NOT:

(A) because "to juggle" is an appropriate infinitive form in combination with "the ability."

(C) because "with aspirations" is a correct idiom for describing those who hope to do a task such as working in a hospital.

(D) because "of working" forms an idiomatic expression with "the aspirations."

Question 20. The best answer is (A) because with a conditional statement of this sort, the past subjunctive "were" should be used rather than the past indicative "was."

The best answer is NOT:

(B) because "could" is correct in describing the circumstance contingent on Frank's availability.

(C) because the present "is" is correct in describing a situation that did exist in the past.

(D) because "to do" correctly refers to Elle's reluctance to make a decision.

Question 21. The best answer is (E) because the sentence correctly describes Acoma Pueblo and its surroundings.

The best answer is NOT:

(A) because the adverb "continuously" accurately describes the Pueblo's history.

(B) because the present tense "sits" appropriately describes the Pueblo's location.

(C) because "offers" is an appropriate verb for describing the existence of views at the Pueblo.

(D) because the participle "surrounding" applies correctly to "countryside."

Question 22. The best answer is (C) because "applied," not "applying" is the correct form to describe a name given in the past and continuing into the present.

The best answer is NOT:

(A) because "scoff" accurately characterizes the actions of historians who do not like the name.

(B) because **moniker** is a synonym for "name."

(D) because "flowering" is the correct form to describe the development or "blossoming" of culture in Harlem.

Question 23. The best answer is (B) because the adverb form "slowly" is necessary to describe how the instructor told the students to drive.

The best answer is NOT:

(A) because the past tense "warned" is correct in this context.

(C) because "entered" is a correct usage to describe an incident occurring in the past.

(D) because the past perfect "had been" is an appropriate usage.

Question 24. The best answer is (C) because the second clause of the sentence calls for the present perfect, not the present, to describe action that could have taken place after the pilot "had been alerted."

The best answer is NOT:

(A) because "had been" is an appropriate use of the past perfect to denote what had to occur before the pilot could take countermeasures.

(B) because the past tense "was" correctly describes a problem about which the pilot could have been alerted.

(D) because the present perfect "would have" describes the result of actions the pilot could have taken had she been alerted.

Question 25. The best answer is (A) because "peaked" is an incorrect form. "Peak" refers to the highest point of something; "peeked" would be correct in this context.

The best answer is NOT:

(B) because "through" is an appropriate preposition for the sentence.

(C) because "could" is appropriate as the past tense of "can."

(D) because "make out" is synonymous with "barely see" and appropriate in this context.

Question 26. The best answer is (B) because a "coma" is a "state of deep unconsciousness," whereas "comma" refers to the mark of punctuation that is relevant here.

The best answer is NOT:

(A) because "of usage" accurately describes the purpose of the rules.

(C) because the plural "are" agrees with "the rules."

D) because **consternation**, meaning "dismay" or "anxiety," accurately describes what some beginning grammar students may feel.

Question 27. The best answer is (C) because in a comparison of two students, the comparative "better" should be used rather than the superlative "best."

The best answer is NOT:

(A) because "comparable" appropriately modifies the girls' grades.

(B) because "but" establishes an appropriate contrast between the girls' similar grades and different skills.

(D) because "the abler" is a correct usage of the comparative degree.

Question 28. The best answer is (E) because although it describes a relatively **convoluted** ("confused") set of circumstances, all of the underlined words and phrases are correct.

The best answer is NOT:

(A) because "was close" accurately describes a race that occurred in the past.

(B) because "to have overtaken" is a correct use of the present perfect to describe an action that would have taken place during the race.

(C) because "would" is appropriate in describing the conditions necessary for Susan to have overtaken Mary.

(D) because "have had to" correctly uses the present perfect. Students may be confused by the fact that the phrase includes "had" as the main verb (indicating an imperative) rather than in its normal use as an auxiliary in the past perfect.

Question 29. The best answer is (D) because "they" does not agree with "everyone." The correct pronouns would be "he or she," or to avoid awkwardness, "before entering" would also be correct.

The best answer is NOT:

(A) because "to combat" germs accurately describes why the lifeguards monitor the level of chlorine.

(B) because "monitor" is a correct plural form that agrees with "the lifeguards."

(C) because "require" is a correct plural form that agrees with "the lifeguards."

IMPROVING PARAGRAPHS – I Miss Billy

Question 30. The best answer is (A) because the sentence is repetitive and does not add significant new information. From the fact that the students were trying to get Mr. Paul "off on a tangent," the reader can infer that they are encouraging him to talk about topics not directly related to class.

The best answer is NOT:

(B) because even in a different place, the sentence adds no new information to the paragraph.

(C) because the sentence adds no new information to the paragraph and would be out of place after sentence 7.

(D) because minor editing such as changing "the" to "our" does not create value in the sentence.

(E) because clarifying with an additional sentence would waste even more space.

Question 31. The best answer is (E) because among responses that accurately convey the necessary information, shorter is better.

The best answer is NOT:

(A) because although it is grammatically correct, this response is too wordy.

(B) because the infinitive "to try" is incorrect following "a game."

(C) because the action of the game was not "seeing" but "trying."

(D) because this response does not make sense.

Question 32. The best answer is (C) because a semicolon connects two clauses that, although they could stand alone as separate sentences, should be more closely connected. The semicolon allows the narrative to be fluid by highlighting the connection between the action in the two sentences.

The best answer is NOT:

(A) because "and" is an unnecessary word that does not contribute to the meaning of the sentence.

(B) because the subject was not "sixteen minutes."

(D) because this response garbles the meaning of the sentence.

(E) because this response is a comma splice.

Question 33. The best answer is (C) because this response offers the most concise clarification of the timeframe in which the action in the paragraph took place, thereby linking sentence 11 to the rest of the paragraph.

The best answer is NOT:

(A) because this phrase does not create a coherent sentence.

(B) because though grammatically correct, this response is too wordy.

(D) because this response leaves unclear whether the boys "learned more" during the particular class in which they wasted sixteen minutes, or during the entire year.

(E) because like response (D), this one leaves unclear the time when the action took place.

Question 34. The best answer is (E) because it correctly uses the present tense to convey the fact that Mr. Paul's knee starts popping when it is going to rain.

The best answer is NOT:

(A) because the past tense "started" does not agree with the present "knows."

(B) because the past perfect "had started" does not agree with the present "knows."

(C) because although this response correctly uses the present tense, "the popping" incorrectly implies that there has been an earlier reference to "popping." The response is also weakened because "popping" is a gerund rather than a verb.

(D) because "popping in his knee" transforms popping from a verb into a noun, thereby weakening the phrase and concealing the source of the popping.

Question 35. The best answer is (B) because this sentence discusses the development of the friendship through tenth grade and prepares the reader for the reference to college in sentence 12.

The best answer is NOT:

(A) because the last paragraph is not about Mr. Paul's class.

(C) because this sentence does not include a transition from the topic of Mr. Paul's class to that of the last paragraph.

(D) because the last paragraph is about the development of a friendship rather than mischief such as that in Mr. Paul's class.

(E) because the last paragraph is not about Mr. Paul.

TEST 2, SECTION 4 – CRITICAL READING

Question 1. The best answer is (D) because given the fact that Eyadema was president for thirty-five years, it is logical to infer that he was a "fixture," and "served" is an active verb for describing the fact that he was president.

The best answer is NOT:

(A) because "overseeing as" is not an appropriate phrase for describing Eyadema's tenure as president.

(B) because "dominator" is an awkward word for describing Eyadema's role in the politics of western Africa. (It might be appropriate to say that he was a "dominant force.")

(C) because "certifying" is not an appropriate word in combination with "as president of Togo."

(E) because although Eyadema may have been chosen as president, he would not have been "chosen for thirty-five years" at any particular time even if he ultimately served for thirty-five years.

Question 2. The best answer is (A) because "zephyr" means "gentle breeze."

The best answer is NOT:

(B) because **gale** means "strong wind," as in a storm.

(C) because **torrent** means "fast-flowing stream."

(D) because **maelstrom** means "confusing or turbulent situation."

(E) because **wisp** means "a thin or faint trace," as in a wisp of smoke.

Question 3. The best answer is (D) because this sentence calls for two words that could be a logical outcome of a worker's efforts with a new supervisor. "Ingratiate" describes Peter's attempt to bring himself into favor with his new supervisor, while "obsequious" describes the result when that effort has gone too far and makes Peter appear excessively compliant or servile.

The best answer is NOT:

(A) because although "acquaint" would be acceptable for the first blank, "oblivious" is not a logical outcome for the second.

(B) because **aspire** means "to seek or hope for" and does not make sense in the first blank. **Noncommittal** means "not willing to be definitive" or "not willing to commit."

(C) because the idiomatic preposition with "introduce" is "to" rather than "with." **Truculent** means "confrontational."

(E) because although **align** ("to become an ally of") might be acceptable for the first blank, but **jovial** ("good-natured") does not make sense for the second.

Question 4. The best answer is (E) because "sedition" means "an action designed to criticize or undermine," generally in reference to a government. It helps to know that "sedition" is a word that was used more commonly before 1900 to describe those who criticized or protested a government, as in the Alien and Sedition Acts in the United States during the presidency of John Adams.

The best answer is NOT:

(A) because **noncompliance** means "failure to obey" rather than "criticizing" or **inciting** rebellion.

(B) because **maliciousness** means "with malice or ill-will." Though maliciousness could be related to criticizing the government, it is not the same concept.

(C) because **interlocution** means "a conversation."

(D) because **interdiction** means "an order prohibiting an action."

Question 5. The best answer is (D) because this sentence calls for two words that express differing degrees of the same concept, the first being more moderate than the second. **Wistful** is a moderate form of "sadness" or "melancholy;" **despondent** is a deeper form of despair.

The best answer is NOT:

(A) because although **pensive** is a synonym of "wistful," **incandescent** means "glowing," or at times can mean "highly emotional."

(B) because "incapacitated" suggests a more extreme distress than "troubled" and therefore this pair of words does not make a logical progression for the two blanks.

(C) because **emphatic** means "forceful" or "definitive" while **overwrought** can mean "nervous" or "agitated." Though these words might be a marginal fit for the blanks, they do not offer as clear a progression as "wistful" and "despondent."

(E) because **distended** means "swollen to an unhealthy degree" while **enthralled** means "captivated."

Question 6. The best answer is (C) because the first blank calls for a word that contrasts with "claimed to welcome opinions," combined with a word in the second blank that modifies "vanity." Given that the first clause casts doubt on whether the subject genuinely welcomes different opinions, it is logical that such opinions should be an affront ("insult") to his **overweening** ("excessive") vanity.

The best answer is NOT:

(A) because "impediment" ("obstacle") does not convey a logical meaning paired with "vanity," and the noun "immodest" is not a logical modifier of "vanity."

(B) because while differing opinions could be an "irritant" to him, they would not logically be an irritant to his vanity. **Noisome** means "offensive."

(D) because **elixir** means "a sweet liquid" or "potion," while **iconoclastic** means "an attacker of icons or institutions."

(E) because the appropriate article for "tribute" is "a" rather than "an." "Tribute" does not make sense when used with "to his vanity."

Question 7. The best answer is (A) because "furtive" means "stealthy" or "hidden."

The best answer is NOT:

(B) because Steve and George would want to avoid sharing a guilty glance so as not to reveal that they were in cahoots.

(C) because "disjointed" means "disrupted" or "lacking in appropriate order."

(D) because **procrastinating** means "unnecessarily delaying."

(E) because although Steve and George want to keep their glance a secret, it would be odd to refer to their glance as "cloaked," meaning "masked" or "covered." "Cloaked" generally refers to physical things that are concealed with a cloak.

Question 8. The best answer is (C) because **phlegmatic** ("calm, unemotional"), the response most nearly the opposite of "outgoing" and "vivacious."

The best answer is NOT:

(A) because **disingenuous** means "consciously misleading" or "pretending to be straightforward."

(B) because **iridescent** means "colorful" or "with luster."

(D) because **immaculate** means "spotlessly clean and orderly."

(E) because **destitute** means "extremely poor."

PASSAGE-BASED READING – Mahalia Jackson

Question 9. The best answer is (D) because "storied" most nearly means "celebrated."

The best answer is NOT:

(A) because "competent" means "capable."

(B) because "creative" implies skill as a composer but not acclaim or recognition.

(C) because "consistent" means "steady" or "in agreement with."

(D) because **concomitant** describes an action or event that happens at the same time as another thing.

Question 10. The best answer is (D) because the passage implies that Jackson was influenced by Bessie Smith but was nevertheless unwilling to sing the blues. By implication, we can infer that Bessie Smith was a blues singer.

The best answer is NOT:

(A) because the passage makes no comparisons between Jackson and Smith.

(B) because the passage states that Jackson refused to join Armstrong's band.

(C) because the passage does not address Armstrong's opinion of Jackson relative to Smith.

(E) because the passage states only that she refused to sing the blues.

PASSAGE-BASED READING – Isle of Eigg

Question 11. The best answer is (C) because most of the passage focuses on Eigg's landscape, geological features, and rocks.

The best answer is NOT:

(A) because although the passage mentions many of Eigg's natural features, it does not mention the island's climate.

(B) because despite the fact that the passage makes reference to Eigg's valleys and open fields, it does not describe the island's vegetation.

(D) because the passage does not describe Eigg's atmosphere aside from its geologic and natural features.

(E) because the passage does not mention Eigg's location beyond the fact that it lies off Scotland's west coast.

Question 12. The best answer is (D) because the passage follows "Singing Sands" with the description of the high-pitched noise that the sands make under foot.

The best answer is NOT:

(A) because the passage makes no comment on the appropriateness of "Singing Sands" as a name.

(B) because the passage does not evaluate whether the Singing Sands is a pleasant beach.

(C) because the passage does not specify the distance between the Singing Sands and the Jurassic fossil bed.

(E) because the passage does not compare the Singing Sands to other beaches.

PASSAGE-BASED READING – The Louisiana Purchase

Question 13. The best answer is **(A)** because "provisional" is a synonym of "temporary."

The best answer is NOT:

(B) because "legitimate" means "credible" or "lawful."

(C) because although "tentative" has a meaning similar to that of "provisional," "tentative" means "not fully worked out" or "not finalized" and generally applies to arrangements that are incomplete or unconfirmed.

(D) because "legal" means "lawful."

(E) because "legislative" applies to people or institutions that make laws.

Question 14. The best answer is **(C)** because Jefferson's plan for slavery in the territories "permitted slavery to continue respect to all slaves, imported or otherwise, for another sixteen years."

The best answer is NOT:

(A) because it was the earlier plan for Virginia, not the plan for the territories, that "applied only to importation of slaves."

(B) because the plan was not adopted.

(D) because the passage does not suggest that Jefferson defined slavery in either case as anything other than involuntary servitude.

(E) because although Jefferson's plan for slavery in the territories was not adopted, the passage does not state definitively whether there was widespread opposition to Jefferson's proposal regarding slavery in the territories, nor does the passage address opposition to Jefferson's plan to limit slavery in Virginia.

Question 15. The best answer is **(E)** because the critics who question Jefferson's decision to propose a sixteen-year delay of abolition in the territories probably believe that the interval would give slavery time to take root. These critics would logically believe that a shorter delay, or none at all, would be a better approach. These critics would also logically infer that Jefferson, a slaveholder, might have proposed a shorter delay had he been more committed to abolition.

The best answer is NOT:

(A) because while it is plausible that the critics might suggest that Jefferson exaggerated the strength of the opposition from fellow Southerners, there is no logical reason for the critics to suggest that he miscalculated it.

(B) because the critics are described as questioning the substance of Jefferson's plan rather than his political skills.

(C) because Jefferson's proposal did, in fact, require new states created from the territories to be bound by the Articles of Confederation.

(D) because in seizing on the sixteen-year delay, the critics are suggesting that Jefferson's plan was too slow, not too hasty, in abolishing slavery.

Question 16. The best answer is (D) because if slaves were considered property, the Articles of Confederation would have allowed slaveholders to freely move them into the territories.

The best answer is NOT:

(A) because the relevant lines do not address whether the new states created in the territories would be "free states."

(B) because the relevant lines do not suggest that Jefferson failed to envision the movement of property.

(C) because the relevant lines make no mention of Jefferson wanting to limit the rights of property owners.

(D) because the relevant lines do not suggest that no one planned to bring slaves into the territories.

Question 17. The best answer is (D) because the first sentence of the fifth paragraph cites the contradiction between Jefferson's plan for eliminating slavery in the territories and the provisions of Articles of Confederation. The passage describes it as "one contradiction between his stated ideals and political reality," implying that there had been other such contradictions.

The best answer is NOT:

(A) because the passage says nothing about whether Jefferson's ideals conflicted with one another, but only that they sometimes conflicted with political reality.

(B) because the passage does not suggest that Jefferson's true beliefs differed from those that shaped his political positions.

(C) because although Jefferson's plan for the territories was not adopted, it is not logical or appropriate to infer that his ideals were unpopular with most Americans.

(E) because although the passage refers to critics of Jefferson, it does not reference "true advocates of abolition" or suggest that anyone living at the time was frustrated by his ideals.

Question 18. The best answer is (B) because "beneficence" means "charitable act" or "charity."

The best answer is NOT:

(A) because "deservedly" means "as appropriate" or "as deserved."

(C) because "enticing" means "tempting" or **alluring**.

(D) because "beneficial" is an adjective that means "giving favor or benefit" that appears similar to the noun **beneficence** but has a different meaning.

(E) because "artifice" means a "stratagem" or "maneuver" that is generally subtle or deceptive.

Question 19. The best answer is (C) because the balance of the passage supports the view that Jefferson treated the Native Americans unjustly, though in describing the views of Professor Wallace, the author uses the words "goes so far as" to suggest that she and other observers might not go as far as Wallace does in describing the idea that Jefferson was a "planner of cultural genocide."

The best answer is NOT:

(A) because the author does not suggest that she disagrees with views held by Professor Wallace, but merely allows that some observers might hold a less extreme view.

(B) because the author does not suggest that she finds Professor Wallace's views "distasteful."

(D) because the author does not suggest that she disagrees with Professor Wallace's views.

(E) because the author does not suggest that Wallace's views are "inflammatory."

Question 20. The best answer is (B) because the passage describes Jefferson's maneuvering to complete a **larcenous** exchange that would allow the United States to take over most of the land that had previously been inhabited by the Kaskaskias tribe.

The best answer is NOT:

(A) because although the passage describes Jefferson as believing that agriculture will improve the Native Americans' quality of life, it makes clear that his true goal is to promote the interests of the United States.

(C) because while Jefferson may envision demonstrating agricultural techniques to the Native Americans, his goal in encouraging them to adopt agriculture is to make more land available for settlement by the United States.

(D) because the passage does not suggest that Jefferson was concerned with assisting the Native Americans develop more unified communities.

(E) because the passage portrays Jefferson's goal of ending the Native Americans' reliance on hunting for subsistence as a policy that would make possible the "larcenous exchange" that would expand the amount of land available for settlement by the United States.

Question 21. The best answer is (A) because the fact that du Coigne named his son after Jefferson, an act of goodwill, contrasts sharply with Jefferson's suggestion that a spy be sent to du Coigne's village and with Jefferson's desire to "take all the tribe's lands and give them a reservation of just 350 acres." Duplicity, meaning "deliberate deceptiveness" or "double-dealing," accurately describes Jefferson's actions as portrayed by Passage 2.

The best answer is NOT:

(B) because Passage 2 suggests that Jefferson did cheat du Coigne and the Kaskaskias tribe.

(C) because Passage 2 highlights the relationship between du Coigne and Jefferson in order highlight Jefferson's duplicity in his dealings with the Kaskaskias.

(D) because Passage 2 does not make reference to any rift in the relationship between du Coigne and Jefferson, but rather suggests that Jefferson moved forward in spite of that relationship.

(E) because Jefferson was not **complicit** ("associated") with du Coigne but instead was duplicitous in seeking a deal that took advantage of du Coigne and the Kaskaskias.

Question 22. The best answer is (D) because "larcenous" means "of or related to larceny," "the crime of theft."

The best answer is NOT:

(A) because **clandestine** means "secret" or "covert."

(B) because **illicit** means "forbidden."

(C) because **laconic** describes a person who seldom speaks, or who speaks with few words.

(E) because **scrupulous** means "honest."

Question 23. The best answer is (A) because "pejorative" means "disparaging" or "expressing disapproval." While Passage 1's largely neutral portrayal of Jefferson gives only one indirect criticism in referencing the conflict between his stated ideals and political reality, Passage 2 is openly disparaging of Jefferson.

The best answer is NOT:

(B) because the Passage 2 does give an admiring portrayal of Jefferson.

(C) because **aphoristic** means "containing aphorisms," which are pithy statements or maxims such as "a penny saved is a penny earned."

(D) because **oxymoronic** means "characterized by oxymoron," which means "combining contradictory terms or items."

(E) because **didactic** means "in a manner to instruct," often with a pretentious or moralizing tone.

Question 24. The best answer is (E) because a major focus of Passage 2 is Jefferson's attitude toward the lifestyle of Kaskaskias tribe and how that attitude was shaped, perhaps unconsciously, by his desire to further the interests of the United States.

The best answer is NOT:

(A) because Passage 2 does not address Jefferson's belief in the inevitability of human progress.

(B) because neither passage suggests that Jefferson preferred compromise over confrontation.

(C) because although Passage 2 portrays Jefferson as an advocate of expanding the land holdings of the United States, it is does not suggest that Jefferson envisions the United States as a global empire.

(D) because although Passage 2 references a critic of Jefferson's treatment of the Kaskaskias tribe, it does not mention critics of American expansionism or Jefferson's response to them.

TEST 2, SECTION 5 – MATH

Question 1. The answer is (D). The total area of the seven larger rooms is equal to x. All of these rooms are of the same size. Therefore, the area of one room is $\frac{1}{7}$ of the total area, x, and the answer is $\frac{x}{7}$.

Question 2. The answer is (B). In an arithmetic sequence, the difference between the values is constant. Therefore, we know that the difference between $y + 6$ and 12 must be the same as that between 12 and y and between y and $y - 3$. Therefore, y is 3 less than 12, $y + 6$ is 3 greater than 12, and $y = 9$.

Question 3. The answer is (A). Since the measure of x is 60°, we know that the area of the shaded sector is $\frac{1}{6}$ the area of the circle. If the circumference, πd, is equal to 12π, the area of the circle must equal 36π. Therefore, the shaded area is 6π.

Question 4. The answer is (B). From the graph, we can see that Acme's sales revenue is

$$\$300,000 + \$200,000 + \$100,000 + \$350,000 + \$250,000 = \$1,200,000$$

Sales of red account for $300,000 or 25 percent of the total.

Question 5. The answer is (C). This is one of those problems that makes eyes roll. If you think of a square divided into 64 smaller squares, you probably have the image of eight squares on each side. So 32 squares border the outside of the big square? Not exactly. If you take a closer look, the squares on the corners border two sides rather than just one. With four squares doing double duty, only 28 rather than 32 border the outside of the big square.

Question 6. The answer is (A). If one angle with vertex O is equal to $80°$, we know that the angle opposite is also equal to $80°$ and that the other two angles are equal to $100°$ (for a total of $360°$). Furthermore, the arc lengths are proportional to the measures of the angles.

If $BD = 20$, then $AC = 20$, $AB = 16$, and $CD = 16$ for a circumference of 72.

Question 7. The answer is (C). Figure III has one extra triangular piece on the left end. The other two figures could be made from the three pieces without cutting or overlapping.

Question 8. The answer is (D). You know that the sum of the angles in every triangle is $180°$. If the ratio of the angles is 10:12:14, then the angle measurements must be $50°$, $60°$, and $70°$. (Hint: the sum of 10, 12, and 14 is 36. Divide each by two to make the sum 18, then multiply each by 10 for the correct angle measurements.) The difference between the largest and smallest is $20°$.

Question 9. The answer is (B). Only if $0 < |x| < 1$ can x, raised to a power less than one, be greater than x (itself) raised to a power greater than 1.

Question 10. The answer is (B). Time to dust off the theory of alternate angles, which says that when a segment intersects two parallel lines, the angles on opposite sides and ends of the segment are equal. By the theory of corresponding angles, we know that $\angle c$ is equal to the angle that is adjacent and to the right of $\angle b$. Hence, $a = b + c$ and $b = a - c$.

Question 11. The answer is (C). This is another problem for which you might be tempted to do a laborious calculation trying to isolate q or p and waste 10 minutes in the process. Look again. You'll find your answer when you figure out how to get 8 from the product of $q \times 1 \times q$. You might think of $q = 2$, but that makes a zero in the denominator of one of the terms in the equation. The next logical option is 4, which gives you:

$$\frac{4}{4-2} \times \frac{1}{4-1} \times \frac{4}{4+1} = \frac{16}{30} = \frac{8}{15}$$

Question 12. The answer is (E). This problem involves two special right triangles: a 45:45:90 triangle, and a 30:60:90 triangle. As you know, the sides of these triangles are in the ratio $1:1:\sqrt{2}$ and $1:\sqrt{3}:2$, respectively. The fact that $\overline{AC}$ and $\overline{BD}$ are perpendicular lets you know that $\overline{AB}$ is the hypotenuse of a right triangle. If $\overline{BC} = \sqrt{2}$, then the short side adjacent to $\overline{AB}$ must have a length of 1. Therefore, $AB = 2$.

Question 13. The answer is (D). Your instinct may be to draw a picture—and you can—but this one is actually a combinations problem masquerading as geometry. If you start at point A and begin drawing segments, you can draw segments to B, C, D, E, and F. That's five. But when you move on to B, you'll only be able to draw four new lines—to C, D, E, and F—because the segment joining A and B already exists. When you move on to C, you'll only be able to draw three segments, and so on. The answer: $5 + 4 + 3 + 2 + 1 = 15$. Our drawing of what this looks like is below:

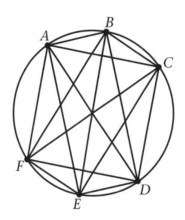

Question 14. The answer is (B). Response II is true because $p \le 5$. Response I is not true because $|q + 5| \le 5$. Response III is not true because $|p|$ will be greater than q in most cases.

Question 15. The answer is (D). Solve this one by plugging in the coordinates of points A, B, C, or D. The latter two are the easiest given that they are on the x axis. If $\overline{CD} = 8$, the coordinates of D must be (4,0). The problem gives you two equations, and you should know by looking that the one with the plus sign opens to the north, the one with the minus sign opens to the south, and that q is the distance from the origin to the point on the y axis at which the points intersect. Therefore, plug (4,0) into $y = q - x^2$ to get $q = 16$.

Question 16. The answer is (E). Since you know the area of the circles, you can work backwards to get the radius of one and use that value to find the area of the square. First divide 225π by 9 to get the area of one circle, 25π. The radius of each circle, therefore, is 5. Here's the tricky part: each side of the square is equal to 6 radii or 30 (not three radii, which would give you 15). Therefore, the area of the square is $30 \times 30 = 900$.

Question 17. The answer is (E). The area of the big circle is $\pi 5^2 = 25\pi$, and the area of one of the small circles is $\pi(.5^2) = .25\pi$. Since there are four small circles, the combined area of the four is π, or $\frac{1}{25}$ th the area of the big circle. Hence, the probability that the point will NOT be inside one of the smaller circles is $\frac{24}{25}$.

Question 18. The answer is (C). A good first move on graphical problems is to locate the y-intercept.

$$\text{If } g(x) = x^2 + bx - c, \text{ then}$$
$$g(0) = (0)^2 + b(0) - c$$

If c is positive, the value of the function when $x = 0$ is negative. Therefore, we can eliminate all but responses A and C. Next, let's see what happens to y when x gets large. Since the value of y is a function of x^2, we know that y will get big faster than $|x|$, corresponding to a graph that opens north.

Question 19. The answer is (B). It takes a little imagination to get this one. Think of a cube with a segment drawn diagonally across it that connects one vertex, A, to another vertex, B, which is diagonally across from A at the point in the cube farthest away from A. The point in the middle of this segment is in the middle of the cube. If you then draw a segment from A down an edge of the cube, you'll have a segment measuring 1. From there, imagine drawing a second segment diagonally across the square that is the bottom of the cube. This segment measures $\sqrt{2}$. Now imagine a third segment that forms the hypotenuse of a triangle that includes the first two segments. Using the Pythagorean Theorem, $c^2 = 12 + (\sqrt{2})^2$. Therefore, $c = \sqrt{3}$ and the answer is $\frac{\sqrt{3}}{2}$.

Question 20. The answer is (B). This question might cause momentary panic until you realize that the squares that end in one particular digit always generate numbers that end in another particular digit. In other words, the square of numbers ending in 7 always end in 9:

$$7^2 = 49, \ 17^2 = 289, \ 27^2 = 729, \text{ and so on}$$

Therefore, you need only concern yourself with digits 1-9, and you can think of the squares of those numbers quickly. The answer is 8.

TEST 2, SECTION 6 – CRITICAL READING

Question 1. The best answer is (B) because the fact that Althea Gibson, an African American, "overcame racial discrimination" suggests that the blank will be filled by a laudatory word. The article "the" just before the blank suggests that the word will be a superlative. Pre-eminent, meaning "greatest" or "best," fills the bill.

The best answer is NOT:

(A) because **redoubtable**, meaning "formidable" or "worthy of respect," does not mesh with the article "the." Gibson may have been a redoubtable female tennis player, but it does not make sense to speak of her as "the" redoubtable female tennis player of the late 1950s.

(C) because **multifarious** means "diverse" or "having many aspects."

(D) because "idealized" means "that which is made into an ideal," or "made to represent a model or perfect specimen."

(E) because **intrepid** means "adventuresome" or "fearless."

Question 2. The best answer is (C) because the blanks suggest a sequence of two closely related words that express degrees of the same concept, with the second a logical outgrowth or amplification of the first. The reference to a **neophyte** ("inexperienced") philosophy student raises the likelihood that the student will be confused. "Byzantine" means "complicated" or "intricate," while "incomprehensible" means "impossible to understand."

The best answer is NOT:

(A) because "elementary" means "simple" or "easily understood."

(B) because although **cryptic** ("mysterious") is a plausible response for the first blank, "irrelevant" does not make sense for the second.

(D) because even though **onerous** ("difficult" or "burdensome") is a possible response for the first blank, "debilitating" ("weakening" or "crippling") is not logical for the second blank. Students may be confused but it is unlikely that they would be debilitated.

(E) because although students might find *Tractatus Logico-Philosophicus* to be "impenetrable," they would not logically find it "inconclusive."

Question 3. The best answer is (E) because being "stultified" ("caused to appear incompetent") is a logical reason for colleagues to be "openly contemptuous," especially after an "incoherent" speech.

The best answer is NOT:

(A) because Representative Peterson would not have "castigated" ("bitterly criticized") himself, even if his speech were **ineffectual** ("lacking in effectiveness").

(B) because **eviscerated** ("having had contents or organs removed") does not make sense in the first blank, despite the fact that **egregious** ("bad" or "offensive") could be acceptable for the second blank.

(C) because **denuded** ("stripped of covering") does not make sense in the first blank. **Intemperate** ("rash" or "hot-headed") would be passable for the second blank.

(D) because **fulminated** ("bitterly attacked") does not make sense in the first blank.

Question 4. The best answer is (A) because the sentence sets up a contrast between the fact that the man was in the psychiatric ward and the fact that the judge saw no reason to question his mental alertness, or **acuity**.

The best answer is NOT:

(B) because "mental mind" is a redundant phrase that does not make sense.

(C) because "derangement" does not create the necessary contrast with the first clause.

(D) because an accused man's "mental attitude" does not form the necessary contrast with the first clause and is not a logical quality for a judge to question.

(E) because since perception comes from the senses, "mental perception" is not a meaningful phrase.

Question 5. The best answer is (D) because "apoplectic" ("uncontrollably furious" or "raging") is the best match for "tirade," especially in light of the fact that Marcy had expected the coach to be upset but was nevertheless surprised by the extent of his tirade.

The best answer is NOT:

(A) because **jocular** refers to a person who jokes.

(B) because **nuanced** means "exhibiting subtle shades of meaning."

(C) because **enigmatic** means "mysterious" or "difficult to understand."

(E) because **mendacious** means "dishonest."

PASSAGE-BASED READING – Environmental Tobacco Smoke

Question 6. The best answer is (D) because both passages cite a significant increase in the risk of lung disease among nonsmokers exposed to environmental tobacco smoke.

The best answer is NOT:

(A) because although both articles cite health risks of environmental tobacco smoke, neither advocates that environmental tobacco smoke be curtailed or eliminated, though Passage 2 does describe the political pressures that led to curtailment of smoking in indoor public places.

(B) because neither passage suggests that the government should regulate environmental tobacco smoke.

(C) because "courtesy and etiquette" is mentioned only in Passage 2 in reference to the tobacco industry's failed attempt to frame the issue of environment tobacco smoke in this way.

(E) because neither article suggests that environmental tobacco smoke is present in most public places, and Passage 2 cites the movement to ban smoking in indoor public places.

Question 7. The best answer is (B) because unlike Passage 2, Passage 1 cites the fact that the combustion end of the cigarette produces higher levels of chemical irritants than the inhaled end, a reason why environmental tobacco smoke is harmful.

The best answer is NOT:

(A) because both passages cite the fact that environmental tobacco smoke causes disease.

(C) because both passages refer to the scientific evidence of environmental tobacco smoke's dangers.

(D) because both passages cite the danger of environmental tobacco smoke to nonsmoking spouses.

(E) because both passages refer to the dangers of environmental tobacco smoke to nonsmokers, the reason why efforts have been made to limit exposure to it.

Question 8. The best answer is (D) because in the second sentence of Passage 2, lines 19-22, the author explains the reason why the debate over environmental tobacco smoke would have enormous implications: "It was one thing for smokers to endanger their own health, and quite another for them to harm innocent bystanders."

The best answer is NOT:

(A) because although smoking in public places has been limited due to the dangers of environmental tobacco smoke, smoking has not been "made illegal."

(B) because Passage 2 does not suggest that smokers would quit smoking if they knew that their smoking was harmful to others.

(C) because the debate over environmental tobacco smoke, and particularly the scientific evidence of its harmfulness to nonsmokers, served to undermine the idea that the issue of smoking in public places could be addressed with common sense and courtesy.

(E) because Passage 2 makes no reference to 1990.

Question 9. The best answer is **(E)** because in referring to the tobacco industry's efforts to suggest that the issue of smoking in public places could be solved with common sense and courtesy, Passage 2 shows that the debate was partly a function of public perception, at least in the view of the tobacco industry.

The best answer is NOT:

(A) because both passages refer to scientific evidence related to the issue of smoking in public places.

(B) because neither passage refers to personal opinion as a factor in the issue of smoking in public places.

(C) because neither passage refers to individual responsibility as a factor in the issue of smoking in public places.

(D) because although Passage 2 refers to the efforts of the tobacco industry to cast the issue of smoking in public places in terms of common sense and courtesy, the passage implies that this effort failed.

PASSAGE-BASED READING – Mary Sue Easterly and Junior Davis

Question 10. The best answer is **(A)** because in this context, "effectively" is synonymous with "in effect" or "having the effect of." By allowing his sperm to fertilize Mary Sue's egg, Mary Sue's lawyer argued, Junior effectively consented to allowing the child to be born, even if he did not explicitly give such consent.

The best answer is NOT:

(B) because "effectively" does not suggest that Junior ever gave his consent and then denied doing so.

(C) because "effectively" does not suggest that Junior gave his consent under duress.

(D) because "effectively" does not imply that Junior's consent would be effective in the future.

(E) because "effectively" does not mean that Junior's consent was "binding in perpetuity."

Question 11. The best answer is **(D)** because the second sentence outlines Mary Sue's argument that Junior had "effectively consented" to allowing her egg to be fertilized with Junior's sperm, and the third sentence outlines Junior's counter-argument that the children should not grow up in a broken home.

The best answer is NOT:

(A) because the third sentence cannot accurately be described as a "disclaimer."

(B) because the second sentence is not a rebuttal ("refutation of another argument") and the third sentence is not an "analysis" but another argument.

(C) because while the second sentence is a statement, the third is not a "query" ("question").

(D) because neither sentence is a "hypothesis" or "theory."

Question 12. The best answer is (C) because the trial judge awarded the embryos to Mary Sue, ruling that they were "children *in vitro*" and therefore it was in their best interests to be born.

The best answer is NOT:

(A) because although the finding that the embryos were really children *in vitro* provided a rationale for awarding them to Mary Sue, this response incorrectly implies that the finding was significant because the embryos were already the property of Mary Sue.

(B) because the passage does not state that Junior based any claims on the fact that the embryos were not children.

(D) because the passage does not state or imply that lower courts had not recognized the embryos as children.

(E) because the passage never states that the trial judge's finding could not be overturned on appeal, and in fact, it was.

Question 13. The best answer is (C) because in this context, **procreation** is synonymous with "reproduction."

The best answer is NOT:

(A) because "creation" ("the act of making") does not apply specifically to reproduction.

(B) because "misconception" means "incorrect idea or belief."

(C) because an **incantation** is "a recitation of charms or spells for magical effect."

(D) because **misogyny** means "hostility toward women."

Question 14. The best answer is (E) because the last sentence of the fourth paragraph, beginning with "therefore," explains the logic of the Tennessee Supreme Court's decision outlined in the preceding sentence.

The best answer is NOT:

(A) because although the Tennessee Supreme Court sided with Junior Davis, the passage does not suggest that Junior's argument was superior to Mary Sue's.

(B) because the sentence addresses why the Tennessee Supreme Court ruled in Junior's favor rather than why he continued to pursue the case.

(C) because the sentence does not address the relevance of the Tennessee Supreme Court.

(D) because the sentence does not discuss the impact of the decision in *Davis v. Davis*.

Question 15. The best answer is (A) because the primary purpose of the passage, as outlined in the last sentence, is to describe a case that "has generally become the standard" for reviewing the rights of individuals "not to become" parents against their will.

The best answer is NOT:

(B) because the passage is concerned with legal precedent relevant to *in vitro* fertilization rather than the process itself.

(C) because the story of Mary Sue and Junior Davis is significant only because their case set a legal precedent.

(D) because the passage is not concerned with the divorce itself but a legal case that established a precedent.

(E) because although the passage mentions reasons why Mary Sue and Junior divorced and entered their legal dispute, the passage is mainly concerned with the legal aspect of their dispute.

PASSAGE-BASED READING – W. H. Auden on W. B. Yeats

Question 16. The best answer is (E) because the author states that he is concerned not with questions such as "How good a poet is Yeats?" but rather with factors that readers should consider, and questions that readers should ask, as they approach the poetry of Yeats.

The best answer is NOT:

(A) because although the passage discusses Yeats's belief in the occult, the author's purpose is less to draw attention to this belief than to suggest how readers should consider this belief as they evaluate the poetry of Yeats.

(B) because although the author outlines factors that readers should consider as they approach the poetry of Yeats, he does not suggest that Yeats is a better poet than most people believe.

(C) because the author examines how readers should interpret Yeats's poetry and does not suggest that it is fruitless to do so.

(D) because the author does not argue that more time must be spent on interpreting Yeats's poetry.

Question 17. The best answer is (D) because after stating in line 5 that his purpose is to consider Yeats "as a predecessor whose importance no one will or can deny," the author uses rhetorical questions to provide examples of the questions he will raise in order to do so.

The best answer is NOT:

(A) because the author is beginning an analysis rather than an interrogation.

(B) because rather than stating a conclusion, the rhetorical questions provide examples that illustrate the author's approach to Yeats and his poetry.

(C) because the rhetorical questions illustrate the author's point of view rather than "dispute" another argument.

(E) because the rhetorical questions provide examples of an approach rather than outline a thesis.

Question 18. **The best answer is (C)** because **cosmology** means "the study of or theories about how the universe works."

The best answer is NOT:

(A) because in the context of the passage, "cosmology" refers not to celestial bodies but to theories about causation and meaning in the world.

(B) because the passage does not speak of any belief that the cosmos has hidden meaning.

(D) because "cosmology" refers not to Yeats's ability to understand the cosmos but rather to the perspective and beliefs from which he found meaning in the cosmos.

(E) because Yeats's cosmology is concerned with meaning and causation rather than surface appearances.

Question 19. **The best answer is (A)** because while the author notes that Yeats's "style and rhythm" are highly influential, "one whole side of Yeats," his concern with the occult, "has left virtually no trace."

The best answer is NOT:

(B) because the author notes that Hardy, Eliot, and Lawrence were influential in both their style and subject matter and does not suggest that Yeats is more influential than any of these.

(C) because the author suggests that Yeats's influence does not extend to his matter—or at least not to his concern with the occult.

(D) because the author suggests that one foreign aspect, Yeats's concern with the occult, has not been influential.

(E) because while the author notes that Yeats's preoccupation with the occult is foreign to most readers, the "curious fact" is that despite Yeats's broad influence, his concern with the occult has not been influential.

Question 20. **The best answer is (B)** because by italicizing "could," the author emphasizes the consternation and disdain of some readers—how *could* Yeats, they ask.

The best answer is NOT:

(A) because italicizing "could" emphasizes the probable reaction of readers rather than an evaluation of whether or not Yeats was silly.

(C) because although readers may associate Yeats's perspective with the lower middle class, the passage does not suggest that Yeats himself identified with the lower middle class.

(D) because while some readers may believe that Yeats's fascination with the occult is incongruous with his skills as a writer, the italicization of "could" emphasizes the reaction of some readers rather than the author's evaluation.

(E) because the passage refers to the reaction of readers in a later era rather than the reaction of Yeats's contemporaries.

Question 21. The best answer is (A) because "or should I say Southern Californian," a humorous aside, draws its impact from a stereotype of Southern Californians that would have been familiar to many readers.

The best answer is NOT:

(B) because a metaphor suggests an analogy between two dissimilar items or states by describing one in terms of another. In this instance, the author merely uses the adjective "Southern Californian" as a descriptor.

(C) because "Southern Californian" is not an example but a description.

(D) because simile suggests a comparison between two dissimilar items or states by using "like" or "as."

(E) because the insertion of "or should I say Southern Californian," does not create **dissonance**, which means "discord" or "inconsistency."

Question 22. The best answer is (A) because ineluctably means "by necessity" or "unavoidably."

The best answer is NOT:

(B) because **indelibly** means "permanently."

(C) because **inscrutably** means "in a manner that is difficult to understand."

(D) because "frequently" means "often."

(E) because "periodically" means "from time to time."

Question 23. The best answer is (C) because with the phrase "an example to me," the author is suggesting that he himself has an obligation to follow his own advice to avoid being judgmental of Yeats, even though aspects of Yeats's worldview seem implausible to some readers, notably the author, who live in a later era.

The best answer is NOT:

(A) because "the example" is a reminder that Yeats should not be dismissed because his worldview is different from that of readers in a later era.

(B) because the author suggests that readers should not look down on Yeats's preoccupation with "mediums, spells, and the Mysterious Orient." The embarrassment felt by some readers betrays an unwarranted feeling of superiority.

(D) because the author's point is not that Yeats's worldview was "provocative and interesting," but that later observers should examine eccentricities in their own worldviews similar to those in Yeats's.

(E) because although the author does believe that Yeats was right to ignore such questions, the phrase "and an example to me" applies to the author's reaction to Yeats rather than whether Yeats was right or wrong in his beliefs.

Question 24. The best answer is (E) because in suggesting that readers "should not claim credit for rejecting what we have no temptation to accept," the author seeks to highlight the fact that each generation has its own myths and beliefs comparable to those of Yeats, and that it is these myths and beliefs that readers should examine rather than those of Yeats's time.

The best answer is NOT:

(A) because the author does not suggest that Yeats's worldview is more accurate than any other.

(B) because although the author suggests that readers should learn more about why Yeats was attracted to Celtic mythology and occult symbolism, he does not advocate general study of these topics nor make any reference to seventeenth-century Ireland.

(C) because the author states that occult symbolism attracted Yeats in his "later" phases.

(D) because the author advocates not that readers should make their belief systems more like that of Yeats, but rather that they should examine facets of their belief systems that are comparable to the "foreign" aspects of Yeats's belief system.

TEST 2, SECTION 8 – MATH

Question 1. The answer is (B). The store is offering customers 5 boxes for the price of 3. For simplicity, let's assume that the price of each is $1.00. That means 5 boxes cost $3.00 and each box costs $.60, a 40 percent discount off of $1.00.

Question 2. The answer is (A). If $f(x) = 3x^2$, then $f(5) = 3(5^2) = 75$. Likewise, if $g(x) = (3x)^2$, then $g(5) = (15)^2 = 225$. Therefore, $75 - 225 = -150$.

Question 3. The answer is (A). From the figure, we know that $6x = 180$. Therefore, $x = 30$.

Question 4. The answer is (B). The first step in solving this problem is to add up the number of students in each organization: $52 + 34 + 28 = 114$. Since 9 students participate in all three organizations, you need to subtract $9 + 9$ to avoid double- and triple-counting them. Since 17 students participate in 2 of the 3 organizations, you'll need to deduct 17 from the total to avoid double-counting them. Therefore, $114 - 18 - 17 = 79$, the total number of students in the three clubs.

Question 5. The answer is (E). This question involves understanding how to combine two rates to get a combined time. If Jenna could paint the fence in 6 hours (or 360 minutes), that means she can paint $\frac{1}{360}$ th of the fence in one minute. Ellen could paint the whole thing in 9 hours (540 minutes) and therefore her rate per minute is $\frac{1}{540}$ th of the fence. We need to add these two rates for our answer, but first we to need to find the least common multiple of 360 and 540 to use as a common denominator. Therefore,

$$\frac{3}{1080} + \frac{2}{1080} = \frac{5}{1080}$$

This tells us that Jenna and Ellen could paint 5 fences of this size in 1080 minutes. To find the time they will need to paint one fence, divide 1080 by 5 for the answer, 216.

Question 6. The answer is (B). To solve, set up two equations and then substitute find Marty's sales. If the total sales of both was 330, let $a + b = 330$. If Joe sold $30 more than Marty, you also know that Marty's sales equal Joe's sales plus 30, i.e. $b = a + 30$. Plugging back in,

$2a + 30 = 330$. Therefore, $a = \$150$. Marty's sales = $150 and Joe's = $180.

Question 7. The answer is (C). Flying into the headwind, the plane flew at 300 miles per hour. On the way back, the plane's speed increased to 400 miles per hour. Since the plane was flying against the wind in the former case and with the wind in the latter, the speed of the wind must have been 50 miles per hour.

Question 8. The answer is (D). This problem should not be difficult. If $a - 12 = 10 - a$, then $2a = 22$ and $a = 11$.

Question 9. The answer is (B). Let the cost of a shoe be x and cost of a pair socks be y. Therefore, $x = 6y$ and $x = 2y + \$12.00$. To solve for y, let

$$6y = 2y + \$12.00$$
$$4y = \$12.00$$
$$y = \$3.00$$

The cost of a pair of shoes is $6(\$3.00) = \$18.00$.

Question 10. The answer is (D). The goal is to satisfy the equation, $*y* = \sqrt{\dfrac{y}{4}} = 2$. Given that 4 is the denominator of the expression, and $\sqrt{4} = 2$, $\sqrt{y}$ must equal 4. Therefore, $*64* = \sqrt{\dfrac{16}{4}} = 2$.

Question 11. The answer is (A). A sleight-of-hand is necessary here to avoid getting bogged down in endless calculations. You are given

$$x^5 = 5 \text{ and } x^4 = \frac{4}{y}$$

Pretty nasty, until you realize that

$$x^5 = x(x^4)$$

That means $x\left(\dfrac{4}{y}\right) = 5$ and $x = \dfrac{5y}{4}$.

Question 12. The answer is (D). This problem hinges on the fact that the longest segment that can be drawn from A to another point on the cylinder must be the hypotenuse of a right triangle. If the volume of the cylinder is 54π and the height is 6, that means r^2 is 9, the radius is 3, and the diameter is 6. Therefore, the two sides of the right triangle are of equal length, meaning that the triangle is a 45:45:90. If the two sides are each 6, the hypotenuse must be $6\sqrt{2}$, which is the distance of the longest segment that can be drawn from A to another point on the cylinder.

Question 13. The answer is (B). There are 360° of arc in a circle. Together, arc AC and arc BD take up 150°, leaving 210°. If $AB = 2(CD)$, then $AB = 140°$ and $CD = 70°$.

Question 14. The answer is (C). The main issue is to isolate a^{-1} from everything else. The original equation is

$$4a^2b^{-2} = 64a$$

Another way to write this is:

$$\frac{4a^2}{b^2} = 64a$$

Combining like terms, we have

$$\frac{4a^2}{a} = 64b^2$$

And

$$a = \frac{64b^2}{4}$$

$$a = 16b^2$$

Finally,

$$a^{-1} = \frac{1}{16b^2}$$

Question 15. The answer is (E). All three of the responses must be true. First, $a > b$ because $\frac{1}{a}$ is always a positive number, and therefore a alone is greater than $a - \frac{1}{a}$. Second, $a - b < 1$ because $0 < \frac{1}{a} < 1$. Finally, since $a > b$, $ab < a^2$.

Question 16. The answer is (D). Time for another round of special right triangles. If the shadow runs 40 feet along the ground, and is 30 feet below, that makes 40 and 30 two sides of a right triangle. The hypotenuse—the distance from the treasure chest to the base of the tree—must therefore be 50 feet.

TEST 2, SECTION 9 – CRITICAL READING

Question 1. The best answer is (D) because while the first clause describes Hemingway's writing style as "direct and concrete," the word "although" implies a contrast between the first clause and the second, which is satisfied by "subtlety."

The best answer is NOT:

(A) because **brevity** means "the act of being brief."

(B) because **lucidity** means "the quality of making sense."

(C) because **gravity** can mean "the force of nature by which bodies exert pull on one another," or it can mean "importance" or "significance."

(E) because **veracity** means "truthfulness."

Question 2. The best answer is (D) because vacillation ("indecisiveness") on the part of the governor would logically raise doubts about his "conviction," the extent to which he is committed to the tax reform initiative.

The best answer is NOT:

(A) because **declaimed** means "to have given a formal oration" and **pulchritude** is a fancy way of saying "beauty," often with respect to women.

(B) because although "wavered" would be appropriate for the first blank, **dogmatism** ("arrogance" or "stubborn adherence to one's opinions or beliefs") is an unflattering quality that would be a dubious choice for the second blank. Some people might argue that this response is correct, but questions like these are often about splitting hairs, and response (D) is the best choice.

(C) because if the governor **expounded** on ("explained in detail") his proposal, it would tend to confirm his passion rather than raise doubts about it.

(E) because **proselytized** means "attempted to convert or persuade," an act that would not logically make aides doubt the governor's "candor."

Question 3. The best answer is **(D)** because "but" implies a contrast between the two clauses, and "spirited" best contrasts with the fact that Chisholm "did not have a realistic chance of winning."

The best answer is NOT:

(A) because **quixotic** means "impractical" or "idealistic without regard for reality."

(B) because "quiet" does not create a logical contrast with "did not have a realistic chance of winning."

(C) because "obliging" does not create a logical contrast with "did not have a realistic chance of winning."

(E) because **disjointed** means "out of sequence" or "lacking logical order."

Question 4. The best answer is **(B)** because **demurred** means "tactfully declined" and therefore makes George an exception to those who offered overwhelming support.

The best answer is NOT:

(A) because "consented" means "agreed." If George had consented, support would have been unanimous.

(C) because "assented" is a synonym of "agreed" and would also have signified George's support.

(D) because "denied" ("refused to admit or agree") does not make sense in combination with "proposal."

(E) because "disengaged" means "not engaged" or the past tense of "the act of ending engagement." Neither makes sense in this context.

Question 5. The best answer is **(E)** because "finesse . . adroit" accurately describes a quality necessary to navigate the obstacle course (**finesse**) and a trait describing those who demonstrate this quality (**adroit**).

The best answer is NOT:

(A) because **shiftless** ("lazy") is not an appropriate descriptor of the contestants who successfully navigated the obstacle course.

(B) because navigating an obstacle course is unlikely to require **introspection** ("self-knowledge " or "exploration of oneself").

(C) because "self-actualization" is a psychological term that means "having fulfilled one's potential," a state that may be important for a happy life but is not likely to be of use in navigating an obstacle course.

(D) because "industriousness" ("the quality of being industrious or hard-working") is a questionable fit for the first blank, and "grounded" ("stable") is a poor one for the second.

Question 6. The best answer is (A) because the blanks require two related words that make idiomatic phrases with "to advice" and "of other people's opinions," and these words must explain why Mr. Franklin is "a difficult colleague." **Impervious** means "unmoved" or "unaffected," often in the context of something that ought to move or affect a reasonable person, and "dismissive" means "contemptuous" or "not disposed to take seriously."

The best answer is NOT:

(B) because **impertinent** is a synonym of "irrelevant," often with connotations of rudeness, while **laudatory** means "that which praises."

(C) because although both words convey reasonably appropriate meanings for the blanks, the appropriate preposition for use with "contemptuous" is "of" rather than "to."

(D) because **impregnable** applies to an entity, usually a building, that cannot be captured by force, and "disliking" is inappropriate for the second blank.

(E) because **histrionic** means "overly dramatic."

PASSAGE-BASED READING – Women during World War II

Question 7. The best answer is (B) because **figuratively** means "in the abstract" and is typically contrasted with "literally." In this case, the author suggests that American society endorsed the figurative idea or symbol of women standing "in the shoes of their missing men," but that the reality of women taking on these roles sometimes caused objections, and that the parameters ("limits") for women in these roles were different than they had been for men.

The best answer is NOT:

(A) because the author does not suggest that people were untruthful when they said they supported having women "in the shoes of their missing men," but rather that societal norms caused the standards of acceptability for women to be different from those for men.

(C) because "only figuratively" refers not to those who wanted to glorify working women, but rather those who were uncomfortable with the reality of women in the workplace.

(D) because even though some "American authorities" may have had misgivings about women taking jobs in factories, their endorsement of that image could not logically be **construed** ("interpreted") as an attempt to prevent women from taking jobs in factories.

(E) because although support for women in the workplace may have been more image than reality, this does not mean that Rosie the Riveter was a poor image.

Question 8. The best answer is (C) because the enhancement of women's "difference" included reference to their "underlying maternal dedication" and their "glamour," both traits that distinguished them from men and served to highlight that women's presence in the workplace was a "temporary sacrifice."

The best answer is NOT:

(A) because the passage contains no reference to the idea that women might be "superior to men in many industrial jobs."

(B) because although women were portrayed as being able to "work in industrial jobs and still be glamorous," the author suggests that the purpose of this portrayal was to maintain distinctions between men and women.

(D) because the article describes how women were viewed through stereotypes rather than as unique individuals, and that they were encouraged to take on new roles out of necessity rather than because of a prior conviction that they were capable of doing so.

(E) because women's difference was "deliberately enhanced" to highlight perceived innate difference.

Question 9. The best answer is (E) because **accoutrements**, meaning "accessories" or "equipment associated with a particular task," is a synonym of "implements."

The best answer is NOT:

(A) because **arraignments** are when people are brought before a court of law to answer charges.

(B) because **denouements** refer to the final chapter or act of a story in which lingering questions are resolved.

(C) because **verisimilitudes** are items or circumstances that appear to be true or real but may not be.

(D) because **battlements** are indentations in a defensive wall that allow defenders to shoot at attackers.

Question 10. The best answer is (C) because the author writes that "when local governments were urged to undertake efforts to help women" with child care, "authorities of many child advocacy programs frequently argued in response that it was in the best interests of the children to have their mothers home."

The best answer is NOT:

(A) because the passage makes no mention of whether child care from the federal government was cost-effective.

(B) because the passage does not mention anyone who argued that child care provided by the government "would be an expensive expansion of the role of government."

(D) because the passage makes reference only to mothers in this context.

(E) because the passage does not make reference to the adequacy of government facilities in this context.

Question 11. The best answer is (B) because the two sentences state that women were criticized for "absenteeism" when they were not at work. At the same time, warnings about "juvenile delinquents" and "latchkey" children were an implicit criticism of the fact that mothers were absent.

The best answer is NOT:

(A) because working mothers were criticized for their "absenteeism" and encouraged to work.

(C) because the two sentences do not address the issue of women's satisfaction.

(D) because the two sentences do not mention the wages women earned.

(E) because the two sentences do not mention financial pressures on women.

Question 12. The best answer is (D) because the passage devotes significant attention to a discussion of the burdens placed on women in wartime America, and to how women were simultaneously criticized for "absenteeism" from work and for neglecting child care.

The best answer is NOT:

(A) because **vitriolic** means "bitter" or "scathing," and while the author clearly believes that the criticism was unfair, she gives no evidence that it could accurately be called "vitriolic."

(B) because "lackadaisical" means "lacking energy or urgency."

(C) because **pragmatic** means "practical" or "realistic."

(E) because **dilatory** means "tending to delay."

Question 13. The best answer is (E) because in line 65, the author describes the number of children in federally funded child care centers as "miniscule," which is a synonym of "tiny."

The best answer is NOT:

(A) because "significant" means "considerable" or "large."

(B) because "large" is the opposite of "miniscule."

(C) because the percentage of working mothers served by federally funded child care was not "proportional" to the number of working mothers.

(D) because although "moderate" suggests that the number was limited, "tiny" is a closer approximation of "miniscule."

Question 14. The best answer is (C) because the relevant sentences describe the increasing demands on women's time from both factory work and child care as reasons why women's time "was suddenly of social significance."

The best answer is NOT:

(A) because the sentences cast the issue in terms of the collective demands on women's time, not the need for women "to devote themselves fully to factory work."

(B) because the sentences make no reference to any need for women to have additional training.

(D) because although the sentences mention a psychiatrist who advocated "shared child care between the partners," this was not the reason why women's time "was suddenly of social significance."

(E) because the sentences do not suggest that women were less suited to physically demanding work than men.

Question 15. The best answer is (B) because lines 93-96 suggest that many women did not have the modern kitchen facilities necessary to make use of pre-prepared and frozen foods. Those who advocated use of these items were unrealistic in their optimism as to the extent to which these new products would be used. In this instance, the author makes use of an alternate definition of "fantastic," meaning "characterized by a fantasy" or "delusional."

The best answer is NOT:

(A) because the excessive optimism for the use of the new products may have been fantastic, but it was not "incomprehensible."

(C) because in this context, "fantastic" is a synonym of "delusional" rather than "extraordinary."

(D) because "supernatural" means "of or related to forces outside this world."

(E) because **ephemeral** means "temporary" or **fleeting**.

Question 16. The best answer is (E) because the sentence that begins with "as late as 1941" cites the antiquated kitchen facilities in many American households to explain why the optimism surrounding the introduction of pre-packaged and frozen food "bordered on the fantastic."

The best answer is NOT:

(A) because the passage does not mention consumer preferences.

(B) because the passage does not address the issue of whether women had time to shop for such foods.

(C) because the passage does not suggest that women had a bias against using pre-prepared food.

(D) because the passage does not address the availability of pre-prepared foods after they were put on the market.

Question 17. The best answer is (B) because the last paragraph notes "other more positive changes," including women experiencing "a new understanding of their worth" and more societal attention to the issue of equal rights for women. The passage perceives the changes set in motion by World War II as largely positive, though the passage does discuss resistance to those changes.

The best answer is NOT:

(A) because the author views the changes as mostly positive rather than **indeterminate**, meaning "unclear" or "not precisely determined."

(C) because most references in the passage, especially in the final paragraph, are to positive changes.

(D) because most of the changes were positive rather than **deleterious** ("harmful" or "injurious").

(E) because by devoting the last paragraph of the passage to a discussion of these changes, the author shows her belief that the changes were significant rather than insignificant.

Question 18. The best answer is (A) because the last paragraph states that "with a new understanding of their worth" after their war-time experiences, many women decided "to renew discussion of long dormant issues of equality."

The best answer is NOT:

(B) because the paragraph speaks of "an new understanding of their worth" rather than "a new understanding of women's advocacy groups."

(C) because while it is true that much of the work for women's rights did not come to fruition until decades later, the main point of the paragraph is that work on issues such as women's equality was spurred by the war-time experience.

(D) because the paragraph implies that the experience of the 1940s created expectations that the role of women *would* change.

(E) because the experience of the 1940s promoted later initiatives for equal rights.

Question 19. The best answer is (D) because the passage begins with a reference to the "new" image of women in the 1940s, explains that image and the factors behind it, and concludes with reference to an era that would follow when women would "renew discussion of long dormant issues of equality."

The best answer is NOT:

(A) because the passage deals with the role of women in particular and is not a "summary" of societal trends in the 1940s.

(B) because the passage does not discuss the issue of whether women felt confined in the 1940s.

(C) because the passage is primarily about women's roles during World War II rather than before or after.

(E) because while the author is clearly an advocate of women's rights, the passage is primarily an historical summary rather than an argument.

TEST 2, SECTION 10 – WRITING

Question 1. The best answer is (D) because the since the statement is about people rather than things, the pronoun "who" is correct. In addition, since "those" is plural, "their memberships" must also be plural.

The best answer is NOT:

(A) because the pronoun "that" applies to a thing rather than to a person.

(B) because the pronoun "that" applies to a thing rather than to a person. The use of "you" and "your" would be acceptable.

(C) because insertion of the preposition "if" requires the addition of a subject for the second clause, as in, "Only if you have renewed your membership in the past six months will <u>you</u> be allowed…"

(E) because "membership" should be plural to agree with "those" and "their."

Question 2. The best answer is (E) because shorter is generally better. Response (E) conveys the idea of the sentence concisely, and all the other responses have unnecessary words or phrases.

The best answer is NOT:

(A) because "which was torrential" is an unnecessary phrase that delays the sentence's development.

(B) because "torrential as it was" is an unnecessary phrase that delays the sentence's development.

(C) because this response contains an awkward adjective, "four-day," and an adjective ("torrential") awkwardly transformed into an adverb. There is also an unnecessary "and" in this response.

(D) because this response includes an unnecessary (and passive) "to be" verb and unnecessary "and."

Question 3. The best answer is (A) because this response correctly conveys that the eucalyptus tree provides a habitat for koala bears and also yields medicinal oil.

The best answer is NOT:

(B) because this phrase transforms "providing" into "a provider," thereby leaving the first clause of the sentence without a verb.

(C) because since the function of providing a habitat for the koala is not related to the fact that eucalyptus leaves yield medicinal oil, a word such as "while" or "in addition to" is necessary to join the two clauses into a meaningful sentence.

(D) because "being a provider" is a roundabout way of saying "providing."

(E) because this response wrongly implies that providing a habitat for the koala is related to yielding medicinal oil.

Question 4. The best answer is (A) because this response accurately describes why cats can draw near to their prey before pouncing. "Therefore" is appropriate to establish that the second clause is an outgrowth of the first. This question is also an example of the fact that the shortest response, when it mangles meaning or usage, is not necessarily correct.

The best answer is NOT:

(B) because this response omits "can," a necessary word since the sentence describes an ability of cats. "After drawing near" is also awkward at the end of a sentence because the "drawing near" should logically come before the "pouncing."

(C) because this response awkwardly places "pouncing" before "drawing near" and omits the conditional "can."

(D) because this response has an unnecessary repetition of "they" and awkwardly places "drawing near" after "can pounce."

(E) because "have the ability" is a wordy substitute for "can" and "drawing" is an unnecessary progressive form awkwardly placed at the end of the sentence.

Question 5. The best answer is (C) because "and remained" is a concise and effective way of linking the clauses of the sentence.

The best answer is NOT:

(A) because "while continuing to remain" is wordy and **redundant** ("repetitive").

(B) because although this response is reasonably good, it includes three unnecessary words—"it," "to," and "be,"—as well as an unnecessary comma.

(D) because "and then continued lowering" is wordy. "Lowering" is not a correct usage in this context.

(E) because this sentence needs a conjunction between the clauses.

Question 6. The best answer is (A) because the sentence correctly describes Margaret Thatcher's approval rating after the Falklands War and includes a modifier, "not surprisingly," that is appropriately placed.

The best answer is NOT:

(B) because "this raised" is awkward in referring to the first clause as its antecedent, and "raised," coming before "approval rating," is likely to create confusion. Instead of "this raised her approval rating," a better order would be "her approval rating rose."

(C) because "not to anyone's surprise" is wordy and misplaced at the beginning of the second clause.

(D) because "was not to anyone's surprise" is wordy and too far removed from "high approval rating."

(E) because this sentence includes an unnecessary use of "being" in a phrase that awkwardly separates "not surprising" from the rest of the sentence.

Question 7. The best answer is (D) because it is the only one that the makes sense. (Instances of this sort are among the few in which the longest response is also the best.) The phrase "most notably" suggests that the gap of eighteen years between Peron's two terms was the most notable reason, but perhaps not the only one why his career was unusual.

The best answer is NOT:

(A) because this sentence is a comma splice with two sentences joined (incorrectly) by a comma.

(B) because this phrase gives an incorrect meaning. This response is made to sound like the seldom-used but acceptable "not least because."

(C) because if Peron's political career is described as "unusual," as it is in the first clause, then "unusual" should apply to Peron's entire career and not just the time "after eighteen years elapsed between his two terms."

(E) because "with eighteen" requires the present form "elapsing" rather than the past "elapsed."

Question 8. The best response is (B) because since the meaning of Lao-tse's name is biographical information rather than an action, it is more appropriately conveyed with an appositive phrase than a participial phrase.

The best answer is NOT:

(A) because "with his name meaning" is an awkward -ing form that should be replaced by an appositive phrase.

(C) because this response is too wordy.

(D) because to speakers of English, the relevant fact is that Lao-tse means "the old master," rather than vice-versa. The sentence is also incorrect because the meaning of Lao-tse's name is not the same as the individual himself and therefore is not appropriate as the subject.

(E) because this response does not convey the fact that Lao-tse means "the old master."

Question 9. The best answer is (D) because since the last part of the sentence cites examples of diversity, the sentence requires "as diverse as" in order to make sense.

The best answer is NOT:

(A) because "diverse professions as" does not make sense. However, "diverse professions such as" would be acceptable though not as good as response (D).

(B) because "of such diversity" is unnecessarily wordy even though its meaning is passable.

(C) because "like" incorrectly implies that each profession in the list is "a diversity of professions."

(E) because this response is too wordy and omits a necessary "as."

Question 10. The best answer is (E) because this response is the only one that includes a construction referring to Poland that is parallel to "the number of immigrants from Spain."

The best answer is NOT:

(A) because in order to be correct, the sentence must compare the immigrants from Spain "with those from Poland."

(B) because this response also includes the parallelism error.

(C) because this response also includes the parallelism error.

(D) because this response also includes the parallelism error.

Question 11. The best answer is (C) because "which influences growth and metabolism" correctly modifies "the pituitary gland" and best states the meaning of the sentence.

The best answer is NOT:

(A) because "influencing on" is not an idiomatic expression.

(B) because "on," not "in," is the correct preposition to use with "influence."

(D) because "where growth and metabolism is influenced" is a passive phrase with a tense error.

(E) because "a growth and metabolism influence" incorrectly changes "growth and metabolism" from the objects of "influence" into adjectives modifying "influence."

Question 12. The best answer is (B) because this response fixes the dangling modifier and creates a logical sequence with the second clause.

The best answer is NOT:

(A) because when a participial phrase modifies a noun—in this case, the people who were soaked by the thunderstorm—that noun must come immediately after the phrase to be grammatically correct.

(C) because the skies cleared "after" we were soaked, not "when" we were soaked.

(D) because "although" incorrectly implies that the fact that the people were soaked would have an impact on whether the skies cleared.

(E) because this response implies that it was the skies that were soaked.

Question 13. The best answer is (D) because the relevant clause in this response concisely and grammatically describes the puffin's bill.

The best answer is NOT:

(A) because this response is wordy and passive.

(B) because "distinctively vertical, flattened" does not convey the same meaning as "distinctive, vertically flattened."

(C) because the inclusion of the verb "has" beside "the puffin" requires "and" before "inhabitants" since "the puffin" is the subject of both verbs.

(E) because this response inappropriately changes the adjective "distinctive" into the adverb "distinctively." The latter has no nearby verb to modify.

Question 14. The best answer is (B) because the sentence is about garments and therefore must compare "garments made of synthetic fabrics" with "those made of cotton."

The best answer is NOT:

(A) because "garments made of synthetic fabrics" cannot reasonably be compared with "cotton."

(C) because "garments made of synthetic fabrics" must be compared with other garments rather than "fabric."

(D) because this response includes the same error as in (A) along with an incorrect preposition ("into").

(E) because changing "absorbs water" to "water-absorbing" does not save this response.

Acknowledgments

We are grateful to all those who assisted in the preparation of this book. We owe our greatest debt to the college counselors in our Advisory Group, and to the hundreds of students who gave us their insight about taking the SAT.

Steve Beamish, math teacher at Sandia Preparatory School, provided timely assistance on both the first and second editions of the book and we are immensely grateful for his help. Alice Perry, chair of the English Department at Sandia Prep, offered her considerable expertise on the first edition. Mary Anne Modzelewski, Bruce's colleague at Sandia Prep, has also been an important source of support, as has Julie Fiske Hogan, production coordinator of the *Fiske Guide to Colleges*. Guy, Jean, and Andrea Hammond provided valuable editing assistance on the second edition.

We are deeply indebted to Carrie Obry for her tireless and good-natured work. We are also grateful to Todd Stocke, Peter Lynch, Heather Otley, Christina Payton, and Dominique Raccah for their dedication to the Fiske guides. Special thanks to Matt Diamond for his excellent work on the design of the book.

We appreciate the efforts of all, but responsibility for the final product is ours alone.

College Counselors Advisory Group

Marilyn Albarelli, Moravian Academy (PA)

Scott Anderson, Mercersburg Academy (PA)

Christine Asmussen, St. Andrew's-Sewanee School (TN)

Bruce Bailey, Lakeside School (WA)

Samuel Barnett, SchoolFutures (VA)

Amy E. Belstra, Cherry Creek H. S. (CO)

Greg Birk, Kinkaid School (TX)

Susan T. Bisson, Advocates for Human Potential (MA)

Robin Boren, Dakota Ridge H. S. (CO)

Clarice Boring, Cody H. S. (WY)

John B. Boshoven, Community High School & Jewish Academy of Metro Detroit (MI)

Mimi Bradley, St. Andrew's Episcopal School (MS)

Nancy Bryan, Pace Academy (GA)

Claire Cafaro, Ridgewood H.S. (NJ)

Nancy Caine, St. Augustine H. S. (CA)

Mary Calhoun, St. Cecilia Academy (TN)

Mary Chapman, St. Catherine's School (VA)

Nedra A. Clark, Montclair High School (NJ)

Anthony L. Clay, Durham Academy (NC)

Kathy Cleaver, Durham Academy (NC)

Alison Cotten, Cy-Fair H. S. (TX)

Alice Cotti, Polytechnic School (CA)

Rod Cox, St. Johns Country Day School (FL)

Kim R. Crockard, C Three: College Counseling Services (AL)

Carroll K. Davis, North Central H. S. (IN)

Renee C. Davis, Rocky River H. S. (OH)

Mary Jo Dawson, Academy of the Sacred Heart (MI)

Christy Dillon, Crystal Springs Uplands School (CA)

Tara A. Dowling, Saint Stephen's Episcopal School (FL)

Dan Feldhaus, Iolani School (HI)

Ralph S. Figueroa, Albuquerque Academy (NM)

Emily E. FitzHugh, The Gunnery (CT)

Larry Fletcher, Salesianum School (DE)

Nancy Fomby, Episcopal School of Dallas (TX)

Daniel Franklin, College Consultant (CO)

Laura Johnson Frey, Vermont Academy (VT)

Phyllis Gill, Providence Day School (NC)

Freida Gottsegen, Pace Academy (GA)

Molly Gotwals, Suffield Academy (CT)

Kathleen Barnes Grant, The Catlin Gabel School (OR)

Madelyn Gray, John Burroughs School (MO)

Amy Grieger, Northfield Mount Hermon School (MA)

Elizabeth Hall, Education Consulting Services (TX)

Andrea L. Hays, Hathaway Brown School (OH)

Rob Herald, Cairo American College (Egypt)

Darnell Heywood, Columbus School for Girls (OH)

Bruce Hunter, Rowland Hall-St. Mark's School (UT)

Deanna L. Hunter, Shawnee Mission East H. S. (KS)

John Keyes, The Catlin Gabel School (OR)

Sharon Koenings, Brookfield Academy (WI)

Joan Jacobson, Shawnee Mission South H. S. (KS)

Gerimae Kleinman, Shaker Heights H. S. (OH)

Laurie Leftwich, Brother Martin High School (LA)

MaryJane London, Los Angeles Center for Enriched Studies (CA)

Martha Lyman, Deerfield Academy (MA)

Brad MacGowan, Newton North H. S. (MA)

Robert S. MacLellan, Jr., The Pingry School (NJ)

Margaret M. Man, La Pietra-Hawaii School for Girls (HI)

Susan Marrs, The Seven Hills School (OH)

Karen A. Mason, Wyoming Seminary (PA)

Lisa Micele, University of Illinois Laboratory H. S. (IL)

Janet Miranda, The Success Planner, Inc. (TX)

Richard Morey, Dwight-Englewood School (NJ)

Joyce Vining Morgan, Putney School (VT)

Daniel Murphy, The Urban School of San Francisco (CA)

Judith Nash, Highland High School (ID)

Stuart Oremus, Wellington School (OH)

Arlene L. Prince, University Preparatory Academy (WA)

Deborah Robinson, Mandarin H. S. (FL)

Julie Rollins, Episcopal H. S. (TX)

William C. Rowe, Thomas Jefferson School (MO)

Bruce Scher, Barrington H. S. (IL)

David Schindel, Vail Mountain School (CO)

Kathy Z. Schmidt, St. Mary's Hall (TX)

Joe Stehno, Bishop Brady H. S. (NH)

Bruce Stempien, Weston H. S. (CT)

Paul M. Stoneham, The Key School (MD)

Audrey Threlkeld, Forest Ridge School of the Sacred Heart (WA)

Ted de Villafranca, Peddie School (NJ)

Scott White, Montclair H. S. (NJ)

Linda Zimring, Los Angeles Unified School District (CA)

About the Authors

In 1980, when he was education editor of the *New York Times*, **Edward B. Fiske** sensed that college-bound students and their families needed better information on which to base their educational choices. Thus was born *Fiske Guide to Colleges*. A graduate of Wesleyan University, Ted did graduate work at Columbia University and assorted other bastions of higher learning. He left the *Times* in 1991 to pursue a variety of educational and journalistic interests, including a book on school reform, *Smart Schools, Smart Kids*. When not visiting colleges, he can be found playing tennis, sailing, or doing research on the educational problems of Third World countries for UNESCO and other international organizations. Ted lives in Durham, North Carolina, near the campus of Duke University, where his wife is a member of the faculty. They are coauthors of *When Schools Compete: A Cautionary Tale* and *Elusive Equality: Education Reform in Post-Apartheid South Africa*.

Since entering Yale in the early 1980s, **Bruce G. Hammond** has devoted much of his time to counseling students about college admissions. At Yale, Hammond was editor-in-chief of the *Insider's Guide to the Colleges*. He subsequently served as managing editor of *Fiske Guide to Colleges*, and is also the author of *Discounts and Deals at the Nation's 360 Best Colleges*. He has been quoted in numerous national publications, including the *New York Times*, the *Wall Street Journal*, *USA Today*, the *Washington Post*, *U.S.News & World Report*, *Business Week*, *Money Magazine*, and *Good Housekeeping*. Bruce lives in Albuquerque, New Mexico, with his wife and stepsons and is director of college counseling at Sandia Preparatory School.

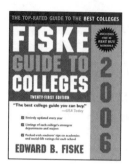

Notes

Notes

Notes

Notes